Ultimate Cardano Smart Contracts

Unlock the Full Potential of the Cardano Blockchain by Developing Real-World Web 3.0 Projects Using Plutus Smart Contracts, and App Development

Lawrence Arthur Ley

www.orangeava.com

First published: June 2024

Published by: Orange Education Pvt Ltd, AVA™

Address: 9, Daryaganj, Delhi, 110002, India

275 New North Road Islington Suite 1314 London,

N1 7AA, United Kingdom

ISBN: 978-81-97396-53-3

www.orangeava.com

Dedicated To

My Children:

Daniel, Sofi, Josie

And their Future

About the Author

Lawrence Arthur Ley has a Computer Science degree from the University of Toronto and over 20 years of IT industry experience. He is passionate about learning new technologies and how they can make a positive impact. His Cardano journey started in 2021 with the Plutus Pioneers program, and he has worked on several open-source Cardano impact projects. Lawrence is a professor in the Blockchain Development Program at George Brown College in Toronto and runs the Cardano Blockchain Toronto monthly meetup with over 500 members.

His professional experience includes IT consulting in the telecommunications, banking, and retail industries. He has a proven track record of building and managing complex, integrated, highly scalable consumer and retail applications. His first experiences with cryptocurrencies involved mining Bitcoin and participating in local meetups where he met Ethereum co-founders Vitalik Buterin and Anthony Di Iorio.

In July 2023, Lawrence was invited to attend the Cardano CIP-1694 Governance Workshop in Edinburgh, Scotland, where he met Cardano co-founder Charles Hoskinson. He was deeply honored to participate in the governance workshops with many highly esteemed individuals from the Cardano ecosystem. He continues to be active in the Cardano community, exploring new technologies and helping others along the way.

About the Technical Reviewer

Venu Kumar Borra is a highly accomplished Technical Architect specializing in distributed computing, smart contracts, and digital assets. He has extensive experience with both public and private blockchains, including Cardano, Ripple, Ethereum, Hyperledger, Corda, and Directed Acyclic Graphs (DAGs). His expertise spans fintech, supply chain, agri-tech, and healthcare.

A strong advocate for Self-Sovereign Identity (SSI) and Zero Knowledge proofs, Venu has practical experience in ZK implementations. He is also a Cryptographic Researcher and Podcast Creator, underscoring his commitment to blockchain technology. Venu's proficiency in tokenization and tokenomics principles enhances business operations and drives innovation.

His technical skills include programming in Solidity, Go-lang, Python, Kotlin, and Haskell, and using development tools like Hardhat and Brownie. Venu is also skilled in emerging technologies such as AI, machine learning, IoT integration, and Distributed Ledger Technology (DLT).

In his current role, Venu focuses on the architecture, design, and development of blockchain systems, emphasizing Explainable AI (XAI), auditability, and transparency solutions. He manages GenAI solutions, leveraging Large Language Models (LLMs) and building Minimum Viable Products (MVPs) using the RAG approach.

As a Board of Trustees member for the Blockchain For Productivity Forum (BCPF), Venu promotes blockchain adoption and implements innovative solutions for social welfare projects in India and internationally. Previously, as the Managing Director of Blocmatrix IT Solutions Pvt Ltd, he delivered cutting-edge solutions across various industries.

Venu holds an MBA in Executive Marketing from NIBM, India, and a Bachelor's degree in Mathematics from the University of Madras, India. His competencies include solution design and development, product management, cloud deployment, consulting, project management, quality assurance, team leadership, training, and technical documentation. Venu excels at translating complex business requirements into innovative technological solutions, consistently driving success and efficiency.

Acknowledgements

I wrote this book to help others learn how blockchain works and create decentralized applications on the Cardano Blockchain. Blockchain is a fascinating technology that can significantly disrupt existing business models. Writing a book about rapidly changing technology, however, is not easy because a lot can change from when you start the book to when it is finally published. Therefore, this book will provide sufficient foundational knowledge and techniques applicable in the foreseeable future, although language features and versions will change over time.

This book only exists because of the true pioneers creating alternative languages such as Aiken and Helios. Although these two projects have different approaches and priorities, both were born out of necessity to create a better Cardano Smart Contract development experience. I am genuinely grateful for this, as is the larger Cardano developer ecosystem.

I wish to thank my family, who endured me constantly working on 'the book.' Their support and understanding were a constant source of inspiration.

Finally, I thank Orange AVA Publishing for their continuous support. This book would not have been possible without them.

Lastly, to the readers, thank you for choosing this book to help you Master Cardano Smart Contracts. May it be an invaluable resource as you discover this new and profound technology.

Preface

Deciding what blockchain to use when building a decentralized application is a big decision. There are many considerations, and switching to a different blockchain may take time and effort. *Ultimate Cardano Smart Contracts* aims to help demonstrate Cardano's features and provide a hands-on approach to writing Smart Contracts. Using this knowledge and insight, you will understand the benefits of building on Cardano and why there is such a large and passionate Cardano community.

This book comprises 14 chapters, each building upon the previous chapters. We will start with the fundamentals of blockchain and then move into writing smart contracts. The book will close with an overview of the Cardano ecosystem and ethos. The book includes technical and non-technical material, so it will appeal to experienced developers and non-technical entrepreneurs looking to improve their knowledge and understanding.

Chapter 1. Blockchain Evolution: This chapter will introduce blockchain and distributed ledger technology, focusing on prior implementations and challenges to overcome. We will look at the Bitcoin and Ethereum whitepapers and how they paved the way for the third-generation blockchain, Cardano. The blockchain trilemma will be examined, along with a review of tokenomics and Cardano's native currency, Ada. Finally, we will finish the chapter by discussing the Cardano roadmap and blockchain use cases.

Chapter 2. Cryptography and Consensus Algorithms Overview: This chapter will briefly introduce cryptography and how it is used in blockchain technology. We will first look at securing a blockchain using the Proof of Work consensus protocol. Then, we will look at Proof of Stake and its benefits over Proof of Work. Finally, we will review Ouroboros, the Proof-of-Stake consensus protocol used by Cardano.

Chapter 3. Transactions: This chapter will examine Cardano addresses and the UTXO architecture. It will also introduce Smart Contracts and explain how they are executed and evaluated. We will see how Redeemers and Datums pass data into Plutus scripts and where Datums are also used for data storage and persistence. Finally, we will examine the transaction Witness Set and how it authorizes the spending of transaction inputs.

Chapter 4. Plutus: In this chapter, we will examine the Plutus core specification, Untyped Plutus Core (UPLC), used for executing Cardano Smart Contracts. We will also explore the different data structures used in Plutus and how to serialize them using the Concise Binary Object Representation (CBOR) format. Next, we will calculate the CPU and memory units using the Plutus cost model and explain why we need to include collateral in a transaction.

Chapter 5. Transaction Builder: This chapter will combine our knowledge of on-chain Plutus scripts and how to lock Ada into a smart contract using off-chain code. We will look at Cardano wallets, the gateway to interacting with the blockchain and smart contracts. Next, we will look at tooling to help build and submit transactions like Demeter. run. Then, we will make a simple, smart contract for vesting using two popular approaches: Helios and Lucid + Aiken.

Chapter 6. Validators: In this chapter, we will look in detail at what a validator is and why they are so important. We will show how to spend UTXOs locked at a validator script address and how to access data provided in a Redeemer or Datum. Next, we will dive deep into understanding what ScriptContext is and how it is used to access all inputs and outputs associated with a transaction. The chapter will review on-chain and off-chain code examples using two different approaches: Helios and Lucid + Aiken.

Chapter 7. Minting: This chapter will examine Cardano native assets and how they differ from Ethereum tokens created using the ERC-20 standard. We will discuss the concept of token bundles and how to optimize coin selection. We will then dive deep into minting Cardano native tokens, the differences between Non-Fungible Tokens (NFTs) and Fungible Tokens (FTs), and the metadata standards CIP-25 and CIP-68. We will combine this with a working minting policy use case and demo.

Chapter 8. Tooling: In this chapter, we will review the tools and service providers you can use for off-chain development. We will look at Cardano Blockchain API providers such as Blockfrost, Maestro, Koios, and Dandelion. Then, we will look at hosted environments with Demeter.run to set up services like Cardano Node, Ogmios, and Kupo. Finally, we will look at how to set up a local Devnet for rapid development and prototyping with the Yaci DevKit.

Chapter 9. Ticket Application Design: This chapter reviews Smart Contract design patterns that leverage and utilize the UTXO architecture. Anti-patterns are also examined, which should be avoided and lead to poor application performance and UTXO contention. We look at Cardano Improvement Proposals (CIPs) and how they apply to the application design. Next, we will create state machine diagrams to model the event ticket application, looking at the inputs and outputs required for a successful transaction. Finally, we will conclude the chapter by reviewing sequence diagrams showing each use case's interaction between system components.

Chapter 10. Ticket Application Implementation: In this chapter, we will walk through the implementation of a ticket application, including blockchain integration. We will look at the application stack, which includes CharkraUI, Next.js, Redis DB, and Blockfrost. Next, we will inspect the front-end off-chain code used to build and submit transactions. Then, we will review the corresponding Smart Contract on-chain code, business logic, and validation rules. Finally, we will run through an end-to-end demo of the application.

Chapter 11. Testing, Security, and Scaling: This chapter will show how to test Smart Contracts and include them in a popular testing framework such as Vitest. We will look at both the traditional testing and property-based testing approaches. Next, we will focus on security and review vulnerabilities identified in real-world Cardano application audits. We will look at code examples of how to make your Smart Contracts more robust and more resilient to any such attacks. Finally, we will close the chapter by discussing scaling and some tools and techniques to improve dApp performance.

Chapter 12. Troubleshooting: This chapter will walk through the debugging tools and techniques for Helios and Aiken. We will look at how to generate CBOR for a transaction and compare data types against the formal specification. We will look at techniques to reduce the computational overhead of a Plutus script that exceeds the execution budget. We will also examine compiler errors and how transaction builders provide robust error-handling support. Finally, we will look at Cardano Node and Browser Wallet errors and how to diagnose them accordingly.

Chapter 13. Cardano Ecosystem: This chapter will review the state of Cardano and the GitHub repositories that contain all of the Cardano source code and specifications. We will look at the Cardano Improvement Process (CIP) and how to make changes and improvements to the Cardano blockchain. Next, we will explore the era of Voltaire and CIP-1694 regarding Cardano governance. We will also review Project Catalyst, one of the largest decentralized innovation platforms that provides grant funding to Cardano projects. Finally, we will look at Cardano partner chain frameworks such as Midnight, a data-protection blockchain.

Chapter 14. Closing Remarks: This chapter will review the ethos of Cardano. We will examine the software industry standards and how these standards fall short for high assurance software. We will see how **IOG (IOHK)** used semi-formal methods to build Cardano and how cryptographic associations like IACR facilitate peer review. Through real-world examples, we will explore Cardano's potential to drive positive social change. We will also discuss regulatory and compliance risks. Finally, we will review the five stages of technology adoption and the Cardano journey.

Downloading the code bundles and colored images

Please follow the links or scan the QR codes to download the
Code Bundles and Images of the book:

https://github.com/ava-orange-education/Ultimate-Cardano-Smart-Contracts

The code bundles and images of the book are also hosted on
https://rebrand.ly/ad614f

In case there's an update to the code, it will be updated on the existing GitHub repository.

Errata

We take immense pride in our work at **Orange Education Pvt Ltd,** and follow best practices to ensure the accuracy of our content to provide an indulging reading experience to our subscribers. Our readers are our mirrors, and we use their inputs to reflect and improve upon human errors, if any, that may have occurred during the publishing processes involved. To let us maintain the quality and help us reach out to any readers who might be having difficulties due to any unforeseen errors, please write to us at :

errata@orangeava.com

Your support, suggestions, and feedback are highly appreciated.

DID YOU KNOW

Did you know that Orange Education Pvt Ltd offers eBook versions of every book published, with PDF and ePub files available? You can upgrade to the eBook version at **www.orangeava.com** and as a print book customer, you are entitled to a discount on the eBook copy. Get in touch with us at: **info@orangeava.com** for more details.

At **www.orangeava.com**, you can also read a collection of free technical articles, sign up for a range of free newsletters, and receive exclusive discounts and offers on AVA™ Books and eBooks.

PIRACY

If you come across any illegal copies of our works in any form on the internet, we would be grateful if you would provide us with the location address or website name. Please contact us at **info@orangeava.com** with a link to the material.

ARE YOU INTERESTED IN AUTHORING WITH US?

If there is a topic that you have expertise in, and you are interested in either writing or contributing to a book, please write to us at **business@orangeava.com**. We are on a journey to help developers and tech professionals to gain insights on the present technological advancements and innovations happening across the globe and build a community that believes Knowledge is best acquired by sharing and learning with others. Please reach out to us to learn what our audience demands and how you can be part of this educational reform. We also welcome ideas from tech experts and help them build learning and development content for their domains.

REVIEWS

Please leave a review. Once you have read and used this book, why not leave a review on the site that you purchased it from? Potential readers can then see and use your unbiased opinion to make purchase decisions. We at Orange Education would love to know what you think about our products, and our authors can learn from your feedback. Thank you!

For more information about Orange Education, please visit **www.orangeava.com**.

Table of Contents

1. Blockchain Evolution **1**

Introduction 1

Structure 1

Distributed Ledger Technology 2

Byzantine Generals Problem 2

Network Consensus 3

Bitcoin Whitepaper 3

Ethereum Whitepaper 4

Charles Hoskinson's Whiteboard Video 6

Scalability 6

Interoperability 6

Sustainability 7

The Blockchain Trilemma 7

Tokenomics 8

Token Allocation 8

Token Distribution 9

Token Allocation Comparison 10

Inflation Rate 11

Cardano Roadmap 11

Blockchain Use Cases 13

Conclusion 13

Points to Remember 13

Multiple Choice Questions 14

Answers 15

Questions 16

Key Terms 16

2. Cryptography and Consensus Algorithms Overview **17**

Introduction 17

Structure 17

Cryptography 18

Public Key Encryption 18

Hashes 19

Digital Signatures 19

Chain of Ownership 21

Proof-of-Work (PoW) 21

Mining 22

Proof-of-Stake (PoS) 22

Probabilistic Finality (Chain-based) 23

Absolute Finality (PBFT) 23

Ouroboros Protocol 24

Ouroboros Classic 24

Ouroboros BFT 24

Ouroboros Praos 25

Ouroboros Genesis 25

Ouroboros Crypsinous 25

Ouroboros Chronos 26

Ouroboros Protocol Lifecycle 26

Time 26

Register 26

Staking 26

Conclusion 27

Points to Remember 28

Multiple Choice Questions 29

Answers 30

Questions 30

Key Terms 30

3. Transactions 31

Introduction 31

Structure 31

Addresses 32

Network Tag 32

Base Address ... 32
Enterprise Address ... 33
Reward (Stake) Addresses ... 33
UTXO ... 35
Transaction Input ... 36
Transaction Output ... 36
Metadata ... 38
Plutus Scripts ... 40
Datums ... 40
Redeemers ... 40
Witness Set ... 41
Conclusion ... 42
Points to Remember ... 42
Multiple Choice Questions ... 43
Answers ... 44
Questions ... 44
Key Terms ... 45
4. Plutus ... 46
Introduction ... 46
Structure ... 46
Plutus Specification ... 47
UPLC Primitive Types ... 48
UPLC Grammar ... 49
UPLC Example ... 50
Concise Binary Representation (CBOR) ... 50
Transaction ... 51
Redeemer ... 53
Plutus Script ... 53
Datum ... 54
Plutus Execution Budget ... 55
Collateral ... 56
Conclusion ... 56

Points to Remember 56
Multiple Choice Questions 57
Answers 58
Questions 58
Key Terms 59
5. Transaction Builder 60
Introduction 60
Structure 60
Transaction Lifecycle 60
Wallets 61
Seed Phrase 62
Testnet Faucet 62
Address Derivation 64
Staking 65
CIP-30 67
Demeter.run 67
Off-Chain Examples 70
Helios 70
Initialize 71
Lock 72
Step 1 72
Step 2 73
Step 3 74
Lucid + Aiken 77
Blockfrost API 77
Initialize 77
Lucid Off-Chain Code 79
Conclusion 80
Points to Remember 81
Multiple Choice Questions 81
Answers 82

Questions....82
Key Terms....83
6. Validators....84
Introduction....84
Structure....84
Validators....84
Helios....85
Helios On-Chain Validator....85
Helios Off-Chain Unlock....87
Off-Chain Cancel....90
Test Drive....91
Aiken....92
Aiken On-Chain Validator....93
Lucid Off-Chain Unlock....94
Lucid Off-Chain Cancel....95
Test Drive....96
Conclusion....96
Points to Remember....97
Multiple Choice Questions....97
Answers....98
Questions....99
Key Terms....99
7. Minting....100
Introduction....100
Structure....100
Tokens....101
Native Assets....101
Token Bundles....101
Minting Policy....102
Fungible Tokens....102
Non-Fungible Tokens....103
Token Registry....103

NFT Metadata Standards ... 103

CIP-25 ... 104

CIP-68 ... 105

Coin Selection ... 105

Minting Policy Use Case ... 106

Helios On-Chain Minting Policy ... 107

Helios Off-Chain Mint ... 108

Helios Off-Chain Burn ... 110

Aiken On-Chain Minting Policy ... 111

Lucid Off-Chain Mint ... 112

Wallet Info ... 114

Setup ... 115

Demo ... 115

Conclusion ... 120

Points to Remember ... 120

Multiple Choice Questions ... 121

Answers ... 122

Questions ... 122

Key Terms ... 122

8. Tooling ... 124

Introduction ... 124

Structure ... 124

Blockchain API/Monitoring Providers ... 124

Blockfrost ... 125

Maestro ... 125

Code Example ... 125

Setup ... 127

Koios ... 127

Dandelion ... 127

Tooling Components ... 127

Cardano Node ... 128

Ogmios ... 133

Kupo ... 136
Code Example ... 137
Setup ... 138
Local Devnet ... 138
Environment ... 139
Install Docker ... 139
Example Test Drive ... 144
Additional Resources ... 146
Conclusion ... 147
Points to Remember ... 147
Multiple Choice Questions ... 148
Answers ... 149
Questions ... 149
Key Terms ... 149
9. Ticket Application Design ... 150
Introduction ... 150
Structure ... 150
Design Patterns ... 151
Thread Token ... 151
Beacon Token ... 152
Order Book ... 152
Anti-Patterns ... 154
Liquidity Pools ... 154
Batchers ... 155
Cardano Improvement Proposals ... 155
CIP-0003 Wallet Key Generation ... 155
CIP-0030 Cardano dApp-Wallet Web Bridge ... 156
CIP-0032 Inline Datums ... 156
CIP-0040 Explicit Collateral Output ... 156
CIP-0068 Datum Metadata Standard ... 156
The Application Architecture ... 158
On-Chain State Machine Diagrams ... 158

Minting Tickets ... 159
Burning Tickets ... 159
Opening Swap ... 160
Updating Swap ... 161
Executing Swap ... 162
Closing Swap ... 163
Print Ticket ... 164
Off-Chain Sequence Diagrams ... 165
Minting Tickets ... 165
Connected Wallet ... 166
Opening Swap ... 166
Viewing Swaps ... 167
Updating Swap ... 169
Executing Swap ... 170
Closing Swap ... 171
Print Ticket ... 171
Verifying Ticket ... 172
Conclusion ... 173
Points to Remember ... 174
Multiple Choice Questions ... 175
Answers ... 176
Questions ... 176
Key Terms ... 176
10. Ticket Application Implementation ... 177
Introduction ... 177
Structure ... 177
Application Stack ... 177
Application Resources ... 178
Common ... 179
Components ... 179
Config ... 179
Init ... 179

Lib 179

Node Modules 179

Pages 179

Pages / API 179

Public 180

Public/Contracts 180

Schema 180

Front-end Application 180

Header and Footer 181

Wallet Connector 181

Swap View 182

Swap Card 184

Event View 185

Event Card 185

My Tickets 185

Print Tickets 186

Transaction Builder 187

Smart Contracts 190

Beacon Minting Policy 190

Ticket Minting Policy 191

Holding Validator 194

Swap Validator 196

Back-end Application 202

Redis DB 202

APIs 203

Redis DB Setup 203

Blockfrost Setup 204

Application Owner Public/Private Key 205

Demo 205

Initial Startup 205

Connect Wallet 206

My Events 206

- *New Event* ... 207
- *Open Swap* ... 208
- *Get Tickets* ... 209
- *Update Swap* ... 210
- *Buy Tickets* ... 211
- *My Tickets* ... 214
- *Print Ticket* ... 215
- *Verify Ticket* ... 216
- *Close Swap* ... 217
- *Search* ... 220
- *Browser Wallet* ... 222
- *Blockchain Benefits* ... 223

Conclusion ... 224
Points to Remember ... 224
Multiple Choice Questions ... 225
- *Answers* ... 226

Questions ... 226
Key Terms ... 227

11. Testing, Security, and Scaling ... 228

Introduction ... 228
Structure ... 228
Testing Frameworks ... 229
- *Testing Strategy* ... 230
- *Test Cases* ... 232
- *Property-Based Testing* ... 235

Secure Smart Contracts ... 236
- *Double Satisfaction* ... 236
- *Invalid Datums* ... 239
- *Token Leakage* ... 241
- *Audits* ... 243

Scaling ... 244
- *Avoiding UTXO Contention* ... 244

Reference Scripts 244
Advanced Smart Contract Designs 246
Hydra 246
Mithril 247
Input Endorsers 247
Conclusion 248
Points to Remember 249
Multiple Choice Questions 249
Answers 250
Questions 250
Key Terms 251
12. Troubleshooting 252
Introduction 252
Structure 252
Trace and Print 252
Helios 253
Aiken 254
CBOR Analysis 255
Helios 255
Lucid + Aiken 255
Execution Budget Errors 256
Compiler Errors 258
Transaction Builder Errors 259
Cardano Node Errors 259
Wallet Errors 260
Conclusion 261
Points to Remember 261
Multiple Choice Questions 262
Answers 263
Questions 263
Key Terms 264

13. Cardano Ecosystem 265
Introduction 265
Structure 265
State of Cardano 266
Cardano GitHub Repositories 267
Cardano Improvement Process (CIP) 268
Member-Based Organization (Intersect) 269
CIP-1694 269
Delegated Representatives (DReps) 270
Stake Pool Operators (SPOs) 270
Constitutional Committee (CC) 270
Stake Pool Operators 271
Project Catalyst 272
Atala Prism (HyperLedger Identus) 273
Midnight 274
Additional Cardano Smart Contract Languages 274
Learning Resources 274
Conclusion 275
Points to Remember 276
Multiple Choice Questions 277
Answers 278
Questions 278
Key Terms 278
14. Closing Remarks 280
Introduction 280
Structure 280
Cardano Ethos 280
Software Industry Standards 281
Blockchain Risks 281
Semi-Formal Methods 282
IACR 283
Potential for Social Good 283

World Mobile 284
Empowa 284
Crypto Green Research 284
Social Good Projects 284
Regulatory and Compliance Risks 285
Technology Adoption 285
The Cardano Journey 286
Conclusion 287
Points to Remember 287
Multiple Choice Questions 288
Answers 289
Questions 289
Key Terms 290
Bibliography **291**
Index **299**

CHAPTER 1
Blockchain Evolution

Introduction

This chapter will introduce blockchain and distributed ledger technology, focusing on prior implementations and challenges to overcome. We will look at the landmark Bitcoin whitepaper and how it ushered in a new era of digital currencies. Next, we will introduce the Ethereum whitepaper, how the concept of smart contracts was born, and the problems that Ethereum was addressing. This chapter will also review the key takeaways from the famous Charles whiteboard video that led many to dig deeper into the Cardano ecosystem. We will then explore the classic Blockchain Trilemma of decentralization, security, and scalability. There will also be a review of tokenomics and Cardano's native currency, Ada. Finally, we will finish the chapter discussing the Cardano roadmap and blockchain use cases.

Structure

In this chapter, we will discuss the following topics:

- Distributed Ledger Technology
- Bitcoin Whitepaper
- Ethereum Whitepaper
- Charles Hoskinson Whiteboard Video
    - Scalability
    - Interoperability
    - Sustainability
- Blockchain Trilemma
- Tokenomics
    - Token Allocation
    - Token Distribution
    - Token Allocation Comparison
    - Cardano Inflation Rate

- Cardano Roadmap
- Blockchain Use Cases

Distributed Ledger Technology

The concept of using a ledger to record credit and debit transactions has existed for thousands of years.[1] With the advent of distributed computing, the concept of the ledger was extended, where multiple parties can see and update a ledger using computers connected to a network. The difference between a centralized and a decentralized distributed ledger, as shown in *Figure 1.1*, is that you no longer have a single central authority. The issue, however, is that you still need a way to ensure the correct ordering of immutable transactions. In 1991, **Stuart Haber** and **W. Scott Stornetta** wrote "*How to Time-Stamp a Digital Document*," which described an approach using timestamps and cryptographic hashes to prove when a digital document had been created or if it had been modified.[2] This approach was used to check for immutability.

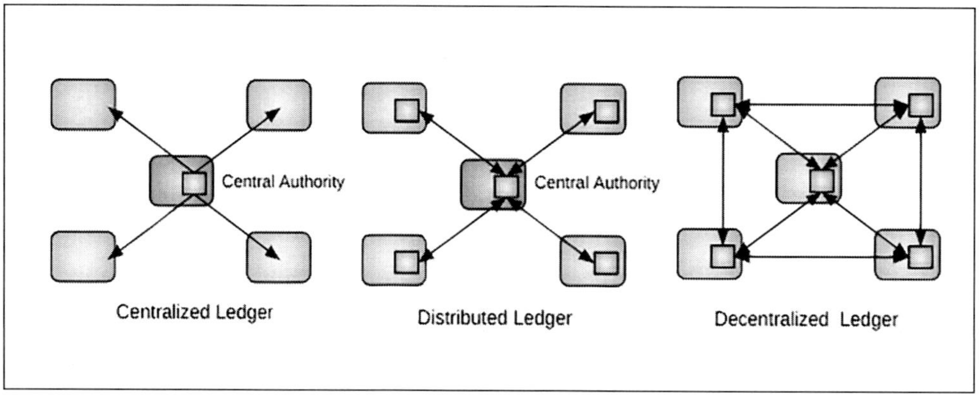

Figure 1.1: *Types of Ledgers*

Byzantine Generals Problem

Another core aspect of distributed ledger technology is ensuring the data stored on each node is correct in a network that may include malicious or unavailable nodes. This problem is known as the Byzantine Generals Problem (BGP).[3] BGP describes a scenario where generals surround a castle for an attack and must communicate and coordinate with each other via messengers. The attack will only succeed if all generals attack simultaneously, using the messengers to signal the attack. The risk, however, is that the attack signal may or may not be received correctly by all generals because the messengers may have been killed or bribed. A network resistant to these types

[1] Lyn Alden, "Broken Money," 1-2.
[2] Stuart Haber et al., "How to Time-Stamp a Digital Document."
[3] Leslie Lampor et al., "The Byzantine Generals Problem."

of failures is called Crash Fault-Tolerant (CFT) and Byzantine Fault-Tolerant (BFT), respectively.

The paper "*Building Secure File Systems Out of Byzantine Storage*" by **Mazières** and **Shasha** introduces a Byzantine fault-tolerant (**BFT**) algorithm that allows a distributed network to reach a consensus on the state of data in an untrusted network.[4] The authors created a consistency protocol called **SUNDR** (Secure Untrusted Data Repository) by leveraging redundancy to handle Byzantine failures and using digital signatures. If a discrepancy is discovered, the protocol will detect malicious behavior and partition file system data blocks into forks.

Network Consensus

For a network to agree on a common state, it needs to use a consensus algorithm that has two key properties:

- **Liveness**: Must continue to make progress in deciding the network state.
- **Safety**: Once honest nodes have confirmed the network state, they must remain committed to this decision.

When dealing with decentralized ledger networks, it is vital for the network's security that the majority of nodes participating in the consensus algorithm are honest. If not, then this is known as a 51% attack, where a single entity controls the majority of nodes. When this happens, the attacker can control the consensus outcome and undo past (or deny future) transactions that may benefit the attacker.

The concept of using computation cycles for solving puzzles in decentralized consensus was first introduced in 1998 by **Wei Dai**'s b-money.[5] The benefit of this approach is that it does not require a centralized authority to create money. "*In 2005, **Hal Finney** introduced the concept of 'reusable proofs of work'*[6]*, a system that uses ideas from b-money together with **Adam Back**'s computationally difficult Hashcash puzzles to create a concept for a cryptocurrency*."[7] This approach, unfortunately, still relied on a trusted back-end,[8] so it did not meet the goal of trustless, decentralized money.

Bitcoin Whitepaper

In 2008, the pseudonym **Satoshi Nakamoto** published "*Bitcoin: A Peer-to-Peer Electronic Cash System*" to address the double spending problem with a decentralized, peer-to-peer electronic cash system, as shown in *Figure* 1.2. In this landmark paper, Satoshi proposed "*a peer-to-peer network using proof-of-work to record a public*

[4]David Mazieres et al., "Building Secure File Systems Out of Byzantine Storage."
[5]Wei Dai, "b-money."
[6]Hal Finney, "RPOW - Reusable Proofs of Work."
[7]Vitalik Buterin, "A Next-Generation Smart Contract and Decentralized Application Platform," 4.
[8]Vitalik Buterin, "A Next-Generation Smart Contract and Decentralized Application Platform," 4.

history of transactions that quickly becomes computationally impractical for an attacker to change if honest nodes control a majority of CPU power."[9] This is accomplished by using network timestamp transactions and "*by hashing them into an ongoing chain of hash-based proof-of-work, forming a record that cannot be changed without redoing the proof-of-work. The longest chain not only serves as proof of the sequence of events witnessed but also as proof that it came from the largest pool of CPU power. As long as a majority of CPU power is controlled by nodes that are not cooperating to attack the network, they'll generate the longest chain and outpace attackers.*"[10]

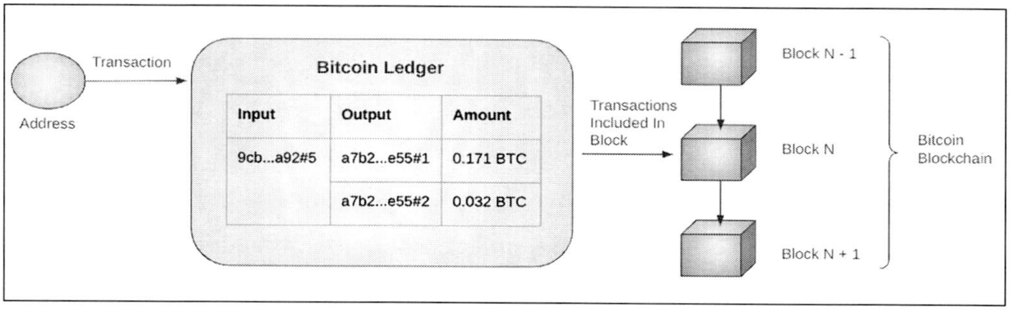

Figure 1.2: *Bitcoin Ledger*

Bitcoin's **Proof-of-Work** implementation was innovative because it solved two problems at the same time. First, it provided a simple and moderately effective consensus algorithm, allowing nodes in the network to collectively agree on a set of canonical updates to the state of the Bitcoin ledger.[11] Second, it provided a mechanism for allowing free entry into the consensus process, solving the political problem of deciding who gets to influence the consensus while simultaneously preventing Sybill attacks.[12]

On January 3rd, 2009, the first Bitcoin block was minted, and a new era of permissionless and trustless digital currency was born. In the subsequent chapters on *Cryptography and Consensus Algorithms Overview* and *Transactions,* we will explore the Bitcoin whitepaper in more detail.

Ethereum Whitepaper

The Ethereum whitepaper by **Vitalik Buterin,** published in 2014, introduced a new way of using blockchain technology to create a more general-purpose distributed computing platform. In particular, he described the concept of a Smart Contract, which can be considered as cryptographic "*boxes*" that contain value and only unlock

[9]Satoshi Nakamoto, "Bitcoin: A Peer-to-Peer Electronic Cash System," 8.
[10]Satoshi Nakamoto, "Bitcoin: A Peer-to-Peer Electronic Cash System," 1.
[11]Vitalik Buterin, "A Next-Generation Smart Contract and Decentralized Application Platform," 4.
[12]Vitalik Buterin, "A Next-Generation Smart Contract and Decentralized Application Platform," 4.

it if certain conditions are met.[13] Unlike Bitcoin scripts, Ethereum Smart Contracts would be Turing-complete and have access to a global state and persistence storage, as shown in *Figure 1.3*. The Smart Contract running in the Ethereum Virtual Machine (**EVM**) would be value-aware and could read the Ether (ETH) amount at the contract account.

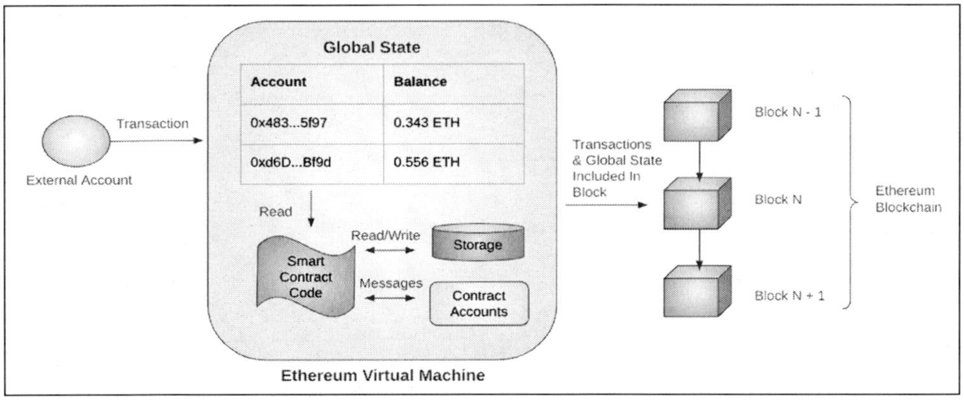

Figure 1.3: *Ethereum Ledger*

The global state in Ethereum contains two types of accounts: externally owned accounts, controlled by private keys, and contract accounts, controlled by their Smart Contract code.[14] Smart Contracts are self-executing since they contain all the information they need within a single node. By using a global state, Ethereum has the advantage that it does not need to recreate all previous transactions to determine the current state of the network. It only has to apply the current transactions in the most recent block to the last global state stored on the node.

Transactions in Ethereum refers to a signed data package that stores a message sent from an externally owned account. Contracts can send messages to other contracts, where messages are virtual objects that are never serialized and exist only in the Ethereum execution environment.[15] Ethereum is also considered non-deterministic because of the use of a global state. In contrast, Bitcoin and Cardano are deterministic since they only use a local state in transactions.

Ethereum smart contracts have the risk of infinite loops because they are Turing-complete scripts. To address this, Ethereum uses the concept of gas fees that are consumed when a smart contract (or chain of smart contracts) is executed. When a transaction is submitted, it must include the maximum amount of gas it will consume to safeguard against an infinite loop code execution.

[13]Vitalik Buterin, "A Next-Generation Smart Contract and Decentralized Application Platform," 13.

[14]Vitalik Buterin, "A Next-Generation Smart Contract and Decentralized Application Platform," 13.

[15]Vitalik Buterin, "A Next-Generation Smart Contract and Decentralized Application Platform," 13.

Charles Hoskinson's Whiteboard Video

The popular whiteboard video by **Charles Hoskinson,** with over 1M views,[16] introduces the concept that Cardano is a third-generation blockchain, with Bitcoin being the first generation and Ethereum being the second generation. Cardano builds upon the first- and second-generation blockchains and addresses some of the key pain points from each, namely:

- Scalability
- Interoperability
- Sustainability

Scalability

Charles indicates that neither Bitcoin nor Ethereum can scale to billions of users, and to improve scalability, one must focus on three key areas:

- **TPS**: Transaction per second.
- **Network**: Network bandwidth required to use and share the network.
- **Storage**: The size of the blockchain that needs to be saved persistently.

Cardano has created, published, and released Ouroboros, a Provable secure Proof-of-Stake Protocol to increase TPS. This protocol requires significantly fewer resources than Proof-of-Work, so parallelism and sidechains can be introduced to increase **TPS**. Cryptographic compression algorithms, in addition to sidechains, will reduce the size of the blockchain that needs to be transmitted and stored, improving both **network** and **storage** scalability. The concept of sidechains allows the base layer of Cardano to act as a settlement layer, while sidechains act as computation layers. When scaling to billions of users, it is not feasible or practicable to broadcast, relay, and store every transaction to all nodes on a settlement layer.

Interoperability

Another area that Cardano aims to address is how a blockchain interacts with other blockchains and legacy systems. In particular, Charles sees a future where multiple blockchains exist, and Cardano can interoperate with each other so value can flow between them. Additionally, there needs to be awareness and the ability to transact with traditional financial systems. To do so, a blockchain needs to have the following capabilities:

- **Metadata**: The story behind a transaction.
- **Attribution**: Identity of senders and receivers.
- **Compliance**: KYC and anti-money laundering.

[16]Charles Hoskinson, "Cardano whiteboard; overview with Charles Hoskinson."

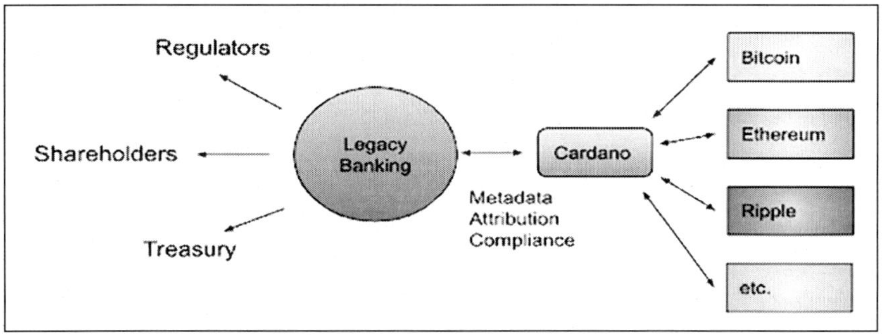

Figure 1.4: *Cardano Interoperability*

Each of these topics is highly sensitive and contentious in the blockchain space. Great care must be exercised when dealing with these items since they may contain personal information stored on an immutable blockchain.

Sustainability

The last area to address is how a blockchain will grow, be funded, and be governed. Will it be a patronage model susceptible to being co-opted by large entities motivated by self-interest? Or will it be a one-time initial coin offering (ICO), which is finite and will run out of funds at some point? The approach taken with Cardano is to build into the protocol a self-sustaining treasury that is funded by initial token supply distribution and ongoing transaction fees. Equally, if not more important, is the question of who decides and how the funds are spent. This falls into the Governance phase in Cardano, which Charles indicates will be the hardest of all the phases in Cardano. The concept is that Ada holders can vote on treasury spending along with governance actions on features or improvements to the protocol over time.

The Blockchain Trilemma

The Blockchain Trilemma refers to a widely held belief that decentralized networks can only provide two of the three benefits at any given time concerning decentralization, security, and scalability.[17]

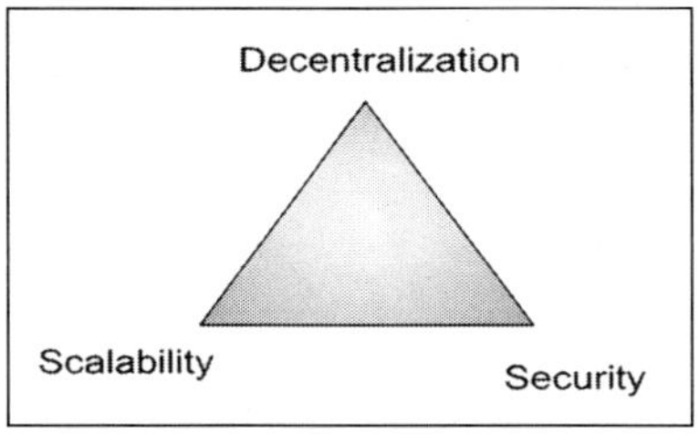

Figure 1.5: *Blockchain Trilemma*

[17]Cryptopedia, "The Blockchain Trilemma: Fast, Secure, and Scalable Networks."

- **Decentralization:** Creating a blockchain that avoids a central point of control.
- **Scalability**: The blockchain must be able to handle an increasing number of users and transactions.
- **Security**: A blockchain must operate as expected, and defend itself from attacks, bugs, and other unforeseen issues.[18]

Cardano aims to address each of these dimensions using the following approaches:

- Promote decentralization by ensuring that a stake pool securing the network can be run with ordinary hardware and a typical internet connection.
- Address scalability with side chains, cryptographic roll-ups, and parallelism (pipelining), increasing the speed at which transactions are processed.
- For high-assurance software and security, use a scientific approach, including a peer review process and formal verification of the Ouroboros Proof-of-Stake protocol.

Tokenomics

The last topic in the chapter is a brief review of tokenomics. A cryptocurrency token is critical in establishing value for a cryptocurrency ecosystem. This is important because running and supporting a network will take real-world resources and costs. Therefore, it is essential to understand the initial token distribution and monetary policy, such as the maximum supply and inflation rate, and how they influence price and market capitalization. Finally, as with the stock market, price and value are frequently misaligned. So, be cautious when evaluating an ecosystem based on the price of the cryptocurrency token. The price may have less to do with the utility or value of that ecosystem and more to do with price manipulation and market sentiment.

Token Allocation

Cardano's native token is Ada, which currently has a circulating supply of 35,125,959,544 ADA and a maximum supply of 45,000,000,000 ADA.[19] The Cardano ICO was completed between October 2015 and January 2017,[20] with the distribution shown in *Figure* 1.6.

[18]https://medium.com/certik/the-blockchain-trilemma-decentralized-scalable-and-secure-e9d8c41a87b3
[19]https://coinmarketcap.com/currencies/cardano/#About
[20]https://cardano.org/genesis/#audit

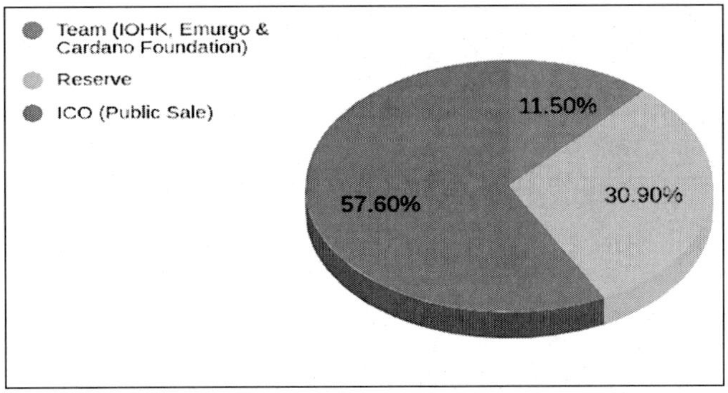

Figure 1.6: *Initial Token Distribution*

There are three founding entities of Cardano:[21]

- **IOHK (IOG)** is a research and engineering company and venture studio that builds blockchain and Web3 products to empower everyone, everywhere.[22]
- **Emurgo** is a for-profit arm that develops, supports, and incubates commercial opportunities and helps integrate businesses into the Cardano blockchain system.
- **Cardano Foundation** is an independent, Swiss-based not-for-profit organization that promotes and advances the Cardano platform for financial and social systems.

Token Distribution

Since there is a maximum supply of Ada, we can see the token distribution at any given time. This is helpful for comparison with other cryptocurrencies because a high allocation of a token not in the circulating supply means there may be downward pressure on the price when the token is released to the public.

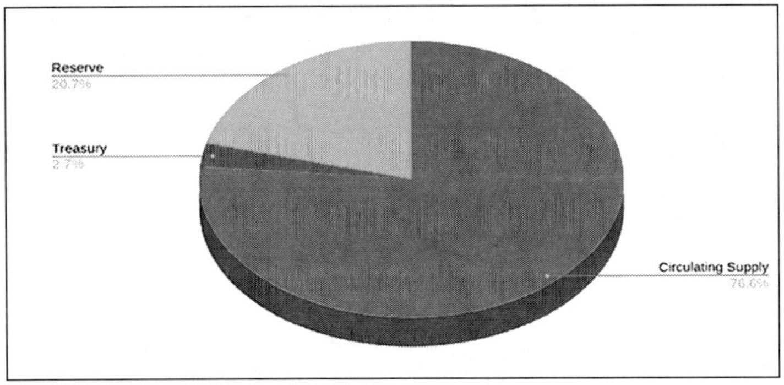

Figure 1.7: *Ada Token Distribution*[23]

[21]https://cardano.org/partners/
[22]https://cardano.org/partners?tab=iog
[23]cardanians.io, "There is 1.23B ADA in Cardano's."

The **reserve** is the amount of Ada used for **staking** rewards and funding the treasury, as shown in *Figure 1.7*. The treasury pays for ecosystem improvements and maintenance. Proof-of-stake networks use staking to allow users to stake their Ada to help secure the network. In return, they receive rewards proportional to the amount of Ada a user stakes vs. all Ada staked in the network. Staking rewards and treasury funding also include transaction fees generated from network activity.

Token Allocation Comparison

Figure 1.8 compares the initial token allocation of the top cryptocurrencies by market capitalization, as of September 27th, 2023. Interestingly, the amount of initial insider + foundation allocation has an upward trend as cryptocurrencies launch over time.

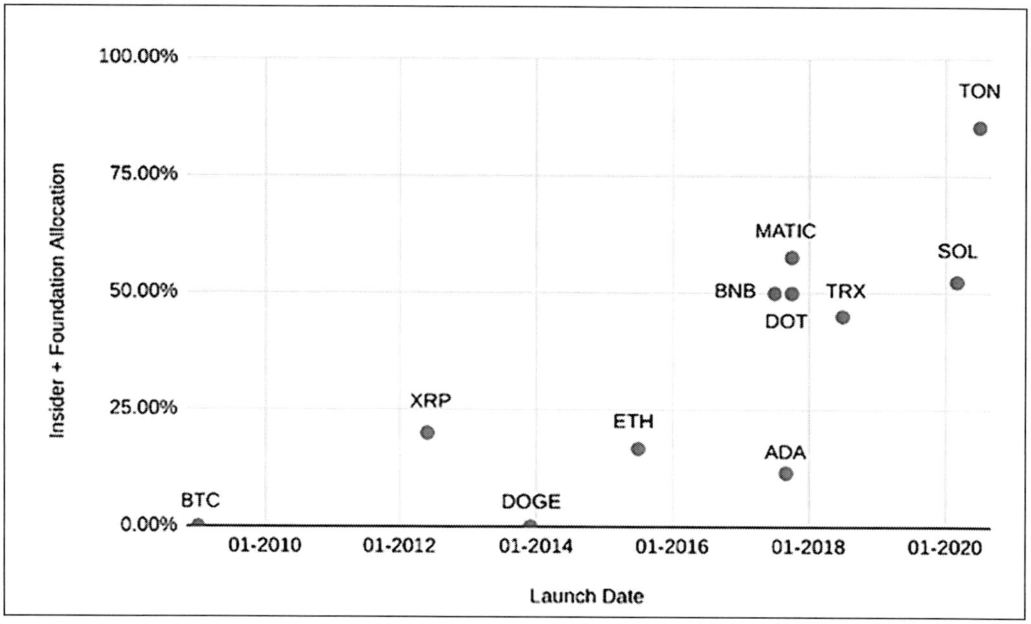

Figure 1.8: *Top 10 Crypto Market Cap Initial Token Allocations*[24]

[24]Source data from:

https://www.investopedia.com/what-is-xrp-6362550#toc-xrp-ledger-and-xrp

https://coinmarketcap.com/currencies/dogecoin/#About

https://www.coingecko.com/en/coins/ethereum/tokenomics

https://coinmarketcap.com/currencies/cardano/#About

https://www.coingecko.com/en/coins/polkadot/tokenomics

https://coinmarketcap.com/currencies/polygon/#About

https://coinmarketcap.com/currencies/bnb/#About

https://coinmarketcap.com/currencies/toncoin/

https://coinmarketcap.com/currencies/solana/#About

Inflation Rate

The last metric we will look at is the Cardano inflation rate of 0.3%.[25] It is the amount of Ada being released from the reserve into the active supply through staking and funding the treasury. The inflation rate for Cardano is similar to that of Bitcoin, which starts out at the highest amount at launch and then exponentially reduces over time, as shown in *Figure* 1.9.

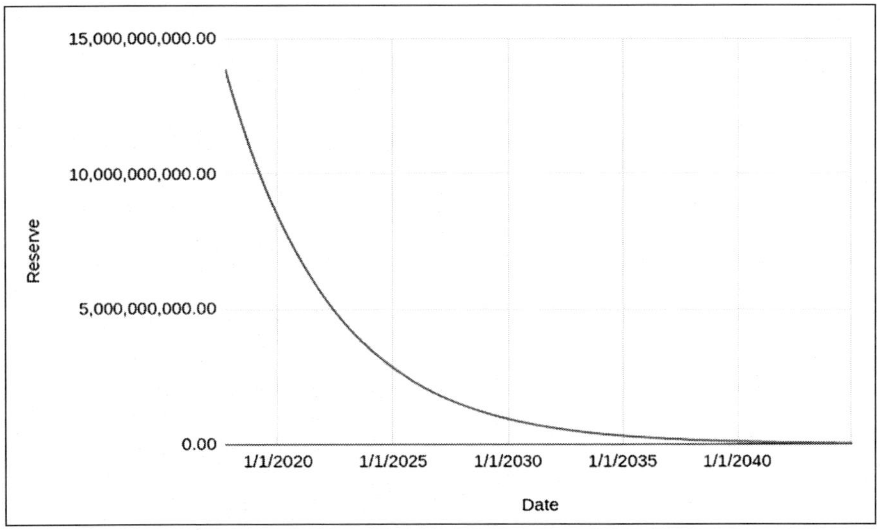

Figure 1.9: *Cardano Inflation Rate*

Cardano Roadmap

The Cardano roadmap has been organized into five themes or phases: Byron, Shelley, Goguen, Basho, and Voltaire.[26] Each theme is focused on a set of capabilities that will be delivered across multiple code releases.[27] Each development theme has one or more eras with a specific set of ledger rules, as shown in *Tables* 1.1 and 1.2.

Phase	Theme	Ledger Era	Description
Byron	Foundation	Byron	The first version of a federated Cardano blockchain using the Ouroboros Proof-of-Stake protocol[28]

[25]https://docs.cardano.org/explore-cardano/monetary-policy/
[26]https://docs.cardano.org/about-cardano/evolution/eras-and-phases/
[27]https://roadmap.cardano.org/en/
[28]https://roadmap.cardano.org/en/byron/

Shelley	Decentralization	Shelley	The roll-out of upgrades improving decentralization and introducing staking delegation and rewards[29]
Goguen	Smart Contracts	Allegra	Introduced token locking support
		Mary	Enabled native tokens and multi-assets
		Alonzo	Launched Smart Contract capability
		Babbage	Implemented features such as inline datums, reference scripts, and reference inputs
Basho	Scaling	N/A	Improve scalability and interoperability of the Cardano network[30]
Voltaire	Governance	Conway	Allow the Cardano blockchain to become a self-sustaining system with network participants using their staked Ada and voting rights to influence the future development of the network[31]

Table 1.1: *Cardano Roadmap*[32]

Date	Phase	Era	Epoch Number	Consensus Mechanism
2017/09	Byron	Byron	0	Ouroboros Classic
2020/02	Byron	Byron	176	Ouroboros BFT
2020/07	Shelley	Shelley	208	Ouroboros Praos
2020/12	Goguen	Allegra	236	Ouroboros Praos
2021/03	Goguen	Mary	251	Ouroboros Praos
2021/09	Goguen	Alonzo	290	Ouroboros Praos
2021/10	Goguen	Alonzo	298	Ouroboros Praos
2022/09	Goguen	Babbage	365	Ouroboros Praos
2023/02	Goguen	Babbage	394	Ouroboros Praos

Table 1.2: *Cardano Timeline*[33]

[29]https://roadmap.cardano.org/en/shelley/
[30]https://roadmap.cardano.org/en/basho/
[31]https://roadmap.cardano.org/en/voltaire/
[32]https://docs.cardano.org/explore-cardano/eras-and-phases/
[33]https://github.com/cardano-foundation/CIPs/blob/master/CIP-0059/feature-table.md

Blockchain Use Cases

To wrap up this introductory chapter, it is helpful to understand some of the blockchain use cases that demonstrate the potential of blockchain technology:

- **Capital Markets**: more efficient flow of capital[34]
- **Tokenization**: representing assets such as gold, stocks, bonds, property, or fiat currencies
- **Rewards:** the ability to use rewards or points to incentivize behavior
- **Decentralized Exchange (DEX)**: non-custodial exchanges for asset and derivative swaps
- **Marketplaces**: to buy and sell tokenized assets
- **Financial Products**: such as lending and borrowing
- **Identity Systems**: Self-Sovereign Identity **(SSI)** solutions
- **Insurance**: using smart contracts and data feeds for claim processing
- **Media and Entertainment**: track and monetize the life cycle of authentic digital content and distribution[35]
- **Decentralized Storage:** leverage token incentivization models for peer-to-peer decentralized storage
- **Decentralized Autonomous Organizations (DAO):** for governance and voting

Conclusion

We should now have a high-level understanding of the evolution of blockchain technology, from the origins of distributed ledgers to the famous Whiteboard Video by Charles Hoskinson, encapsulating the purpose and goals for Cardano. We introduced the Bitcoin and Ethereum whitepapers and will examine both Proof-of-Work and Proof-of-Stake consensus models in more detail in the next chapter. Additionally, we reviewed fundamental blockchain concepts such as the Blockchain Trilemma, tokenomics, Cardano roadmap, and blockchain use cases. In the next chapter, we will take a deeper technical dive into cryptography and consensus algorithms and explore how they make a blockchain secure.

Points to Remember

- Networks can be either centralized or decentralized.
- The difficulty of a decentralized network is that it must not have a central authority.

[34]https://consensys.io/blockchain-use-cases/capital-markets
[35]https://consensys.io/blockchain-use-cases/media-and-entertainment

- A Byzantine fault is where a network node is either unavailable or trying to harm the network.
- A network uses a consensus algorithm to agree on the correct state of the network.
- A 51% attack occurs when a single entity controls the majority of nodes in a decentralized ledger network.
- The Bitcoin whitepaper solved two problems at the same time:
    - Provided a simple and efficient consensus algorithm.
    - Anyone can participate in the consensus algorithm, eliminating the need for a central authority.
- The Ethereum whitepaper introduced the concept of Turing-complete scripts that can access the ledger's global state.
- Cardano is considered a third-generation blockchain with the goals of addressing scalability, interoperability, and sustainability.
- The price and value of a token are frequently misaligned, so when evaluating a cryptocurrency, it is important to consider fundamental principles such as decentralization, security, and scalability.
- Cardano has five development themes or phases: Byron, Shelley, Goguen, Basho, and Voltaire.

Multiple Choice Questions

1. What kind of network does not need central authority?
    a. Centralized
    b. Decentralized
    c. Distributed
    d. Anonymous
2. What innovative concept did Wei Dai publish that Bitcoin uses today?
    a. Computation work by solving puzzles
    b. Computation work by CPU power
    c. Computation work by network power
    d. Computation work by consensus
3. Why was Hal Finney's "*reusable proofs of work*" not widely adopted?
    a. It was based on Proof-of-Work (POW)
    b. It was not decentralized

   c. Relied on a trusted back-end
   d. Insecure cryptography
4. Bitcoin's Proof-of-Work was innovative because it was:
   a. A time-based consensus algorithm
   b. A hash-based consensus protocol
   c. A time- and hash-based consensus protocol
   d. An efficient and open consensus protocol
5. Why Turing-complete scripts were not used in Bitcoin?
   a. There was no suitable computer language to write it at the time
   b. There was a risk of an infinite loop
   c. It needed to be a functional programming language
   d. Bitcoin does not use scripts
6. What are the three key pain points of the first- and second-generation blockchains?
   a. Scalability, Interoperability, Sustainability
   b. Scalability, Decentralization, Sustainability
   c. Decentralization, Scalability, Consensus
   d. Sustainability, Consensus, Programmability
7. What are the three dimensions of the Blockchain Trilemma?
   a. Security, Consensus, Decentralization
   b. Programmability, Security, Consensus
   c. Decentralization, Scalability, Security
   d. Security, Scalability, Programmability

Answers

1. b
2. a
3. c
4. d

5. b
6. a
7. c

Questions

1. What problems are decentralized ledgers trying to solve?
2. Why is decentralization so crucial to a consensus protocol?
3. What is a Byzantine fault and how to mitigate it?
4. What was the motivation for the Bitcoin whitepaper?
5. Why did Vitalik Buterin write the Ethereum whitepaper?
6. What are the goals of Cardano?
7. Why is tokenomics important?

Key Terms

- **Attribution:** Identity of senders and receivers.
- **BFT:** Byzantine fault-tolerant
- **CFT:** Crash fault-tolerant
- **Compliance:** KYC and anti-money laundering.
- **Consensus:** The ability of network nodes to agree on the network state.
- **Decentralized**: A network that does not have a central authority.
- **Metadata:** The story behind a transaction.
- **Reserve:** The amount of cryptocurrency used for staking rewards over time.
- **Scalable**: The ability of a blockchain system to scale network transactions.
- **Secure**: The ability of a blockchain to remain trustworthy.
- **Attribution**: Identity of senders and receivers.
- **Staking**: Using Ada to help secure the Cardano blockchain and receive Ada rewards.
- **Treasury**: The amount of Ada that is used for maintenance and upgrades.

CHAPTER 2
Cryptography and Consensus Algorithms Overview

Introduction

In this chapter, we will introduce cryptography and cryptographic hashes. We will show how cryptographic hashes are made and used in blockchain technology. Next, we will explore the Proof-of-Work consensus protocol used by the Bitcoin blockchain. We will show how a prover and verifier work together to secure a blockchain. Next, we will examine Proof-of-Stake and its benefits over Proof-of-Work. Finally, we will review Ouroboros, Cardano's Proof-of-Stake consensus protocol.

Structure

In this chapter, we will discuss the following topics:

- Cryptography
  - Public Key Encryption
  - Hashes
- Digital Signatures
  - Chain of Ownership
- Proof-of-Work
  - Mining
- Proof-of-Stake
  - Probabilistic Finality (Chain-based)
  - Absolute Finality (PBFT)

- Ouroboros
    - Ouroboros Classic
    - Ouroboros BFT
    - Ouroboros Praos
    - Ouroboros Genesis
    - Ouroboros Crypsinous
    - Ouroboros Chronos
    - Ouroboros Protocol Lifecycle

Cryptography

"*The first recorded use of cryptography for correspondence was by the Spartans, who, as early as 400 BC, employed a cipher device*"[1] for secret communication. A cipher is any method of transforming a message to conceal its meaning.[2] Before the mid-1970s, all cipher systems used symmetric key algorithms, in which the same cryptographic key is used with the underlying algorithm by both the sender and the recipient, who must both keep it secret.[3] The challenge with **symmetric** encryption is that the secret key must be transmitted securely beforehand, which does not scale when there are many keys to manage or a prior secure channel does not exist.[4] This limitation was addressed by **asymmetric** encryption, used in **public key encryption** and **digital signatures**.

Public Key Encryption

The first step in the process of using public key encryption is to generate a pair of public and private keys using a mathematically based one-way cryptographic algorithm.[5] The classic cryptography example refers to Alice trying to send an encrypted message to Bob in *Figure 2.1*. In this case, Alice needs to use Bob's public key to encrypt the message. The message is unreadable to everyone except for Bob, who holds the private key. When Bob receives the encrypted message, he decrypts it using his private key and reads the original message sent by Alice.

---

[1]Gustavus J. Simmons, "History of cryptography."
[2]Encyclopaedia of Britannica, "cipher."
[3]https://en.wikipedia.org/wiki/Public-key_cryptography
[4]A. Menezes, "Handbook of Applied Cryptography," 283.
[5]A. Menezes, "Handbook of Applied Cryptography," 286.

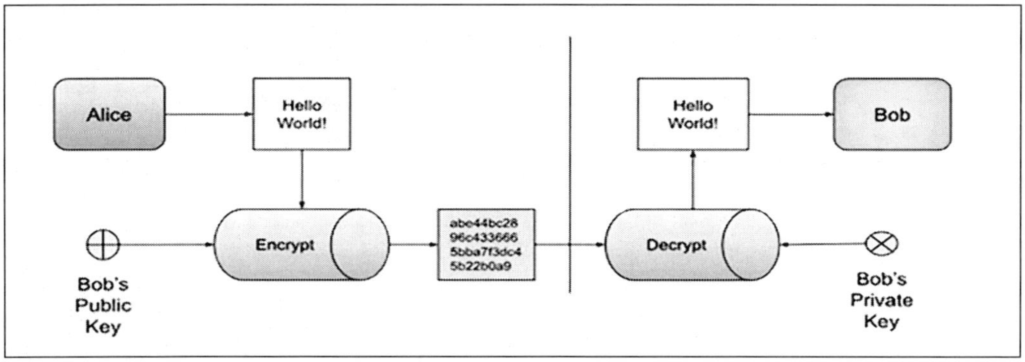

***Figure 2.1**: Public Key Encryption*

Hashes

Cryptographic hashes are generated using a mathematical function that takes an input of arbitrary size and generates a fixed-length output.[6] This is known as a one-way hash and cannot be decoded to reveal the original contents of the input. The generated output will always be the same for the same set of inputs. If there is even the smallest change in the inputs, the generated hash will be entirely different, known as the avalanche effect.[7] The avalanche effect ensures collision resistance and tamper detection, which is used extensively in blockchains.

The BLAKE2b-256 cryptographic hash algorithm is used in Cardano to generate an address,[8] and BLAKE2b-224 is used to generate public key hashes. Hash functions are also used in blockchains to generate a hash of a block containing the list of transactions. This helps check and ensure immutability since any change in the transactions contained in a block will change the block hash.

Digital Signatures

Digital signatures provide a way for Alice to sign a message so that the signature can be later verified by anyone using Alice's public key.[9] The message is not encrypted like public key encryption, instead, a digital signature proves that Alice and only Alice signed this message. In the context of blockchain, the message is a transaction and Alice is the owner of a blockchain address. When a transaction is signed by Alice's private key, anyone else on the blockchain can verify by using Alice's public key, as shown in *Figure* 2.2.

---

[6]Prashant P. Pittalia, "A comparative study of hash algorithms in cryptography," 147.
[7]Darshana Upadhyay, et al., "Investigating the Avalanche Effect of Various Cryptographically Secure Hash Functions and Hash-Based Applications," 112472–112486.
[8]https://docs.cardano.org/learn/cardano-addresses/
[9]Shafi Goldwasser, "Chapter 10: Digital signatures" (PDF). Lecture Notes on Cryptography," 168.

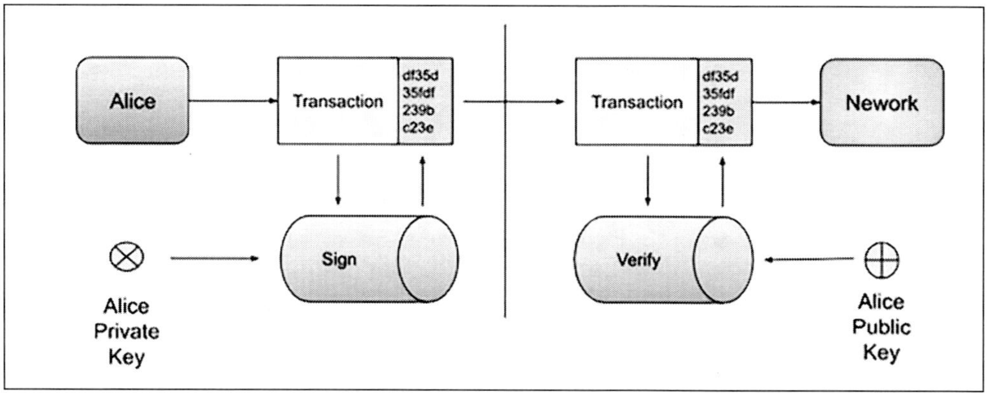

Figure 2.2: *Digital Signatures*

The first commonly used digital signature was Rivest-Shamir-Asleman (RSA), created in 1977, which uses the property that factoring two large primes is difficult. In 1991, the Digital Signature Algorithm (DSA) was created, leveraging the fact that solving the discrete log problem (x ^ y = z) is difficult. Given x and z, solving for y is difficult when y is a large enough number. An elliptic curve signature algorithm was added to DSA, creating the Elliptic Curve Digital Signature Algorithm (ECDSA), which has a smaller key size and faster operations.[10] Cardano uses the Edwards-curve Digital Signature Algorithm (EdDSA), which has the following benefits[11]:

- Fast signing and verification
- High level of security
- Small signatures
- Small keys

Table 2.1 summarizes the different signature algorithms used in Bitcoin, Ethereum, and Cardano:

Blockchain	**Signing Algorithm**	**Elliptic Curve**	**Hash Function**
Bitcoin	ECDSA	Secp256k1	SHA-256
Ethereum	ECDSA	Secp256k1	Keccak-256
Cardano	EdDSA	Curve25519	BLAKE2b

Table 2.1: *Digital signatures*[12]

[10]https://academy.cardanofoundation.org/, "Different Digital Signature Algorithms."
[11]Daniel, J. Bernstein, et. al. "High-speed high-security signatures." J Cryptogr Eng 2, 77–89 (2012).
[12]https://www.susanka.eu/coins-crypto/

Chain of Ownership

An electronic coin, as defined in the Bitcoin whitepaper, is a chain of digital signatures.[13] A Bitcoin is transferred digitally by signing the previous transaction's hash and the next owner's public key. A transaction will only be approved if the signature matches the public key included in the previous transaction. By linking these together, the **chain of ownership** can be verified, as shown in *Figure* 2.3.

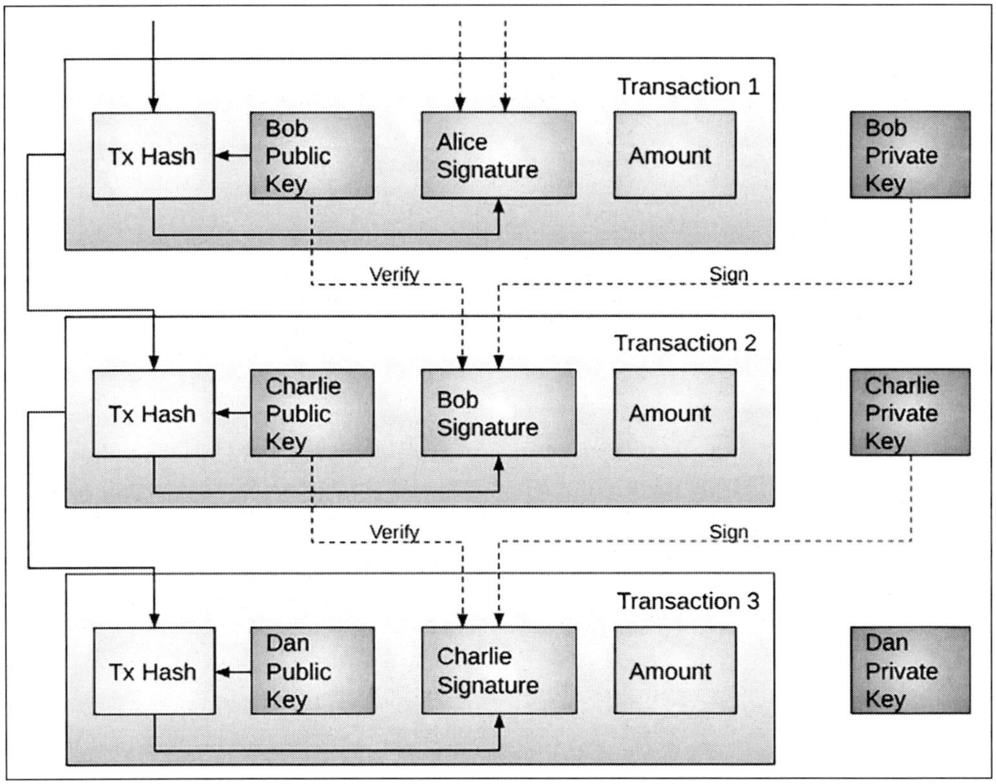

***Figure 2.3**: Chain of Ownership*[14]

Proof-of-Work (PoW)

In the Bitcoin whitepaper, the double-spend problem is where Bob tries to create two transactions to spend the same amount twice. To solve this issue, a timestamp or timeline is introduced. Each block hash is linked to the previous block hash, creating a chain of blocks and ordering transactions, as shown in *Figure* 2.4. The ledger can now confirm if a transaction is trying to double-spend outputs that have already been spent and reject it accordingly.

[13]Satoshi Nakamoto, "Bitcoin: A Peer-to-Peer Electronic Cash System," 2.
[14]Satoshi Nakamoto, "Bitcoin: A Peer-to-Peer Electronic Cash System," 2.

To help regulate the frequency of block production, a nonce is used and incremented to find a block hash with a required number of zero bits. The Bitcoin network monitors the pace of block production, and if blocks are produced too fast, the number of required zero bits increases. Conversely, if the number of blocks being produced takes too long, the number of required zero bits decreases. The adjustment of the required number of zero bits is also known as **difficulty**.[15] The level of CPU effort increases exponentially as the **difficulty** increases. Because the blocks are chained together, undoing a previous transaction requires changing all the previous blocks, which becomes practically impossible as more blocks are confirmed by the network.

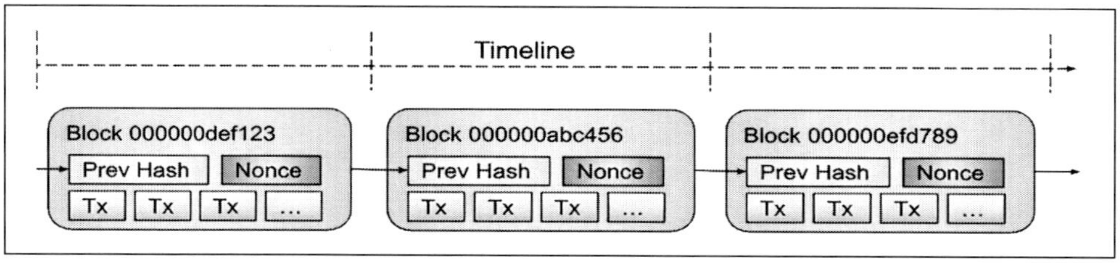

Figure 2.4: *Proof-of-Work*

Mining

The last issue to solve is to provide an incentive for creating new blocks called mining and encourage miners to be honest and not attack the network. This is accomplished by distributing new Bitcoins in the first transaction in each block to the miner who created the block. The number of new Bitcoins created decreases exponentially over time, which controls Bitcoin's inflation rate. Additionally, if the output value of the transaction is less than the input value, this is considered a transaction fee and awarded to the miner.[16] The new Bitcoins plus the transaction fee will make it more profitable for the miner to act honestly rather than try to subvert the network with an invalid block.

Proof-of-Stake (PoS)

With the growing popularity of Bitcoin, the difficulty has increased exponentially. As a result, the **PoW** consensus protocol requires a lot of energy for miners to produce a block. **PoS**, on the other hand, is significantly more energy efficient by selecting block producers randomly and proportionally to the amount of Ada they have staked on the network. Stakeholders can delegate their stake to a Stake Pool Operator (**SPO**) to aggregate Stake together and increase the chances for block production. In a PoS protocol, there is no need to generate computationally intensive puzzles; meanwhile, the security and permissionless properties are still comparable to **PoW**.[17]

---

[15]Satoshi Nakamoto, "Bitcoin: A Peer-to-Peer Electronic Cash System." 2.
[16]Satoshi Nakamoto, "Bitcoin: A Peer-to-Peer Electronic Cash System," 4.
[17]Aggelos Kiayias, et al., "Ouroboros: A Provably Secure Proof-of-Stake Blockchain Protocol," 1.

PoS, however, introduces a different threat vector for determining the block (slot) leader. To achieve a fair randomized election among stakeholders, **entropy** must be introduced into the system and may be prone to manipulation by an adversary.[18] Ouroboros **PoS** protocol mitigates this risk by using an entropy parameter that represents something unpredictable outside the Cardano ecosystem.[19] *"The value of this parameter is calculated based on events that could not have been known in advance, or that anyone could have had insider information about."*[20]

We will look into the Ouroboros protocol in more detail in the next section and will complete the **PoS** overview by examining the two major categories of **PoS** protocols:[21]

- **Probabilistic Finality** (Chain-based)
- **Absolute Finality** (PBFT)

Probabilistic Finality (Chain-based)

Probabilistic or chain-based finality attempts to simulate the **PoW** Nakamoto consensus protocol used in Bitcoin. As more blocks are linked together, they form the longest chain and become probabilistically final.[22] Typically, waiting until 6 blocks have been linked together is sufficient for probabilistic finality, with a high likelihood that a transaction will not be reverted or rolled back. One of the key advantages of a probabilistic finality mechanism is that it prioritizes network **availability** for continuous and permissionless access.

Absolute Finality (PBFT)

In an **Absolute Finality** or Practical Byzantine Fault Tolerant (**PBFT**) protocol, a validator is randomly chosen to propose a new block. The validators then vote on the inclusion of this new block, and consensus is achieved when the required number of validators agree on accepting a new block.[23] Additionally, **PoS** blockchains like Ethereum implement an economic penalty that makes it prohibitively expensive for validators who are unavailable or act maliciously against the network. By using **Absolute** and **Economic Finality**, the protocol prioritizes the **consistency** of the network and would halt the network rather than accept an invalid transaction for any length of time.[24]

---

[18]Aggelos Kiayias, et al., "Ouroboros: A Provably Secure Proof-of-Stake Blockchain Protocol," 1.
[19]https://docs.cardano.org/explore-cardano/cardano-entropy/
[20]https://docs.cardano.org/explore-cardano/cardano-entropy/
[21]Alexis Gauba, "Finality in Blockchain Consensus."
[22]Shehar Bano, et al., "SoK: Consensus in the Age of Blockchains," 2.
[23]Shehar Bano, et al., "SoK: Consensus in the Age of Blockchains," 4.
[24]Alexis Gauba, "Finality in Blockchain Consensus."

Ouroboros Protocol

Ouroboros is the first provably secure **PoS** protocol and the first blockchain protocol based on peer-reviewed research.[25] It consists of a family of PoS protocols, including:

- Ouroboros Classic
- Ouroboros BFT
- Ouroboros Praos
- Ouroboros Genesis
- Ouroboros Crypsinous
- Ouroboros Chronos

Ouroboros Classic

Ouroboros Classic was the first Ouroboros protocol published in July 2017.[26] The paper defined the protocol as an energy-efficient rival to **PoW**, introduced the mathematical framework to analyze PoS, and introduced a novel incentive mechanism to reward participants in a PoS setting.[27] What distinguishes Ouroboros from other blockchain protocols is its ability to generate unbiased randomness in its leader selection algorithm with security assurances.[28] Let's examine this in more detail.

"*Ouroboros divides time on Cardano into epochs, where each epoch is divided into slots. A slot is a short period of time in which a block can be created, and grouping slots into epochs is central to adjusting the leader election process to the dynamically changing stake distribution. A slot leader is elected for each slot, responsible for adding a block to the chain and passing it to the next slot leader. To protect against adversarial attempts to subvert the protocol, each new slot leader must consider the last few blocks of the received chain as transient: only the chain that precedes the prespecified number of transient blocks is considered settled.*"[29]

Ouroboros BFT

The Ouroboros Byzantine Fault Tolerance (**BFT**) was a simplified protocol[30] based on Ouroboros Classic and was used primarily to help with one of the most significant

[25]https://docs.cardano.org/learn/ouroboros-overview/
[26]Aggelos Kiayias, et al., "Ouroboros: A Provably Secure Proof-of-Stake Blockchain Protocol," 1.
[27]Olga Hryniuk, "From Classic to Chronos: the implementations of Ouroboros explained."
[28]https://docs.cardano.org/learn/ouroboros-overview/
[29]Olga Hryniuk, "From Classic to Chronos: the implementations of Ouroboros explained."
[30]Aggelos Kiayias, et al., "Ouroboros-BFT:A Simple Byzantine Fault Tolerant Consensus Protocol," 1.

milestones in Cardano known as the Shelly release. It transitioned the network to a federated model to avoid requiring all nodes to be online all the time.[31]

Ouroboros Praos

Praos introduces a verifiable random function (**VRF**) on the current timestamp and a nonce for a specific epoch.[32] Given a private key and an input, a **VRF** outputs a pseudo-random number and a proof.[33] The corresponding public key can verify the proof and random number. Additionally, this approach prevents anyone except the proposed slot leader from knowing the slot leader for a specific slot in advance. This is important to avoid **DDoS** or targeted attacks, where a slot leader is publicly known in advance.[34]

Ouroboros Genesis

The Bitcoin **PoW** consensus protocol has the advantage that any participant can join the network and participate using only the Genesis block. This is a very important feature of any blockchain, as it does not rely on any trusted notion or checkpoints of the correct state of the network. Ouroboros Genesis addresses this limitation with the Ouroboros **PoS** protocols by using a novel chain selection rule that allows new or offline participants to join the network using only the genesis block.[35] This approach is called "*bootstrapping from genesis*," and the Ouroboros Genesis paper proves that it can still retain the prior security assurances while using this approach. The paper also provides proof of the protocol's Universal Composability, showing that it retains its security properties even when used in different protocol configurations.[36]

Ouroboros Crypsinous

Ouroboros Crypsinous is the first formally analyzed privacy-preserving PoS blockchain protocol.[37] Using SNARKs and key-private forward secure encryption, the paper uses a novel coin evolution technique to prove the network is secure against adaptive attacks.[38] This protocol is not intended to be implemented on the main Cardano settlement layer but may be used in a side chain such as Midnight, a privacy-preserving blockchain.

---

[31]Olga Hryniuk, "From Classic to Chronos: the implementations of Ouroboros explained."
[32]Bernardo David, et al. "Ouroboros Praos: An adaptively-secure, semi-synchronous proof-of-stake blockchain"
[33]LLFOURN, "Introduction To Ouroboros."
[34]Peter Gaži, "Presenting Ouroboros at MIT."
[35]Christian Badertscher, et al., "Ouroboros Genesis: Composable Proof-of-Stake Blockchains with Dynamic Availability," 1.
[36]Olga Hryniuk, "From Classic to Chronos: the implementations of Ouroboros explained."
[37]Thomas Kerber, et al., "Ouroboros Crypsinous: Privacy-Preserving Proof-of-Stake," 1.
[38]Thomas Kerber, "Ouroboros Crypsinous: Privacy-Preserving Proof-of-Stake," 1.

Ouroboros Chronos

Ouroboros Chronos demonstrates how blockchain protocols can synchronize clocks securely via a novel time synchronization mechanism, thereby becoming independent of external time services.[39] The paper aims to make the ledger more resistant to attacks that target time information.[40]

Ouroboros Protocol Lifecycle

Let's walk through the Ouroboros protocol lifecycle to provide a step-by-step example of how everything fits together.

Time

The first block in the Cardano blockchain is the genesis block, which is the beginning of time from a blockchain perspective. Cardano uses the concept of slots, which occur approximately every second, where at most one block can be created. The expected block production frequency is 0.05, meaning that, on average, a block will be produced every 20 seconds.[41] Only a slot leader can create a block for a given slot. There are precisely 432,000 slots in every epoch, equivalent to every 5 days.

Register

The first step in participating in the Cardano network is registering the stake key associated with the Ada to be staked. This typically refers to the registration of Ada to a specific Stake Pool Operator **(SPO)**. The amount staked is used to calculate rewards and distribute proportionally back to the staking addresses. The **SPO** will handle (among other things) the stake pool registration process, as shown in *Figure* 2.5:

1. Synchronize with the network ledger.
2. Obtain the current slot.
3. Obtain the global random oracle.

Staking

1. At the start of each epoch, each stake pool operator queries the blockchain to obtain the stake distribution of a previous block, which was two epochs ago.

[39]Olga Hryniuk, "From Classic to Chronos: the implementations of Ouroboros explained."
[40]Christian Badertscher, et al., "Ouroboros Chronos: Permissionless Clock Synchronization via Proof-of-Stake," 1.
[41]Arnaud Bailly, "Time handling on Cardano, part 1. About Ouroboros and the importance of determinism."

2. Using a **VRF** generated from the first ⅔ slots in the previous epoch, the stakeholder with their private key can produce an output in the current epoch to determine if they can be a slot leader.[42]
3. If the **VRF** output value is below a certain threshold, they can become the slot leader for that block.
4. Slot Leader Responsibilities:[43]
   a. Assemble the transactions that should be included in the block.
   b. Include in the block the random value (v) and proof (π) obtained from the VRF output.
   c. Generate a new private key and delete the old one so it is impossible to forge signatures with the old private key.
   d. Broadcast the new block to the network.
5. The rewards are calculated at the end of the epoch and then distributed to the reward addresses in the next block.

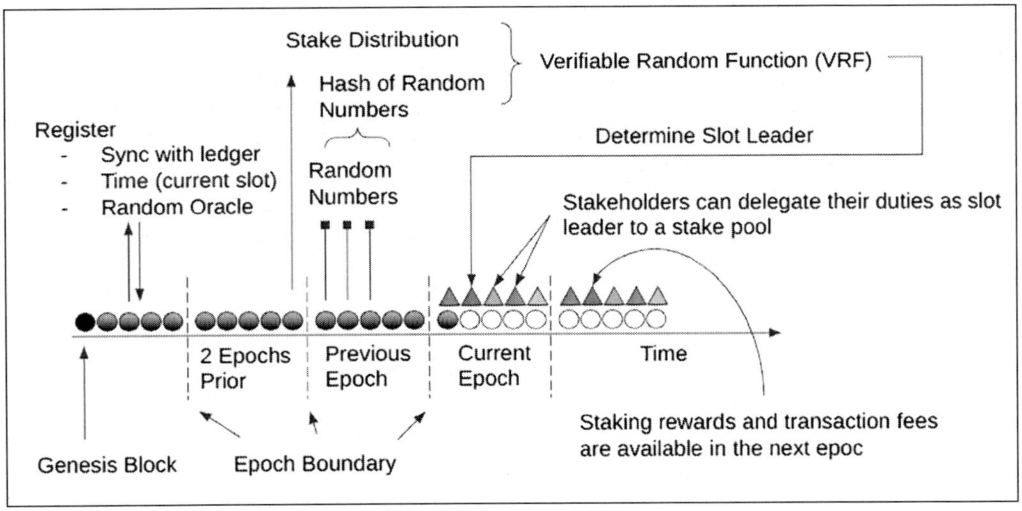

Figure 2.5: *Ouroboros Protocol Lifecycle*

Conclusion

This chapter introduced cryptography with a focus on public key hash algorithms. We saw how this extended to a concept called digital signatures, which underpins cryptocurrencies today. By linking digital signatures, a blockchain can create

[42]Crypto Carlos, "Ourobors protocol. The heart of Cardano."
[43]https://developers.cardano.org/docs/operate-a-stake-pool/introduction-to-cardano/

proof-of-ownership for the movement of a digital coin like Bitcoin. We looked deeper at Proof-of-Work and how mining a block incentivizes miners to be honest and prevent network attacks. We then looked at the energy-efficient Proof-of-Stake and how to mitigate the risk associated with predicting random number generation, along with the differences and tradeoffs between Probabilistic and Absolute Finality. Finally, we reviewed the Ouroboros family of protocols and the current protocol lifecycle on the Cardano Mainnet today. Using our knowledge of cryptography and how **PoS** blockchains work, we will explore how to transfer value using transactions in the next chapter.

Points to Remember

- Using public key encryption requires generating a pair of public and private keys.
- If a transaction is signed by a private key, anyone on the blockchain can verify it using the corresponding public key.
- Bitcoin is transferred digitally by signing the previous transaction's hash and including the next owner's public key.
- To solve the double-spend problem, a timestamp is included in the hash of each block, and more timestamps are included in the chain of blocks, securing the prior blocks.
- Bitcoin mining incentivizes honest behavior by distributing new Bitcoins and transaction fees as the first transaction in each block to the miner who created the block.
- Proof-of-Stake is significantly more energy efficient than Proof-of-Work.
- Proof-of-Stake selects block producers (validators) randomly and proportionally to the native currency they have staked on the network.
- Entropy must be introduced into the system to achieve a fair randomized election among Proof-of-Stake stakeholders.
- With security assurances, Ouroboros can generate unbiased randomness in the protocol's leader selection algorithm.
- Probabilistic finality occurs as more blocks are linked, forming the longest chain.
- Validators vote on including a new block, and the outcome is considered final, achieving Absolute Finality.

Multiple Choice Questions

1. What type of encryption does public key cryptography use?
    a. Symmetric
    b. Asymmetric
    c. Bi-Symmetric
    d. Anonymous
2. How do you verify a signature?
    a. Use both private and public keys
    b. Use the private key
    c. Use the symmetric key
    d. Use the public key associated with the private key
3. How did Bitcoin solve the double-spend problem?
    a. Used timestamps to order transactions
    b. Used a distributed ledger to record transactions
    c. Used cryptography to sign a transaction
    d. Used blocks to record transactions
4. Proof-of-Stake is more energy efficient because:
    a. Block leader selection is not needed
    b. Randomness is not needed
    c. Solving computational puzzles is not needed
    d. Forming the longest chain is not needed
5. What risk occurs in both Proof-of-Stake and Proof-of-Work?
    a. Centralization
    b. Randomness Bias
    c. Plutocracy
    d. Environmental

Answers

1. b
2. d
3. a
4. c
5. a

Questions

1. Why is cryptography important to blockchains?
2. What problems did the Bitcoin whitepaper solve?
3. How much more energy efficient is Cardano PoS compared to Bitcoin PoW?
4. What are the advantages and disadvantages of Absolute Finality?
5. Why is it essential that Ouroboros is provably secure?
6. How does Ouroboros ensure the correct chain is chosen when a client joins the network?

Key Terms

- **Block:** Contains zero or more transactions.
- **Chain of Ownership:** Links digital signatures together.
- **DDos:** Distributed denial of service.
- **Difficulty:** The increasing rate of computation required to create a block.
- **Digital Signature:** Signed message using a private key.
- **Entropy:** The amount of randomness in a system.
- **Epoch:** A unit of time that contains a fixed number of slots.
- **Finality:** A state that can be considered final and irreversible.
- **Mining:** Incentives paid to miners for creating a block.
- **Public Key Encryption:** Generates a pair of public and private keys.
- **PoS:** Proof-of-Stake
- **PoW:** Proof-of-Work
- **Slot:** Occurs every second and may contain at most one block.
- **SPO:** Stake Pool Operator
- **VRF:** Verifiable Random Function

CHAPTER 3
Transactions

Introduction

In this chapter, we will first look at Cardano Addresses, how they are built, and the data inside them. Next, we will look at the UTXO architecture and show how transactions are created, along with optional metadata. We will also introduce how Smart Contracts, known as Plutus scripts, are executed and evaluated. We will see how Redeemers pass data into Plutus scripts and how Datums are used for data storage and persistence. Finally, we will look at the transaction Witness Set and how it authorizes the spending of transaction inputs.

Structure

In this chapter, we will discuss the following topics:

- Addresses
  - Network Tag
  - Base Address
  - Enterprise Address
  - Reward (Staking) Address
- UTXO
  - Transaction Inputs
  - Transaction Outputs
- Metadata
- Plutus Scripts
- Datum
- Redeemer
- Witness Set

Addresses

A Cardano (Shelly) address is a sequence of bytes encoded using Bech32.[1] There are three types of addresses that you will typically interact with on Cardano:

- Base Addresses
- Enterprise Addresses
- Reward (Stake) Addresses

The structure of a Cardano address is shown in *Figure 3.1*:

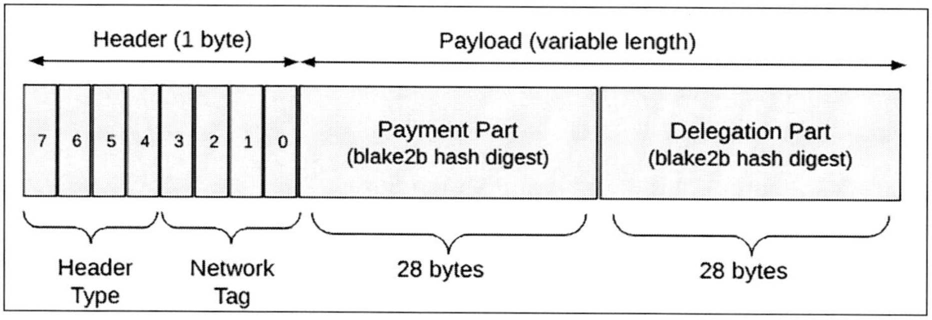

***Figure 3.1**: Cardano Address Structure*

The header type indicates what type of address (or payload), and the network tag indicates what network this address is associated with.

Network Tag

Header Bits	Network
`xxxx0000`	Testnet(s)
`xxxx0001`	Mainnet

***Table 3.1**: Network Tag*

Base Address

A base address is the most common type of address, as shown in *Table 3.2*. When the payment part is a **`PaymentKeyHash`**, the transaction must be signed with the corresponding private key for this address. When the payment part is a **`ScriptHash`**, a script with a matching hash must be executed and evaluated to true to spend from this address. The delegation part is similar to the payment part but is used to register (and delegate) a staking certificate for Ada that is locked at this address. As we recall from

[1]https://github.com/cardano-foundation/CIPs/tree/master/CIP-0019

the previous chapter, staking is the mechanism that helps secure a Proof-of-Stake blockchain and receive rewards for doing so.

Header Bits	Payment Part	Delegation Part
`0000xxxx`	`PaymentKeyHash`	`StakeKeyHash`
`0001xxxx`	`ScriptHash`	`StakeKeyHash`
`0010xxxx`	`PaymentKeyHash`	`ScriptHash`
`0011xxxx`	`ScriptHash`	`ScriptHash`

Table 3.2: *Base Address*

Enterprise Address

An enterprise address is similar to a base address, except there is no delegation part. The header types for enterprise addresses are listed in *Table* 3.3.

Header Bits	Payment Part	Delegation Part
`0110xxxx`	`PaymentKeyHash`	N/A
`0111xxxx`	`ScriptHash`	N/A

Table 3.3: *Enterprise Address*

Reward (Stake) Addresses

Reward addresses are used to distribute rewards for staking in the Proof-of-Stake protocol and have the following properties:[2]

- It uses account-style accounting and not UTXO.
- Account balances are only increased when staking rewards are distributed.
- To transfer out the Ada locked at a Reward Address, a withdrawal-type transaction is required to release the funds and zero out the balance of the rewards address.
- A one-to-one relationship exists between a registered staking key and a reward account address.

Header Bits	Stake Reference
`1110xxxx`	`StakeKeyHash`
`1111xxxx`	`ScriptHash`

Table 3.4: *Reward (Stake) Address*

To put it all together, the following output is generated by the **`cardano-address address inspect`** command line tool. Note that in an address, a chain pointer may

[2]https://docs.cardano.org/learn/cardano-addresses/

exist that refers to an on-chain location containing a stake key registration certificate.[3] Pointers, however, are rarely used, and, in the following example, we can see that the **`stake_reference`** is **"by_value"**, indicating that the staking certificate is at this staking address and not a pointer.

Shelly Base Address (base 32):

```
addr_test1qqq40ucy70wms9p7tku6ntcamzuuxnsaejal7p82qcahh3ryswkc5djr3z37lh
v3zjytgyfpf8en2pa4cfuvqdz4za8syv5dnc
```

```
$ echo addr_test1qqq40ucy70wms9p7tku6ntcamzuuxnsaejal7p82qcahh3ryswkc-
5djr3z37lhv3zjytgyfpf8en2pa4cfuvqdz4za8syv5dnc | cardano-address address
inspect
{
  "address_style": "Shelley",
  "address_type": 0,
  "network_tag": 0,
  "spending_key_hash": "0157f304f3ddb8143e5db9a9af1dd8b9c34e1dccbbff04
  ea063b7bc4",
  "spending_key_hash_bech32": "addr_vkh1q9tlxp8nmkupg0jahx5678wch8p5
  u8wvh0lsf6sx8daug8cyak6",
  "stake_key_hash": "6483ad8a364388a3efdd911488b4112149f33507b5c278c0
  3455174f",
  "stake_key_hash_bech32": "stake_vkh1vjp6mz3kgwy28m7ajy2g3dq3y9ylxdg8
  khp83sp525t57tzwkxk",
  "stake_reference": "by value"
}
```

Convert a Raw Base Address (base 16) with the header bits in bold:

```
$ bech32 <<<
addr_test1qqq40ucy70wms9p7tku6ntcamzuuxnsaejal7p82qcahh3ryswkc5djr3z37lh
v3zjytgyfpf8en2pa4cfuvqdz4za8syv5dnc
000157f304f3ddb8143e5db9a9af1dd8b9c34e1dccbbff04ea063b7bc46483ad8a364388a
3efdd911488b4112149f33507b5c278c03455174f
```

Convert a Raw Stake Address (base 16) with the header bits in bold:

```
$ bech32 <<< stake_test1upjg8tv2xepc3gl0mkg3fz95zys5nue4q76uy7xqx323wncx
v6f68
e06483ad8a364388a3efdd911488b4112149f33507b5c278c03455174f
```

[3] https://github.com/cardano-foundation/CIPs/tree/master/CIP-0019

Hex	Binary	Hex	Binary	Hex	Binary	Hex	Binary
0	0	4	100	8	1000	C	1100
1	1	5	101	9	1001	D	1101
2	10	6	110	A	1010	E	1110
3	11	7	111	B	1011	F	1111

Table 3.5: *Hexadecimal Conversion*

UTXO

Cardano and Bitcoin use a similar unspent transaction output (UTXO) model, whereas a blockchain like Ethereum uses an account-based model. In a UTXO model, a transaction consumes one or more UTXOs as inputs and then produces one or more UTXOs as outputs, where each UTXO is locked at an address. A UTXO can only be spent (used) once and is no longer an *unspent* transaction output if it has already been used as a transaction input. The amount of assets at an address is the sum of all the UTXOs at a particular address. Additionally, only Alice can spend the UTXO at Alice's address because she has the private key and can create a **`signature`** to prove it.

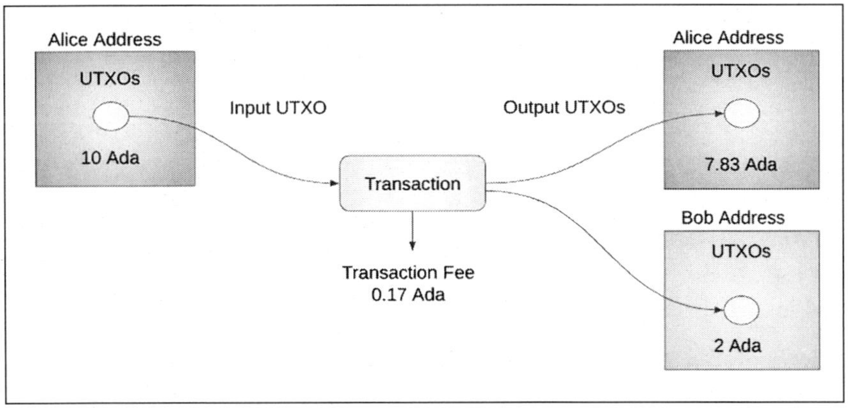

Figure 3.2: *UTXO Model*

In *Figure* 3.2, Alice has a UTXO with 10 Ada and wants to send 2 Ada to Bob. A transaction is created, and the UTXO with the 10 Ada is used as the input, and 2 new UTXOs are created as the outputs. The UTXO with 2 Ada will go to Bob's address, 0.17 Ada will pay for transaction fees, and the remaining Ada (change) will be the UTXO that goes back to Alice. This works the same way as using a physical wallet when trying to pay with a 10-dollar bill at a store for a 2-dollar bottle of water.

Using a blockchain explorer, we can see what this transaction looks like on the Cardano blockchain, as shown in *Figure* 3.3: `https://preprod.cexplorer.io/tx/c9e6dc1e7ecdf7110747c91d0d638ce896435a504e745025996230533ae9f548`

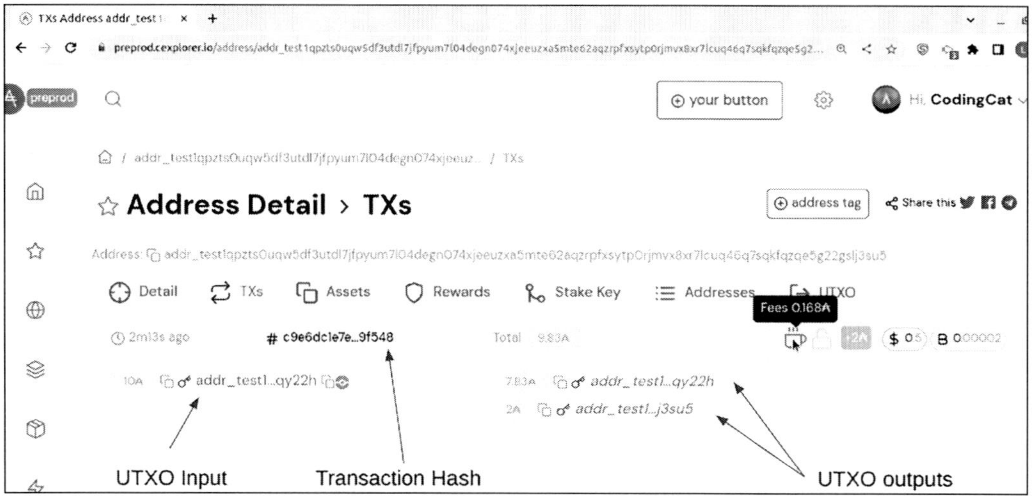

Figure 3.3: *Block Explorer Transaction View*

Transaction Input

A transaction input simply points to a transaction hash on the ledger and index since there may be more than one transaction output for a specific transaction.

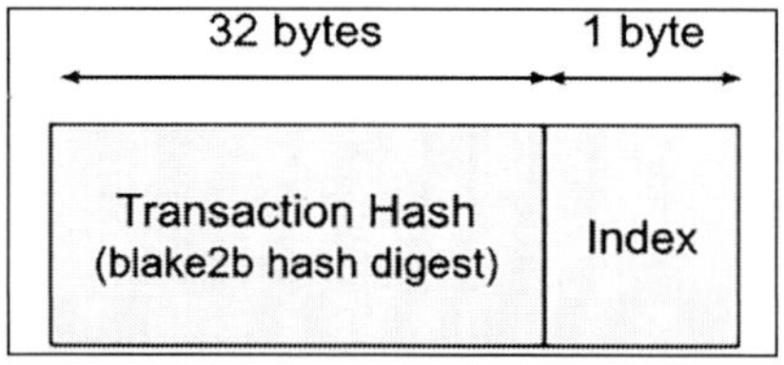

Figure 3.4: *Transaction Input*

The ledger specification[4] for an input is defined as:

```
transaction_input = [ transaction_id : $hash32
                    , index : uint
                    ]
```

Transaction Output

Before the Alonzo Era of smart contracts, a transaction output contained the following:

- Address that the output is locked at
- Value of Ada and any Cardano native tokens
- Optional **`datum`** used for storing a persistent data hash

[4]https://github.com/IntersectMBO/cardano-ledger/blob/master/eras/conway/impl/cddl-files/conway.cddl

The ability to store a **`datum`** value with a UTXO is how Cardano uses a EUTXO model, whereas Bitcoin only uses a UTXO model.

Here is an example of 2 EUTXOs at an address on Cardano*:

```
$ cardano-cli query utxo --address addr_test1vzu...dxn7 --cardano-mode
--testnet-magic 1

TxHash TxIx Amount

--------------------------------------------------------------------

158...925 0 3551912116 lovelace + TxOutDatumNone

b4e...0d2 0 5000000 lovelace + TxOutDatumNone
```

**Please note that the address and TxHash have been truncated for formatting.*

Observations:

- In this example, there are 2 UTXOs.
- Transaction hash 158...925 with index 0 has 3,551,912,116 lovelace.
- Transaction hash b4e...0d2 with index 0 has 5,000,000 lovelace.
- There is 1,000,000 lovelace in 1 Ada.
- The amount of Ada locked at the address is:

  ```
  3,551.912116
     + 5.000000
  3,556.912116
  ```
- There is no datum associated with these UTXOs.

Post Alonzo, additional fields were added to the outputs. In the current Conway Era, we have the following output fields:

- Address that the output is locked at
- Amount of Ada and any Cardano native tokens
- Optional **`datum`** used for storing a persistent data hash on-chain
- Optional **`inline datum`** used for storing persistent data value on-chain
- Optional **`reference script`** that allows a smart contract to be stored on-chain

Here is an example of a UTXO in the Conway era:

```
$ cardano-cli query utxo --tx-in 5f07cfe475c846a7a644850f7174d98d281b09
d3a780a0e51d06d1adff0cdcf7#4 --cardano-mode --testnet-magic 1 --out-file
utxo.out

$ cat utxo.out

{
```

```
    "5f07cfe475c846a7a644850f7174d98d281b09d3a780a0e51d06d1adff0cdcf7#4"
    : {
        "address":
"addr_test1qrazs4ngp8vl0h2qaexugnm4lhjts0g7l94d780pyx99f87m76rh0cewyp03f
8w9e2lemp96jtqk0hyjqtg5528pn9tsyqhfr5",
        "datum": null,
        "datumhash": null,
        "inlineDatum": null,
        "referenceScript": null,
        "value": {
            "lovelace": 981840654
        }
    }
```

The `datum` field contains the datum value attached to a transaction when it is submitted to the Cardano blockchain. If an **`inlineDatum`** is used, the datum value is stored on-chain, otherwise, only the **`datumhash`** is recorded on-chain.

Looking at the ledger specification,[5] the output is defined as follows:

```
post_alonzo_transaction_output =
  { 0 : address
  , 1 : value
  , ? 2 : datum_option ; datum option
  , ? 3 : script_ref   ; script reference
  }


datum_option = [ 0, $hash32 // 1, data ]
```

Metadata

A transaction can have metadata and is optionally included when submitting a transaction to the network. Only the hash of the metadata contents is stored on-chain and *is not* accessible to smart contracts. Blockchain indexers, however, capture, store, and retrieve the full contents of the transaction metadata, which are used for off-chain transaction building. CIP-25,[6] using label 721, was the first transaction metadata standard for minting transactions of Non-Fungible Tokens or NFTs.

[5] https://github.com/IntersectMBO/cardano-ledger/blob/master/eras/conway/impl/cddl-files/conway.cddl

[6] https://github.com/cardano-foundation/CIPs/tree/master/CIP-0025

A minimal structure for an NFT using CIP-25, version 1, is as follows:

```
{
      "721": {
        "<policy_id>": {
          "<asset_name>": {
            "name": <string>,
            "image": <uri | array>
          }
        }
      }
    }
```

An example of this standard being used and viewed with a blockchain explorer[7] is shown in *Figure 3.5*:

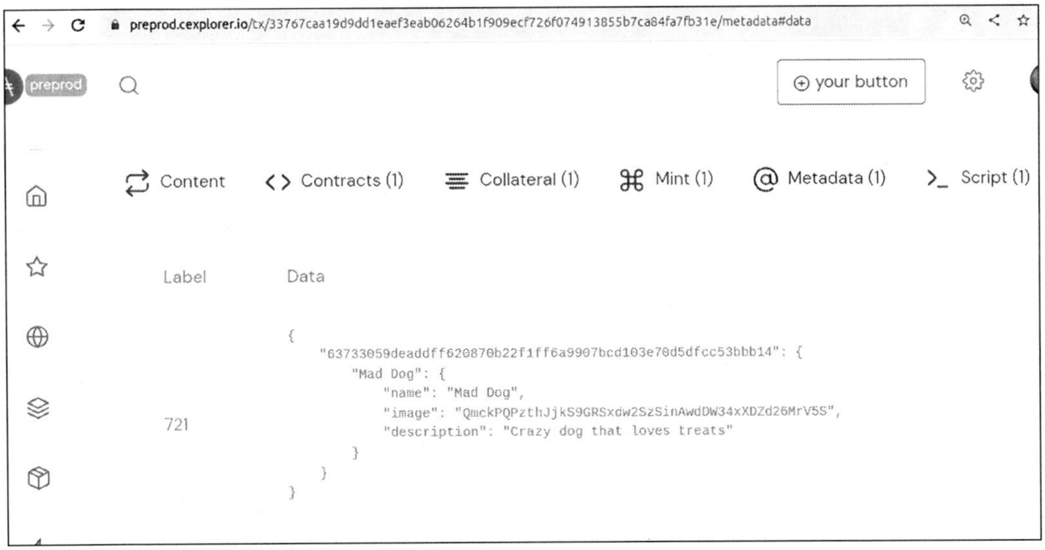

Figure 3.5: *Transaction Metadata*

Where:

- `policy_id` is `63733059deaddff620870b22f1ff6a9907bcd103e70d5dfcc53bbb14`
- `asset_name` is `Mad Dog`
- **NFT** name is `Mad Dog`

[7]https://preprod.cexplorer.io/tx/33767caa19d9dd1eaef3eab06264b1f909ecf726f074913855b7ca84fa7fb31e

- **NFT** `image` is `QmckPQPzthJjkS9GRSxdw2SzSinAwdDW34xXDZd26MrV5S`
- **NFT** `description` is `Crazy dog that loves treats`

Plutus Scripts

Up to this point, we have only looked at transactions that send (spend) assets from an address owned by a user with a corresponding public and private key. In Cardano, we have Smart Contracts that use a Turing-complete scripting language called Plutus. A Plutus script can spend or mint successfully only if the evaluated result returns true. The script is included when submitting a transaction so it can be evaluated by the **Plutus Core Evaluator** inside a Cardano node. As we recall, the network comprises connected nodes that form a consensus on valid blocks. So, when a transaction is submitted, each node must execute the included script and confirm the result. If true, the node will accept the transaction into the block and become part of the blockchain.

Typically, a Plutus script is either a **`spending` (validator)** or a **`minting`** script. A **`spending`** script involves spending UTXOs locked at a script address. The script address is simply a hash of the script itself and the appropriate address header byte value. A **`minting`** script involves minting (adding) or burning (removing) native tokens in the Cardano ledger. When a minting script is used to mint, the new tokens must be included in a UTXO(s) as output(s) and sent to an address. Conversely, when a minting script is used to burn, the tokens must be included in UTXO(s) as input(s).

Datums

When we looked at transaction outputs, we observed that you can include a datum value for data persistence. This datum value can be read by a Plutus spending script that examines the transaction UTXO input. Since a UTXO can only be spent once as an input, the datum value must be recreated and included in the UTXO output if used by another script. If using a reference input, however, the UTXO is read-only, so the datum value can be reused for any number of transactions serially or in parallel.

Redeemers

Redeemers can provide information to a Plutus script during script evaluation within a transaction. For example, the ability to specify what type of mint operation (minting or burning) a transaction will execute. Redeemers can also pass information to a Plutus script that is only known at run time and does not need to be persistent.

The following are the different types of Redeemers from the ledger specification[8]:

```
redeemer_tag =
    0 ; Spending
  / 1 ; Minting
  / 2 ; Certifying
  / 3 ; Rewarding
  / 4 ; Voting
  / 5 ; Proposing
```

We reviewed the **`Spending`** and **`Minting`** Reedmer tags, so now let's look at `Certifying` and **`Rewarding.`** A **`Certifying`** Redeemer is used for publishing certificates to the network. This is used, for example, when registering a staking key to the network for staking. A `Rewarding` Redeemer is used for withdrawing staking rewards locked at a stake key address. Recall that a staking address is not a UTXO-based address and is only used to receive staking rewards. At the time of writing, Voting and Proposing Redeemer tags will be used for on-chain governance and voting.

Putting this all together is a simplified diagram (without a transaction fee), as shown in *Figure* 3.6, of the inputs and outputs to create a transaction using a Plutus Script, which spends 2 Ada.

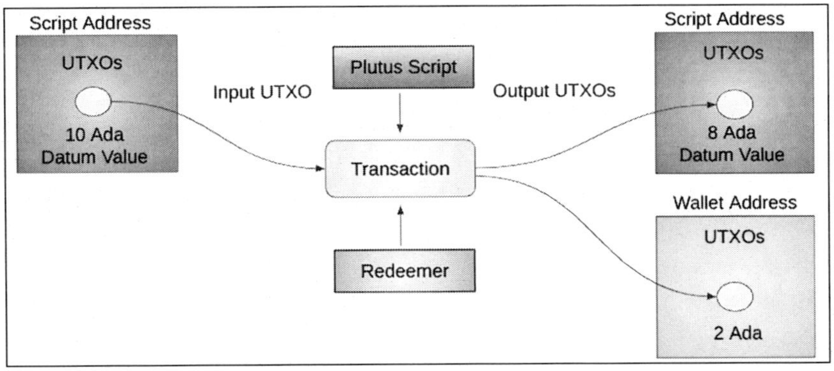

***Figure* 3.6**: *Simplified Script Transaction*

Witness Set

All transactions include a witness set that includes the witnesses required to spend a UTXO. In this chapter, we have focused on the following types of witnesses:

- Signature
- Redeemer

[8]https://github.com/IntersectMBO/cardano-ledger/blob/master/eras/conway/impl/cddl-files/conway.cddl

- Datum
- Plutus Script

Therefore, when looking at the ledger specification,[9] all transactions must have the following high-level structure:

```
transaction =
  [ transaction_body
  , transaction_witness_set
  , bool
  , auxiliary_data / null
  ]
```

Where:

- **`Transaction_body`** contains, among other things, a fee, the UTXO inputs and outputs, metadata hash, script hash, and minting value if any.
- **`Transaction_witness_set`** contains any witnesses required for spending UTXO inputs
- **`Bool`** indicates if this is a valid transaction
- **`Auxiliary_data`** optionally contains transaction metadata

Conclusion

We reviewed the different types of Cardano addresses and how they are constructed and deconstructed. We looked at the UTXO architecture, how inputs and outputs are used, and how UTXOs are locked at an address. We looked at an example of transaction metadata and how it is stored and linked to an on-chain transaction. Next, we looked at the Datum and Redeemer and how it provides information to a Plutus script as part of a transaction. Finally, we reviewed the concept of a Witness Set that allows a transaction to spend UTXO inputs. In the next chapter, we will look at Plutus scripts in more detail and how to use them in a transaction.

Points to Remember

- There are three main types of addresses: Base, Enterprise, and Reward.
- A transaction header type determines the type of address.
- A transaction network tag determines the network a transaction is associated with (Mainnet or Testnet).

---

[9]https://github.com/IntersectMBO/cardano-ledger/blob/master/eras/conway/impl/cddl-files/conway.cddl

- A transaction contains a Payment Part and an optional Delegation Part.
- The Payment or Delegation Part can be either a **`PaymentKeyHash`** (public key hash) or a **`ScriptHash`**.
- A reward address is a special type of account-based address only used for staking rewards.
- A transaction consumes one or more UTXOs as inputs and must produce one or more UTXOs as outputs.
- A signature is proof that the transaction was signed by the correct private key.
- A transaction input includes an index because there may be more than one output UTXO for a given transaction.
- A Datum is used to store persistent data on-chain and is included in a UTXO.
- A Datum value can be stored as a hash or in full as an inline datum.
- The Plutus Core Evaluator evaluates a Plutus script to see if it returns true.
- A Plutus script is typically a spending (validator) or minting script.
- A Plutus spending (validator) script spends UTXOs locked at a script address.
- A Plutus minting script is used to mint or burn Cardano native tokens.
- A UTXO can also be a reference input, a read-only UTXO that cannot be spent.
- A redeemer provides information to a script during a transaction evaluation.
- The witness set may contain a signature, redeemer, datum, or Plutus scripts.

Multiple Choice Questions

1. What is not a valid Cardano Address?
   a. Base
   b. Enterprise
   c. Reward
   d. UTXO
2. A script address is derived from?
   a. Public key hash
   b. Plutus script hash
   c. Private stake key hash
   d. Private key hash

3. What does a signature prove?
    a. A transaction is signed with a valid public key
    b. A transaction is signed with a valid staking key
    c. A transaction is signed with a valid private key
    d. A transaction is signed with a valid reward key
4. A Plutus script evaluates to?
    a. A boolean value
    b. A binary value
    c. A hexadecimal value
    d. Non-zero value
5. What is a Redeemer?
    a. Used for identifying reference scripts
    b. Used for transaction balancing
    c. Provides information to a script at runtime
    d. Halts a transaction if false

Answers

1. d
2. b
3. c
4. a
5. c

Questions

1. Why can't you lock a UTXO at a reward address?
2. What is the process for claiming staking rewards?
3. Why do you include a Plutus script as a witness in the witness set and what can it prove?
4. Why not store all metadata data on-chain, not just the metadata hash?
5. Why is a Plutus spending script also known as a validator?

Key Terms

- **Base Address:** Address that includes both the payment and staking keys.
- **Datum:** It is used to store the datum hash on-chain.
- **Enterprise Address:** Address that only includes the payment key.
- **Inline datum:** It is used to store the actual datum value on-chain.
- **Metadata:** Data that describes a transaction.
- **Minting script:** A Plutus script used to mint or burn Cardano native tokens.
- **NFT:** Non-Fungible Token.
- **PaymentKeyHash:** The hash digest of a public key.
- **Plutus Core Evaluator:** The component in a node that evaluates a plutus script.
- **Plutus script:** A Turing-complete language that is executed on the node.
- **Redeemer:** Redeemer is used to pass information into a script at runtime.
- **Reference script:** A read-only UTXO that cannot be spent .
- **Reward Address:** It is used for distributing and receiving staking rewards.
- **ScriptHash:** The hash digest of a Plutus script.
- **Signature:** The cryptographic hash signature of a transaction hash.
- **Spending (validator) script:** A Plutus script used to spend UTXOs locked at a script address.
- **UTXO:** An unspent transaction output.
- **Witness:** It provides proof that the transaction can spend UTXO inputs.

CHAPTER 4
Plutus

Introduction

Plutus, the Smart Contract language for Cardano, is compiled and executed as an Untyped Plutus Core (**UPLC**) program. The first Plutus smart contracts were written in Haskell using the PlutusTx Haskell module. Unfortunately, PlutusTx was not optimized and created a very challenging development experience when Cardano smart contracts first launched. Shortly thereafter, alternative Plutus scripting languages, such as Aiken (https://aiken-lang.org/) and Helios (https://github.com/Hyperion-BT/helios), emerged, which were significantly more performant and used syntax and coding styles similar to popular programming languages like Rust or C.

In this chapter, we will look at the Plutus core specification in detail and how the Cardano ledger executes a Lambda Calculus program. We will examine the different data structures used in Plutus and how the data is serialized and transmitted using the Concise Binary Object Representation (**CBOR**) format. Next, we will look at the Plutus cost model and how it is used to calculate the CPU and memory units, which must not exceed the maximum values. Finally, we will discuss collateral and its role in a transaction.

Structure

In this chapter, we will discuss the following topics:

- Plutus Specification
- Concise Binary Representation (**CBOR**)
  - Transaction
  - Redeemer
  - Plutus Script
  - Datum
- Plutus Execution Budget
- Collateral

Plutus Specification

The first generation of scripts on Cardano were **native scripts**,[1] followed by Plutus.[2] Native (phase-1) scripts have very limited functionality and are executed internally within the ledger. Plutus, a Turing-complete scripting language, executes outside the ledger but requires a successful evaluation to spend a UTXO locked by a Plutus script.[3] The ledger must support multiple Plutus script versions, so each script includes the version number in the script itself. This way, the ledger will know how to evaluate a script, each with its own version. *Table* 4.1 summarizes the Plutus versions known at the time of writing, and we will only focus on **PlutusV2** and **Plutus Core Version 1.0.0** for this book.

Era	Ledger Language (Id)	Plutus Core Version	Protocol Version	Date
Alonzo	PlutusV1 (0)	1.0.0	5.0	Sep, 2021
Vasil	PlutusV2 (1)	1.0.0	7.0	Jun, 2022
Valentine	PlutusV2 (1)	1.0.0	8.0	Feb, 2023
Conway	PlutusV3 (2)	1.1.0	9.0	Upcoming

***Table* 4.1**: *Plutus Versions*

The objective of the Plutus specification was to create a simple scripting language that can be evaluated with minimal (and constrained) computational footprint on the Cardano Node. Unlike the Ethereum Virtual Machine, which has a long and complicated proof, the Plutus abstract state machine is short and succinct.[4] This is a very desirable property when building a highly stable blockchain to minimize hard fork upgrades. Plutus scripts are written using a language called Untyped Plutus Core or **UPLC**, which was derived from System F, a form of **Lambda Calculus**.[5] Fortunately, Smart Contract Plutus development uses **higher-level programming** languages that compile and generate the **UPLC** for us.

Note: Learning **UPLC** or Lambda Calculus is not required to write Cardano smart contracts. The remainder of this section is optional but may be helpful to readers looking for more details on how generated UPLC code maps to the Plutus Core specification. For an introduction to Lambda Calculus, please look at the video "*Lambda Calculus - Fundamentals of Lambda Calculus & Functional Programming in JavaScript*."[6]

---

1 https://github.com/cardano-foundation/CIPs/tree/master/CIP-0029
2 lutus Core Team, "Formal Specification of the Plutus Core Language." 24.
3 Andre Knispel, et al., "A Formal Specification of the Cardano Ledger integrating Plutus Core," 3.
4 Philip Wadler, "Functional smart contracts on Cardano."
5 James Chapman, et al., "System F in Agda, for fun and profit."
6 Gabriel Lebec, "Lambda Calculus - Fundamentals of Lambda Calculus & Functional Programming in JavaScript."

UPLC Primitive Types

UPLC uses a simple language syntax with a limited set of atomic types, listed in *Table 4.2*:

Type	Syntax
integer	-?[0-9]+
bytestring	#([0-9A-Fa-f][0-9A-Fa-f])*
string	UTF-8 characters, enclosed in double quotes " "
bool	True | False
unit	()
Type	**Denotation**
Data	data Data = Constr Integer [Data] | Map [(Data, Data)] | List [Data] | I Integer | B ByteString

Table 4.2: *UPLC Atomic Types*

In addition to the atomic data types, there are two types of operators included in UPLC, as shown in *Table* 4.3:

Operator op	|op|	Denotation
list	1	[list(t)] = [t]
pair	2	[pair(t1,t2)] = [t1] x [t2]

Table 4.3: *UPLC Type Operators*

The **con** keyword defines constants, followed by the type declaration and the value. *Table* 4.4 provides some usage examples:[7]

Type	Example
unit	con unit ()
bool	con bool False
integer	con integer 123
bytestring	con bytestring #abc123

[7]Plutus Core Team, "Formal Specification of the Plutus Core Language," 26.

`string`	`con string "GM Cardano"`
`pair`	`con pair<bool, integer> [True, 123]`
`list`	`list<bytestring> [#0d, #f3]`

Table 4.4: *UPLC Type Examples*[8]

A lambda function uses the keyword **`lam`** and is passed a variable name and returns a term that can be either a constant, a function, or a well-formed value of any type. The UPLC program must not contain any free variables and, therefore, be considered a "*closed term*."[9] For example, **`(program 1.0.0 (lam x x))`** is a valid program, but **`(program 1.0.0 (lam x y))`** is not. Please note that all Plutus scripts must include a **`program`** and **`version`.**

Plutus Core has no arithmetic operators but uses built-in functions for arithmetic operations. Some **`builtin`** functions are domain-specific to the Cardano blockchain, while other **`builtin`** functions may be added over time. The last items we will review are the **`force`** and **`delay`** directives. The `force` directive is applied to a polymorphic function to force the instantiation of a typed parameter.[10] The **`delay`** directive is used for **lazy evaluation** of a branch condition, which preserves type abstraction.[11] **Lazy evaluation** allows for more efficient code execution because values are only computed if they are used. This also allows for the creation of infinite data structures that are impossible to create in languages like C.

UPLC Grammar

Putting this all together, we define the grammar of a **UPLC** program, as shown in *Figure 4.1*:

Term *L, M, N*	::=	*x*	variable
		(con T *c*)	constant
		(builtin *b*)	builtin
		(lam *x M*)	λ abstraction
		[*M N*]	function application
		(delay *M*)	delay execution of a term
		(force *M*)	force execution of a term
		(error)	error
Program *P*	::=	(program *v M*)	versioned program

Figure 4.1: *UPLC Grammar (Plutus Core Version 1.0.0)*[12]

[8] https://aiken-lang.org/uplc/syntax#primitive-types
[9] Plutus Core Team, "Formal Specification of the Plutus Core Language," 6.
[10] Plutus Core Team, "Formal Specification of the Plutus Core Language," 11.
[11] https://aiken-lang.org/uplc/syntax#delay--force
[12] Plutus Core Team, "Formal Specification of the Plutus Core Language," 6

UPLC Example

Looking at a simplified example, we can see how a higher-level language, such as Aiken, generates a UPLC program. *Table* 4.5 has a simple validator script that always returns true. The program uses lambda (**`lam`**) functions to evaluate and return the constant **`True`**.

Higher Level Language

```
validator {
  fn main(_datum, _redeemer, _context) -> Bool {
    True
  }
}
```

UPLC Code

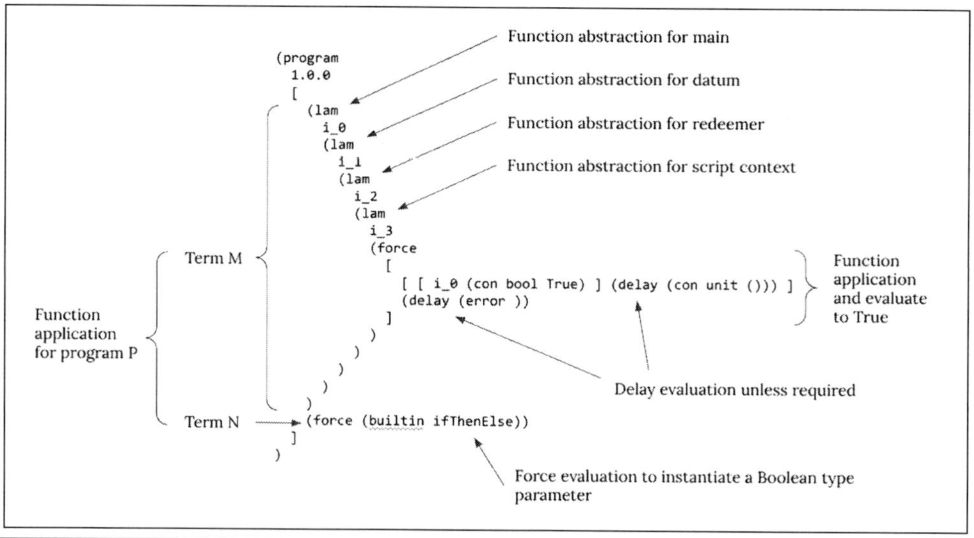

Table 4.5: *UPLC Example*

Concise Binary Representation (CBOR)

CBOR is a binary and encoding format defined in the Internet standard RFC 8949.[13] In the previous chapter on *Transactions*, we looked at the Cardano ledger **CDDL** specification,[14] which defines the format of a transaction. When a transaction is

[13]https://www.rfc-editor.org/rfc/rfc8949.html

[14]https://github.com/IntersectMBO/cardano-ledger/blob/master/eras/conway/impl/cddl-files/conway.cddl

submitted to the network, the entire transaction and all relevant data are **serialized** and encoded in **CBOR**. We will examine a transaction in detail and **deserialize** it to see the UPLC Plutus code and related data (redeemer and datum).

For example, *Figure 4.2* shows a transaction executing a Plutus validator script:

https://preprod.cexplorer.io/tx/99c529355ebd1f410517457b6ff04e66c2de28b8667b9428ec232e03efa22c29

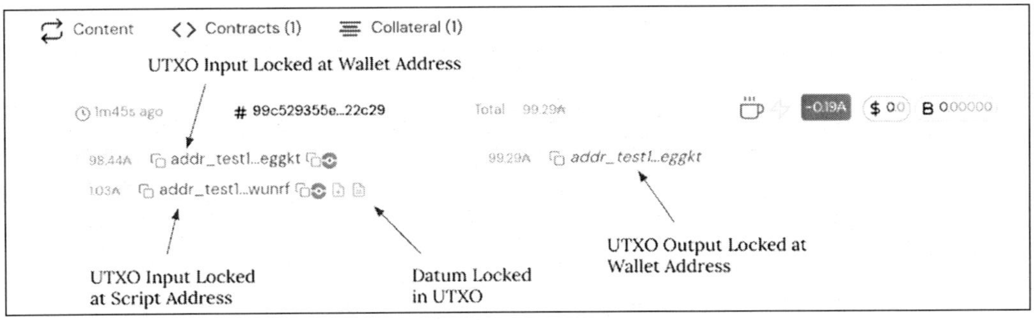

Figure 4.2: *Transaction Example*

Transaction

The **CBOR** hexadecimal format for this transaction that was submitted to the network is as follows:


```
84a80082825820d9b02da5897bd1ff9e2fdab008334d2804ea1accab
c7c3962e33771ed9f1a8d500825820d9b02da5897bd1ff9e2fdab008334d2804ea1a
ccabc7c3962e33771ed9f1a8d501018182581d606d04be153546d63c8a33
e0c11ec44cf790803f31c2f893fc241529531a05eb1244021a0002
d9250b582031e6c463846e3c0afe2aebfc9993355dbe8ce4dab892a7
af0e397a75df3509b90d81825820d9b02da5897bd1ff9e2fdab008334d2804ea1a
ccabc7c3962e33771ed9f1a8d5010e81581c6d04be153546d63c8a33e0c11e
c44cf790803f31c2f893fc24152953108258 1d606d04be153546d63c8a33e0c11
ec44cf790803f31c2f893fc241529531a05d9dd11111a000445b8a30081825820
fc6500742705cfe8c2f0822e73e2ab09c43285973adffe8aa06bd12d1fa6051f584
0ec7f53a69852e6daa868a3f221114435544ab2851bc6f2f42abe9772507b30064a1
f012ddab23153644703047ea2faf9132390e91937b82389626404d7adfd0105818
40000d8799f4d48656c6c6f2c20576f726c6421ff821977151a009daaac068158f258
f0010000323232323232323222232325333008323232533300b002100114a066446
4660020020644a66602200229404c8c94ccc040cdc78010028a51133004004001 3
014002375c60240026eb0c038c03cc03cc03cc03cc03cc03cc03cc020c008c0
20014dd7180118040 0399b8f375c6002600e00a91010d48656c6c6f2c20576f726
c6421002300d001149858c94ccc020cdc3a40000226464a66601a601e0042930b1ba
e300d00130060041630060033253330073370e900000899192999806180700 10a4
c2c6eb8c030004c01401058c01400c8c014dd5000918019baa0015734aae7555cf2a
b9f5742ae89f5f6
```

When we decode this to a diagnostic form using https://cbor.nemo157.com/, we can see the transaction details, as illustrated in *Figures* 4.3 and 4.4. *Figure* 4.3 shows the UTXO inputs and outputs and the required signatures for this transaction:

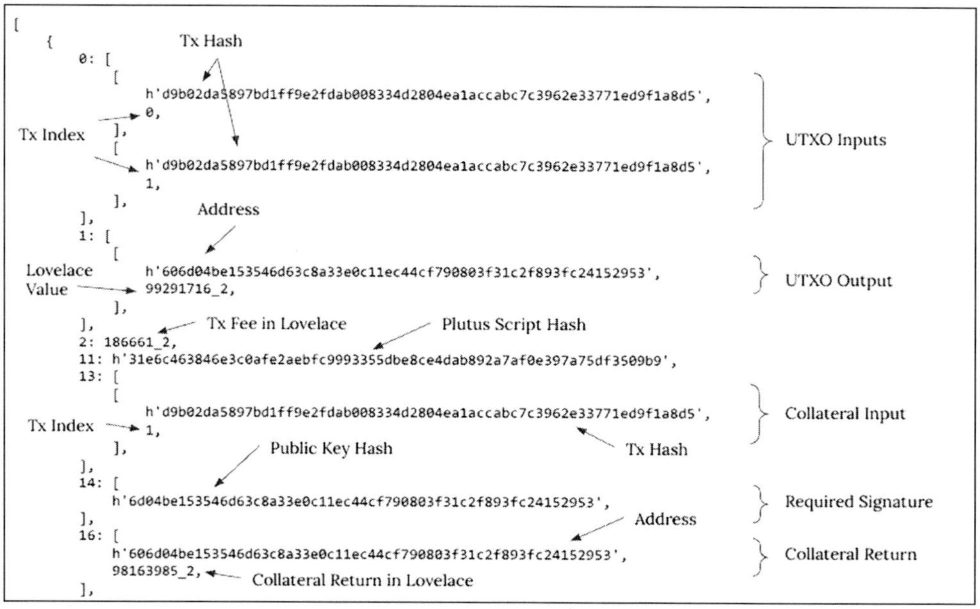

Figure 4.3: *CBOR Transaction Part 1*

Figure 4.4 shows the collateral required, the public key, Redeemer, and Plutus script witnesses. This transaction does not contain auxiliary data or metadata, and the transaction validity flag is set to true.

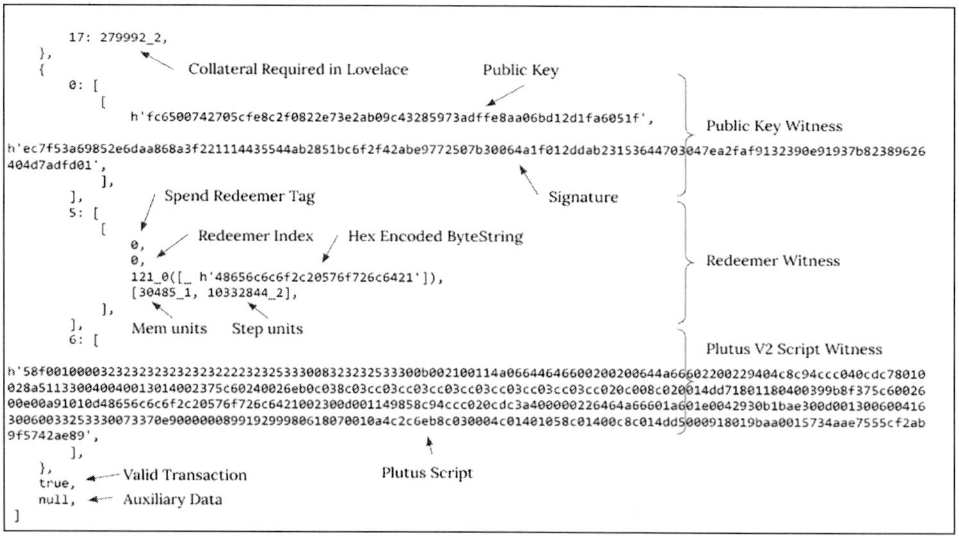

Figure 4.4: *CBOR Transaction Part 2*

Redeemer

To get a human-readable version of the Redeemer, we need to convert from the Hex ByteString to a UTF-8 string. Plutus, however, will use the ByteString directly during script execution. Here is an example of using `xxd` to convert a Hex-encoded ByteString to a normal string:

```
$ echo 48656c6c6f2c20576f726c6421 | xxd -p -r
$ Hello, World!
```

Plutus Script

The Plutus script is double encoded (CBOR + flat), meaning we need to deserialize it twice to get it into UPLC. So, the first step is to decode it using a CBOR decoder,[15] and save it to a file called **`plutus.flat`**:

```
$ cat plutus.flat
01000032323232323232322222323253330083232325333300b002100114a066446466002
00200644a66602200229404c8c94ccc040cdc78010028a5113300400400130140023 75c
60240026eb0c038c03cc03cc03cc03cc03cc03cc03cc020c008c020014dd7180118
0400399b8f375c6002600e00a91010d48656c6c6f2c20576f726c6421002300d0011498
58c94ccc020cdc3a400000226464a66601a601e0042930b1bae300d0013006004163006
00332533300733 70e90000089919299980618070010a4c2c6eb8c030004c01401058c0
1400c8c014dd5000918019baa0015734aae7555cf2ab9f5742ae8
```

Next, we need to convert it from hex to UPLC using the Aiken utility tool to decode it:

```
$ aiken uplc decode --hex plutus.flat
(program
  1.0.0
  [
    (lam
      i_0
      [
        (lam
          i_1
          ...
        )
        (force (builtin headList))
      ]
```

[15] https://cbor.nemo157.com/

```
    )
    (force (builtin tailList))
  ]
)
```

Datum

Next, we will look at a Datum in *Figure* 4.5 using **`cexplorer.io`**:[16]

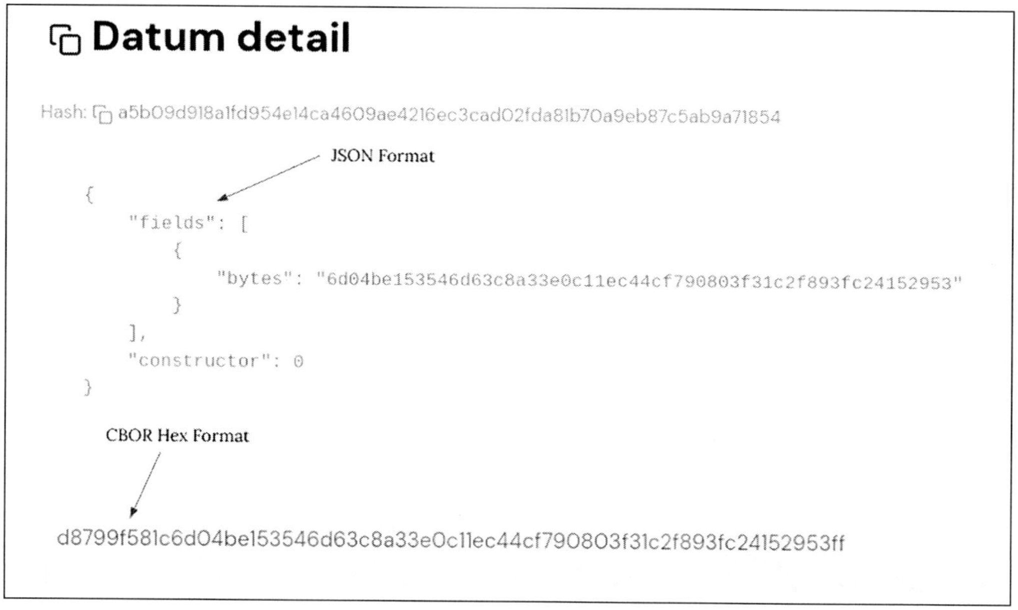

Figure 4.5: *Datum Example*

The datum in *Figure* 4.5 is an inline datum, so the value is stored on-chain and locked at a UTXO that we want to spend. If we look at the UTXO, we will see that the value is encoded in CBOR hex format:

```
d8799f581c6d04be153546d63c8a33e0c11ec44cf790803f31c2f893fc24152953ff
```

When we decode the datum CBOR hex value, we get the following output of a byte array:

```
121_0([_
    h'6d04be153546d63c8a33e0c11ec44cf790803f31c2f893fc24152953',
])
```

In this example, the datum value represents a public key hash.

[16] https://preprod.cexplorer.io/datum/a5b09d918a1fd954e14ca4609ae4216ec3cad02fda81b70a9eb87c5ab9a71854

Plutus Execution Budget

Looking at the Redeemer Witness of the transaction in *Figure* 4.4, we will notice an execution budget for the attached plutus script:

```
[30485_1, 10332844_2]
```

These values refer to the memory and CPU (steps) execution units, which are defined in the Plutus ledger specification:

```
ex_units = [mem: uint, steps: uint]
```

The **mem** and **steps** are calculated and submitted with the transaction, then verified by the Plutus Core Evaluator during script execution. If either of the values exceeds the maximum limits during script execution, then an error will be raised:

```
Error: The budget when the machine terminated was:\n({ cpu: -84834\n|
mem: 17553\n}
```

In this example, the **cpu/steps** value was exceeded and resulted in a negative number. As a result, the execution was halted, and the validation failed. To calculate the **mem** and **cpu/step** costs for a given Plutus script, a **cost model**[17] is used to map the **execution cost** for each Plutus operation. The cost model is located in the network protocol parameters and can be changed over time via network updates. To see the **protocol parameters**, you can use the `cardano-cli` tool:

```
$ cardano-cli query protocol-parameters --testnet-magic 1
{
    "collateralPercentage": 150,
    "costModels": {
    ...
            "PlutusScriptV2": {
             "addInteger-cpu-arguments-intercept": 205665,
             "addInteger-cpu-arguments-slope": 812,
             "addInteger-memory-arguments-intercept": 1,
             "addInteger-memory-arguments-slope": 1,
    ...
    "maxTxExecutionUnits": {
        "memory": 14000000,
        "steps": 10000000000
```

[17]https://plutus-apps.readthedocs.io/en/latest/reference/cost-model-parameters.html

```
},
"maxTxSize": 16384,
...
```

The protocol parameters specify, among other things, the execution cost of each Plutus operation, the maximum **memory** and **steps** units per transaction, and the maximum overall transaction size (**maxTxSize**) in KB.

Collateral

The last topic we will look at is collateral included in a transaction. Collateral is a small amount of Lovelace (1.5 × Transaction Fee) that will be used if there is a phase-2 Plutus script failure.[18] Any change left over from the collateral inputs is returned to the user and is called the **collateral return**. However, Plutus script evaluation is usually done locally before submitting it to the network. This will catch and prevent the submission of an invalid Plutus script. The role of collateral is to help protect the network from malicious or spam transactions.

Conclusion

The reader should now understand the Plutus core specification and the **UPLC** code used for Plutus script execution and evaluation. We examined a **CBOR** transaction, how to deserialize it, and looked into the transaction details. We also looked at the Plutus script execution budget and how it is calculated using the **cost model**. Lastly, we discussed collateral, which is used during a phase-2 Plutus script evaluation failure. The next chapter will explore the off-chain code used to create and submit a transaction. We will also look at the user wallet, which is the gateway to interacting with the Cardano blockchain and smart contracts.

Points to Remember

- The first generation of scripts on Cardano was native scripts that were evaluated inside the ledger.
- A Plutus script is a phase-2 script that evaluates outside of the ledger.
- Untyped Plutus Core or UPLC is a form of Lambda Calculus.
- UPLC is the low-level language that is executed on the node.
- Writing smart contracts is done with a higher-level language that generates the low-level UPLC.
- UPLC programs must be closed with all terms properly defined.

[18] Andre Knispel, et al., "A Formal Specification of the Cardano Ledger integrating Plutus Core," 6.

- A UPLC program can take advantage of the lazy evaluation found in Lambda Calculus.
- CBOR is a binary standard for serializing and deserializing data structures.
- Cardano transactions are serialized to CBOR when submitted to the network and deserialized during Cardano node validation.
- The Redeemer in a transaction contains the memory and step/cpu units that a script will consume.
- During Plutus script evaluation, the script will halt and fail if the memory or step/cpu units exceed the maximum allowable units.
- The cost model in the network parameters contains the cost for each Plutus operation and the maximum memory and step/cpu unit allowed in a transaction.
- Collateral must be provided in a transaction and is designed to protect the network from malicious and spam transactions.

Multiple Choice Questions

1. The first generation of scripts on Cardano are?
    a. PlutusV1
    b. PlutusV2
    c. Native Scripts
    d. Smart Scripts
2. What statement is false about Native Scripts and Plutus Scripts?
    a. Both must be evaluated to be true to spend a UTXO locked by the script
    b. Both can create a multi-sig script address
    c. Both are Turing-complete
    d. Native scripts are a phase-1 script
3. What is `lam` in UPLC?
    a. A lambda function abstraction
    b. A lambda function application
    c. A lambda function permutation
    d. A lambda function association

4. Why is lazy evaluation desirable?
    a. Less efficient code execution
    b. More efficient code execution
    c. Forces evaluation of all declared variables
    d. Cannot create infinite data structures
5. Where is the current Plutus cost model located?
    a. Node configuration
    b. Plutus script configuration
    c. Plutus evaluator configuration
    d. Protocol parameters

Answers

1. c
2. c
3. a
4. b
5. d

Questions

1. What are the advantages of Lambda Calculus?
2. Are Turing-complete and Lambda Calculus programs formally equivalent?
3. What are the differences between CBOR and flat encoding?
4. Why are the memory and cpu/step units included in the Redeemer in a transaction?
5. What are the similarities and differences between step-1 and step-2 scripts?
6. What inputs can be used for collateral?

Key Terms

- **CBOR**: Concise Binary Object Representation
- **Collateral Return:** The amount of Ada change returned if collateral is used during a transaction.
- **CDDL:** Concise Data Definition Library
- **Cost Model:** The execution cost parameters for each Plutus operation.
- **Deserialize:** The process of decoding code and data structures from a binary format.
- **Execution Cost:** The amount of memory and cpu/step units used for each Plutus operation.
- **Higher Level Programming:** A language that allows the use of more complex functions and data structures to make the code more readable.
- **Lambda Calculus:** A minimal language to define functions and applications.
- **Lazy Evaluation:** Only instantiate variables that are used in code execution.
- **Native Scripts:** Simple scripts that are used in phase-1 evaluation.
- **Protocol Parameters:** A file with parameters and settings that is used by the network.
- **Serialize:** The process of encoding code and data structures to a binary format.
- **UPLC:** Untyped Plutus Core

CHAPTER 5
Transaction Builder

Introduction

This chapter will combine our knowledge of on-chain Plutus scripts and how to lock Ada into a smart contract using off-chain code. We will look at Cardano wallets, the gateway to interacting with the blockchain and Smart Contracts. Next, we will look at some of the tools to help build and submit transactions, such as **`Demeter.run`**. Then, we will build a simple vesting smart contract using two popular approaches: Helios and Lucid + Aiken.

Structure

In this chapter, we will discuss the following topics:

- Transaction Lifecycle
- Wallets
  - Seed Phrase
  - Testnet Faucet
  - Address Derivation
  - Staking
  - CIP-30
- Demeter.run
- Off-Chain Code Examples
  - Helios
  - Lucid + Aiken

Transaction Lifecycle

In the previous chapter, we looked at how the Cardano node and ledger evaluate a Plutus script. This chapter will focus on how to build and submit a transaction that includes a Plutus script. The building of a transaction is assembling the UTXO inputs and outputs, attaching scripts we want to run, and adding redeemers, datums, and metadata, if any. Once the transaction is assembled, we must get it signed and include the signature as a witness. *Figure* 5.1 shows the off-chain steps of building, signing, serializing, and submitting a transaction to the network.

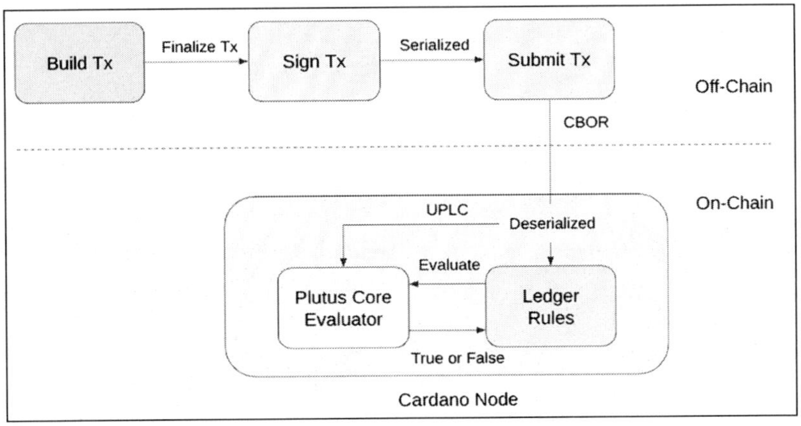

***Figure* 5.1**: *Transaction Lifecycle*

Wallets

In cryptocurrencies, a wallet is the user interface that interacts with the blockchain. A wallet typically allows users to create an account, which is a collection of UTXOs locked at a public key address. This type of **account abstraction** helps users visualize familiar concepts such as account balances and transaction history. Many wallets also allow users to select stake pools and register their stake key to collect staking rewards. *Table* 5.1 lists some of the wallet providers on the Cardano network in alphabetical order.

Name	Full Node	Hardware Wallet Support	Mobile App	Open Source
`Daedalus`	✓	✓	✕	✓
`Eternl`	✕	✓	✓	✕
`Flint`	✕	✓	✓	✓
`GameChanger`	✕	✕	✕	✓
`GeroWallet`	✕	✓	✕	✕
`Lace`	✕	✓	✕	✓
`Ledger`	✕	✓	✕	✓
`Nami`	✕	✕	✕	✓
`NuFi`	✕	✓	✕	✕

Typhon	✗	✓	✗	✓
VESPR	✗	✗	✓	✓

***Table 5.1**: Cardano Wallets*[1]

Full Node: A wallet that includes a full Cardano node and does not use any third-party service to look up transactions on the blockchain.

Hardware Wallet Support: A wallet that supports hardware devices in signing transactions.

Mobile App: A wallet with a native mobile app on iOS or Android devices.

Open Source: The wallet's open-source code is available on GitHub.

Seed Phrase

To create an account with a wallet, you must either create a new seed phrase or import an existing one. If we recall from *Chapter 3, Transactions*, a private key is needed to sign a transaction. To create this private key, wallets typically use a **seed phrase** to generate a random private key. This is a two-step process, whereby, a mnemonic sentence or a group of words is used to create a random seed.[2] This random seed is then used to derive the public and private key pairs.[3]

Testnet Faucet

Cardano typically has two Testnets used for end-to-end testing before Mainnet.[4] Please be mindful of what network you are connecting to when sending and receiving funds.

- **Preview Testnet:** The epoch has been shortened to 1 day and is ahead of a Mainnet fork by at least 4 weeks.
- **Preprod Testnet:** This network is used for release candidate testing for mainnet launches. It mimics production as closely as possible and is the more stable Testnet network.

We will use the Testnet faucet to acquire test Ada and send it to our wallet address. In this book, we will use the `Eternl` wallet, and *Figure* 5.2 shows how to get an address to receive funds.

[1]https://www.cardanocube.com/cardano-ecosystem-interactive-map
[2]https://github.com/bitcoin/bips/blob/master/bip-0039.mediawiki
[3]https://github.com/bitcoin/bips/blob/master/bip-0032.mediawiki
[4]https://book.world.dev.cardano.org/environments.html

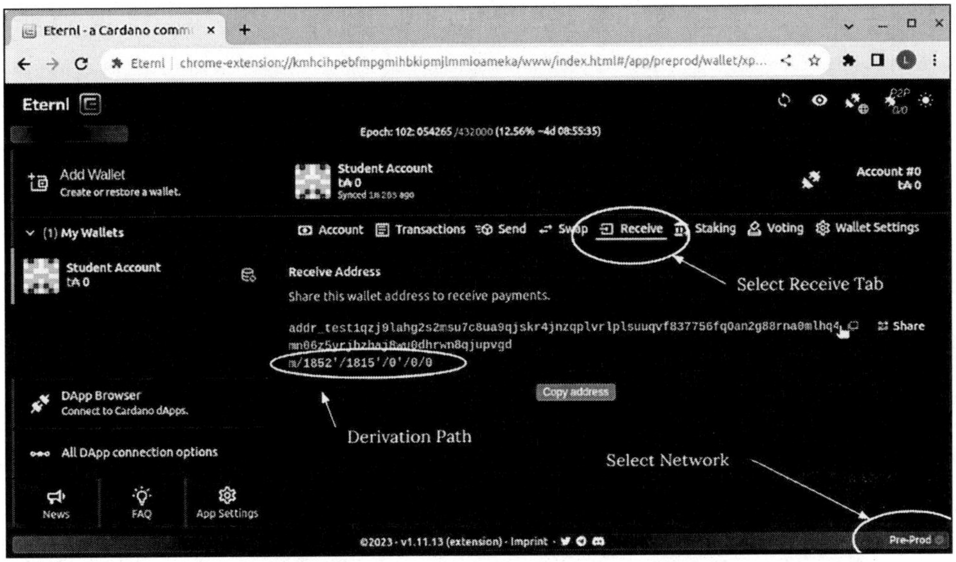

***Figure* 5.2**: *Eternl Wallet Receives Funds*

Copy the address and paste it into the Testnet faucet form on https://docs.cardano.org/cardano-testnet/tools/faucet/, as shown in *Figure* 5.3.

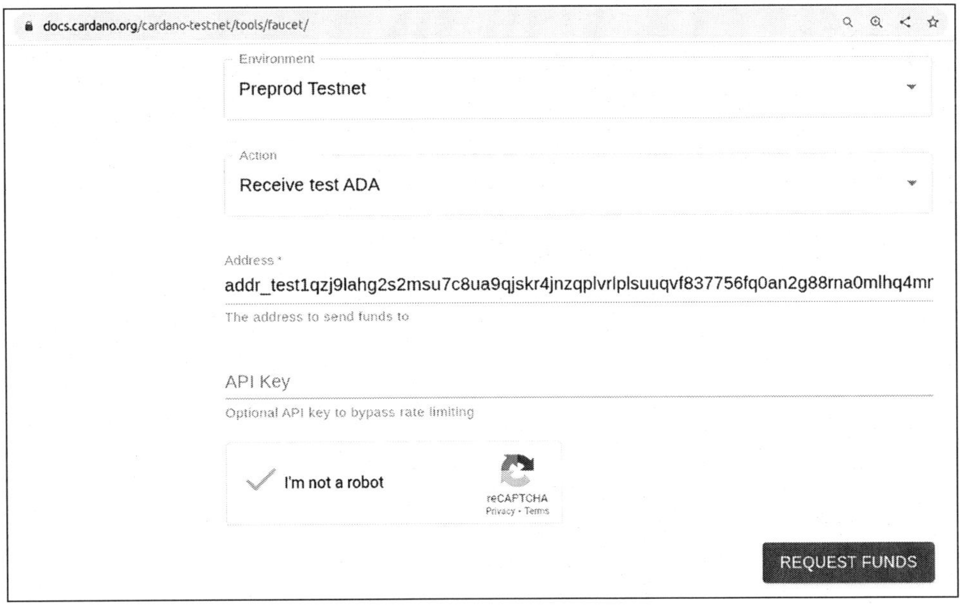

***Figure* 5.3**: *Testnet Faucet Request*

Select "**`Request Funds`**," and you should see the "**`Success`**" message, which includes a transaction hash that you can use on https://preprod.cexplorer.io/ to verify the status.

Success
Your transaction has been successful and test funds have been sent to
addr_test1qzj9lahg2s2msu7c8ua9qjskr4jnzqplvrlplsuuqvf837756fq0an2g88rna0mlhq4mn06z5yrjhzhaj8wu0dhrwn8qjupvgd.
Please verify the following transaction hash:
2db4baf31e3abf57311633ad594f5458bb14a8c09aade700618b6cd53e7f9c43

***Figure 5.4**: Testnet Faucet Submitted*

After 10–60 seconds, you should see 10,000 test Ada (**`tAda`**) in the **`Eternl`** wallet.

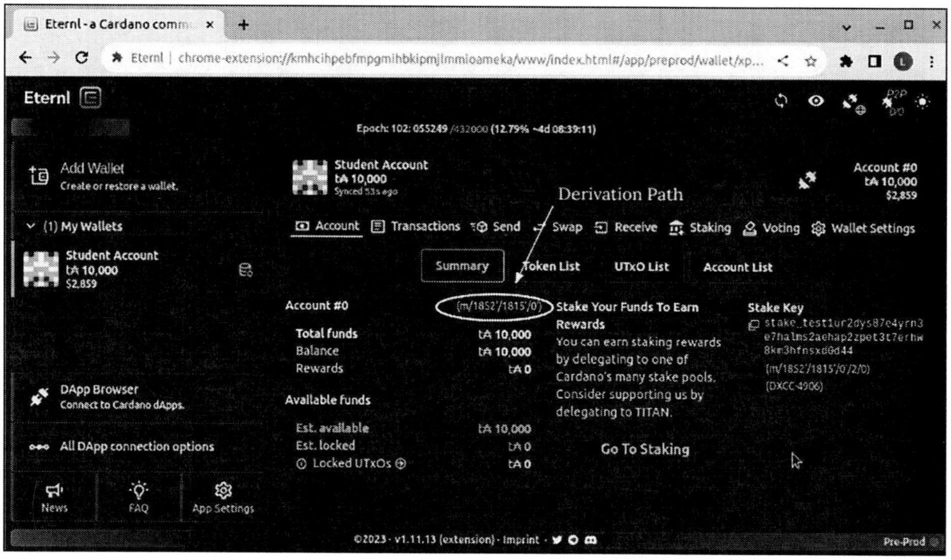

***Figure 5.5**: Eternl Wallet Account Summary*

Address Derivation

The **Hierarchy for Deterministic** (**HD**) wallets, such as **`Eternl`**, follows the specification in CIP-1852[5] for the derivation path:

```
m / purpose' / coin_type' / account' / role / index
```

In *Figure* 5.5, we can see the derivation path for the receiving address is:

```
m/1852'/1815'/0'/0/0
```

Table 5.2 explains each of the derivation path elements:

Name	Value	Notes
Purpose	1852	Specification name (for example, CIP-1852)
Coin Type	1815	Different value for each cryptocurrency (for example, Ada Lovelace birth)

[5]https://github.com/cardano-foundation/CIPs/tree/master/CIP-1852

Account	0	Allows for creating separate wallet accounts
Role	0	0 = External Chain (receiving payments) 1 = Internal Chain (change address) 2 = Staking Key
Index	0	Address index starting at 0

Table 5.2: *Derivation Path*

You can create different addresses for the same private key to receive payments (and change) using HD wallets. In practice, however, using a "`single address mode`" is generally preferable, where the same address is re-used. Creating a new address for each transaction helps anonymize it so it cannot be linked to the wallet account. With Cardano, however, as soon as a stake key is registered for a wallet address, all transactions from that address can be linked via the stake key. Having multiple addresses for the receiving and change addresses adds additional dApp complexity, which is why some wallets only support single address mode. To switch (or keep) `Eternl` to use single address mode is shown in *Figure* 5.6.

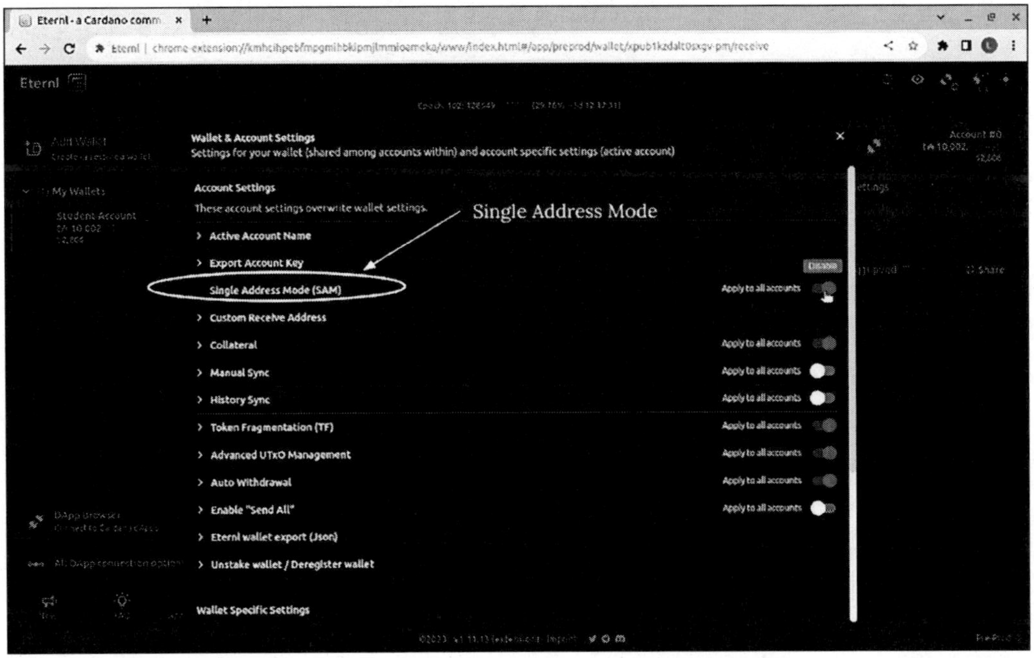

Figure 5.6: *Eternl Single Address Mode*

Staking

One of the most important features of the Cardano network is the ability to stake from your wallet easily. This is known as liquid, non-custodial staking, and it is why

Cardano has a high level of staking on the network, which contributes to its security and decentralization. To stake, a user goes to the staking tab, chooses a stake pool, and selects "**`Delegate`**," as shown in *Figure* 5.7.

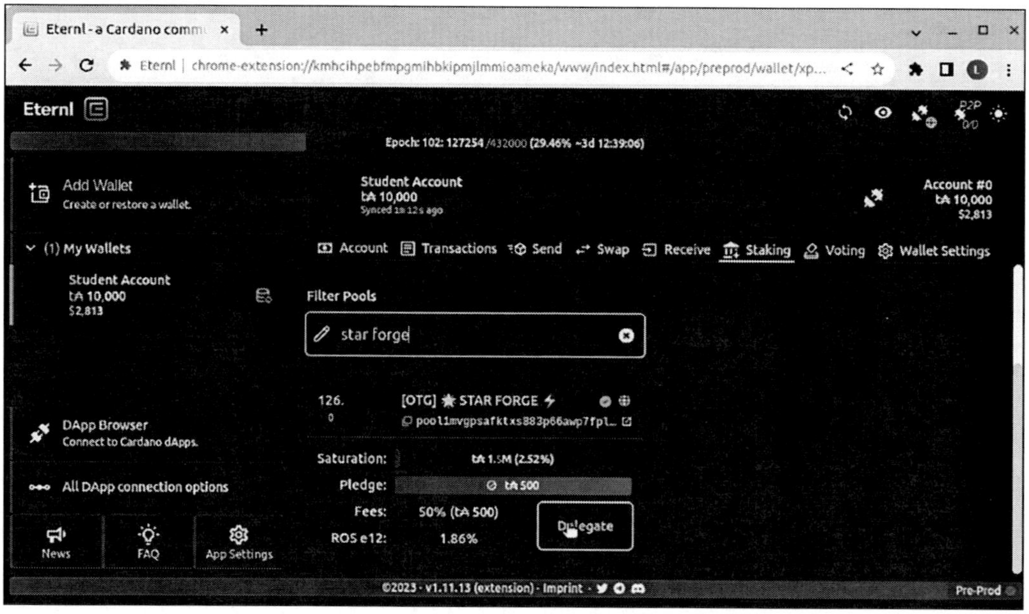

***Figure* 5.7**: *Stake Pool Delegation*

Next, the user must sign a transaction that registers the stake key and stake pool delegation to the network, as shown in *Figure* 5.8.

***Figure* 5.8**: *Stake Pool Registration*

When a transaction with the stake key registration certificate and stake pool delegation certificate has been confirmed, the user will receive staking rewards as per the

Ouroboros lifecycle discussed in *Chapter 2, Cryptography and Consensus Algorithms Overview.*

CIP-30

For a dApp to connect to a browser extension wallet such as **`Eternl`**, the dApp should follow the CIP-30 standard.[6] This standard describes a webpage-based communication bridge to allow webpages to interact with the browser extension wallet. This is implemented by injecting JavaScript code into the webpage that is being rendered. The webpage or dApp can then call the JavaScript code with predefined public methods to retrieve and submit data to the wallet. In the off-chain code examples, we will see how to interact with the wallet using CIP-30 later in this chapter.

Demeter.run

Before we dive into our first off-chain smart contract examples, we must get an environment up and running quickly. This is where **`Demeter.run`** can help. It is a fully hosted solution that can spin up a variety of Cardano environments. Cardano is fully open source, so you can install and run Cardano components locally or in a cloud environment. For this book, we will use **`Demeter.run`** to focus more on the concepts and application logic and spend less time on environment setup and configuration.

To set up an environment to be used for the examples in this book, follow these steps:

1. Go to https://demeter.run/
2. Start a free trial.
3. Sign-up/login.
4. Create an organization.
5. Create a new project, as shown in *Figure* 5.9.

[6]https://cips.cardano.org/cips/cip30/

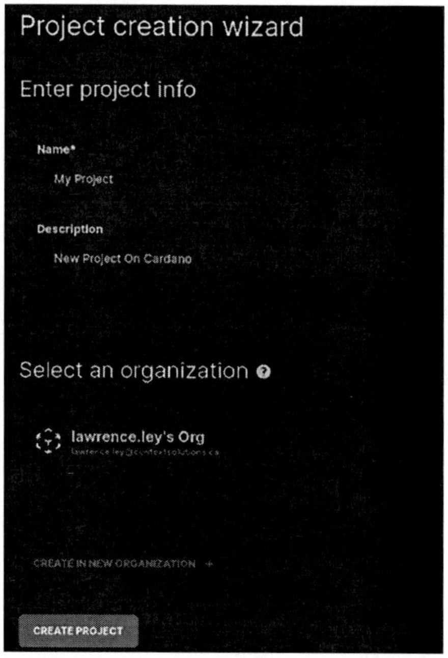

Figure 5.9: *Demeter.run New Project*

6. You can start with a free tier, but depending on usage, you may need to move to a paid tier or buy additional DCUs. Each plan purchased is associated with a specific project.

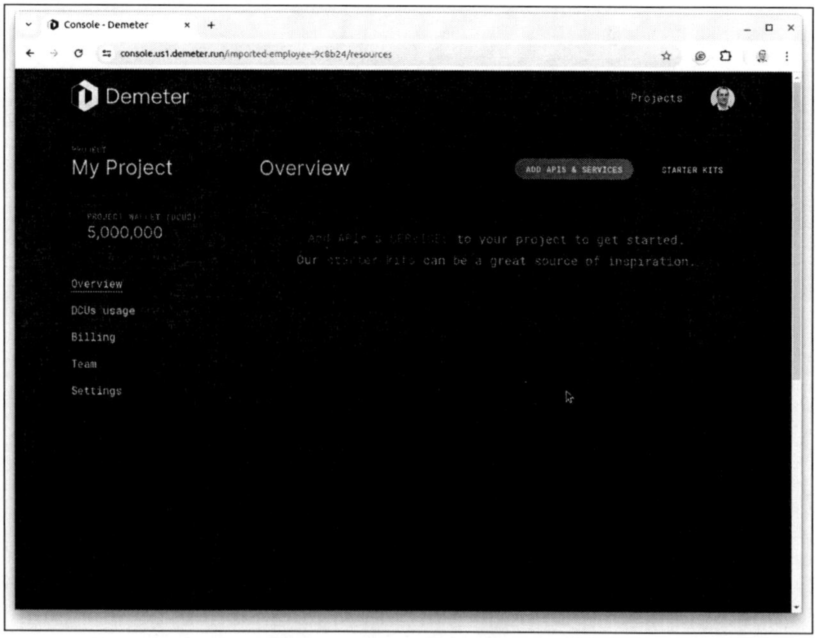

Figure 5.10: *Demeter.run Project View*

7. Select **ADD APIS & SERVICES**, as shown in *Figure* 5.10.
8. Scroll down and create a new workspace.
9. Select "**Clone an existing repository**".
10. Paste the GitHub URL in the text box:
    `https://github.com/ava-orange-education/Mastering-Cardano-Smart-Contracts.git`
11. Keep the branch default as the main.
12. Select Node.js as the toolchain.
13. Select Workspace **small** size.
14. Select the **Pre-prod** network.
15. Select **Create** at the bottom of the page.
16. If you scroll to the top of the page, you will see the workspace being provisioned and will be completed, as shown in *Figure* 5.11.

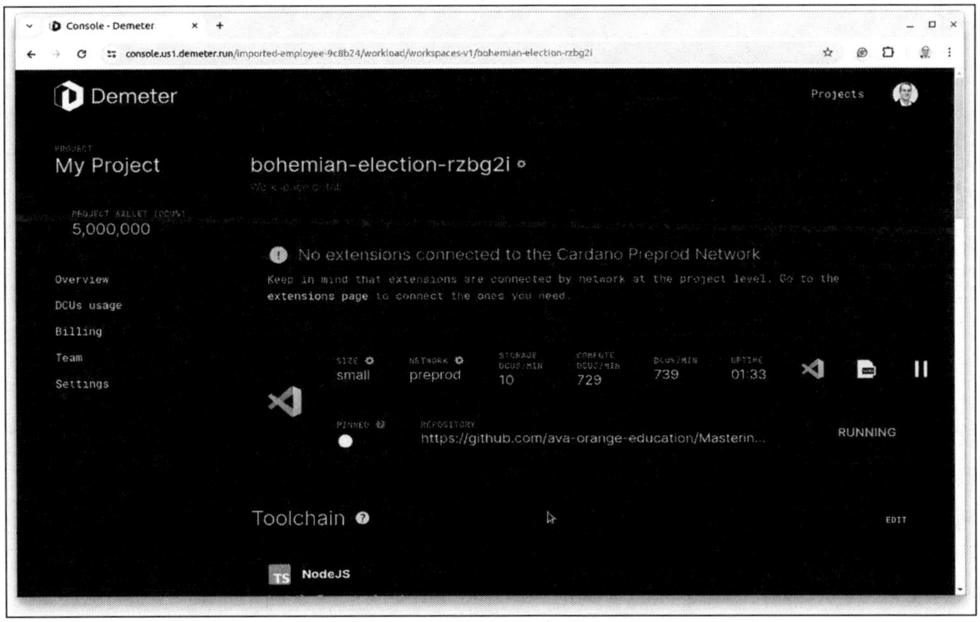

Figure 5.11: *Demeter.run Project Provisioning*

17. Scroll down the page and **EDIT** Exposed Ports.
18. Enter Name as **Next.js**.
19. Enter Number **3000**.
20. Select **Expose**.

21. Scroll back up to the top of the page and select the VS code icon to launch the VS code editor.
22. Authorize trusted access so you can use VS code web to edit your code.
23. Select **`Terminal`** -> **`New Terminal`** to create a terminal window to execute commands on the common line, as shown in *Figure* 5.12.

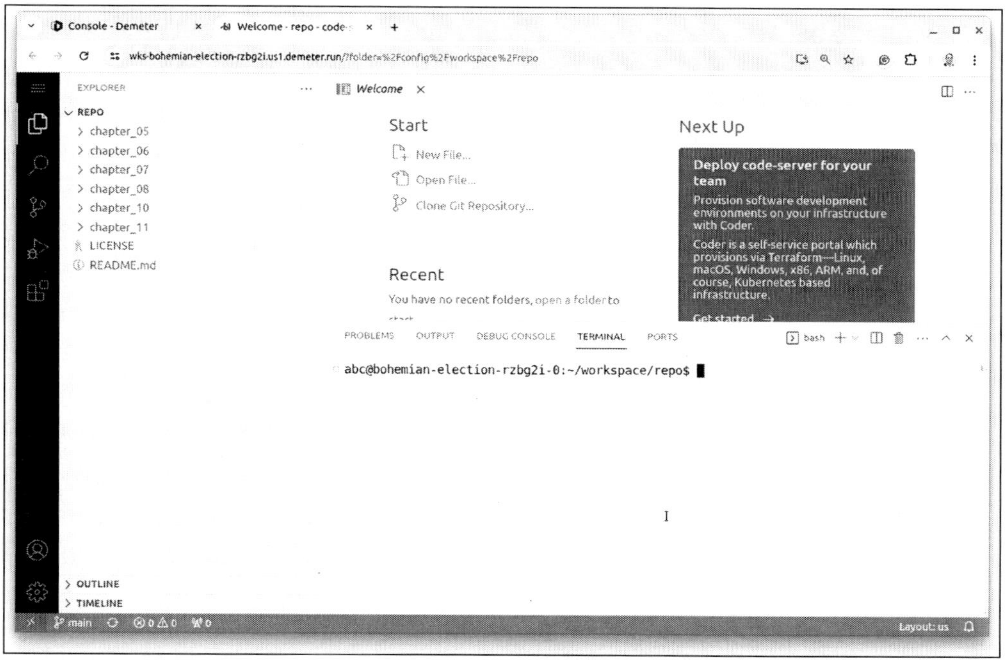

***Figure* 5.12:** *Visual Studio Code Web*

Off-Chain Examples

This section will show two approaches to building the off-chain code for a simple vesting smart contract. Each approach will use Next.js for the application framework. For more information on Next.js, the reader is encouraged to check out the Next.js documentation at https://nextjs.org/docs.

Helios

Helios is both an off-chain JavaScript/TypeScript SDK and an on-chain functional, strongly typed programming language. It prioritizes readability and ease of use for an optimal developer experience. One of the main advantages of Helios is that it is a single JavaScript file with no third-party libraries, which improves the auditability and transparency of the smart contract being executed.

Initialize

We will refer to the GitHub code examples with a fully functional end-to-end example to execute your first off-chain code. In the Visual Studio web setup in the prior section with a Demeter.run workspace, select a new Terminal window and perform the following steps:

```
$ cd chapter_05/helios/vesting
$ nvm install 18.17.0
$ npm install
$ npm run dev
```

This will start up Next.js and run on the default port of 3000. Ignore any prompts from Visual Studio about port forwarding, since we will access the port using the exposed port URL. You can go into the workspace on **Demeter.run** and select the URL for the exposed port to access the Next.js web application. In your browser, you should see something like *Figure 5.13*.

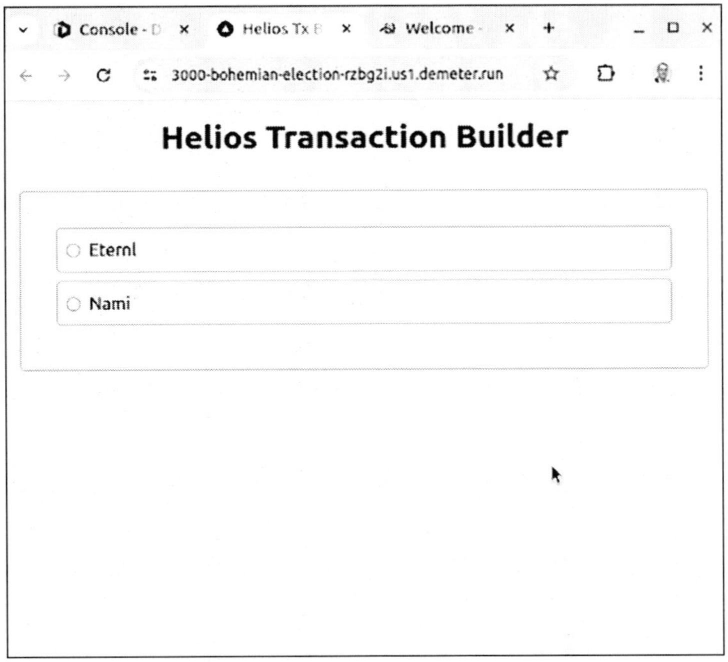

Figure 5.13: *Helios Transaction Builder*

Please ensure you have either **Eternl** (or Nami) browser wallet extensions installed on your Chrome browser before selecting a wallet. You may need to refresh the page if you just installed or enabled the browser wallet extension. On the **Helios Tx Builder** page, when a wallet is selected, the wallet will prompt the user to confirm if it is okay to connect to this site if has not already connected to it previously. Confirm ok, and then you will see the wallet balance of the selected wallet, as shown in *Figure 5.14*.

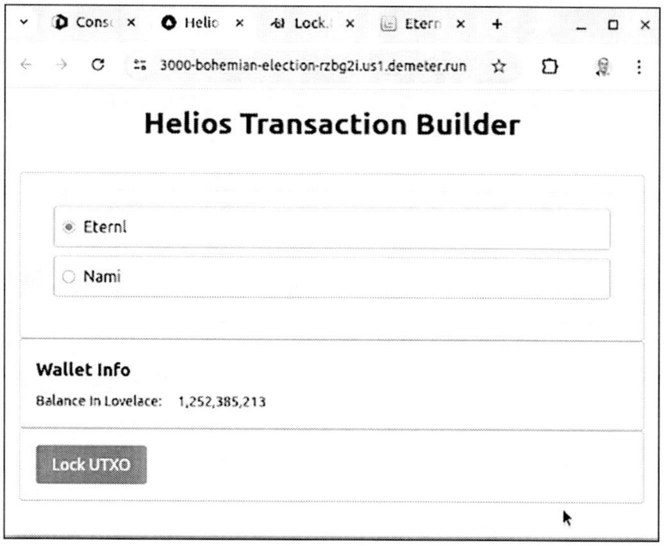

Figure 5.14: *Helios Wallet Selector*

Lock

In *Figure* 5.14, you will notice a "**`Lock UTXO`**" button at the bottom of the screen. This button will create an off-chain transaction to lock 2 Ada and a Datum at a script address. Let's look at the code required to submit an on-chain transaction in the following steps.

Step 1

To connect to the browser wallet API, we will create a **`WalletConnector.tsx`** component within the Next.js application. In *Figure* 5.15, on lines 52 and 53, the code first confirms if the browser plugin exists. If yes, then it updates the **`walletAPI`** state variable on line 56 so that the rest of the application can access it.

```
51      const enableWallet = async (walletChoice: string) => {
52        const walletName = walletDetails[walletChoice]?.api;
53        if (walletName) {
54          try {
55            const walletAPI = await window.cardano[walletName].enable();
56            onWalletAPI(walletAPI);
57            return true;
58          } catch (err) {
59            console.error("enableWallet error", err);
60          }
61        }
62        return false;
63      };
```

Figure 5.15: *Wallet API*[7]

[7]https://github.com/ava-orange-education/Mastering-Cardano-Smart-Contracts/blob/main/chapter_05/helios/vesting/components/WalletConnector.tsx

Step 2

Once we have access to the **`walletAPI`**, we can query the wallet for available UTXOs and change the address, as seen on lines 89 and 92 in *Figure* 5.16. Helios uses a **`walletHelper`** class that wraps the **`walletAPI`** object to provide convenience functions and automatic conversions to Helios data types.

```
88      // Get wallet UTXOs
89      const utxos = await walletHelper.pickUtxos(minAdaVal);
90
91      // Get change address
92      const changeAddr = await walletHelper.changeAddress;
93
94      // Start building the transaction
95      const tx = new Tx();
96
97      // Add the UTXO as inputs
98      tx.addInputs(utxos[0]);
```

***Figure* 5.16**: *Helios WalletHelper*[8]

Next, we must compile the Plutus script to confirm the script address. This can be done via client-side JavaScript, as seen on line 104 in *Figure* 5.17. On line 107, we can see how easy it is to import the Datum structure from the on-chain code and create the appropriate Datum off-chain. Next, we construct the UTXO output on lines 113 to 117 using the script address and the amount of Lovelace (2 Ada), and attach the Datum as an inline datum.

```
100     // Load in the vesting validator script (program)
101     const vestingProgram = new VestingValidator();
102
103     // Compile the vesting validator
104     const compiledProgram = vestingProgram.compile(optimize);
105
106     // Construct the vesting datum
107     const vestingDatum = new (vestingProgram.types.Datum)(
108       changeAddr.pubKeyHash
109     )
110
111     // Construct the output to send the minAda
112     // and the inline datum to the script address
113     tx.addOutput(new TxOutput(
114       Address.fromHashes(compiledProgram.validatorHash),
115       new Value(minAdaVal.lovelace),
116       Datum.inline(vestingDatum)
117     ));
```

***Figure* 5.17**: *Helios Program*[9]

[8]https://github.com/ava-orange-education/Mastering-Cardano-Smart-Contracts/blob/main/chapter_05/helios/vesting/pages/index.tsx
[9]https://github.com/ava-orange-education/Mastering-Cardano-Smart-Contracts/blob/main/chapter_05/helios/vesting/pages/index.tsx

Step 3

The last step before we sign the transaction is to get the current network parameters, including the current epoch, cost model, max **`tx`** size, and more. This is needed for internal validation of the script while it is being constructed. In this example, we are simply sending (locking) Ada at the script address, so we do not need to evaluate the Plutus script. We will, however, evaluate the Plutus script in the next chapter on *Validators*. On line 124 in *Figure* 5.18, the transaction is finalized, which balances the transaction inputs and outputs and returns any change to the wallet if needed. Once the transaction has been finalized, we ask the wallet to prompt the user to sign the transaction. The fully signed transaction is submitted to the network on line 131.

```
119        // Read in the network parameter file
120        const networkParamsJson = await getNetworkParams(network);
121        const networkParams = new NetworkParams(networkParamsJson);
122
123        // Send any change back to the buyer
124        await tx.finalize(networkParams, changeAddr, utxos[1]);
125
126        // Sign the unsigned tx to get the witness
127        const signatures = await cip30WalletAPI.signTx(tx);
128        tx.addSignatures(signatures);
129
130        // Submit the signed tx
131        const txHash = await cip30WalletAPI.submitTx(tx);
```

***Figure* 5.18**: *Helios Submit Transaction*[10]

The user is prompted to sign the transaction using the **`Eternl`** wallet, as shown in *Figure* 5.19.

[10]https://github.com/ava-orange-education/Mastering-Cardano-Smart-Contracts/blob/main/chapter_05/helios/vesting/pages/index.tsx

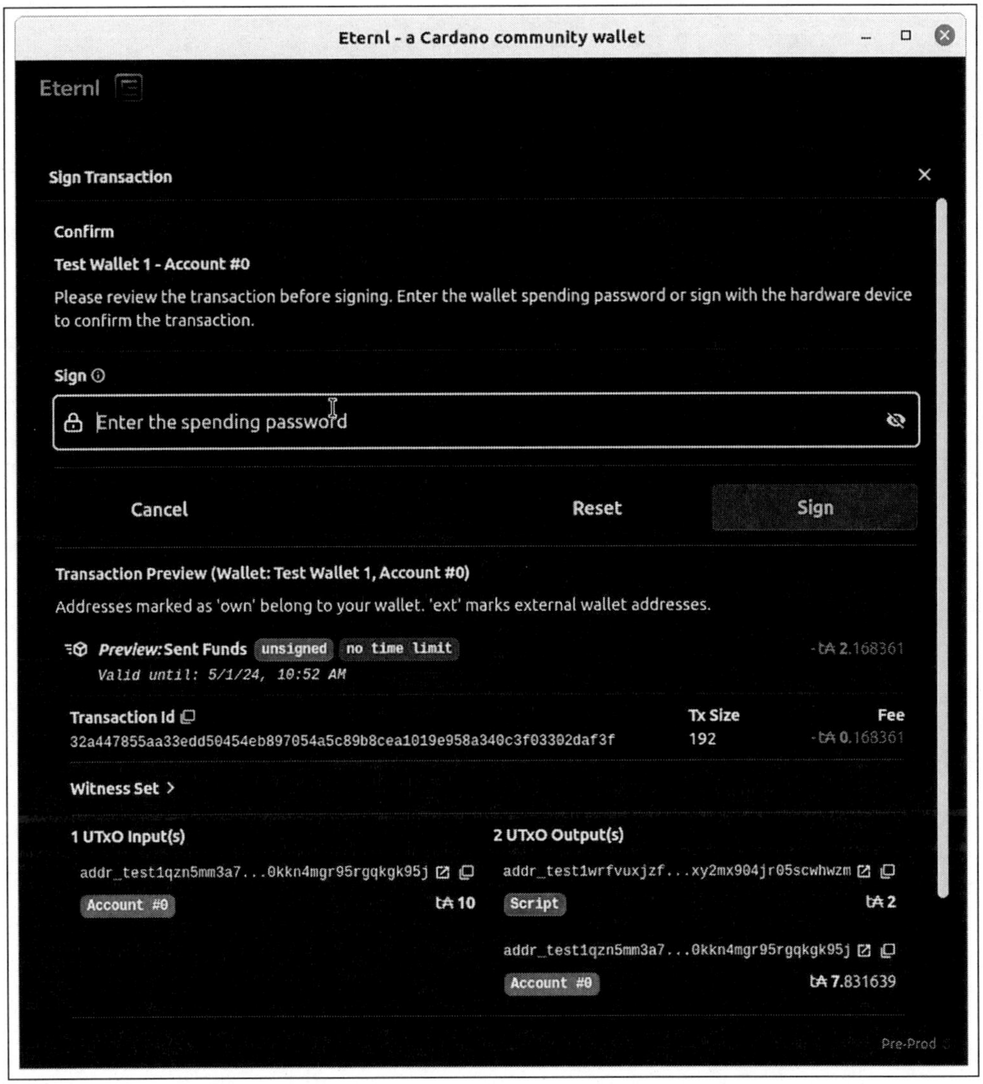

Figure 5.19: *Eternl Wallet Sign Transaction*

After successfully signing the transaction with the browser wallet, a transaction hash (**`TxId`**) will be shown with a link to a blockchain explorer, as shown in *Figure* 5.20.

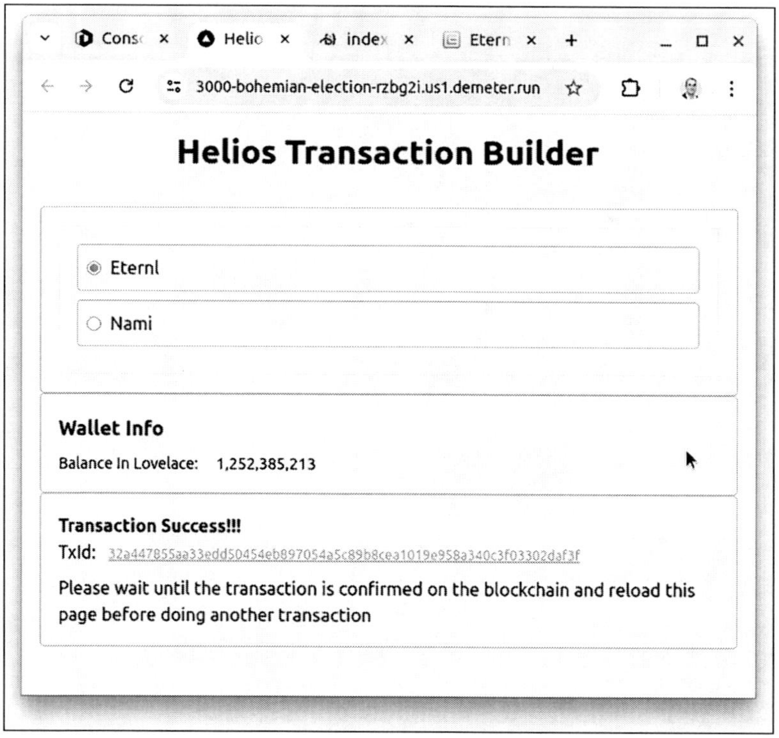

Figure 5.20: *Transaction Successful*

If we select the link to the blockchain explorer, we can see the transaction including the attached inline datum, as shown in *Figure 5.21*.

Figure 5.21: *Blockchain Explorer*[11]

[11]https://preprod.cexplorer.io/tx/32a447855aa33edd50454eb897054a5c89b8cea1019e958a340c3f03302daf3f

Lucid + Aiken

Lucid + Aiken combo has the advantage of broader adoption and usage within the Cardano community. The Aiken team has also been focused on excellent developer experience and has created several utilities to help the Smart Contract developer lifecycle. This section will focus on building an off-chain transaction using Lucid to lock a UTXO at an Aiken script address.

Unlike Helios, which has the option to compile a Plutus script at run-time, Aiken follows the more typical two-phase deployment process:

1. Compile an Aiken script using the Rust-based Aiken compiler to generate artifacts such as the compiled Plutus script and script hash into a file known as a **blueprint**.
2. The Lucid off-chain code reads the compiled script in the **blueprint** file and any contract parameters that may be required.

Blockfrost API

In our examples, we will use Blockfrost API to interact with the Cardano Preprod network. Therefore, you must obtain an API key and set it as an environment variable.

1. Go to https://blockfrost.io/
2. Create a free account and create an API key for the Cardano Preprod network.

Initialize

For the Lucid off-chain code example, we will refer to the GitHub code that can be run with the following steps:

```
$ cd chapter_05/aiken/vesting
$ nvm install 18.17.0
$ npm install
$ echo export NEXT_PUBLIC_BLOCKFROST_API=https://cardano-preprod.block-
frost.io/api/v0 >> ~/.bashrc
$ echo export NEXT_PUBLIC_BLOCKFROST_KEY=your-blockfrost-API-key >>
~/.bashrc
$ source ~/.bashrc
$ npm run dev
```

This will launch Next.js and provide the same experience we saw using the Helios Transaction Builder. For this chapter, the Aiken contract has already been pre-compiled, and we will discuss the Aiken installation and build steps in *Chapter 6, Validators*.

Figures 5.22, 5.23, and 5.24 show the blueprint file's contents. It describes the Aiken Validator and the datum and redeemer data types.

```
{
  "preamble": {
    "title": "aiken-lang/contracts",
    "description": "Aiken contracts for project 'aiken-lang/contracts'",
    "version": "0.0.0",
    "plutusVersion": "v2",
    "compiler": {
      "name": "Aiken",
      "version": "v1.0.20-alpha+49bd4ba"
    },
    "license": "Apache-2.0"
  },
  "validators": [
    {
      "title": "vesting.vesting",
      "datum": {
        "title": "datum",
        "schema": {
          "$ref": "#/definitions/vesting~1Datum"
        }
      },
      "redeemer": {
        "title": "redeemer",
        "schema": {
          "$ref": "#/definitions/vesting~1Redeemer"
        }
      },
      "compiledCode": "590109010000323232323232323222232325333008325333009
      "hash": "f6048678791f061c1860f66c2371b1954e6fc525bff86b058937d163"
    }
  ],
```

Figure 5.22: *Aiken Blueprint Validator*

```
"definitions": {
  "ByteArray": {
    "dataType": "bytes"
  },
  "vesting/Datum": {
    "title": "Datum",
    "description": "Create a datum with the owner PubKeyHash
    "anyOf": [
      {
        "title": "Datum",
        "dataType": "constructor",
        "index": 0,
        "fields": [
          {
            "title": "owner",
            "$ref": "#/definitions/ByteArray"
          }
        ]
      }
    ]
  },
```

Figure 5.23: *Aiken Blueprint Datum Definition*

```
"vesting/Redeemer": {
  "title": "Redeemer",
  "description": "The vesting contract can be either
  "anyOf": [
    {
      "title": "Cancel",
      "dataType": "constructor",
      "index": 0,
      "fields": []
    },
    {
      "title": "Claim",
      "dataType": "constructor",
      "index": 1,
      "fields": [
        {
          "title": "msg",
          "$ref": "#/definitions/ByteArray"
        }
      ]
    }
  ]
```

***Figure* 5.24**: *Aiken Blueprint Redeemer Definition*

Lucid Off-Chain Code

The **WalletConnect.tsx** component will get the **walletAPI** the same way as the Helios off-chain code example. The difference with Lucid is that it also needs to use a blockchain API provider such as **Blockfrost**. Once the provider has been created on lines 32-35 in *Figure* 5.25, the **walletAPI** is passed to it on line 118 in *Figure* 5.26.

```
22  const blockfrostAPI = process.env.NEXT_PUBLIC_BLOCKFROST_API as string;
23  const blockfrostAPIKey = process.env.NEXT_PUBLIC_BLOCKFROST_API_KEY as string;
24
25  if (!blockfrostAPI && !blockfrostAPIKey){
26    throw console.error("NEXT_PUBLIC_BLOCKFROST_API or \
27                         NEXT_PUBLIC_BLOCKFROST_API_KEY not set");
28  }
29
30  // Create lucid object and connect it to a
31  // blockfrost provider
32  const lucid = await Lucid.new(
33    new Blockfrost(blockfrostAPI, blockfrostAPIKey),
34    network,
35  );
```

***Figure* 5.25**: *Lucid Blockfrost Provider*[12]

The Datum is manually constructed, and the Plutus validator script is read from the blueprint file on lines 126 and 129, respectively, in *Figure* 5.26. Finally, the transaction is built, signed, and submitted on lines 133, 139, and 142.

[12]https://github.com/ava-orange-education/Mastering-Cardano-Smart-Contracts/blob/main/chapter_05/aiken/vesting/pages/index.tsx

```
    lucid.selectWallet(walletAPI);

    // Get the pkh from the wallet
    const publicKeyHash = lucid.utils.getAddressDetails(
      await lucid.wallet.address()
    ).paymentCredential?.hash;

    // Construct the datum
    const datum = Data.to(new Constr(0, [publicKeyHash!]));

    // Read in the validator script and determine the script address
    const validator = await readValidator();
    const contractAddress = lucid.utils.validatorToAddress(validator);

    // Build the tx
    const tx = await lucid
      .newTx()
      .payToContract(contractAddress, { inline: datum }, { lovelace })
      .complete();

    // Sign the unsigned tx to get the witness
    const signedTx = await tx.sign().complete();

    // Submit the signed tx
    const txHash = await signedTx.submit();
```

Figure 5.26: *Lucid Submit Transaction*[13]

Tip: *If you only have 1 UTXO in your wallet, the balance may show 0 lovelace because your wallet has excluded it and reserved it for collateral. For Lucid, you must explicitly set collateral in your wallet. For Eternl, you can set collateral by going to the Wallet Settings tab, selecting the Collateral dropdown, and then pressing the Set Collateral button.*

Conclusion

We started the chapter with a walkthrough of the transaction lifecycle and the wallets typically used in Cardano. We then proceeded into off-chain transaction building using two different approaches: Helios and Lucid + Aiken. The same user experience was created for each approach to highlight the code differences between them. We also demonstrated how useful tools like **`Demeter.run`** are used for standing up a development environment and how you register your stake to a stake pool using a wallet. Looking ahead, we are ready to review the on-chain code and execute it as part of a transaction.

[13]https://github.com/ava-orange-education/Mastering-Cardano-Smart-Contracts/blob/main/chapter_05/aiken/vesting/pages/index.tsx

Points to Remember

- The transaction lifecycle involves building, signing, and submitting.
- Transactions are serialized when submitted to the network using the CBOR format.
- Wallets are the gateway to the blockchain and Smart Contracts.
- A seed phrase is used to generate a private key.
- A Testnet faucet is used to get test Ada (**`tAda`**) for the preview and pre-prod networks.
- Address derivation is used to derive multiple addresses using the same private key.
- Staking from a wallet will submit a stake registration and stake pool delegation certificate.
- CIP-30 is a Cardano standard for connecting to browser extension wallets.
- Demeter Run is an on-demand hosting platform for Cardano environments.
- Helios is both an off-chain and on-chain library.
- Helios and Lucid can be used in a client browser.
- Blueprints are created during the Aiken build process and contain the compiled script, metadata, and type definitions for the Datum and Redeemer.

Multiple Choice Questions

1. What is required to delegate to a stake pool?
   a. Stake pool delegation certificate
   b. Withdraw certificate
   c. Use a wallet
   d. Stake registration certificate
2. Which statement is true regarding a receiving and a change address?
   a. Both are internal addresses
   b. One is an internal and the other is a variable
   c. One is external and the other is internal
   d. Both are external addresses

3. What CIP among the following is a Cardano browser wallet connection standard?
    a. CIP-22
    b. CIP-42
    c. CIP-30
    d. CIP-32
4. What is used when generating a private key?
    a. Network
    b. Seed phrase
    c. Password
    d. None of the above
5. What is the Aiken blueprint used for in Lucid?
    a. UTXOs locked at a script address
    b. Current Epoch
    c. Compiled Plutus script and parameters
    d. ADA price

Answers

1. a
2. c
3. c
4. b
5. c

Questions

1. What are the advantages and disadvantages of Single Address Mode wallets?
2. Can Helios or Lucid + Aiken be used in a server-side model?
3. What other languages and frameworks can you use to write Cardano off-chain code?

4. Why are Aiken blueprints helpful?
5. Are seed phrases required to make a private key?

Key Terms

- **Assembled Transaction**: Create a transaction with inputs, outputs, Datums, and Redeemers.
- **Account Abstraction**: Create a view or model of an account with a balance and transaction history.
- **Full Node:** A Cardano node and does not use any third-party service to look up transactions on the blockchain.
- **Seed Phrase**: Used to help generate a private key.
- **Hierarchy for Deterministic Walle**t: Used to derive multiple addresses from the same private key.
- **Single Address Mode:** Reuses the same network address.
- **Auditability:** The ability to confirm that the smart contract has been audited.
- **Transparency:** How to ensure the smart contract being executed is the correct one.
- **WalletAPI:** JavaScript object to interact with CIP-30 compliant browser wallet.
- **Blockfrost:** An API service provided to query the Cardano blockchain.

CHAPTER 6
Validators

Introduction

This chapter will examine what a validator is and why they are so important. We will show how to spend UTXOs locked at a validator script address and how to access data provided in a Redeemer and Datum. Next will be a deep dive into understanding the `ScriptContext` and how it is used to access inputs and outputs associated with a transaction. The chapter will also review code examples using two different approaches: Helios and Lucid + Aiken.

Structure

In this chapter, we will discuss the following topics:

- Validators
- Helios
  - Helios On-Chain Validator
  - Helios Off-Chain Unlock
  - Helios Off-Chain Cancel
- Lucid + Aiken
  - Aiken On-Chain Validator
  - Lucid Off-Chain Unlock
  - Lucid Off-Chain Cancel

Validators

Validators are fundamental to Cardano Smart Contracts because they specify the on-chain conditions required to spend a UTXO locked at a script address. Once a validator is on-chain, it is immutable where code becomes "*law*". A typical use case for validators is a vesting contract where funds are locked into a contract until the specific condition(s) are met. We will further build on our vesting example in the upcoming chapters and look at both the on-chain and off-chain codes. Validators consist of two components: the on-chain code that defines the rules and logic, and the off-chain code that creates and submits the transaction.

Helios

We first saw how to build an off-chain transaction using Helios in *Chapter* 5, *Transaction Builder*. In this chapter, we will first look at the code to build the on-chain validator and then the off-chain code required to spend a UTXO locked at the script address. The Helios language for on-chain code is a strongly typed, functional programming language with similar code quality benefits from languages like Haskell or Aiken. The Helios compiler, however, is written in JavaScript and has the unique advantage of compiling at run-time using only JavaScript. This makes the setup and installation trivial since all you need is a recent version of Node.js, which is widely available on many operating systems.

Helios On-Chain Validator

The first line of a Helios on-chain validator specifies the purpose of the Plutus script. In this case, it is a **`spending`** script, and the name of the script is called **`vesting.`** In *Figure* 6.1, on line 7, a Datum is defined as a **`struct`** with an **`owner`** variable using a **`PubKeyHash`** data type. This will be stored on-chain within a UTXO locked at the script address. We previously saw an example of this type of Datum in *Chapter* 4, *Plutus*, *Figure* 4.5. On line 15 in *Figure* 6.1, there is a Redeemer with an **`enum`** data type that contains two elements: **`Cancel`** and **`Claim`**. The **`Claim`** element has a **`msg`** variable that is used to pass a message to the validator at runtime.

```
1   spending vesting
2   const VERSION: String = "v0.0.1"
3   /*
4    Create a datum with the owner PubKeyHash that will be included
5    into each UTXO locked at this script address.
6   */
7   struct Datum {
8       owner: PubKeyHash
9   }
10
11  /*
12   The vesting contract can be either cancelled by the owner
13   or claimed by the beneificiary
14   */
15  enum Redeemer {
16      Cancel
17      Claim {
18          msg: String
19      }
20  }
```

***Figure 6.1**: Helios On-Chain Validator Declarations*[1]

[1] https://github.com/ava-orange-education/Mastering-Cardano-Smart-Contracts/blob/main/chapter_06/helios/vesting/contracts/vesting.hl

Note: When running locally, a Helios Visual Studio Code extension (**`ext:hl`**) is available for syntax highlighting. For Visual Studio Web, you must associate the **`.hl`** extension with C #.

On line 23 in *Figure* 6.2, a **contract parameter `MESSAGE`** is declared that will be hard coded into the Plutus script. A **contract parameter** is a UPLC value that precedes the main validator function and can be updated dynamically at compile time or run-time if required.

```
22  // Add message constant as a contract paramater
23  const MESSAGE: String = "Hello World!"
24
25  // Define the main validator function
26  func main(datum: Datum, redeemer: Redeemer, ctx: ScriptContext) -> Bool {
27      tx: Tx = ctx.tx;
28      print(VERSION);
29
30      // Depending on the redeemer provided in the transaction, process accordingly.
31      redeemer.switch {
32          Cancel => {
33              // Tx must be singed by pkh in datum
34              tx.is_signed_by(datum.owner)
35          },
36          red: Claim => {
37              // Redeemer must match the message to spend this UTXO
38              red.msg == MESSAGE
39          }
40      }
41  }
```

Figure 6.2: *Helios On-Chain Validator Body*[2]

The main validator function is defined on line 26 in *Figure* 6.2. We can see that three parameters, **`Datum`**, **`Redeemer`**, and **`ScriptContext`**, are passed to the main function. A validator may use none or any of these arguments depending on the validator logic. We have already discussed **`Datum`** and **`Redeemer`** in *Chapter* 4, *Plutus*, so we will look into the **`ScriptContext`** in more detail. The **`ScriptContext`** includes the script purpose and all information related to the submitted transaction, except for **auxiliary data (metadata)**.

As we recall from *Chapter* 3, *Transactions*, a script purpose is specified in the redeemer for each UTXO locked at a script address. Therefore, the four script purposes that may be used in the **`ScriptContext`** are as follows:

- **`Spending`**: used for validating the spending of a UTXO locked at a script address.
- **`Minting`**: used for minting or burning native tokens.
- **`Certifying`**: used for stake key registration and delegating stake to a stake pool.
- **`Rewarding`**: used for withdrawing staking rewards.

[2]https://github.com/ava-orange-education/Mastering-Cardano-Smart-Contracts/blob/main/chapter_06/helios/vesting/contracts/vesting.hl

In *Figure* 6.2, line 27, we define a local variable **`tx`**, which gets all of the transaction information from the current transaction being executed. This will then be used to extract the required signers of this transaction. Next, we use a **`switch`** statement on the Redeemer to execute different codes based on the value of the Redeemer. If the Redeemer is a **`Cancel`**, then we look at the required signatures in the transaction to see if they match the public key hash in the datum. If this is true, the validator allows the owner to do whatever he wants with this UTXO. If the Redeemer is a **`Claim`,** then we return **`true`** if the message in the redeemer matches the contract parameter **`MESSAGE`** value. If the Redeemer does not match either a **`Cancel`** or **`Claim`** or returns a false value, the validator will return **`false`** and the transaction will fail.

Helios Off-Chain Unlock

First, we will create an **`Unlock.tsx`** component that will allow the user to enter the text for the Redeemer and select a button to build the unlock transaction, as shown in *Figure* 6.3.

```
    return (
        <form onSubmit={onSubmit}>
        <div className="p-4 border">
            <span>Redemeer Message</span>
                <label className="flex items-center space-x-2">
                    <input
                        type="text"
                        name="message"
                        id="message"
                        placeholder="Enter Redeemer Text Message"
                        value={message}
                        onChange={(e) => handleChange(e)}
                    />
                </label>
        </div>
```

Figure 6.3: *Unlock UI Component*[3]

Then, we create the unlock function in our main **`index.tsx`** page that takes the Redeemer parameter and builds the transaction. The unlock function in *Figure* 6.4 is similar to the lock function, but we need to get a receiving address on line 171 to send the unlocked funds. On line 186, we attach the validator script to the transaction to be included as a script witness.

[3]https://github.com/ava-orange-education/Mastering-Cardano-Smart-Contracts/blob/main/chapter_06/helios/vesting/components/Unlock.tsx

```
// Get wallet UTXOs
const utxos = await walletHelper.pickUtxos(minAdaVal);

// Get change address
const changeAddr = await walletHelper.changeAddress;

// Get receiving address(es)
const receivingAddr = await walletHelper.allAddresses;

// Start building the transaction
const tx = new Tx();

// Add the UTXO as inputs
tx.addInputs(utxos[0]);

// Load in the vesting validator script (program)
const vestingProgram = new VestingValidator();

// Compile the vesting validator
const vestingCompiledProgram = vestingProgram.compile(optimize);

// Add the script as a witness to the transaction
tx.attachScript(vestingCompiledProgram);
```

Figure 6.4: *Unlock Function Vesting Program*[4]

Next, in *Figure* 6.5, we need to get a UTXO locked at the script address on line 189 and construct the Redeemer on line 193. In Helios, we can simply import the Redeemer type from the on-chain code and generate the UPLC code with the **`_toUplcData()`** function. We then add the UTXO input and the Redeemer on line 198, which will be linked together as a Redeemer witness. A UTXO output on line 206 is also created for 2 Ada to be sent to the receiving address once the UTXO locked at the script address is spent.

```
188  // Get the UTXO(s) locked at the vesting contract (if any)
189  const vestingUtxo = await getVestingUtxo(
190                    Address.fromHashes(vestingCompiledProgram.validatorHash));
191
192  // Create the vesting claim redeemer
193  const vestingRedeemer = (new vestingProgram .types.Redeemer.Claim(message))
194                          ._toUplcData();
195
196  // Check that UTXO input exists
197  if (vestingUtxo) {
198    tx.addInput(vestingUtxo, vestingRedeemer);
199  } else {
200    throw console.error("No UTXOs found at vesting contract address: ",
201                        Address.fromHashes(vestingCompiledProgram.validatorHash)
202                        .toBech32);
203  }
204
205  // Construct the output to send the unlocked funds to
206  tx.addOutput(new TxOutput(
207    receivingAddr[0], // send to the frist receiving address
208    new Value(minAdaVal.lovelace)
209  ));
```

Figure 6.5: *Unlock Function Inputs and Outputs*[5]

[4]https://github.com/ava-orange-education/Mastering-Cardano-Smart-Contracts/blob/main/chapter_06/helios/vesting/pages/index.tsx

[5]https://github.com/ava-orange-education/Mastering-Cardano-Smart-Contracts/blob/main/chapter_06/helios/vesting/pages/index.tsx

The **getVestingUtxo** function on line 189 makes a network call to a Next.js API created to query the blockchain for UTXOs at the script address. The Next.js API uses **Blockfrost**, a third-party Blockchain API provider, and is executed on the server. There are other providers and approaches to querying the Cardano blockchain, such as Maestro, Ogmios, and Koios. We will review other blockchain API providers in *Chapter* 8, *Tooling*. The advantage of using the **Blockfrost** API server-side is that it avoids API key leakage when calling the API directly from the browser. Additionally, this avoids network calls to a different domain, which can result in browser CORS errors. *Figure* 6.6 shows the code of the Next.js **vestingUtxo** API that is called by the function **getVestingUtxo** in **index.tsx**.

```
export default async function handler(
  req: NextApiRequest,
  res: NextApiResponse ) {

    const getVestingUtxo = async (vestingValidatorAddr: string): Promise<TxInput> => {
        const apiKey = process.env.BLOCKFROST_API_KEY as string;
        if (!apiKey) {
            throw console.error("BLOCKFROST_API_KEY not set");
        }
        const blockfrostAPI = new BlockfrostV0(network, apiKey);
        const vestingUTXOs = await blockfrostAPI.getUtxos(
                                        Address.fromBech32(vestingValidatorAddr));
        if (vestingUTXOs.length < 1) {
            throw console.error("No UTXOs found at vesting address: ",
                                vestingValidatorAddr);
        }
        return vestingUTXOs[0];  // only return the first UTXO
    }
    try {
        const txInput = await getVestingUtxo(req.body.addr);
        res.status(200).send(txInput.toFullCbor());
    }
    catch (err) {
        res.status(500).json("getVestingUtxo API error: " + err);
```

Figure 6.6: *getVestingUtxo* API[6]

The remainder of the unlock function is the same as the lock function, which assembles, signs, and submits the transaction to the network. The new UI with the Unlock button and the Redeemer message input is shown in *Figure* 6.7.

[6]https://github.com/ava-orange-education/Mastering-Cardano-Smart-Contracts/blob/main/chapter_06/helios/vesting/pages/api/vestingUtxo.ts

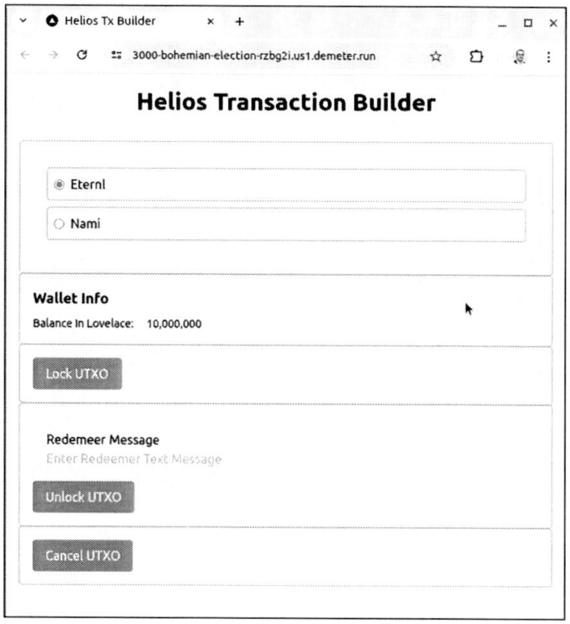

Figure 6.7: *Helios Unlock UTXO*

Off-Chain Cancel

We create a **`Cancel.tsx`** component and a cancel function inside **`index.tsx`**, which will be almost identical to the **`Lock.tsx`** component and the **`unlock`** function. There are only a few changes between the unlock and the cancel function. Can you spot the differences in *Figure 6.8*?

```
    // Construct the output to send the unlocked funds to
    tx.addOutput(new TxOutput(
      receivingAddr[0], // send to the frist receiving address
      new Value(minAdaVal.lovelace)
    ));

    // Add the public key hash as a required signer to the transaction
    tx.addSigner(receivingAddr[0].pubKeyHash!)

    // Read in the network parameter file
    const networkParamsJson = await getNetworkParams(network);
    const networkParams = new NetworkParams(networkParamsJson);

    // Send any change back to the buyer
    await tx.finalize(networkParams, changeAddr, utxos[1]);

    // Sign the unsigned tx to get the witness
    const signatures = await cip30WalletAPI.signTx(tx);
    tx.addSignatures(signatures);

    // Submit the signed tx
    const txHash = await cip30WalletAPI.submitTx(tx);
```

Figure 6.8: *Helios Cancel UTXO*[7]

[7]https://github.com/ava-orange-education/Mastering-Cardano-Smart-Contracts/blob/main/chapter_06/helios/vesting/pages/index.tsx

One difference is that we must explicitly add the required signer for the transaction. The **`.addSigner()`** function, on line 294, will add the wallet's public key hash to the transaction and include it as a required signer. The Cardano Node will ensure that any required signers have a corresponding valid signature in the witness set. The on-chain code then looks up the public key hash in the list of required signers to see if there is a match.

Test Drive

To run the demo, you need to execute the following commands; unless you change the version number or the **`vesting`** script, the validator script address will be the same for everyone:

```
$ cd chapter_06/helios/vesting
$ npm install
$ echo export BLOCKFROST_KEY=your-blockfrost-API-key >> ~/.bashrc
$ echo export NEXT_PUBLIC_ENV="dev" >> ~/.bashrc
$ echo export NEXT_PUBLIC_HOST="demeter-run-host" >> ~/.bashrc
$ echo export NEXT_PUBLIC_PROTOCOL="https" >> ~/.bashrc
$ echo export NEXT_PUBLIC_PORT="" >> ~/.bashrc
$ source ~/.bashrc
$ npm run dev
```

You should now be able to access the application using the exposed port URL. You can lock the 2 Ada and either claim (unlock) using the correct Redeemer value or cancel it. *Figure* 6.9 shows a successful transaction claiming the 2 Ada using the correct Redeemer value.

Figure 6.9: *Helios Vesting Claim*[8]

[8]https://preprod.cexplorer.io/address/addr_test1wp4gwgtnyp8grwhzjj47qy7k60hxfv9p2wymjcwkzgw6r9cp0ctvs/tx#data

Aiken

Aiken is a functional programming language with a compiler written in Rust, and we will compile an Aiken script using the **aiken build** command. This generates the compiled Plutus code and a **blueprint** file containing metadata and type definitions. To install Aiken in your **Demeter.run** workspace, you first need to download the installer:

```
$ curl -sSfL https://install.aiken-lang.org | bash
$ echo export PATH=:/config/.aiken/bin:$PATH >> ~/.bashrc
$ source ~/.bashrc
```

Then, run the following command:

```
aikup
```

With **aiken** installed, you can use the help switch to see the following available options:

```
$ aiken --help
```

```
Cardano smart contract language and toolchain


Usage: aiken <COMMAND>


Commands:
  new          Create a new Aiken project
  fmt          Format an Aiken project
  build        Build an Aiken project
  address      Compute a validator's address
  check        Type-check an Aiken project
  docs         Build the documentation for an Aiken project
  add          Add a new project package as dependency
  blueprint    Commands for working with Plutus blueprints
  packages     Managing project dependencies
  tx           Commands for working with transactions
  uplc         Commands for working with untyped Plutus-core
  completion   Generates shell completion scripts
  help         Print this message or the help of the given subcommand(s)
```

You can create a new project with the following command:

```
aiken new aiken-lang/new-project
```

This will create the following project files and folders:

```
└── new-project
    ├── aiken.toml
    ├── lib
    │   └── new-project
    ├── README.md
    └── validators
```

`aiken.toml` contains information about your project, including libraries and the GitHub repo. The validators folder contains the on-chain Aiken source code, and the lib directory contains any project libraries needed or created for this project. You can run a quick test to confirm everything is installed correctly by executing **`aiken build`** and **`aiken check`** inside the new-project directory.

In the examples in this book, we place all of the Aiken on-chain validator code and artifacts in the **`contracts`** directory within each chapter project(s). For example:

```
chapter_06/aiken/vesting/contracts
```

If you want to learn more about setup and installation tasks including IDE language configurations, please refer to the Aiken online documentation.[9]

Aiken On-Chain Validator

Now, we are ready to look at our first Aiken validator script, as shown in *Figure 6.10*:

```
use aiken/hash.{Blake2b_224, Hash}
use aiken/list
use aiken/string
use aiken/transaction.{ScriptContext}
use aiken/transaction/credential.{VerificationKey}
const version: ByteArray = "v1.0.0"

/// Create a datum with the owner PubKeyHash that will be included
/// into each UTXO locked at this script address.
type Datum {
  owner: Hash<Blake2b_224, VerificationKey>,
}
/// The vesting contract can be either cancelled by the owner
/// or claimed by the beneificiary
type Redeemer {
  Cancel
  Claim { msg: ByteArray }
}

// Add hard coded message constant
const message: ByteArray = "Hello World!"
```

Figure 6.10: *Aiken On-Chain Validator Declarations*[10]

[9]https://aiken-lang.org/installation-instructions
[10]https://github.com/ava-orange-education/Mastering-Cardano-Smart-Contracts/blob/main/chapter_06/aiken/vesting/contracts/validators/vesting.ak

The first 5 lines, in *Figure* 6.10, are the explicit import of classes we will use, followed by the Datum and Redeemer types. The Datum includes a Hash object, which contains a **`Blake2b_224`** and **`VerificationKey`** object. It should be noted that this is stored on-chain as a single **`ByteArray`** representing the public key hash. On line 15, the Redeemer contains two conditions (Cancel and Claim) to spend the UTXOs locked at this script address. The Claim redeemer also contains a **`msg`** payload using the **`ByteArray`** data type. On line 21, we hard-coded the "**`Hello World!`**" message as a script constant.

Next, in *Figure* 6.11, we define the validator function on line 23 and create the vesting function with the **`Datum`**, **`Redeemer`**, and **`ScriptContext`** as arguments:

```
23  validator {
24    fn vesting(datum: Datum, redeemer: Redeemer, context: ScriptContext) -> Bool {
25      trace string.from_bytearray(version)
26      when redeemer is {
27        Cancel ->
28          // Tx must be singed by pkh in datum
29          list.has(context.transaction.extra_signatories, datum.owner)
30        Claim { msg } ->
31          // Redeemer must match the message to spend this UTXO
32          msg == message
33      }
34    }
35  }
```

Figure 6.11: *Aiken On-Chain Validator Body*[11]

On line 26, we determine the type of Redeemer provided for a particular transaction. In the case of Cancel, the code on line 29 looks through the list of required signers and confirms if there is a public key hash matching the public key hash in the datum. If true, then the validator evaluates to true and allows the spending of the UTXO locked at the script address. If the Redeemer is a Claim, we compare the **`msg`** payload to the hard-coded message constant on line 32. If there are no matches for the Redeemer, then the validator will fail and not allow the spending of the UTXO locked at the script address.

Lucid Off-Chain Unlock

We will create the same **`Unlock.tsx`** component that we did with Helios and an **`unlock function`** in **`index.tsx`**. We need to create a Redeemer for the unlock function but don't need to create a Datum since it is already part of the UTXO we want to spend. The Redeemer on line 172, in *Figure* 6.12, creates a Plutus Data object corresponding to the UPLC Datatypes we saw in *Chapter* 4, *Plutus*. In this case, we are creating a **`Constr`** at index 1, containing a hexadecimal-encoded string. When the script is evaluated, this hexadecimal-encoded string will be converted into the Redeemer Claim ByteArray payload. We specify an index of 1 because the Redeemer **`Cancel`** was the first Redeemer

[11] https://github.com/ava-orange-education/Mastering-Cardano-Smart-Contracts/blob/main/chapter_06/aiken/vesting/contracts/validators/vesting.ak

defined in the Plutus script with an index of 0. The next Redeemer in order will have an index of 1, the Claim Redeemer.

```
171      // Construct the Claim redeemer
172      const vestingRedeemer = Data.to(new Constr(1, [fromText(message)]));
173
174      // Get the UTXO(s) locked at the vesting contract (if any)
175      const utxo = (await lucid.utxosAt(contractAddress));
176      if (utxo.length < 1) {
177        throw console.error("No UTXOs exist at the vesting contract address: ",
178                            contractAddress);
179      }
180      const tx = await lucid
181        .newTx()
182        .collectFrom([utxo[0]], vestingRedeemer)
183        .attachSpendingValidator(validator)
184        .complete();
185
186      // Sign the unsigned tx to get the witness
187      const signedTx = await tx.sign().complete();
188
189      // Submit the signed tx
190      const txHash = await signedTx.submit();
```

Figure 6.12: *Lucid Off-Chain Unlock*[12]

On line 175, the UTXOs locked at the script address are obtained by calling the **`lucid.utxosAt`** function, which uses the Blockfrost API to query the blockchain. Next, we build the transaction and specify the input UTXO on line 182 and the Validator script on line 183. The lucid transaction can now be assembled using the **`.complete()`** method. There is a lot of activity behind the scenes to assemble and finalize a transaction. We will focus on the more commonly used **`lucid tx`** methods to build and submit a transaction. Once the transaction has been finalized, the wallet will ask the user to sign it and submit it to the network.

Lucid Off-Chain Cancel

Lastly, we will create a new **`Cancel.tsx`** component and a cancel function in **`index.tsx`**. The **`Cancel.tsx`** component is almost identical to the Lock.tsx component, the main difference being the required signatures in the transaction on line 226 in *Figure* 6.13. This is needed because the on-chain code looks to see if the required public key hash matches the public key hash stored in the datum.

[12]https://github.com/ava-orange-education/Mastering-Cardano-Smart-Contracts/blob/main/chapter_06/aiken/vesting/pages/index.tsx

```
// Construct the Cancel redeemer
const vestingRedeemer = Data.to(new Constr(0,[]));

// Get the UTXO(s) locked at the vesting contract (if any)
const utxo = (await lucid.utxosAt(contractAddress));
if (utxo.length < 1) {
  throw console.error("No UTXOs exist at the vesting contract address: ",
                      contractAddress);
}
const tx = await lucid
  .newTx()
  .collectFrom([utxo[0]], vestingRedeemer)
  .addSigner(await lucid.wallet.address())
  .attachSpendingValidator(validator)
  .complete();

// Sign the unsigned tx to get the witness
const signedTx = await tx.sign().complete();

// Submit the signed tx
const txHash = await signedTx.submit();
```

Figure 6.13: *Lucid Off-Chain Cancel*[13]

Test Drive

To try out the example, run the following steps:

```
$ cd chapter_06/aiken/vesting/contracts
$ aiken build
$ cd ..
$ echo export NEXT_PUBLIC_BLOCKFROST_API=https://cardano-preprod.block-
frost.io/api/v0 >> ~/.bashrc
$ echo export NEXT_PUBLIC_BLOCKFROST_KEY=your-blockfrost-API-key >>
~/.bashrc
$ source ~/.bashrc
$ npm install
$ npm run dev
```

Conclusion

We looked at our first on-chain Plutus validators built using the languages Helios and Aiken. We then looked at the corresponding off-chain code to execute these validators using Helios and Lucid, respectively. We looked at how to initialize a project using Aiken and how to compile an Aiken Smart Contract. Then, the **`ScriptContext`** was examined and how it contains key transaction information such as inputs, outputs, script purpose, and more. We also looked at the Datum and Redeemer definitions on-chain and how they are accessed during script execution. The creation of an Off-chain

[13]https://github.com/ava-orange-education/Mastering-Cardano-Smart-Contracts/blob/main/chapter_06/aiken/vesting/pages/index.tsx

Redeemer and required signers was also demonstrated in the examples. The next chapter will dive into Minting Policies, parameterized smart contracts, and minting native tokens.

Points to Remember

- Helios is used for both on-chain and off-chain code.
- Helios on-chain code can be compiled on the fly because the Helios compiler is written in JavaScript.
- Aiken is used for on-chain code and is compiled prior to run-time using the rust-based **`aiken`** compiler.
- Aiken also generates a blueprint file that contains Plutus script metadata and type definitions.
- The **`aiken`** program has several convenient utility functions that may be used during smart contract development.
- Lucid is used for the off-chain code and is frequently used in combination with Aiken.
- Lucid and Helios off-chain code rely on a blockchain API provider to obtain blockchain information such as UTXOs locked at a script address.
- The Helios off-chain code can import the Helios on-chain code, allowing for sharing type definitions.
- Helios off-chain code does not require any third-party libraries and is consolidated into one JavaScript file.
- When spending a UTXO, a Redeemer must be provided for each UTXO locked at a script address.
- A required signer must include a signature in the witness set for a transaction.

Multiple Choice Questions

1. What is required to spend a UTXO at a Plutus script address?
   a. Datum Only
   b. Minting Script
   c. Datum and Redeemer
   d. Epoch

2. What activity must occur during transaction finalization?
    a. Balance the inputs and the outputs
    b. Specify the Redeemer
    c. Specify the Datum
    d. Sign the transaction
3. How does off-chain code access blockchain data?
    a. Makes a direct RPC call to the node
    b. Usually not needed
    c. Uses an API provider (for example, **`Blockfrost`**, **`Ogmios`**, and more)
    d. CIP-30 wallet connector
4. What is the typical sequence for on-chain code execution?
    a. Local evaluator, Node for **`tx`** submission, All blockchain nodes
    b. All blockchain nodes only
    c. Node for **`tx`** submission only
    d. Local evaluator then All blockchain nodes
5. What are the four different script purposes?
    a. `Validate`, `Mint`, `Reward`, `Cert`
    b. `Spend`, `Burn`, `Cert`, `Reward`
    c. `Spend`, `Mint`, `Burn`, `Context`
    d. `Spend`, `Mint`, `Cert`, `Reward`

Answers

1. c
2. a
3. c
4. a
5. d

Questions

1. How could you improve the auditability of a smart contract that is executed?
2. Why are most smart contracts deployed before run-time?
3. What is the role of `Datum` and `ScriptData` hashes?
4. Why must you always specify a redeemer when executing a smart contract?
5. How are the Plutus cost models retrieved by off-chain frameworks such as Lucid and Helios?
6. What is the CDDL specification identifier for the required signers of a transaction?

Key Terms

- **Auxiliary Data:** Metadata about the transaction where only the metadata hash is stored on-chain.
- **Blake2b:** A hash algorithm that generates a hash based on an input of bytes.
- **Blueprint:** An Aiken-generated file that contains Plutus script metadata and type definitions .
- **`Blockfrost`:** An API Provider for blockchain data.
- **`ByteArray`:** An array of bytes encoded using a hexadecimal format.
- **Contract Parameter:** A variable on-chain that can be updated during compilation or at run-time.
- **`Enum`:** A data type that can be enumerated and used in a switch/case statement.
- **`ScriptContext`:** Contains all information about the current transaction being evaluated except for Auxiliary Data.
- **`Spending script`:** Type of validator for spending UTXO locked at a script address.
- **`Switch` Statement:** Used to evaluate different Enum combinations.
- **`VerificationKey`:** The public key of the corresponding private key.

CHAPTER 7
Minting

Introduction

In this chapter, we will examine Cardano native assets and how they are different from tokens on Ethereum created using the ERC-20 and ERC-721 standards. We will discuss the concept of token bundles and how to optimize coin selection. Next, we will deep dive into how Cardano native tokens are minted and the differences between Non-Fungible Tokens (NFTs) and Fungible Tokens (FTs). We will also review the NFT and FT metadata standards CIP-25 and CIP-68 and how to implement them when minting. Finally, we will introduce the Cardano Token Registry and explore its benefits for the end-user wallet experience. We will put this all together with a working minting policy use case and demo.

Structure

In this chapter, we will discuss the following topics:

- Tokens
    - Native Assets
    - Token Bundles
- Minting Policy
    - Fungible Tokens
    - Non-Fungible Tokens
    - Token Registry
    - NFT Metadata Standards
        - CIP-25
        - CIP-68
- Coin Selection
    - Minting Policy Use Case

Tokens

On March 1st, 2021, as part of the Mary hard fork, Cardano was upgraded to a multi-asset ledger. This was a significant event because custom native tokens can now leverage the secure, peer-reviewed, ledger rules used for Ada, Cardano's native currency. This is much different than in Ethereum, which requires a custom ledger code for each token following either the ERC-20 or ERC-721 standards. Additionally, there are no requirements for special fees or additional event-handling logic to track transactions associated with a Cardano native asset.[1]

Native Assets

A Native asset is a custom token on Cardano that operates in the same manner as the base layer currency, Ada. The only requirement is that a native asset must always have a minimum amount of Ada included. CIP-55[2] simplified the minimum Ada calculation and used the number of CBOR bytes of a UTXO, which includes all of the native assets locked in a particular UTXO.

Assets represent value such as 1 Ada (1,000,000 lovelace) or 100 gold coins. Each asset token is always made of three components*:

- **Policy Identifier (ID):** A unique identifier that is the hash of the Minting Policy Plutus script.
- **Asset Name:** An immutable token name on-chain for a specific minting policy.
- **Quantity**: The accounting unit.

* Ada is the only asset token where the Policy ID is an empty string.

Token Bundles

A token bundle is a collection of tokens that may be the same or different from each other. Token bundles organize tokens into a particular structure that properly defines the Minting Policy ID, Token Name, and quantity of each of the tokens in a **collection**. Let's look at the following example:

```
{
    "lovelace": "1646420",
    "assets": {
        "Game Monetary Policy ID": {
            "Gold": "100",
```

[1]https://github.com/IntersectMBO/cardano-ledger/blob/master/doc/explanations/features.rst

[2]https://github.com/cardano-foundation/CIPs/tree/master/CIP-0055

```
            "Silver": "1,000",
            "Bronze": "10,000",

        },
        "Game Character Policy ID": {
            "Dracula": "1"
    }
}
```

In the preceding example , we have a collection of tokens that each represents value locked at a UTXO. The **`Game Monetary Policy ID`** is a unique Minting Policy ID, and the player holds a collection of 100 Gold, 1,000 Silver, and 10,000 Bronze tokens. So, a user would be able to spend up to 100 Gold, up to 1,000 Silver, and up to 10,000 Bronze tokens in a single transaction. Since this player only has 1 Dracula token, they can only send (spend) 1 Dracula token to another player. There always needs to be a minimum amount of Ada in a token bundle, and in this case, it is 1,646,420 lovelace.

Minting Policy

There are two different types of minting policies on Cardano:

- A native script minting policy that is created using the **`cardano-cli`** tool and uses a private and public key.
- A minting policy that is a plutus script.

The **`cardano-cli`** approach[3] was first used before smart contracts were introduced, but this approach is still used today because it is a proven and secure technique. Using **`cardano-cli`** with native script provides the ability to specify time-locks and multi-signature conditions.[4]

A minting policy is written in a similar way to how we would write a validator script. The difference between a validator script and a minting policy is that a minting policy uses a **`minting`** script purpose and does not use a datum. The **`minting`** script purpose allows the minting policy to mint or burn native tokens as part of a transaction. Only the conditions to mint or burn are defined in the custom logic of a minting policy.

Fungible Tokens

You may want to create a **monetary policy** with a fixed supply of 1,000,000 tokens. The minting policy would only allow a one-time minting of 1,000,000 tokens, with each

[3]https://developers.cardano.org/docs/native-tokens/minting/
[4]https://github.com/IntersectMBO/cardano-node/blob/1.35.7/doc/reference/simple-scripts.md

token having the same name. This allows each to token be fungible or tradable with each other, similar to how fiat currency operates today.

Non-Fungible Tokens

A Non-Fungible Token (**NFT**) is where each token is unique and distinct. There are two approaches to making a unique token on Cardano.

- **Option 1**: Time-lock, where a token can only be minted before a specific date and time.
- **Option 2**: Minting Policy logic that checks for the existence of a UTXO in the input that has to be spent.

The second option is preferred because it leverages the unique properties of the Cardano UTXO architecture. Once a UTXO is spent, it can never be spent again, and there will not be another UTXO with the same hash. By hard coding this condition into the minting policy and also ensuring that only one token is minted, we guarantee that the token is unique. A time-lock approach was used before smart contract functionality was available, but this method is still used when creating large NFT collections.

Token Registry

The Token Registry[5] is used to store off-chain metadata for a minting policy ID and token name. A minting policy ID is a hexadecimal hash value, so it is helpful to have a mapping of human-readable information about a specific Minting Policy and token. The registry provides an API that wallets and other applications can use to look up a token image URL, decimal precision, and other metadata. With the adoption of CIP-68 increasing, the need for a centralized off-chain token registry will be phased out over time. For a step-by-step guide to register a token, please visit the following URL:

https://github.com/cardano-foundation/cardano-token-registry/wiki

NFT Metadata Standards

When minting an NFT, you can take advantage of transaction metadata that can be included in any transaction on the Cardano network. The first Cardano metadata standard was documented in CIP-25[6], which specifies the standard fields for NFT metadata. A notable difference between the Ethereum ERC-721 token metadata is that CIP-25 metadata is linked to the minting transaction and not the minting policy. So, the process to look up the metadata using CIP-25 is to look at the original minting transaction for a particular minting policy.

---

[5]https://github.com/cardano-foundation/cardano-token-registry
[6]https://github.com/cardano-foundation/CIPs/tree/master/CIP-0025

CIP-25

The format for CIP-25 NFT metadata is illustrated in *Figure 7.1*:

```
{
      "721": {
        "<policy_id>": {
          "<asset_name>": {
            "name": <string>,

            "image": <uri | array>,
            "mediaType": image/<mime_sub_type>,

            "description": <string | array>,

            "files": [{
              "name": <string>,
              "mediaType": <mime_type>,
              "src": <uri | array>,
              <other_properties>
            }],

            <other properties>
          }
        },
        "version": <version_id>
      }
    }
```

Figure 7.1: *CIP-25 NFT Metadata Format*

The label 721 indicates that this is token metadata, and the format is flexible, allowing you to add additional elements as required. To test out and verify valid transaction metadata in production, you can use a tool like **`Pool.pm`** test metadata tool.[7]

[7]https://pool.pm/test/metadata

CIP-68

The disadvantage of CIP-25 is that it is created with the original Mint transaction and is not updateable or accessible to a Plutus script. CIP-68[8] addresses this by using the concept of a reference token that is created at the same time when an **NFT** or **FT** is created. The reference token can be either locked at an unspendable script address to be immutable, or locked at a spending script address if there is a requirement for it to be updateable. The metadata is stored in a datum included with the reference token UTXO output. Therefore, it can be accessible to a Plutus script by reading the datum values. With the Vasil hard fork in September 2022, **reference inputs** were introduced that allowed a Plutus script to include a UTXO input as read-only and not have to spend it. Therefore, any number of transactions (even in parallel) can include a read-only CIP-68 reference token UTXO without any concurrency issues.

In *Figure* 7.2, we can see how a mint transaction generates a user token and a reference token, which are linked using the same token name and minting policy ID. The token name is prefixed with 222 to indicate an NFT token, and 100 to indicate a reference token. For fungible tokens, the prefix of 333 is used. It should be noted that the reference token and the NFT or FT tokens do not need to be minted at the same time.

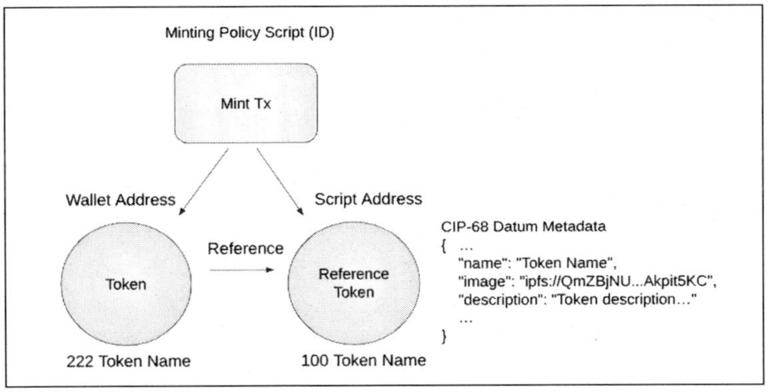

***Figure* 7.2**: *CIP-68 Datum Metadata*

In *Chapter 9, Ticket Application Design*, we will discuss the process of creating and using CIP-68 metadata datum in more detail, with a real-world example.

Coin Selection

Coin selection is the process of determining what UTXO inputs are required to cover the cost of the UTXO outputs, including network fees. There are a number of constraints that we need to be aware of during the coin selection process, which are as follows:[9]

[8]https://github.com/cardano-foundation/CIPs/tree/master/CIP-0068
[9]https://github.com/cardano-foundation/CIPs/tree/master/CIP-0002

- The maximum size limit of a transaction is where each UTXO, either as an input or an output, increases the overall transaction size.
- The accumulation of very small UTXOs (**dust**) that are unspendable because you can't combine enough of them together to cover the transaction cost.
- A UTXO cannot be partially spent; it must be fully spent as part of a transaction.

Therefore, the goal of a coin selection algorithm is to avoid **dust** and create usable UTXOs. Coin selection algorithm considerations apply to both Ada and native tokens. The most common approaches for coin selection are Largest-first and Random Improve.[10] Largest-first selects UTXO inputs in the order from the largest value to the smallest value. The Random Improve algorithm uses two phases. The first phase cycles through a descending ordered list of UTXO inputs, and randomly selects UTXOs until the required amount of output value is obtained. In the second phase, the algorithm again chooses randomly from the descending order list of UTXO inputs until it is approximately twice the amount of output value. Coin selection is typically implemented by the wallet and/or the transaction builder framework. That said, it is important to understand the coin selection algorithms when selecting UTXO inputs. Also, you need to be aware that users may run into issues related to **dust** or UTXO fragmentation caused by too many UTXOs required as inputs.

Minting Policy Use Case

Next, we are going to look at a real-world use case for minting on the Cardano blockchain. In this example, we will use a minting policy to create a fixed number of tickets for an event.

Minting event ticket tokens have the following blockchain advantages, outlined in *Table 7.1*:

Blockchain Feature	**Who**	**Benefit**
Number of tickets minted is fixed and cannot be changed	Performer	Knows exactly how many tickets were issued for a particular event
	Attendee	The value of a ticket cannot be diluted by additional tickets being created after the initial allocation

[10]https://github.com/cardano-foundation/CIPs/tree/master/CIP-0002#algorithms

Minting and Cardano ledger rules	Attendee	If an attendee has a valid ticket, then this is a genuine ticket and cannot be fake
	Seller	For secondary market sales, the ticket can be verified by examining the blockchain to confirm that it is a genuine ticket
	Performer	The movement of tickets is recorded on the blockchain so it is easy to audit how many tickets have actually been sold or canceled (burned)

***Table 7.1**: Minting Use Case Benefits*

Helios On-Chain Minting Policy

The on-chain Helios minting policy on line 1, *Figure* 7.3, states the purpose of the script as **`minting`** and the name of the script called **`ticket.`** There are two Redeemer conditions, Mint and Burn, on lines 7 and 8. The contract parameters on lines 11–16 will be updated dynamically at run-time. So, for now, they are initialized with dummy values and will be updated in the off-chain code.

```
1   minting ticket
2
3   /*
4    The minting policy can either mint or burn an ticket
5    */
6    enum Redeemer {
7       Mint
8       Burn
9   }
10
11  const TX_ID: ByteArray = #abc123
12  const tx_id: TxId = TxId::new(TX_ID)
13  const TX_IDX: Int = 0
14  const output_id: TxOutputId = TxOutputId::new(tx_id, TX_IDX)
15  const TN: String = ""
16  const QTY: Int = 1
```

***Figure** 7.3: Helios On-Chain Minting Redeemer and Parameters*[11]

Next, in *Figure* 7.4, we can see the main function contains the minting policy logic. First, note that only a **`Redeemer`** and **`ScriptContext`** are passed as arguments. On line 20, we create the **`MintingPolicyHash`** dynamically, which takes into account the contract parameters that have been passed into the script at run-time. We then create an **`AssetClass`** that will be used to verify what is minted. On line 25, we pull out the

[11]https://github.com/ava-orange-education/Mastering-Cardano-Smart-Contracts/blob/main/chapter_07/helios/ticket/contracts/ticket.hl

minted value that was part of this transaction. Now, we have the information we need to handle the Redeemer conditions.

```
18  func main(redeemer: Redeemer, ctx: ScriptContext) -> Bool {
19      tx: Tx = ctx.tx;
20      mph: MintingPolicyHash = ctx.get_current_minting_policy_hash();
21      tn_assetclass: AssetClass = AssetClass::new(
22          mph,
23          TN.encode_utf8()
24      );
25      value_minted: Value = tx.minted;
26      redeemer.switch {
27          Mint => {
28              // Check that contract parameter UTXO is included in the inputs
29              // and that the minted amount is equal to the quanty given
30              (value_minted == Value::new(tn_assetclass, QTY)).trace("NFT1: ") &&
31              tx.inputs.any((input: TxInput) -> Bool {
32                                  (input.output_id == output_id).trace("NFT2: ")
33                                  }
34                              )
35          },
36          Burn => {
37              // Allow any quantity of the token to be burned in a transaction
38              (value_minted.get(tn_assetclass) < 0).trace("NFT3: ")
39          }
40      }
41  }
```

Figure 7.4: *Helios On-Chain Minting Logic*[12]

On line 30, in *Figure* 7.4, we confirm that the token minted in the transaction matches the token name and amount in the contract parameters. Lines 31 and 32 check that the UTXO specified in the contract parameter is included in the inputs. Since a UTXO can only be spent once, the minting policy will only allow it to be minted once, which guarantees uniqueness. Finally, on line 38, we allow the burning as long as the token belongs to the minting policy and has a negative quantity.

Helios Off-Chain Mint

We will highlight the differences between the off-chain code in this example and the previous validator example was shown in *Chapter* 6, *Validators*. On line 119 in *Figure* 7.5, we create the minting policy program and then apply the contract parameters on lines 120–123. Only after the parameters have been applied, can we compile the script and attach it to the transaction on line 129. We also construct the Mint Redeemer on line 132, which uses the Redeemer type specified in the on-chain code.

[12]https://github.com/ava-orange-education/Mastering-Cardano-Smart-Contracts/blob/main/chapter_07/helios/ticket/contracts/ticket.h

```
// Read in the ticket minting policy and apply the contract parameters
const utxoId = utxos[0][0].outputId.txId.hex;
const utxoIdx = utxos[0][0].outputId.utxoIdx;
const ticketMinting = new NFTMinting();
ticketMinting.parameters = {["TX_ID"] : utxoId};
ticketMinting.parameters = {["TX_IDX"] : utxoIdx};
ticketMinting.parameters = {["TN"] : name};
ticketMinting.parameters = {["QTY"] : BigInt(qty)};

// Compile the helios minting script
const ticketCompiledMinting = ticketMinting.compile(optimize);

// Add the script as a witness to the transaction
tx.attachScript(ticketCompiledMinting);

// Create the minting claim redeemer
const mintRedeemer = (new ticketMinting.types.Redeemer.Mint())
                                ._toUplcData();
```

Figure 7.5: *Helios Off-Chain Contract Parameters*[13]

In *Figure* 7.6, an array of tokens on line 136 uses the ticket name and qty passed in from the user input to create the assets that we will mint, as shown on lines 139–141. Next, we specify the tokens to mint in the transaction on line 145. We use the **`MintingPolicyHash`** from the compiled script and include both the tokens and the Redeemer created previously. We also create an output, where we send the minted ticket tokens to an **`address`** from the user input, as shown on lines 153–156.

```
135 // Create the minted tokens
136 const tokens = [[textToBytes(name), BigInt(qty)]] as [[number[], bigint]];
137 
138 // Create the minted assets
139 const assets = new Assets([[ticketCompiledMinting.mintingPolicyHash,
140                             tokens
141                 ]])
142 
143 // Add the new minted token to the transaction which includes
144 // the minting policy hash, the token name, amount and the redeemer
145 tx.mintTokens(
146     ticketCompiledMinting.mintingPolicyHash,
147     tokens,
148     mintRedeemer
149 )
150 
151 // Construct the output to send ticket token(s) to the address
152 // from the user input
153 tx.addOutput(new TxOutput(
154   Address.fromBech32(address),
155   new Value(minAdaVal.lovelace, assets)
156 ));
```

Figure 7.6: *Helios Off-Chain Mint Tokens*[14]

[13]https://github.com/ava-orange-education/Mastering-Cardano-Smart-Contracts/blob/main/chapter_07/helios/ticket/pages/index.tsx
[14]https://github.com/ava-orange-education/Mastering-Cardano-Smart-Contracts/blob/main/chapter_07/helios/ticket/pages/index.tsx

In this minting use case, we also make use of transaction metadata following the CIP-25 standard. On line 160 in *Figure* 7.7, we make a call to **`generateMetadata`**, which returns a JSON-like record for the data passed in the arguments. The **`name, qty, utxoId,`** and **`utxoIdx`** will be stored in the metadata and can be used to reconstruct the minting policy later if burning is required. The **`mintingPolicyHash`**, **`name`**, **`description`**, and **`image`** are used off-chain for displaying the token in wallets, dApps and blockchain explorers.

```
158    // Attached the metadata for the minting transaction
159    tx.addMetadata( 721,
160                    generateMetadata(
161                        ticketCompiledMinting.mintingPolicyHash.hex,
162                        name,
163                        description,
164                        image,
165                        BigInt(qty),
166                        utxoId,
167                        utxoIdx
168                    )
169      );
```

Figure 7.7: *Helios Off-Chain Metadata*[15]

Helios Off-Chain Burn

There may be a scenario requiring the burning of unsold ticket tokens. Since the Cardano ledger tracks and avoids any double spending of native assets, the burning of ticket tokens can only be done if the ticket tokens actually exist in the transaction inputs. Therefore, the only way to burn a token is to actually have possession of that token in your wallet, so it can be spent as a transaction input.

We will first look at line 230 in *Figure* 7.8, which queries the blockchain to get the mint metadata for a particular token. As we recall, we need the token **`name`**, **`qty`**, **`utxoId`**, and **`utxoIdx`** as contract parameters to rebuild the correct minting policy. Now that we have the contract parameters, we can compile the script and attach it to the transaction. We also create a Burn Redeemer on line 246 that allows the burning of the ticket tokens accordingly.

[15]https://github.com/ava-orange-education/Mastering-Cardano-Smart-Contracts/blob/main/chapter_07/helios/ticket/pages/index.tsx

```
// Get the NFT metadata needed for the script parameters
const ticketMetadata = await getTicketMetadata(policyId, tokenName);

// Load in the ticket program and set contract parameters
const ticketMinting = new NFTMinting();
ticketMinting.parameters = {["TX_ID"] : ticketMetadata.utxoId};
ticketMinting.parameters = {["TX_IDX"] : Number(ticketMetadata.utxoIdx)};
ticketMinting.parameters = {["TN"] : tokenName};
ticketMinting.parameters = {["QTY"] : BigInt(ticketMetadata.qty)};

// Compile the helios minting script
const ticketCompiledMinting = ticketMinting.compile(optimize);

// Add the script as a witness to the transaction
tx.attachScript(ticketCompiledMinting);

// Create the vesting claim redeemer
const mintRedeemer = (new ticketMinting.types.Redeemer.Burn())
                                 ._toUplcData();
```

Figure 7.8: *Helios Off-Chain Metadata Query*[16]

Lastly, we build the **`MintingPolicyHash`** from the **`policyId`** stored in the metadata and then add the token to burn by using a negative **`qty`** number on line 252, as shown in *Figure* 7.9.

```
245 // Create the vesting claim redeemer
246 const mintRedeemer = (new ticketMinting.types.Redeemer.Burn())
247                                  ._toUplcData();
248
249 const ticketMPH = MintingPolicyHash.fromHex(policyId);
250
251 // Create the burn tokens
252 const tokens = [[textToBytes(tokenName), BigInt(-1 * qty)]] as [[number[], bigint]];
253
254 // Add the new minted token to the transaction which includes
255 // the minting policy hash, the token name, amount and the redeemer
256 tx.mintTokens(
257   ticketMPH,
258     tokens,
259     mintRedeemer
260 )
```

Figure 7.9: *Helios Off-Chain Burn Tokens*[17]

Aiken On-Chain Minting Policy

The Aiken on-chain minting policy uses **`token_name, qty,`** and **`utxo_ref`** as contract parameters that are applied during run-time on line 15, as shown in *Figure* 7.10. Only the Redeemer and **`ScriptContext`** are passed to the ticket function, which contains the minting policy logic. On line 18, the expect statement is used to create a new binding

[16]https://github.com/ava-orange-education/Mastering-Cardano-Smart-Contracts/blob/main/chapter_07/helios/ticket/pages/index.tsx
[17]https://github.com/ava-orange-education/Mastering-Cardano-Smart-Contracts/blob/main/chapter_07/helios/ticket/pages/index.tsx

for **policy_id** from the script **purpose**. On line 19, we deconstruct the Transaction type and pull out both the inputs and the minted value from the transaction. We then use the expect statement on line 22 to bind **asset_name** and **amount** with a tuple from the mint value and match the **policy_id**. Now we have all the information we need to execute the Redeemer conditions. On lines 31 and 32, we check that the input contains the **utxo_ref** that was passed in the contract parameter. On line 34, we confirm that the asset name and amount match what was provided as contract parameters. The Burn Redeemer on line 37 allows the burning of any negative amount as long as the **asset_name** within this script minting policy is included in the transaction.

```
15  validator(token_name: ByteArray, qty: Int, utxo_ref: OutputReference) {
16    fn ticket(redeemer: Redeemer, ctx: ScriptContext) -> Bool {
17      let ScriptContext { transaction, purpose } = ctx
18      expect tx.Mint(policy_id) = purpose
19      let Transaction { inputs, mint, .. } = transaction
20      // Check that the asset value is what is being minted
21      // with this transaction
22      expect [(asset_name, amount)] =
23        mint
24          |> value.from_minted_value
25          |> value.tokens(policy_id)
26          |> dict.to_list()
27
28      when redeemer is {
29        Mint -> {
30          // Check that that the utxo_ref is included as input
31          expect Some(_input) =
32            list.find(inputs, fn(input) { input.output_reference == utxo_ref })
33          // Confirm that both the token name and qty are correct
34          amount == qty && asset_name == token_name
35        }
36        // Allow burning of any number of tokens per transaction
37        Burn -> amount < 0 && asset_name == token_name
38      }
```

Figure 7.10: *Aiken On-Chain Minting Policy*[18]

Lucid Off-Chain Mint

The Lucid off-chain code is very similar to the Helios off-chain code, and we will only show the differences between the two approaches. In particular, the way contract parameters are applied is different, as shown in *Figure 7.11*. On line 89, a custom function takes in the contract parameters and then applies them to the Plutus minting policy script on line 96. The Plutus script is read from the blueprint file, which was generated from the **aiken build** command.

[18]https://github.com/ava-orange-education/Mastering-Cardano-Smart-Contracts/blob/main/chapter_07/aiken/ticket/contracts/validators/ticket.ak

```
// Read in the minting script and apply the contract parameters
async function readValidator( tokenName: string,
                              qty: bigint,
                              outRef: Data): Promise<SpendingValidator> {
  const validator = JSON.parse(props.blueprint).validators[0];

  return {
    type: "PlutusV2",
    script: applyParamsToScript(validator.compiledCode, [
                                  fromText(tokenName),
                                  BigInt(qty),
                                  outRef],)
  };
}
```

Figure 7.11: *Lucid Applied Contract Parameters*[19]

In *Figure* 7.12, the validator (minting policy) is returned on line 132 using the **`name`**, **`qty`**, and **`outRef`** calculated from the UTXO in the wallet. On line 135, the **`Redeemer`** is manually constructed to match the **`Redeemer`** in the on-chain Aiken code. The **`policyId`** and **`assetName`** are constructed using the **`validator`** Script and **`name`**, respectively, on lines 138 and 139.

```
121  // Select wallet UTXOs and use the first one
122  const utxos = await lucid?.wallet.getUtxos()!;
123  const utxo = utxos[0];
124
125  // Create the UTXO that must be spent as part of this tx
126  const outRef = new Constr(0, [
127    new Constr(0, [utxo.txHash]),
128    BigInt(utxo.outputIndex),
129  ]);
130
131  // Read in the minting validator with applied parameters
132  const validator = await readValidator(name, BigInt(qty), outRef);
133
134  // Construct the Mint redeemer
135  const mintRedeemer = Data.to(new Constr(0, []));
136
137  // Derive the minting policy id & asset name
138  const policyId = lucid.utils.validatorToScriptHash(validator);
139  const assetName = `${policyId}${fromText(name)}`;
```

Figure 7.12: *Lucid Minting Policy ID and Asset Name*[20]

The last step is to generate the metadata on line 142, in *Figure* 7.13, and build the transaction on lines 150–160. The validator script, metadata, and minted assets are attached to the transaction on lines 153, 154, and 155 accordingly. Finally, the output is created to send the ticket tokens to the address provided by the user input on line 159.

[19]https://github.com/ava-orange-education/Mastering-Cardano-Smart-Contracts/blob/main/chapter_07/aiken/ticket/pages/index.tsx
[20]https://github.com/ava-orange-education/Mastering-Cardano-Smart-Contracts/blob/main/chapter_07/aiken/ticket/pages/index.tsx

```
// Generate the metadata
const metadata = generateMetadata(policyId,
                                  name,
                                  description,
                                  image,
                                  BigInt(qty),
                                  utxo.txHash,
                                  utxo.outputIndex);

const tx = await lucid
  .newTx()
  .collectFrom([utxo])
  .attachMintingPolicy(validator)
  .attachMetadata(721, metadata)
  .mintAssets(
    { [assetName]: BigInt(qty) },
    mintRedeemer
  )
  .payToAddress(address, { [assetName]: BigInt(qty) })
  .complete();
```

Figure 7.13: *Lucid Minting Metadata*[21]

The Lucid-off chain Burn is similar to Mint, except that **`mintAssets()`** uses a negative quantity and has no metadata or transaction output.

Wallet Info

Since we are dealing with native assets, we modified the **`WalletInfo`** component to show both Lovelace and any native assets at the user's wallet address. This requires calling the **`Blockfrost`** API to get the list of assets and then populating an array that will be displayed on the UI, as shown in *Figure* 7.14.

[21] https://github.com/ava-orange-education/Mastering-Cardano-Smart-Contracts/blob/main/chapter_07/aiken/ticket/pages/index.tsx

```
    const getWalletInfo = async ( address: string) : Promise<WalletInfo> => {

        const apiKey = process.env.NEXT_PUBLIC_BLOCKFROST_API_KEY as string;
        const API = new BlockFrostAPI({
            projectId: apiKey
          });
        // Call blockfrost API to get assets at the wallet address
        const addrInfo = await API.addresses(address);
        let balance = [] as any;

        addrInfo.amount.forEach(({unit, quantity}) =>
                // Check to see if the unit is lovelace, if not
                // then slice out the policy id and token name
                balance.push({mph: unit.length > 56 ? unit.slice(0,56): '',
                              tn: unit.length > 56 ? toText(unit.slice(56)): unit,
                              qty: quantity}))

        const walletInfo = new WalletInfo(
            address,
            balance
        );
       return walletInfo;
```

Figure 7.14: *Lucid getWalletInfo*[22]

Setup

To set up the **`Demeter.run`** environment to run the Lucid + Aiken demo, please execute the following commands in a terminal window (if you have not already done so from *Chapter 6, Validators*).

```
$ echo export NEXT_PUBLIC_BLOCKFROST_API=https://cardano-preprod.block-
frost.io/api/v0 >> ~/.bashrc
$ echo export NEXT_PUBLIC_BLOCKFROST_KEY=your-blockfrost-API-key >>
~/.bashrc
$ echo export NEXT_PUBLIC_ENV="dev" >> ~/.bashrc
$ echo export NEXT_PUBLIC_HOST="demeter-run-host" >> ~/.bashrc
$ echo export NEXT_PUBLIC_PROTOCOL="https" >> ~/.bashrc
$ echo export NEXT_PUBLIC_PORT="" >> ~/.bashrc
$ source ~/.bashrc
$ npm install
$ npm run dev
```

Demo

Figure 7.15 shows the new **`WalletInfo`** component with 100 "**`Dog Show 1`**" ticket tokens already at the wallet address.

[22]https://github.com/ava-orange-education/Mastering-Cardano-Smart-Contracts/blob/main/chapter_07/aiken/ticket/pages/api/getWalletInfo.ts

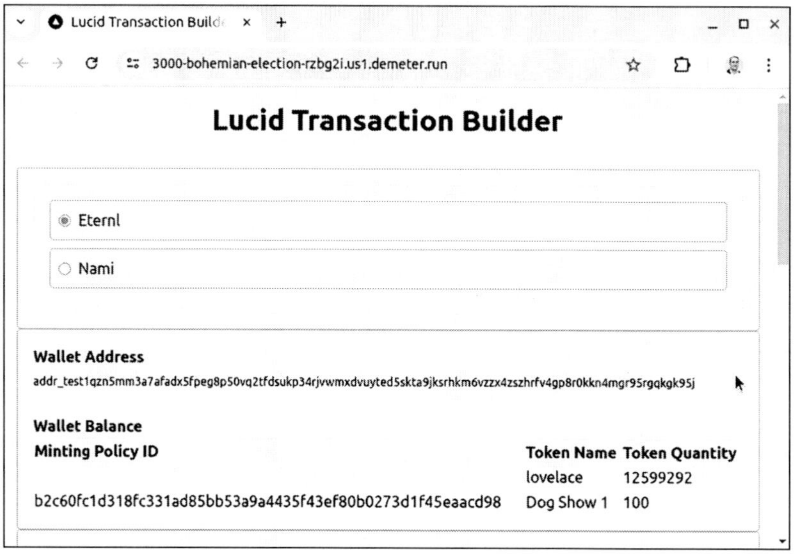

Figure 7.15: *Lucid Wallet Info*

To mint a new batch of tickets, the user enters the destination address, token name, token description, **IPFS** image content identifier, and quantity, as shown in *Figure* 7.16:

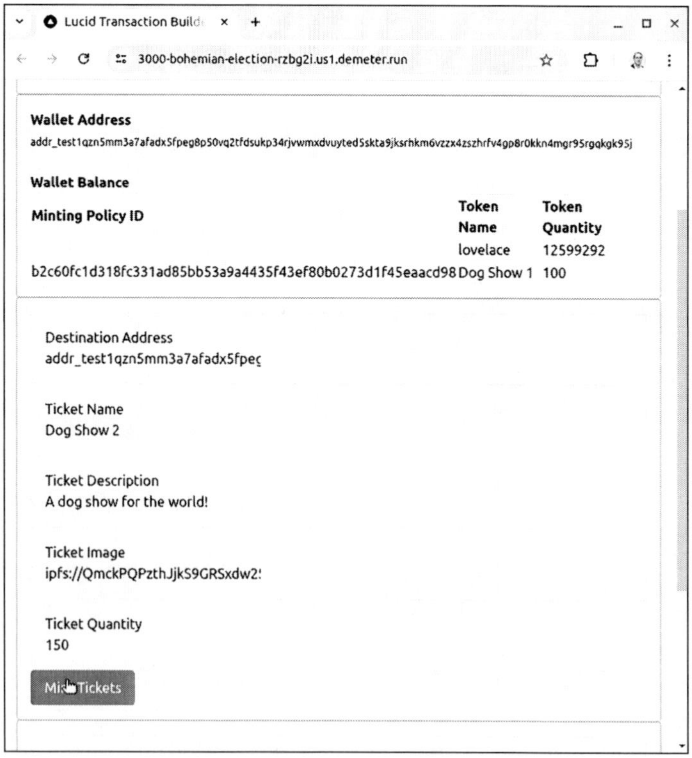

Figure 7.16: *Lucid Mint*

After selecting the `Mint Ticket` button and signing the transaction with your wallet, as shown in *Figure* 7.16, a transaction success message should appear.

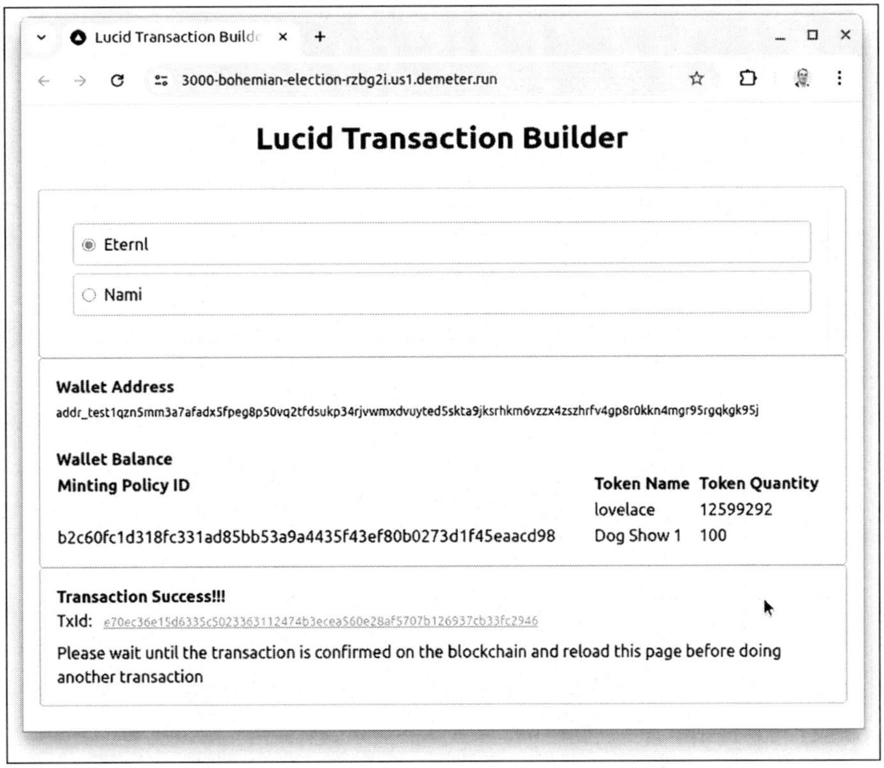

Figure 7.17: *Lucid Mint Transaction Success*

If you select the `TxId` link, you will be able to see the transaction on Preprod once it has been confirmed on the network. In *Figure* 7.18, you can see that a new 150 **`Dog Show 2`** tokens were created and sent back to the wallet address.

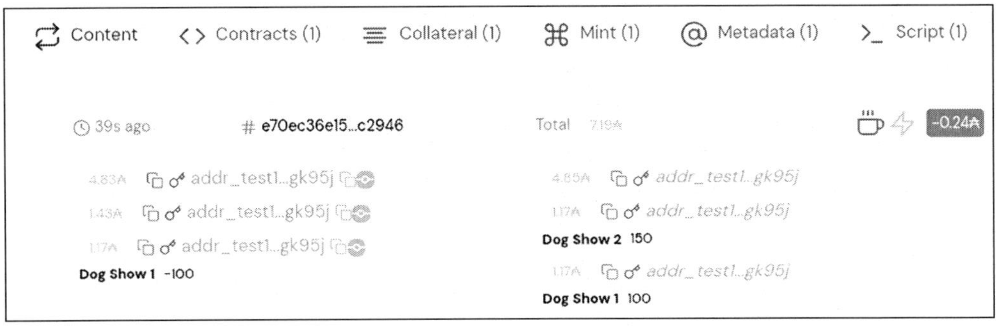

Figure 7.18: *Cardano Explorer Mint Transaction Detail*[23]

[23]https://preprod.cexplorer.io/tx/e70ec36e15d6335c5023363112474b3ecea560e28af5707b126937cb33fc2946

We can also verify the metadata on the Cardano Explorer in *Figure* 7.19:

Figure 7.19: *Cardano Explorer Mint Transaction Metadata*[24]

Next, we will try to burn (cancel) 20 tickets because they needed to make more room for the dogs at the event. The user needs to enter the Minting **`Policy ID`**, the **`Token Name`**, and the amount of tokens to burn, as shown in *Figure* 7.19. This will only succeed if the user has the event tokens in their wallet.

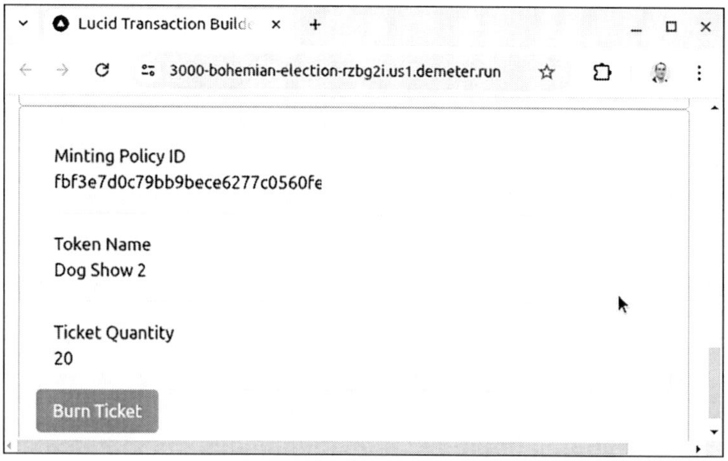

Figure 7.20: *Lucid Burn Token*

[24]https://preprod.cexplorer.io/tx/e70ec36e15d6335c5023363112474b3ecea560e28af5707b126937cb33fc2946/metadata#data

A successful transaction message should appear, and the transaction can be seen on the Cardano Explorer link. In *Figure* 7.21, 20 ticket tokens have been burned, with only 130 remaining.

Figure 7.21: *Burn Token Transaction*[25]

The blockchain explorers and APIs can be queried to find the total number of assets in circulation, as shown in *Figure* 7.22.

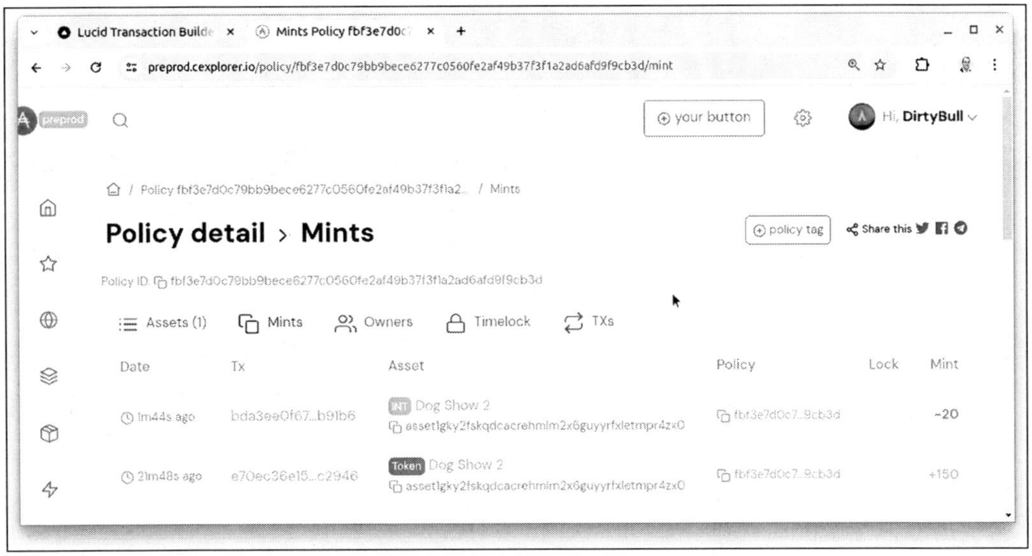

Figure 7.22: *Minting Policy Asset Accounting*[26]

[25]https://preprod.cexplorer.io/tx/bda3ee0f670f4a334116969867a46d9fe509939f893d274d3a98489e44cb91b6

[26]https://preprod.cexplorer.io/policy/fbf3e7d0c79bb9bece6277c0560fe2af49b37f3f1a2ad6afd9f9cb3d/mint

Conclusion

We reviewed what a Cardano native asset is and how it is different from an Ethereum ERC-20 token. We explored the concept of token bundles and how they are used to group a collection of tokens together inside a UTXO. Next, we understood the role of the minting policy and how to mint Cardano native asset tokens. The differences between Non-Fungible Tokens (**NFT**s) and Fungible Tokens (**FT**s) were discussed, where **NFT**s represent a unique asset and **FT**s represent assets that are identical to each other. The CIP-25 and CIP-68 metadata standards were also reviewed with examples of what CIP-25 metadata looks like. We briefly discussed the role of the Token Registry, as well as the importance of using an optimal coin selection algorithm. We finished up the chapter by looking at a real-world use case involving minting ticket tokens for an event. The next chapter will focus on Cardano tooling used for blockchain development, queries, and monitoring.

Points to Remember

- Cardano native assets use the Cardano ledger to prevent double spending of tokens.
- A minting policy hash will be unique if a UTXO is used as a contract parameter and is spent in the mint transaction.
- A token bundle includes one or more tokens and must always include a minimum amount of Ada.
- Tokens are included in a UTXO and can be locked at a Base, Enterprise, or Plutus Script address.
- A minting policy only controls the minting or burning of tokens.
- A minting policy does not manage the ledger state of the token or the circulating supply.
- An off-chain code is required to determine the circulating supply by examining all the mint and burn operations for a specific minting policy.
- Non-fungible tokens (**NFT**s) are unique and distinct assets that are not interchangeable with each other.
- Fungible Tokens (**FT**s) are identical and can be exchanged with each other.
- CIP-25 is a metadata standard that is used when submitting a transaction.
- CIP-68 uses a reference token and a datum value that can be either immutable or updateable, depending on the use case.
- The Token Registry registers a minting policy and token name to provide metadata about the token, which is used by wallets, blockchain explorers, and exchanges.

- Using a proper coin selection algorithm is important to avoid dust, which is a small amount of UTXOs that cannot be spent because the cost of doing so exceeds their combined value.

Multiple Choice Questions

1. Which of the following statements is false?
   a. Cardano native tokens are identical to ERC-20 Tokens
   b. Cardano native assets use the base ledger to avoid double spending
   c. A Cardano minting policy typically uses less code than an ERC-20 contract
   d. A Cardano minting policy is typically more secure than an ERC-20 contract
2. How does a one-time Minting Policy create the initial circulating supply?
   a. Custom code inside the minting policy
   b. Queries the Cardano ledger
   c. Queries the minting policy metadata
   d. None of the above
3. How is CIP-25 metadata stored on-chain?
   a. As a hash value on-chain and included as auxiliary data as part of a transaction
   b. In JSON format and stored fully on-chain
   c. Nothing is stored on-chain
   d. Content is stored in a UTXO datum
4. How do you specify the precision units of a Fungible Token (FT)?
   a. Only possible using CIP-25
   b. In the Token Registry or CIP-68
   c. Inside the minting policy
   d. None of the above

5. What is UTXO fragmentation?
    a. There are too many UTXOs on the blockchain
    b. There are too many UTXO needed as inputs to satisfy the outputs
    c. There are too many UTXO outputs
    d. There are too many assets locked into one UTXO

Answers

1. a
2. a
3. a
4. b
5. b

Questions

1. What are some other possible use cases for minting on Cardano?
2. In what situations would you use CIP-25 or CIP-68?
3. What are the ways to make a Minting Policy ID or Token Name unique?
4. For a given native token, is it possible to know the current Address where the UTXO is locked at and how can this be done?
5. Can you describe other coin selection algorithms besides Largest-first and Random Improve?

Key Terms

- **Asset Name**: An immutable token name on-chain of a specific minting policy.
- **CIP-25:** Metadata standard using transaction metadata.
- **CIP-68**: Metadata standard using a reference token and datum.
- **Collection:** The grouping of tokens together in a token bundle.
- **Dust:** A very small value UTXO that cannot be spent.
- **ERC-20:** Ethereum FT token standard
- **ERC-721:** Ethereum NFT token standard

- **Monetary Policy**: Specifies the amount of tokens in circulation and the inflation or deflation rate.
- **Policy Identifier (ID):** A unique identifier that is the hash of a Minting Policy script.
- **Quantity:** The accounting unit.
- **Reference Inputs**: Read-only UTXOs that are included as transaction inputs but cannot be spent.

CHAPTER 8
Tooling

Introduction

Developing smart contracts often involves working with code that exists outside the blockchain (off-chain) and integrating it seamlessly with the Cardano network. In this chapter, we will review some of the tools and **service providers** you can use to help accomplish these tasks. First, we will delve into Cardano Blockchain API providers such as Blockfrost, Maestro, Koios, and Dandelion. Next, we will explore hosted environments with `Demeter.run` to set up services like Cardano Node, Ogmios, and Kupo. Finally, we will learn how to set up a local Devnet for rapid development and prototyping with the Yaci DevKit.

Structure

In this chapter, we will discuss the following topics:

- Blockchain API/Monitoring Providers
    - Blockfrost
    - Maestro
    - Koios
    - Dandelion
- Tooling Components
    - Cardano-node
    - Ogmios
    - Kupo
    - Local Devnet
    - Additional Resources

Blockchain API/Monitoring Providers

The examples throughout this book demonstrate the use of Blockfrost API to query the blockchain and submit transactions. In this section, however, we will look at additional widely used blockchain service providers and tooling that help avoid a centralized point of failure within the Cardano ecosystem.

Blockfrost

Blockfrost (https://blockfrost.io/) was one of the first providers in Cardano and has earned the trust of a large user base with over 100M+ daily requests and 20K+ developers.[1] Blockfrost has excellent API documentation and a wide range of services, from simple blockchain queries to **webhook** callbacks for your application. They have free entry-level plans that allow you to test out APIs for your application. You can make HTTP REST calls to their API or use their convenient **SDKs** for Node.js, Python, Rust, C#, Go, and more. Blockfrost supports Mainnet, Preprod, and Preview networks, and you can run your own instance from their GitHub Repo.[2]

Maestro

On July 19, 2023, Maestro (https://www.gomaestro.org/) released V1 of their dApp platform with new features that significantly improved Cardano blockchain integration:[3]

- **Turbo Transactions**: Accelerate **transaction finality** with Maestro's transaction propagation system.
- **New Blockchain Indexer**: High performance, low latency, optimized Cardano blockchain indexer with convenient and efficient APIs.
- **Transaction Manager:** A transaction monitoring system with automatic retries and zero-delay pending, on-chain, and rollback notifications.[4]

Code Example

In our vesting and ticket examples, we change the Lucid provider in `pages/index.tsx` to use Maestro, which is included in the Lucid library, as shown in *Figure* 8.1.

[1]https://blockfrost.io/
[2]https://github.com/blockfrost/blockfrost-backend-ryo
[3]https://www.gomaestro.org/dapp-platform
[4]https://twitter.com/GoMaestroOrg/status/1681685533314142209

```
// Define the Cardano Network
const network = "Preprod";
const maestroAPIKey = process.env.NEXT_PUBLIC_MAESTRO_API_KEY as string;

// Create lucid object and connect it to the maestro provider
const lucid = await Lucid.new(
  new Maestro({
    network: network,
    apiKey: maestroAPIKey,
    turboSubmit: true
  }),
  network,
);
```

Figure 8.1: *Lucid Maestro Provider*[5]

For the ticket minting example, we also needed to change the blockchain query in **`getTicketMetadata.ts`** in the **`pages/api`** folder. We use the Node.js API provided by Maestro, as shown in *Figure* 8.2.

```
18  let maestroClient = new MaestroClient(
19    new Configuration({
20      apiKey: apiKey,
21      network: "Preprod",
22    })
23  );
24
25  const getMetadata = async (asset: string): Promise <AssetInfo|undefined> => {
26
27    const assetInfo = await maestroClient.assets
28    .assetInfo(asset)
29    .catch((error) => {
30      if (error.response) {
31        console.error("Status Code Error", error.response);
32      } else if (error.request) {
33          console.error("Network Error", error.request);
34      } else {
35          console.error("Client Error", error.message);
36      }
37    });
38    if (assetInfo) {
39        return assetInfo.data.data;
40    }
41  }
```

Figure 8.2: *Maestro TypeScript API*[6]

In *Figure* 8.2, on line 18, we create the Maestro client and then call **`maestroClient.assets`** on line 27 to get the metadata for the asset.

[5]https://github.com/ava-orange-education/Mastering-Cardano-Smart-Contracts/blob/main/chapter_08/maestro/ticket/pages/index.tsx
[6]https://github.com/ava-orange-education/Mastering-Cardano-Smart-Contracts/blob/main/chapter_08/maestro/ticket/pages/api/getTicketMetadata.ts

Setup

To set up the Demeter.run environment to run the Maestro demo, execute the following commands in a terminal window:

```
$ export NEXT_PUBLIC_MAESTRO_API_KEY=your-maestro-key-here
$ export NEXT_PUBLIC_ENV="dev"
$ export NEXT_PUBLIC_HOST="your-demeter-run-host"
$ export NEXT_PUBLIC_PROTOCOL="https"
$ export NEXT_PUBLIC_PORT=""
```

Koios

Koios[7] is a distributed, open-source, **RESTful** APIs for querying and submitting to the Cardano blockchain. It is built and maintained by the highly respected Cardano Stakepool Guild Operators.[8] Koios promotes decentralization by using distributed processing architecture, a core value of Cardano. A typescript Koios provider client can also be used directly from the Helios library.

Dandelion

Dandelion[9] is a collection of Cardano Blockchain APIs as a free community service. The services include:

- GraphQL[10]
- Ogmios[11]
- Cardano DB Sync/Postgres API [12]
- Rosetta API[13]

Tooling Components

One of the major benefits of Cardano is that the code is open source, and you have the ability to download, build, and run all the required components yourself. Or, you can use a third-party provider to manage and host these components. We have already seen how to set up an environment for the examples in this book with Demeter.run, but they offer many other Cardano components and services. We will look at some of the more popular components used for Cardano blockchain integration.

---

[7]https://koios.rest/
[8]https://cardano-community.github.io/guild-operators/
[9]https://dandelion.link/
[10]https://github.com/cardano-foundation/cardano-graphql
[11]https://ogmios.dev/
[12]https://github.com/IntersectMBO/cardano-db-sync
[13]https://github.com/cardano-foundation/cardano-rosetta

Tooling components are used to query, react, or transact with a blockchain. A typical, off-chain tooling setup is illustrated in *Figure* 8.3, where Cardano DB Sync processes blocks from a Cardano Node and stores data in a Postgres Database. An application can then query the database or react to blockchain events accordingly.

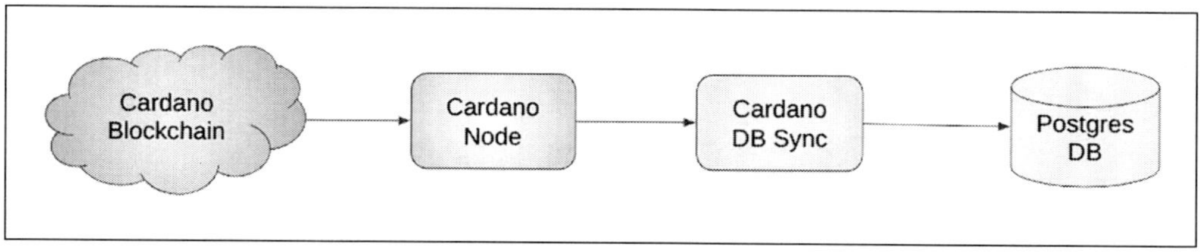

***Figure* 8.3:** *DB Sync Off-Chain Indexing*

The challenge with DB Sync is that it is difficult to set up and requires significant hardware resources for Mainnet. Fortunately, Demeter.run provides hosted instances that you can easily deploy with no manual configuration. This is great for networks like Mainnet or Preprod but not well-suited for custom networks or local testing environments.

Cardano Node

The core component of the Cardano blockchain is the Cardano Node and the source code is located on GitHub.[14] You can download and compile the source code, run the static binaries, or use docker containers. Demeter.run also has an extension to provision a Cardano Node as follows:

1. Go to https://demeter.run/
2. Choose the project you want to deploy to. We will enable this extension for a workspace already created in *Chapter* 5, *Transaction Builder*.
3. Once the workspace is provisioned in *Figure* 8.4, you must enable the Cardano Node by selecting the Connected Extensions by scrolling down the page.

[14]https://github.com/IntersectMBO/cardano-node

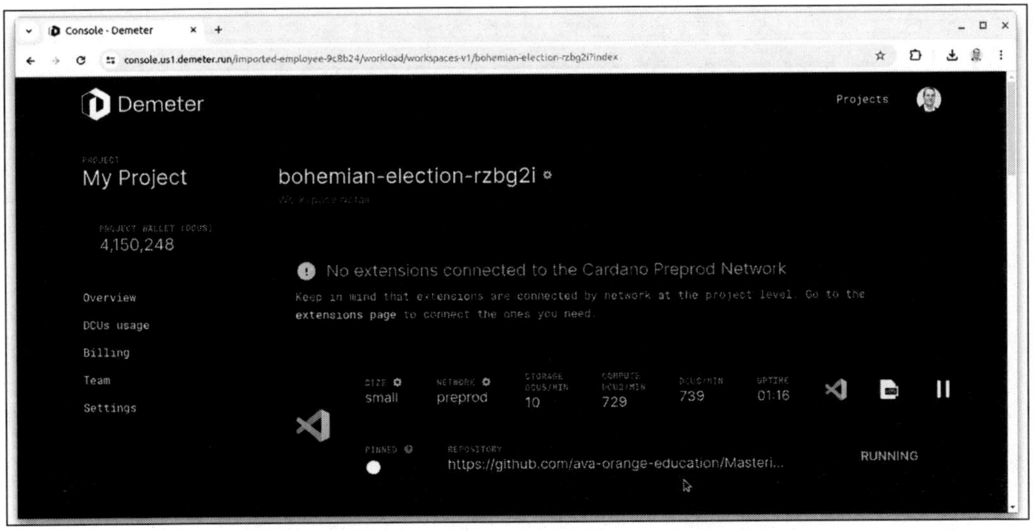

Figure 8.4: *Demeter.run Cardano Workspace*

4. Select Browse Extensions.
5. Find the Nodes box, select **`Deploy`**, and then **`Provision Resource`**.
6. Scroll down, select **`Preprod`**, and select the **`Create Resource`** button at the bottom of the page.
7. When you go back to the **`Project Overview`** you should see the Node extension connected, as shown in *Figure* 8.5.

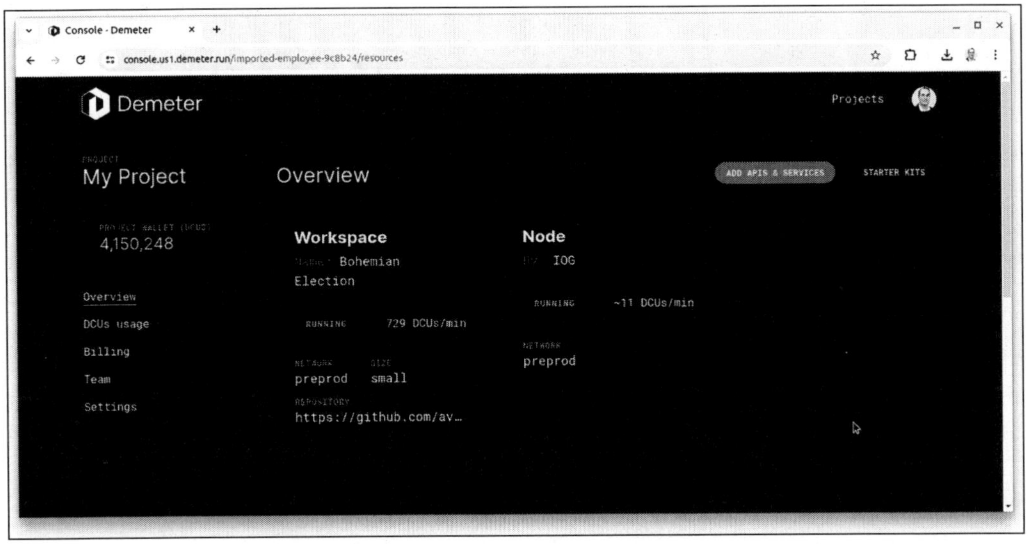

Figure 8.5: *Demeter.run Cardano Node Connected*

8. Select the workspace you previously provisioned.
9. Select the **Visual Studio Code** icon on the workspace to launch the Visual Studio web client.
10. From the hamburger menu, select **Terminal** -> **New**.

To verify that your cardano-node is connected to the network, type the following command and you should see **syncProgress** at 100%.

```
~/workspace/repo$ cardano-cli query tip --testnet-magic 1
{
    "block": 1595041,
    "epoch": 106,
    "era": "Babbage",
    "hash": "ed3be308f9538fe59241f5d90b333de06ddc581ee783ba0002d0c911b3b
    df3f6",
    "slot": 44370786,
    "slotInEpoch": 220386,
    "slotsToEpochEnd": 211614,
    "syncProgress": "100.00"
}
```

Most of the tooling that connects to the **Cardano Node** uses a socket and you can find out the location of the socket by printing out the shell environment variable:

```
~/workspace/repo$ echo $CARDANO_NODE_SOCKET_PATH
/ipc/node.socket
```

The **cardano-cli** is the Swiss army knife of Cardano and there are lots of resources on its usage and would suggest starting here.[15] Type **cardano-cli** to see the following list of top-level common options. Use the **--help** flag to get additional usage info for each command.

```
~/workspace/repo$ cardano-cli
cardano-cli - General purpose command-line utility to interact with
cardano-node. Provides specific commands to manage keys, addresses, build
& submit transactions, certificates, etc.
```

[15]https://github.com/input-output-hk/cardano-node-wiki/blob/main/docs/getting-started/cli.md

```
Usage: cardano-cli (Era based commands | byron | ping | version)

Available options:
  --version                Show the cardano-cli version
  -h,--help                Show this help text

Era based commands
  address                  Payment address commands
  stake-address            Stake address commands
  key                      Key utility commands
  transaction              Transaction commands
  node                     Node operation commands
  stake-pool               Stake pool commands
  query                    Node query commands.
                           Will query the local node whose
                           Unix domain socket is obtained from the
                           CARDANO_NODE_SOCKET_PATH environment variable.
  genesis                  Genesis block commands
  governance               Governance commands
  text-view                Commands for dealing with Shelley TextView files.
                           Transactions, addresses
                           etc are stored on disk as
                           TextView files.

Byron specific commands
  byron                    Byron specific commands

Available commands:
  ping                     Ping a cardano node either using
                           node-to-node or node-to-client protocol. It
                           negotiates a handshake and keeps sending
                           keep alive messages.

Miscellaneous commands
  help                     Show all help
  version                  Show the cardano-cli version
```

You can now access command-line utility tools such as **cardano-address** and **bech32**.

```
~/workspace/repo$ cardano-address
Usage: cardano-address ((-v|--version) | COMMAND)
  Command-line for address and key manipulation in Cardano.

Available options:
  -h,--help                Show this help text
  -v,--version             Show the software current version and build
                           revision.

Available commands:
  version                  Show the software current version and build
revision.
  recovery-phrase          About recovery phrases
  key                      About public/private keys
  address                  About addresses
  script                   About scripts


~/workspace/repo$ bech32 --help
Usage: bech32 [PREFIX]

  Convert to and from bech32 strings. Data are read from standard input.

Available options:
  -h,--help                Show this help text
  PREFIX                   An optional human-readable prefix (e.g. 'addr').
                             - When provided, the input text is decoded
                             from various encoding formats and re-encoded
                             to bech32 using the given prefix.
                             - When omitted, the input text is decoded
                             from bech32 to base16.
  -v,--version              output version information and exit
```

```
Supported encoding formats: Base16, Bech32 & Base58.

Examples:
  To Bech32:
    $ bech32 base16_ <<< 706174617465
    base16_1wpshgct5v5r5mxh0

    $ bech32 base58_ <<< Ae2tdPwUPEYy
    base58_1p58rejhd9592uusa8pzj2

    $ bech32 new_prefix <<< old_prefix1wpshgcg2s33x3
    new_prefix1wpshgcgeak9mv

  From Bech32:
    $ bech32 <<< base16_1wpshgct5v5r5mxh0
    706174617465
```

Ogmios

Ogmios[16] is one of the most widely used and popular tools for Cardano developers, and it has excellent documentation. It is a translation layer that exposes the Cardano node capability via a REST API or Web RPC interface. Ogmios is open source and can be downloaded, built, and installed locally from GitHub,[17] or by a docker container. We will deploy the hosted version using Demeter.run, so we can quickly demonstrate how to interact with it using our examples.

To add an Ogmios extension:

1. Go to the **`Project`** page, scroll down, and select **`BROWSE EXTENSIONS`**, as shown in *Figure* 8.6.

[16]https://ogmios.dev/
[17]https://github.com/CardanoSolutions/ogmios

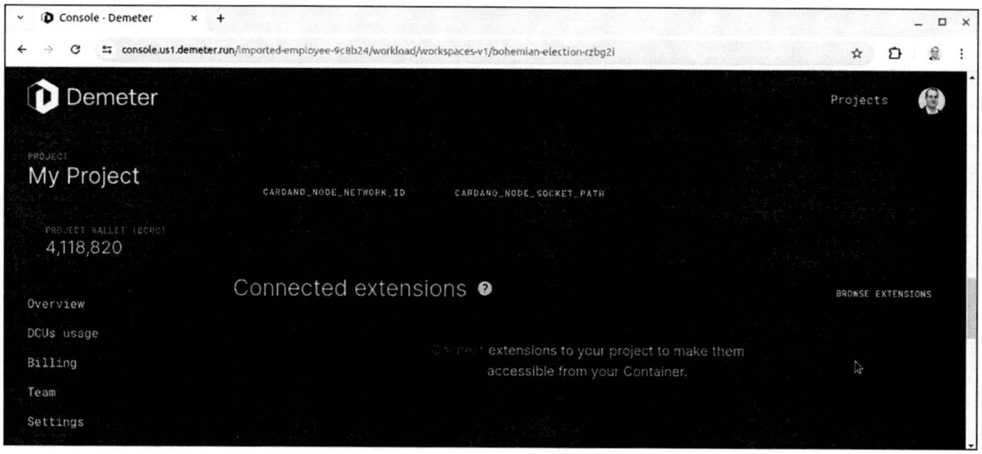

Figure 8.6: *Demeter.run Project View*

2. Select Ogmios Deploy.
3. Select **`Create Resource`** and the **`Preprod`** network.
4. Select v5 as the version and the **`CREATE RESOURCE`** button.
5. You see the instance running, as shown in *Figure* 8.7.

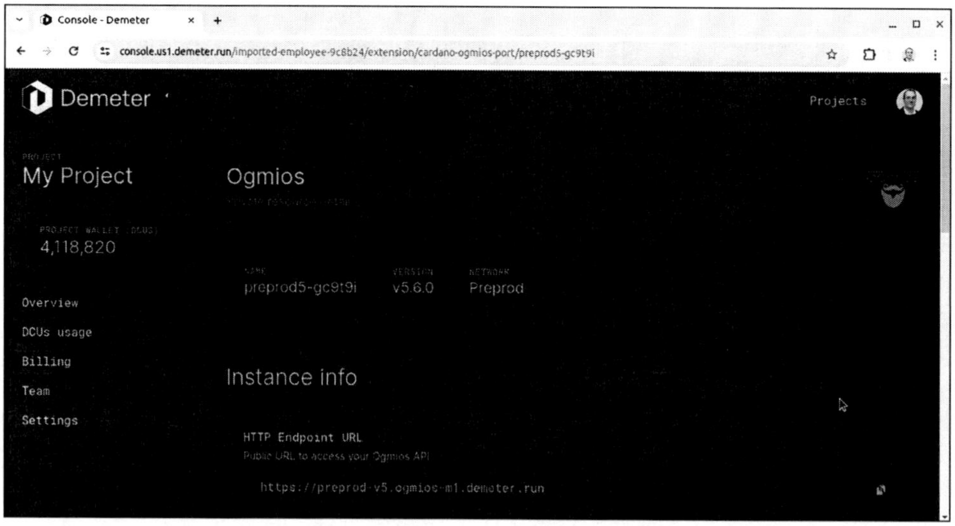

Figure 8.7: *Demeter.run Ogmios Live*

Now, let's try out the **`Ogmios`** API using a web tool like Hoppscotch.[18]

1. Go to the URL: https://hoppscotch.io/realtime/websocket.
2. Paste in the public https hostname for Ogmios and prefix wss:// to the address.

[18]https://hoppscotch.io/

3. Select **Connect**.
4. Then paste the following query and select **Send**:

```
{
    "type": "jsonwsp/request",
    "version": "1.0",
    "servicename": "ogmios",
    "methodname": "Query",
    "args": {
        "query": "ledgerTip"
    }
}
```

5. You should see the successful result, as shown in *Figure 8.8*.

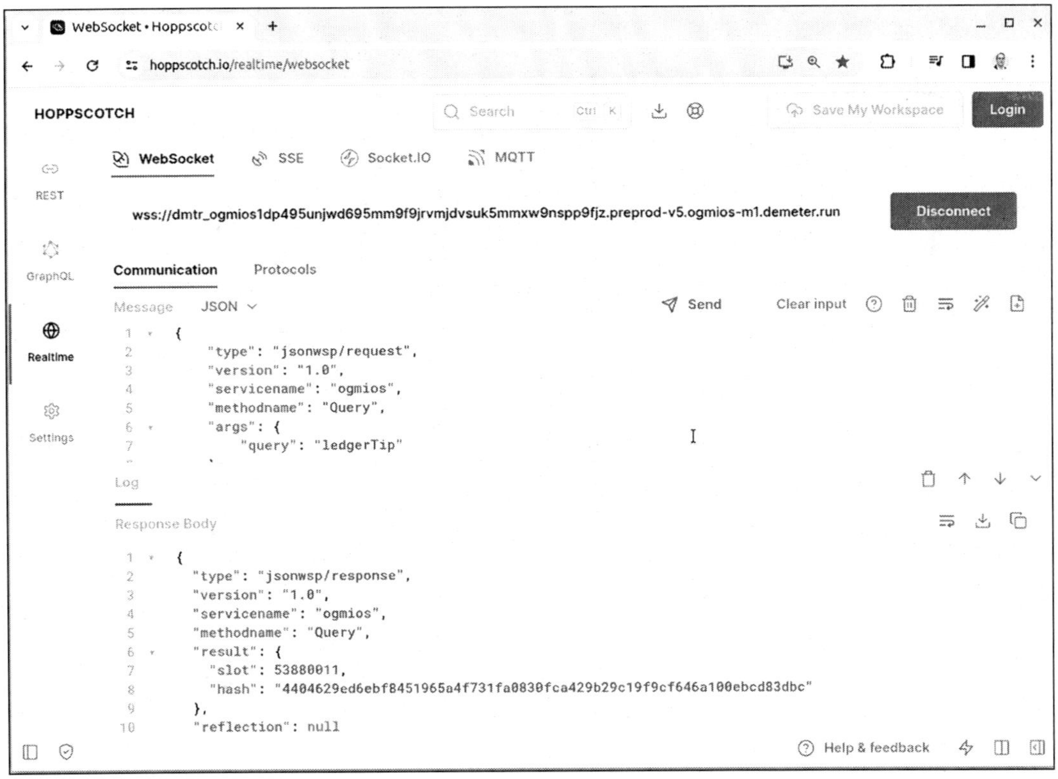

Figure 8.8: *Hoppscotch Ogmios Success*

Kupo

Kupo[19] is an open-source Cardano blockchain indexer that is fast, lightweight, and configurable. The API documentation[20] is excellent and is the go-to choice for many Cardano development teams who prefer to use in-house tools. Blockchains are designed to be a sequence of blocks connected together, forming a chain. This, however, makes it very difficult to perform efficient data queries. This is why we have indexers that take in blockchain data and store it in a database. This data can be indexed and then queried, filtered, and analyzed. Kupo can be downloaded, built, and installed locally, but it can also be set up as a hosted service using Demeter.run.

We will again go to the Project page and add another resource, this time a Kupo resource. Select deploy and create the resource for the preprod network. Next, copy the https URL for future reference. We should see four resources: Workspace, Node, Ogmios, and Kupo, as shown in *Figure* 8.9.

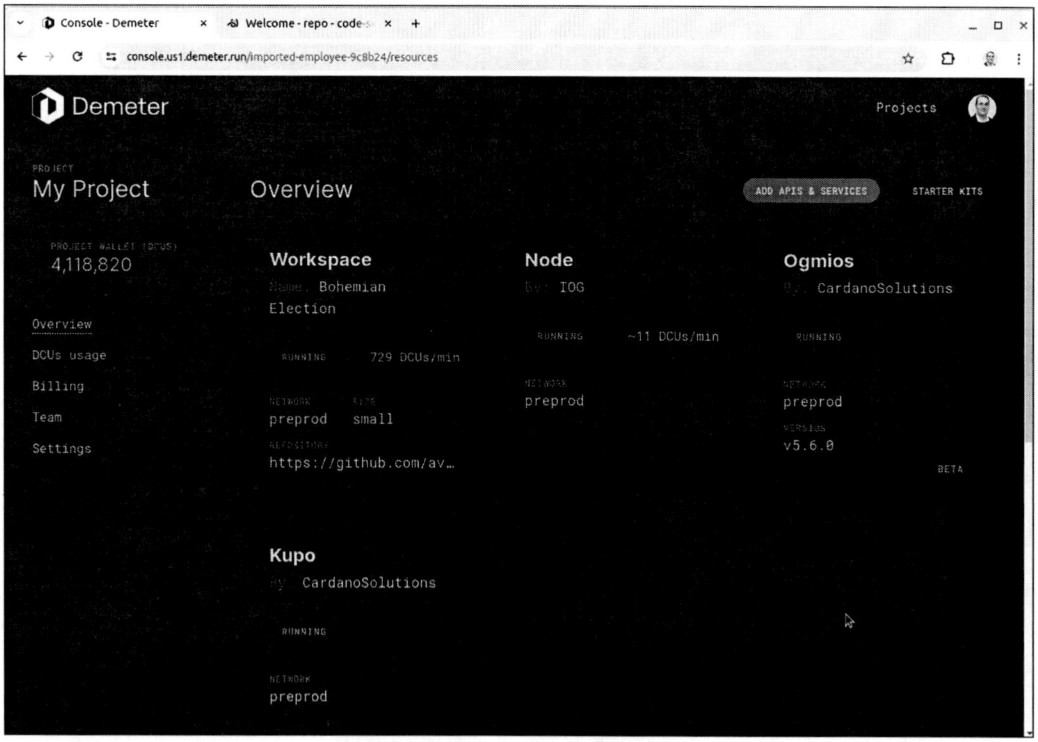

Figure 8.9: *Demeter.run Resources*

To do a quick test to confirm Kupo is working correctly, you can execute the following command and replace the hostname with the hostname copied from the **`Demeter.run`** Kupo resource.

[19]https://github.com/CardanoSolutions/kupo
[20]https://cardanosolutions.github.io/kupo/

```
$ curl -fsSL https://dmtr_kupo12e…mph005.preprod-v2.kupo-m1.demeter.run/
health
# TYPE kupo_configuration_indexes gauge
kupo_configuration_indexes  1.0
# TYPE kupo_connection_status gauge
kupo_connection_status  1.0
# TYPE kupo_most_recent_checkpoint counter
kupo_most_recent_checkpoint  59235759
# TYPE kupo_most_recent_node_tip counter
kupo_most_recent_node_tip  59235759
```

In this case, the Kupo instance is healthy and you can see the most recent **`checkpoint`** and **`node tip`**. Checkpoints are blocks on-chain that have been processed by Kupo and are mainly used to synchronize with the blockchain after a restart.[21]

Code Example

Now, we are ready to update the vesting and ticket code examples to use Ogmios and Kupo together. Lucid has a provider we can use for this exact purpose, called **`kupmios`**, as shown in *Figure* 8.10.

```
// Define the Cardano Network
const network = "Preprod";
const KUPO_API = process.env.NEXT_PUBLIC_KUPO_API as string;
const OGMIOS_API = process.env.NEXT_PUBLIC_OGMIOS_API as string;

if (!KUPO_API && !OGMIOS_API) {
  throw console.error("NEXT_PUBLIC_KUPO_API or NEXT_PUBLIC_OGMIOS_API not set");
}

// Create lucid object and connect it to the kupo + ogmios provider
const lucid = await Lucid.new(
  new Kupmios(
    KUPO_API,
    OGMIOS_API),
  network,
);
```

***Figure* 8.10:** *Lucid Kupmios*[22]

The vesting example will work without any other changes by switching to the Kupmios provider. The ticket example, however, requires changes to the pages/API **`getTicketMetadata.ts`**, as shown in *Figure* 8.11.

[21]https://cardanosolutions.github.io/kupo/#tag/Checkpoints
[22]https://github.com/ava-orange-education/Mastering-Cardano-Smart-Contracts/blob/main/chapter_08/ogmios-kupo/vesting/pages/index.tsx

```
64 const getTicketMetadata = async (ticketPolicyId: string,
65                                  ticketTokenName: string): Promise<TicketInfo> => {
66
67     const asset = ticketPolicyId + fromText(ticketTokenName);
68
69     // Call Kupo API to first get the transaction id of the mint
70     const transaction = await getTransaction(asset);
71
72     // Now call Kupo API to get the metadata using the mint tx
73     const metadata = await getMetadata( transaction[0].created_at.slot_no,
74                                         transaction[0].transaction_id);
75
76     const name = metadata[0].schema['721'].map[0].v.map[1].k.string as string;
77     const description = metadata[0].schema['721'].map[0].v.map[1].v.map[1].v.string as
78     const image = metadata[0].schema['721'].map[0].v.map[1].v.map[2].v.string as strin
79     const qty = metadata[0].schema['721'].map[0].v.map[1].v.map[5].v.string as string;
80     const utxoId = metadata[0].schema['721'].map[0].v.map[1].v.map[6].v.string as stri
81     const utxoIdx = metadata[0].schema['721'].map[0].v.map[1].v.map[7].v.string as str
```

Figure 8.11: *Kupo getMetadata*[23]

To retrieve metadata from Kupo, first get the transaction associated with the mint transaction. The token asset is provided on line 70, and the results are sorted by the order of the transactions that occurred on the blockchain. Therefore, the mint is the first transaction, so use the first transaction ID and then look up the metadata on that specific transaction on line 73. Lines 76–81 parse the metadata object and return the results to the front end.

Setup

To set up the Demeter.run environment to run the Kupo + Ogmios demo, please execute the following commands in a terminal window.

```
$ export NEXT_PUBLIC_KUPO_API=https://dmtr_kupo12e…mph005.preprod-v2.
kupo-m1.demeter.run
$ export NEXT_PUBLIC_OGMIOS_API=wss://dmtr_ogmios1v…g0t6mk.preprod-v5.
ogmios-m1.demeter.run
$ export NEXT_PUBLIC_ENV="dev"
$ export NEXT_PUBLIC_HOST="your-demeter-run-host"
$ export NEXT_PUBLIC_PROTOCOL="https"
$ export NEXT_PUBLIC_PORT=""
```

Local Devnet

Thanks to the awesome work from BoxBean[24]; it is now easy to install a local Devnet, similar to Hardhat for Ethereum. The Yaci Devkit uses lightweight components for indexing and querying blockchain data. In particular, BoxBean created Yaci, a modular, Java-based Ouroboros min-protocol that listens to incoming blocks, monitors the

[23]https://github.com/ava-orange-education/Mastering-Cardano-Smart-Contracts/blob/main/chapter_08/ogmios-kupo/ticket/pages/api/getTicketMetadata.ts
[24]https://github.com/bloxbean

local mempool, and submits transactions.[25] The team also created Yaci Store, a Java-based solution that provides an API to query indexed data and handle rollbacks.[26] To enable integration with a browser extension wallet like Nami and Helios for off-chain transaction building, the local Devnet will also use a local Cardano DB Sync to feed blockchain data to a local Blockfrost API provider.

The following five steps are required to set up a local devnet:

1. Set up YaciDevkit[27]
2. Set up Cardano DB Sync
3. Set up Blockfrost backend RYO (Run Your Own)
4. Build and install Nami browser wallet with a local Testnet network
5. Top up wallet with funds

Environment

The following setup instructions have been tested on Ubuntu Linux 20.04.1. You may require additional setup for other operating systems.

Install Docker

```
$ sudo apt -y install apt-transport-https ca-certificates curl
software-properties-common

$ curl -fsSL https://download.docker.com/linux/ubuntu/gpg | sudo gpg
--dearmor -o /usr/share/keyrings/docker-archive-keyring.gpg

$ echo "deb [arch=amd64 signed-by=/usr/share/keyrings/docker-ar-
chive-keyring.gpg] https://download.docker.com/linux/ubuntu $(lsb_
release -cs) stable" | sudo tee /etc/apt/sources.list.d/docker.list > /
dev/null

$ sudo apt update

$ sudo apt -y install docker-ce docker-ce-cli containerd.io

$ sudo usermod -aG docker $USER

$ newgrp docker

$ docker run hello-world
```

Step 1: Setting up Yaci Devkit

Once docker is installed, you can cd into the **`yaci-devit`** directory, so that we can

[25]https://github.com/bloxbean/yaci
[26]https://github.com/bloxbean/yaci-store/blob/main/docs/design.md
[27]https://github.com/bloxbean/yaci-devkit

install the following two docker images.[28] We will install the following images as part of the setup process:

```
REPOSITORY              TAG             IMAGE ID        SIZE
bloxbean/yaci-cli       0.0.20-beta1    0b5f0541f396    1.2GB
bloxbean/yaci-viewer    0.0.9           73b52df24dfb    579MB
```

```
$ git clone https://github.com/ava-orange-education/Mastering-Carda-
no-Smart-Contracts.git --recurse-submodules
$ cd Mastering-Cardano-Smart-Contracts/chapter_08/local-devnet/yaci
-devkit
$ sudo ./start.sh
$ sudo ./yaci-cli.sh
```

To start up a new cluster, use the command `create-node -o --start`

```
yaci-cli:>create-node -o --start
[Success] Delete existing folder
[Success] Create cluster folder !!!
[Success] Slot length updated in genesis.json
[Success] Updated configuration.yaml
[Success] Update ports
[Success] Create Cluster : default

###### Node Details (Container) ######
[Node port] 3001
[Node Socket Paths]
/clusters/default/node-spo1/node.sock
[Submit Api Port] 8090
[Protocol Magic] 42
[Block Time] 1.0 sec
[Slot Length] 1.0 sec
[Start Time] 0


#################### URLS (Host) ####################
[Yaci Viewer] http://localhost:5173
[Yaci Store Swagger UI] http://localhost:8080/swagger-ui.html
[Yaci Store Api URL] http://localhost:8080/api/v1/
```

[28]https://hub.docker.com/r/bloxbean/yaci-cli/tags

```
[Pool Id] pool1wvqhvyrgwch4jq9aa84hc8q4kzvyq2z3xr6mpafkqmx9wce39zy
```

...

```
[OK] Yaci Store Started
devnet:default>
```

For more information regarding startup options and configuration, please consult the GitHub repository: https://github.com/bloxbean/yaci-devkit.

Step 2: Starting DB Sync

In a new terminal window:

```
$ cd chapter_08/local-devnet/yaci-devkit
$ ./start-db-sync.sh
```

If successful, you should see the following output.

...

```
cardano-db-sync_1    | [db-sync-node:Info:65] [2024-05-08 10:15:13.01 UTC] Insert Babbage Block: epoch 0, slot 244, block 244, hash 74ec222296e80d0dae52fd7723c7317746928144fdbf8b9f5fd31a7ca6daf095

cardano-db-sync_1    | [db-sync-node:Info:65] [2024-05-08 10:15:14.00 UTC] Insert Babbage Block: epoch 0, slot 245, block 245, hash e13b22299709d612d8381bc6292a75ef04f5fa912a308c97ad8f804c8044fc94

cardano-db-sync_1    | [db-sync-node:Info:65] [2024-05-08 10:15:15.00 UTC] Insert Babbage Block: epoch 0, slot 246, block 246, hash 888f504744cef550755ebd88a6cd6e9b5ad27f3ddcba11076ac8a00a9d04a258

cardano-db-sync_1    | [db-sync-node:Info:65] [2024-05-08 10:15:16.00 UTC] Insert Babbage Block: epoch 0, slot 247, block 247, hash be35c0eb-241b0369af4a869480e9340a6c079fc25a3e8f96273fa633a22b4da9
```

...

Step 3: Starting The Blockfrost-RYO

In another new terminal window:

```
$ cd chapter_08/local-devnet/blockfrost-backend-ryo

$ nvm install 20.9.0.

$ yarn install

$ yarn run dev-testnet
```

Step 4: Installing the Nami Local Devnet Version

Open up another terminal window and go into the Nami directory.

```
$ cd chapter_08/local-devnet/nami
$ nvm use 20.9.0
$ npm install
$ npm run build
```

This will create a build directory that can be loaded into the Chrome browser. Open a Chrome browser tab extension window **`chrome://extensions/`** and select "Load Unpacked" at the top left side of the window. Then navigate to the **`nami/build`** directory that was just created and select it. The Nami wallet should now be installed, and you can launch the browser extension. It will first ask you to create a new wallet and a passphrase. You will need to switch to the Testnet network and can do that by selecting the avatar at the top right of the window. Next, select Settings, Network, and choose Testnet from the Network dropdown menu, as shown in *Figure* 8.12. Also, enable Custom Node and enter **`http://localhost:8090/api/submit/tx`** as the URL. You can confirm you are on the correct network by seeing the Testnet label on the bottom left of the Nami pop-up window.

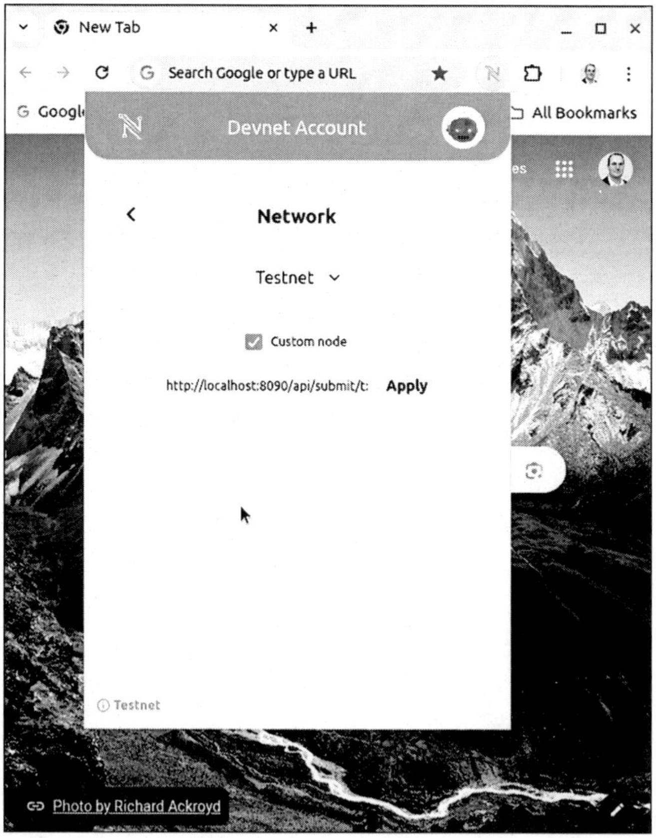

Figure 8.12: *Nami Wallet Devnet*

Tip: *If you installed the Nami wallet using the unpack method and closed down the browser, you may need to follow the unpack instructions again. If you have also re-*

created the new local Devnet network, then you will need to create a new Nami account or explicitly remove the Nami wallet browser plugin to clear cached Nami account data.

Step 5: Top Up Wallet with Funds

With the Nami wallet open, select the receive button, and copy the receiving address. Then, go into the **`yaci-cli`** terminal, type the **`topup`** command, and paste the receiving address and the amount of Ada to send, as shown in *Figure 8.13*.

Figure 8.13: *Yaci DevKit Top-up*

You can confirm in your Nami wallet that you have received this amount, as presented in *Figure 8.14*.

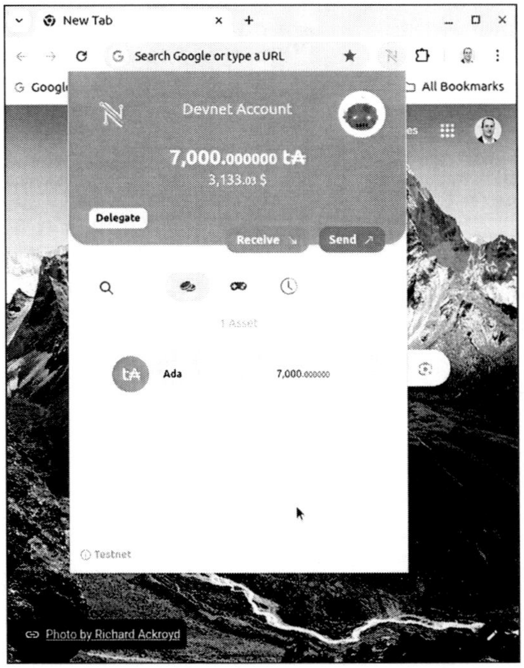

Figure 8.14: *Nami Wallet Top-up*

Example Test Drive

Now we can try out a previous ticket example using the local devnet. Using another terminal window, execute the following commands:

```
$ cd chapter_08/local-devnet/ticket
$ npm install
$ npm run dev
```

Next, mint some new tickets on the local devnet, as illustrated in *Figure* 8.15.

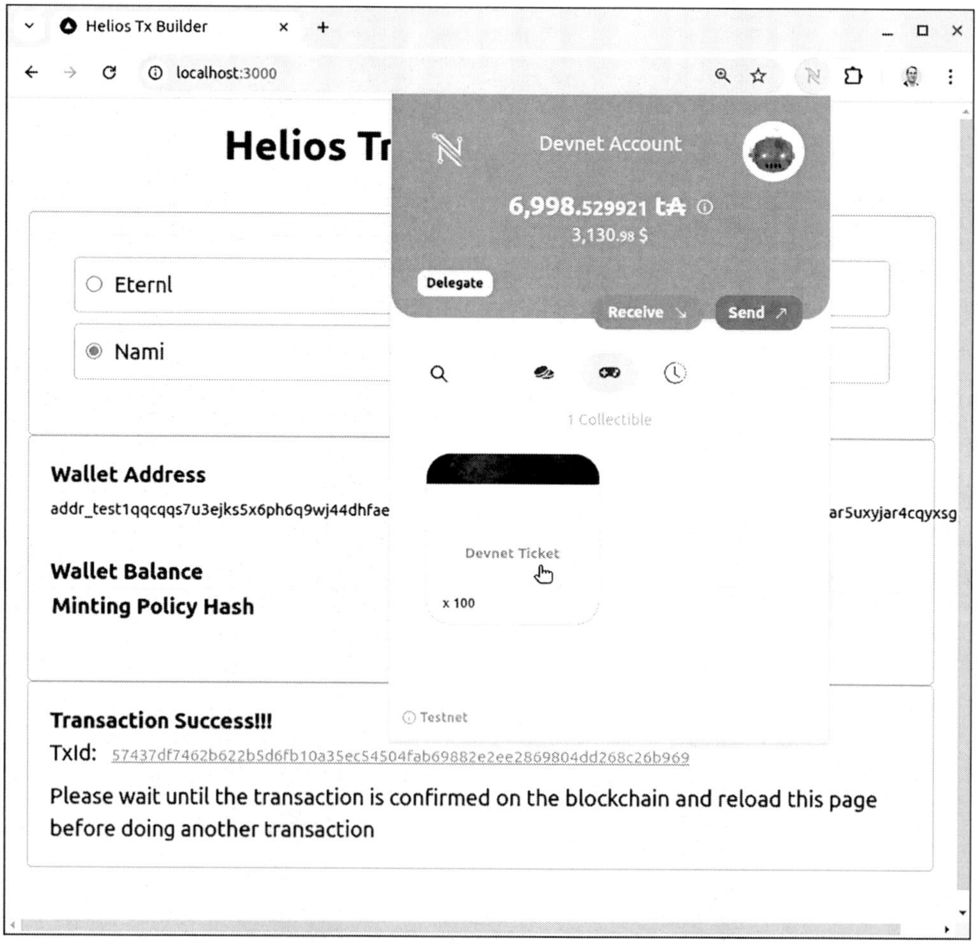

Figure 8.15: *Minting on Local Devnet*

We can now see the transaction details on the local Yaci DevKit blockchain explorer under the transactions tab, as shown in *Figure* 8.16.

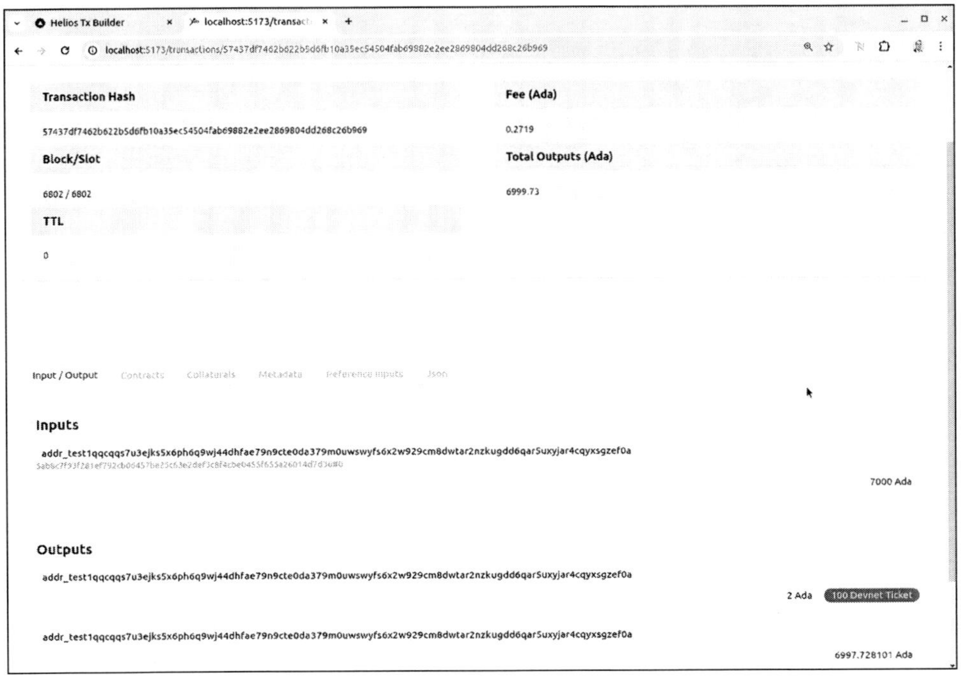

Figure 8.16: *Local Devnet Explorer Transaction View*

We can also view the smart contract details including the Redeemer values in *Figure* 8.17.

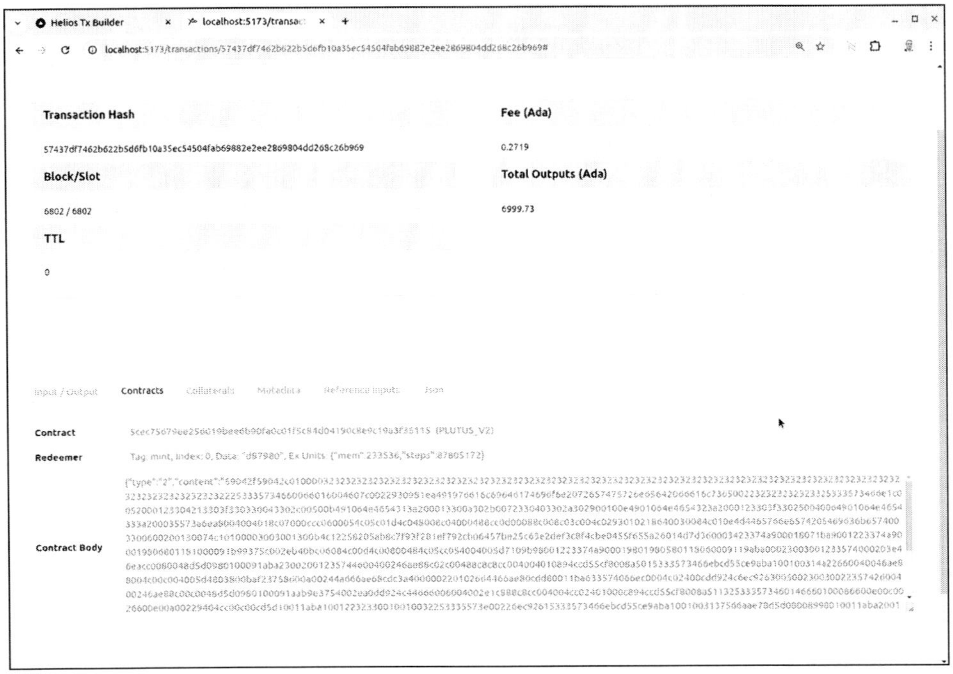

Figure 8.17: *Local Devnet Explorer Contract View*

Additional Resources

Additional approaches and solutions exist to query and react to Cadano blockchain data. *Table 8.1* provides an overview of the more popular Cardano tooling options.

Name	**Description**	**Technology Stack**
DB Sync[29]	Cardano Blockchain Indexer	Haskell Postgress SQL DB
Kupo[30]	Cardano Blockchain indexer	Haskell
Ogmios[31]	Lightweight interface to Cardano Node	Haskell
Yaci Store[32]	Cardan Blockchain indexer and real-time monitoring	Java, RDBMS or Redis/ MongoDB
Carp[33]	Cardano Blockchain indexer	Rust, Typescript, Oura, Cardano Multiplatform Lib, PostgresDB
Scrolls[34]	Blockchain crawler, aggregator with real-time updates	Rust, Redis
Ouroboros Network JS[35]	Ouroboros network library written in typescript with Node. js streaming for chain sync, tx monitoring and submission	Typescript
GraphQL[36]	Cross-platform, typed, and queryable API for Cardano	Typescript, Cardano DB Sync
Oura[37]	Realtime blockchain monitoring and alerting	Rust, Pallas[38]

Table 8.1: *Blockchain Tooling*

[29]https://github.com/IntersectMBO/cardano-db-sync
[30]https://github.com/CardanoSolutions/kupo
[31]https://ogmios.dev/
[32]https://github.com/bloxbean/yaci-store
[33]https://github.com/dcSpark/carp
[34]https://github.com/txpipe/scrolls
[35]https://github.com/StricaHQ/ouroboros-network-js
[36]https://github.com/cardano-foundation/cardano-graphql
[37]https://github.com/txpipe/oura
[38]https://github.com/txpipe/pallas

Conclusion

This chapter provided an overview of some of the more popular Cardano off-chain providers and tooling available to developers. First, we explored Cardano Blockchain providers such as Blockfrost, Maestro, Koios, and Dandelion. Next, we understood some of the Cardano infrastructure components and tooling, such as Cardano Node, Ogmios, and Kupo, and how to provision them with Demeter.run. We also learned how to deploy a local devnet using Yaci DevKit to test both the on-chain and off-chain code. Finally, we provided an overview of the most popular tooling components for completeness. We are now ready for the next chapter to use our knowledge of off-chain tooling to build a complete end-to-end blockchain application.

Points to Remember

- Multiple blockchain API service providers and tooling options help promote decentralization and avoid a single point of failure in the ecosystem.
- Blockfrost was one of the first Cardano API service providers and is the most used API service provider in the Cardano ecosystem.
- Maestro recently launched a new version of its APIs with low latency, high-performance chain index queries, transaction state management, and optimized transaction submission.
- Koios is a decentralized, distributed platform that provides Cardano Blockchain API services.
- Off-chain tooling components are used to query, react, or submit blockchain data.
- Cardano Node can be run from a docker container, static binaries, or by compiling the source code.
- Demeter.run has resources such as Cardano Node that can be run and attached to a workspace
- **`cardano-cli`** is the Swiss army knife of Cardano with multiple uses and functionality
- Ogmios is popular because it exposes Cardano node functionality using REST APIs or a Web RPC interface.
- Kupo is also a popular open-source Cardano Blockchain indexer that captures and saves blockchain data quickly to an in-memory database.
- Lucid has a built-in Kupo and Ogmios provider that can connect to a Kupo and Ogmios instance for blockchain data lookups and transaction submissions.
- Yaci DevKit can set up a local devnet similar to Hardhat for Ethereum.

Multiple Choice Questions

1. Why is blockchain tooling needed?
   a. Used by on-chain in validator logic
   b. Used by the Cardano Ledger
   c. Needed to start/stop the Cardano Blockchain
   d. Access blockchain data efficiently
2. What functionality cannot be done using **`cardano-cli`**?
   a. Start/Stop a cardano node
   b. Submit a transaction
   c. Query the Cardano Blockchain tip
   d. See the contents of a UTXO
3. How do you access Ogmios?
   a. Node socket
   b. SQL query
   c. HTTP REST API
   d. HTTP REST API or RPC Web Socket
4. What are some of the features of the Yaci Devkit?
   a. A blockchain explorer, Kupo and Ogmios APIs
   b. Token registry
   c. Mainnet network
   d. GraphQL
5. Which tool can submit a transaction?
   a. Kupo
   b. Oura
   c. Carp
   d. ouroboros-network-js

Answers

1. d
2. a
3. d
4. a
5. d

Questions

1. What are the centralization risks to any blockchain?
2. Why is blockchain technology generally not efficient for direct data access?
3. How does tooling speed up access to data queries?
4. What did Maestro do to help improve the finality times for a submitted transaction?
5. What are some of the advantages of using a local Testnet or devnet?

Key Terms

- **Node Tip:** The latest (highest) confirmed block in the blockchain.
- **RESTful:** It uses HTTP requests to access and set data between a client and server.
- **SDK**: Software Development Kit makes it more convenient for developers to access service providers' APIs.
- **Service Provider**: A company that provides off-chain blockchain API services.
- **Transaction Finality:** The time it takes to finalize a transaction on the blockchain.
- **Webhook:** A callback function that will make a network call to an application when a certain condition is met.

CHAPTER 9
Ticket Application Design

Introduction

This chapter will discuss Smart Contract design patterns that leverage and utilize the Cardano UTXO architecture. **Anti-patterns** are also examined which should be avoided and lead to poor application performance and **UTXO contention**. We will discuss Cardano Improvement Proposals (CIPs) and where they will be applied to the application design. Next, we will examine a state machine diagram to see how the entire event ticket lifecycle works. Then we will explore state transitions looking at the inputs and outputs required for a successful transaction. Finally, we will summarize the chapter by reviewing sequence diagrams showing each use case's interaction between system components.

Structure

In this chapter, we will discuss the following topics:

- Design Patterns
  - Thread Token
  - Beacon Token
  - Order Book
- Anti-Patterns
  - Liquidity Pools
  - Batchers
- Cardano Improvement Proposals
  - CIP-0003 Wallet Key Generation
  - CIP-0030 Cardano dApp-Wallet Web Bridge
  - CIP-0032 Inline Datums

    - CIP-0040 Explicit Collateral Output
    - CIP-0068 Datum Metadata Standard
- The Application Architecture
    - On-Chain State Machines
    - Off-Chain Sequence Diagrams

Design Patterns

By now, you are aware of the significant differences between a UTXO and an account model blockchain. In particular, many account-based blockchain design patterns are not optimal for UTXO blockchains and are called anti-patterns. Let's first examine common UTXO design patterns and then contrast them with anti-patterns.

Thread Token

One of the first and most common design patterns involves using a thread token. A unique token is minted and included in a UTXO locked at a script address. The script can only be spent if the transaction includes this thread token, as shown in *Figure* 9.1. It is critical that this token is unique, so it is created using a minting policy that requires a specific UTXO as an input. By leveraging the underlying uniqueness of UTXOs, it can only be spent once, and we can guarantee that the thread token will be unique.

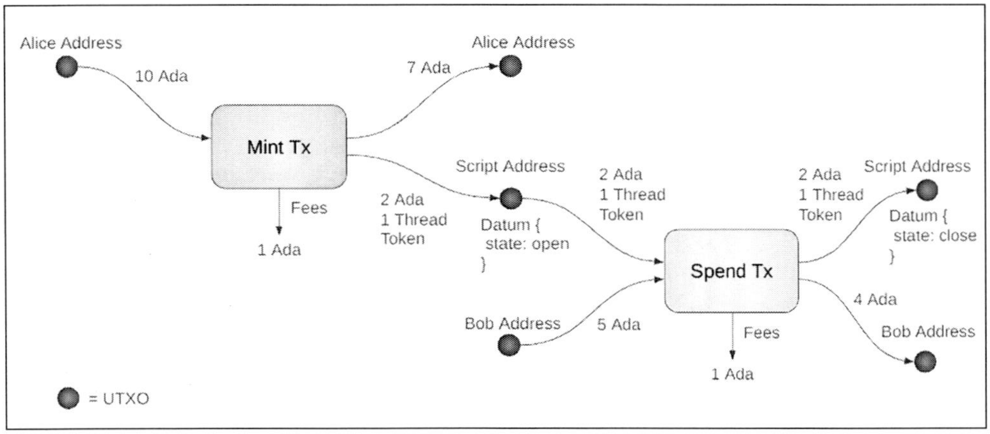

Figure 9.1: *Thread Token Example*

A thread token can be used to control the sequence of validator script execution. Every transaction must include the thread token, guaranteeing that only one transaction can be executed at any time. This is useful if you are trying to update some type of state and need the validator to ensure the correct before and after state transitions (refer to *Figure* 9.1). This is also useful to confirm preconditions such as whether a token has been minted in a separate transaction. By using a thread token, Smart Contracts can communicate with each other using the existence (or absence) of a particular token in a transaction.

Beacon Token

A Beacon Token[1] is used to easily identify the address of a specific UTXO that contains a Beacon Token. There are many examples where UTXOs are created, and the off-chain application needs to keep track of these UTXOs. As we saw in *Chapter 8, Tooling*, chain indexers can capture the minting transaction information and record the UTXO and address containing a token. The indexers can also monitor token movement and be able to provide the current address where a token resides. This is useful if you need to provide a list of UTXOs that match a specific Beacon Token. A Beacon Token can also be used as a Thread Token, combining both the Thread Token and Beacon Token design patterns.

Order Book

To take advantage of the EUTXO model for concurrency and scalability, you need to design your application, which will scale as the number of users grows. Fortunately, the EUTXO architecture can facilitate this because it uses local state and is fully deterministic. This means that multiple concurrent users can interact with your application, each with their own UTXOs that are independent of each other. Therefore, as more users use the application, there is no centralized access that will limit throughput as in global state systems. Additionally, local state is well suited for creating **state channels** and **zero-knowledge proofs** to segment a set of UTXOs for scaling solutions.[2] We will discuss scaling solutions such as Hydra in *Chapter 11, Testing, Security, and Scaling.*

An Order Book design is an example of leveraging EUTXO architecture's benefits. In particular, the design involves a three-step process:

Step 1: Place an order on-chain with a UTXO locked at a contract script address

Step 2: Identify or monitor the orders off-chain for a match

Step 3: Submit a transaction to fill (or cancel) the order

In a simplified example, as shown in *Figure* 9.2, a swap script address uses a parameter to record the asked asset, the offered asset, Beacon Token and the public key hash (**PKH**) of the user wallet. This creates a unique swap address for each asset pair. The **PKH** is used, so only the wallet that placed the order can cancel it. A unique Beacon Token is attached to each order UTXO so that off-chain code can easily find all swaps when looking for order matches.

[1] https://github.com/cardano-foundation/CIPs/pull/466
[2] Jarek Hirniak, "Axo Protocol Whitepaper: The New era of trading"

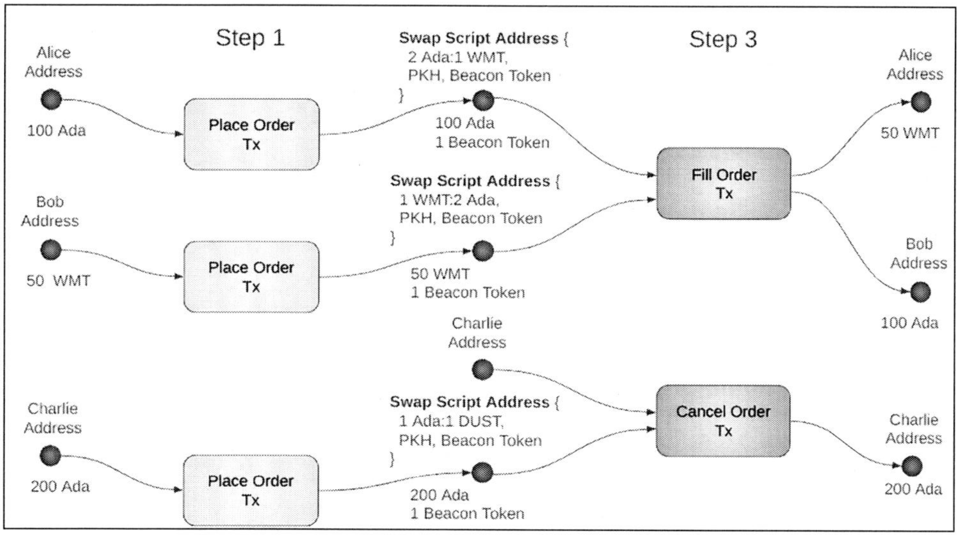

Figure 9.2: *Simplified Order Book Example*

Alice and Bob have positions that can be swapped without any third-party intermediary. A swap position can be partially filled, or swap positions can be aggregated together to fill multiple swaps. This is known as composability, and teams like Cardano Swaps[3] advocate order book design standards to enable swap composability across the Cardano ecosystem.

In *Figure* 9.2, Alice offers 100 Ada for 50 WMT tokens, and Bob offers 50 WMT tokens for 100 Ada. This valid swap is detected off-chain, and a Fill Order transaction is submitted on-chain to execute the swap. Once the Fill Order is completed, the Ada and WMT tokens in the swaps are transferred to each party. Bob gets 100 Ada, and Alice receives 50 WMT tokens. Charlie decides to cancel his swap position without any third-party intermediary and is allowed to do so because he can sign the transaction with the required public key hash (**PKH**).

The Order Book design pattern works well because of the following Cardano EUTXO architecture principles[4]:

- Local state
- Independent and unique wallet UTXOs and smart contracts
- Immutable UTXOs
- Determinism
- On-chain verification and Off-chain computation
- Parallel transaction processing

[3]https://github.com/fallen-icarus/cardano-swaps
[4]Lars Brunjes et al., "Building UTxO optimized Dapps"

An Order Book design can be applied to many different use cases that involve exchanging value between two or more parties.

Anti-Patterns

Now that we have looked at design patterns that take advantage of EUTXO architecture, let's look at some design patterns we should avoid. Most of the anti-patterns are design approaches that come from an account model such as Ethereum.

Liquidity Pools

The concept of a centralized liquidity pool was introduced, where users can pool their liquidity in trading pairs. This would create an automated market maker (AMM) for market orders, as shown in *Figure* 9.3.

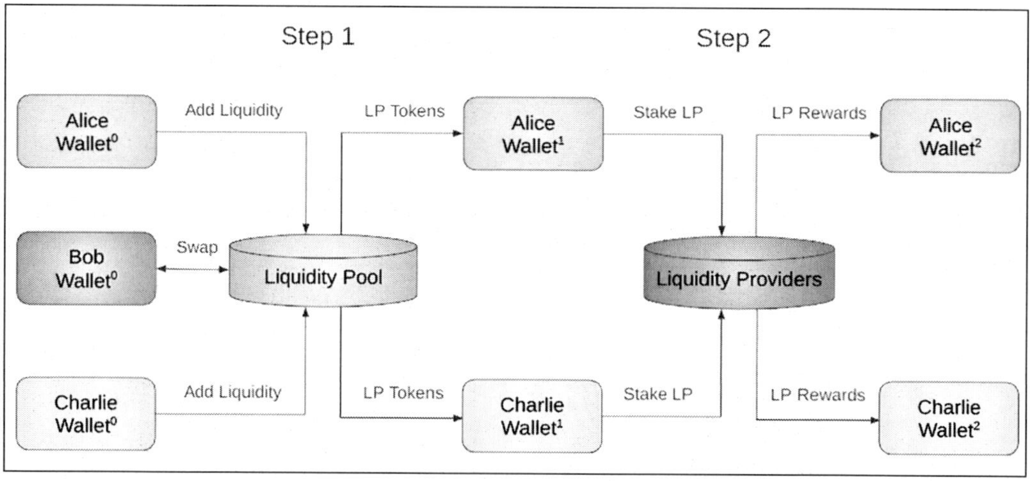

Figure 9.3: *Liquidity Pools*

The disadvantage of this approach is that liquidity is aggregated into a centralized pool and typically involves custodial ownership. It means that someone else has the keys to spend your funds and you no longer have direct control over them. This also makes for an excellent attack vector, which is why we saw over $3.1 billion USD stolen in 2022 from DeFi protocols.[5] In this model, we must also introduce **Liquidity Provider (LP)** pools where LP tokens are staked to incentivize liquidity providers. This is not required in an order book design pattern and adds complexity. Finally, the negative side effect of impermanent loss only occurs with centralized AMM pools. This worsens the more significant change (+/-) in the price of an asset pair being provided as liquidity.[6]

[5]Chainalysis, "2022 Biggest Year Ever For Crypto Hacking with $3.8 Billion Stolen..."
[6]Jarek Hirniak, "Axo Protocol Whitepaper: The New era of trading", 19

Batchers

To make matters worse, when this design pattern is used in an EUTXO architecture, the centralized liquidity pools create UTXO contention and scalability is impacted as more users are added. To mitigate this, another anti-pattern involves Batchers processing an order on the user's behalf, as shown in *Figure* 9.4.

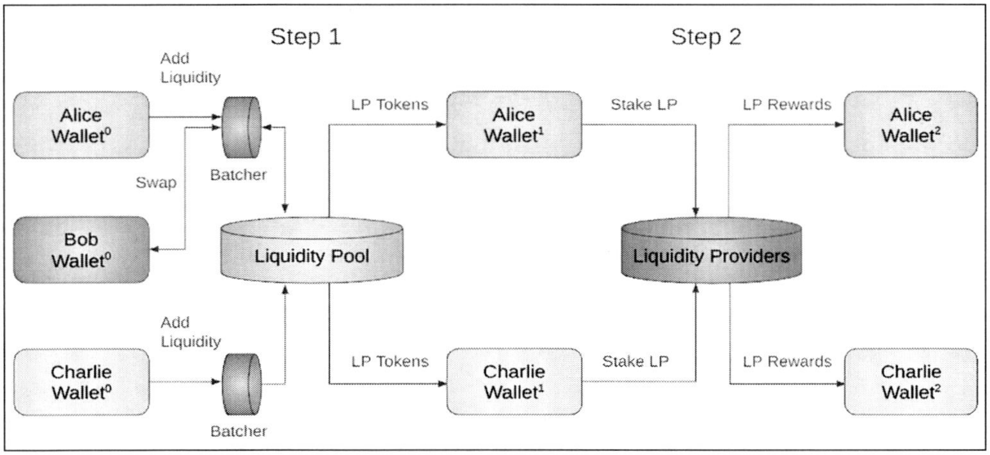

Figure 9.4: *Batchers*

Batchers, unfortunately, introduces centralization where typically only approved entities can run a Batcher and add liquidity to a pool or execute a swap. This can also lead to front-running transactions to the detriment of users trying to get the best price for a swap. On Ethereum, this is known as miner extractable value (MEV).

Cardano Improvement Proposals

Cardano Improvement Proposals (CIPs)[7] are standards or references for design and implementation best practices. We will review the following CIPs and how they apply to our application design.

CIP-0003 Wallet Key Generation

In our ticket application design, the application will need to sign a transaction in addition to the signatures from the end user. For an application to sign a transaction, we must create a private and public key following the standards defined in CIP-0003.[8] CIP-0003 references BIP-39 which uses a mnemonic seed phrase to generate a wallet and is used for entropy. The CIP also references HD Wallets already covered in *Chapter 3, Transactions.*

[7]https://cips.cardano.org/

[8]https://github.com/cardano-foundation/CIPs/tree/master/CIP-0003

CIP-0030 Cardano dApp-Wallet Web Bridge

CIP-0030[9] is a standard for browser-based, wallet integration. It specifies the JavaScript APIs that are injected into the browser window and how a web application can interact with them. We will use CIP-0030 in our application design, but it should be noted that there is a newer standard under review that allows for **P2P** wallet communication and is documented in CIP-0045.[10]

CIP-0032 Inline Datums

CIP-0032[11] improved Cardano Smart Contract development and efficiency. Before CIP-0032, only a Datum hash could be stored on-chain, not the actual Datum values. This meant that an application would have to recreate the Datum value, which made it challenging for other Smart Contracts to use it. With CIP-0032, the Datum value can reside on-chain so applications can simply reference the on-chain value. The Datum value is locked inside a UTXO, which Smart Contracts can access as part of a transaction. Combining CIP-0032 and CIP-0031 (reference inputs) allows for read-only data values on-chain and is frequently used by Oracle data providers today.

CIP-0040 Explicit Collateral Output

A new type of output, called Collateral Outputs, was introduced with CIP-0040.[12] Collateral, as we recall from *Chapter 4, Plutus*, is required as a deposit that is used if a Plutus script phase two evaluation fails. Although this helps to protect the network against spam or malicious attacks, it also introduces an additional Ada requirement to submit a transaction. Using collateral outputs, a transaction can be constructed so that we can use any UTXO as collateral, but only consume the deposit amount if needed and return the change as a collateral return output. Before CIP-0040, a pure UTXO with only Ada could only be used as the collateral input.

CIP-0068 Datum Metadata Standard

CIP-0068[13] is a standard that defines a way to store token metadata using a datum. This is different from CIP-0025, which stores token metadata using transaction metadata. The advantage of using a Datum is that it can be updated and read directly by a smart contract. This standard applies to Non-Fungible Tokens (**NFT**s) or Fungible Tokens (**FT**s). CIP-0068 involves creating a reference token linked to the original token(s)

---

[9]https://github.com/cardano-foundation/CIPs/tree/master/CIP-0030
[10]https://github.com/cardano-foundation/CIPs/pull/395
[11]https://github.com/cardano-foundation/CIPs/tree/master/CIP-0032
[12]https://github.com/cardano-foundation/CIPs/tree/master/CIP-0040
[13]https://github.com/cardano-foundation/CIPs/tree/master/CIP-0068

minted, as shown in *Figure* 9.5. This design allows the **NFT**s or **FT**s to move around on the blockchain, but the reference token remains in one location.

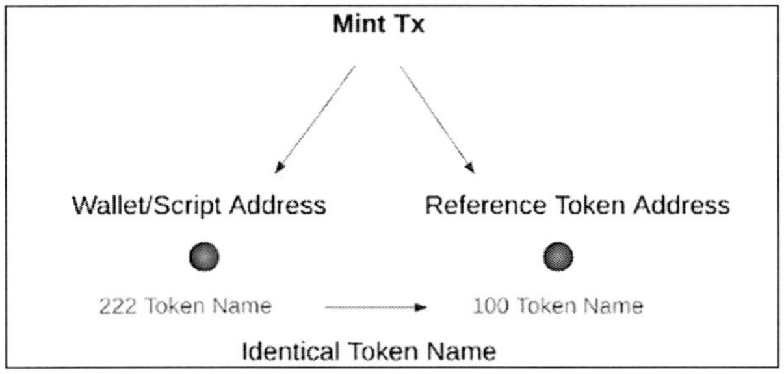

***Figure* 9.5:** CIP-0068

The token naming convention is to prefix hex-encoded labels such as 222 for **NFT**s and 100 for the reference token. The common labels to prefix are listed in *Table* 9.1.

Label	Class	Description	Hex Encoded Label
100	NFT	Reference Token located at reference token address	`000643b0`
222	NFT	Non-Fungible Token at wallet or script address	`000de140`
333	FT	Fungible Token at wallet or script address	`0014df10`
444	RFT	Rich-Fungible Token at wallet or script address. This can be used to represent fractional NFT ownership	`001BC280`

***Table* 9.1:** CIP-0068 *Labels*[14]

The token name must be identical, allowing the two tokens to be linked to or reference each other. For more detailed information and with basic examples, please review CIP-0068 on GitHub.[15]

The steps to create your own label are[16]:

1. Convert the decimal label to hex[17]
2. Get the checksum of the hex[18]
3. Drop the 0x and use the last 2 digits
4. Concat the 4-digit hex and the 2-digit checksum, then add a zero to the start and end

[14]https://developers.cardano.org/docs/governance/cardano-improvement-proposals/cip-0068/
[15]https://github.com/cardano-foundation/CIPs/tree/master/CIP-0068
[16]https://github.com/inimrod/cip68-fungible-token-demo/blob/main/src/lib/init-vars.ts
[17]https://www.rapidtables.com/convert/number/decimal-to-hex.html
[18]https://crccalc.com/

The Application Architecture

Using our knowledge of EUTXO design patterns and standards, we are now ready to create the application architecture for a ticket application where users can mint, burn, buy, sell and redeem event tickets.

On-Chain State Machine Diagrams

The complete **state machine** diagram for the ticket token lifecycle is shown in *Figure* 9.6. We will look at how the application transitions to each state in detail.

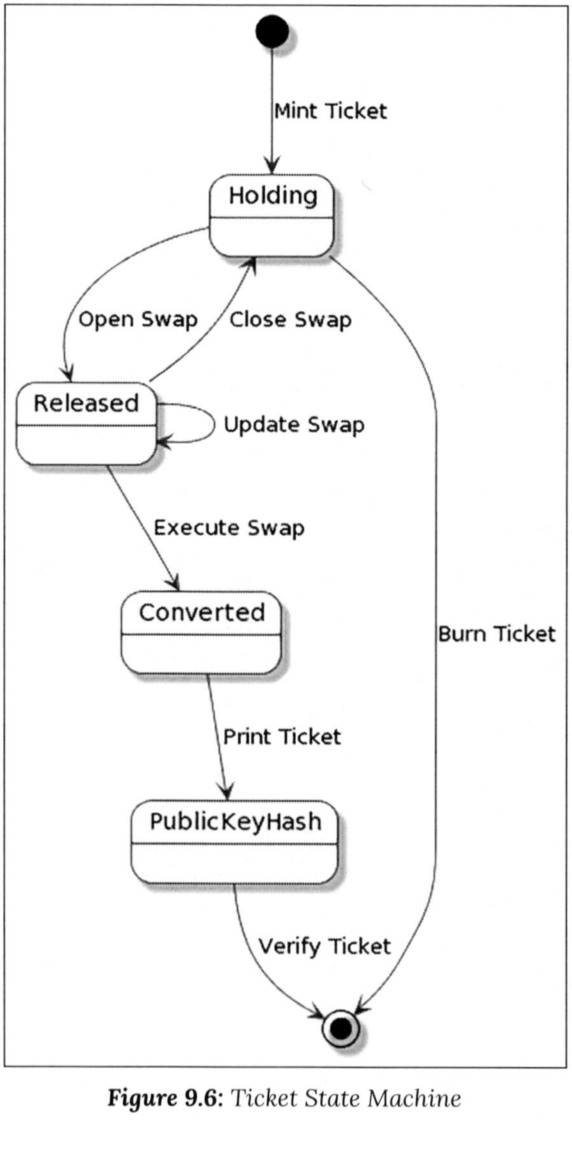

Figure 9.6: *Ticket State Machine*

Minting Tickets

Tickets for an event must be first minted and sent to the holding validator script, as shown in *Figure* 9.6. The Ticket Minting Policy in *Figure* 9.7, shows the script parameters that will be used including the UTXO input, name of event, show time, number of tickets minted, stake and payment **PKH**, holding validator address, and the minimum amount of lovelace. The ticket holding script requires the stake key signature to move the ticket tokens locked at this script address. Transaction metadata is created to record the minting policy script parameters which can be used for future minting policy-related transactions (for example, burn or convert). The payment PKH will be used for the payment address when the ticket is sold (converted).

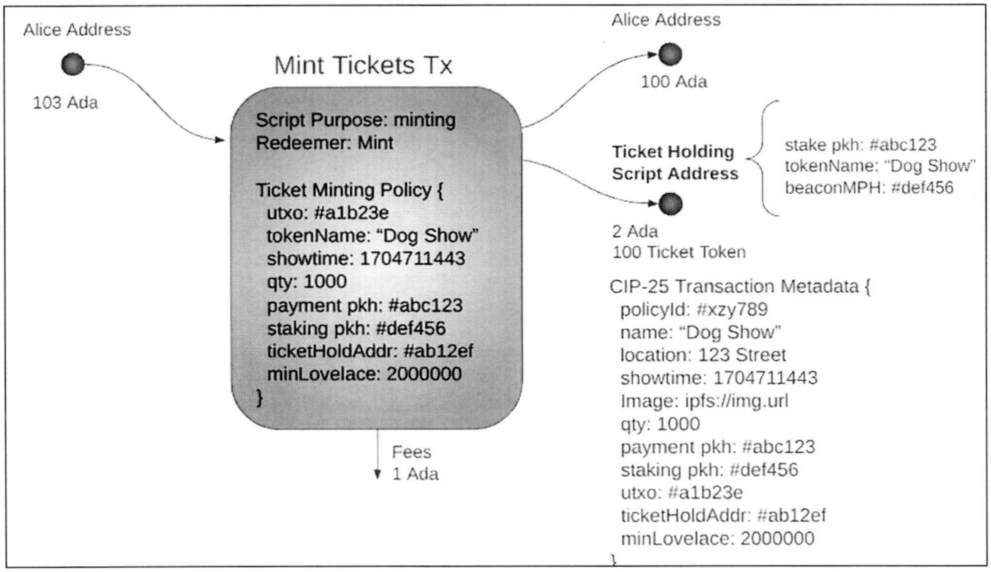

Figure 9.7: *Mint Tickets Transaction*

Burning Tickets

The minting policy will allow the burn of any token that belongs to the minting policy, as shown in *Figure* 9.8. Unsold tickets may be burned to reduce the supply of event tickets. The mint is a one-time event, but the burn can happen any time after the mint. Typically, however, an event organizer will not want to burn purchased/converted ticket tokens, which could be used for rewards, special access to content, or future events.

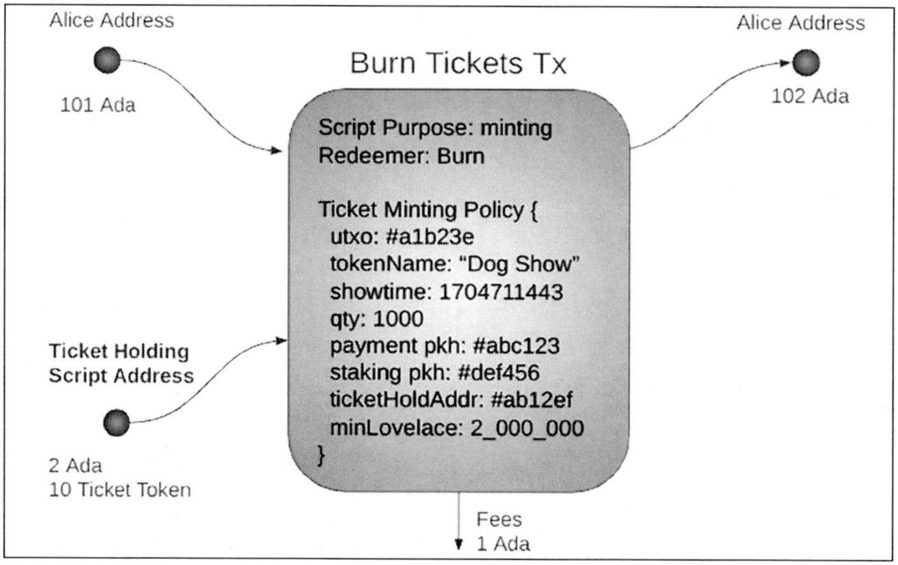

Figure 9.8: *Burn Ticket Transaction*

Opening Swap

Opening a swap requires executing both a spending and a minting script within the same transaction. In this case, we must execute Transfer Tickets, as detailed in *Figure* 9.9, and Mint Beacon outlined in *Figure* 9.10. The price of the swap is specified in the Datum and is updateable. For example, if the **`askedAsset`** is set to 10 Ada, the swap can only be executed if 10 Ada is paid for each ticket token.

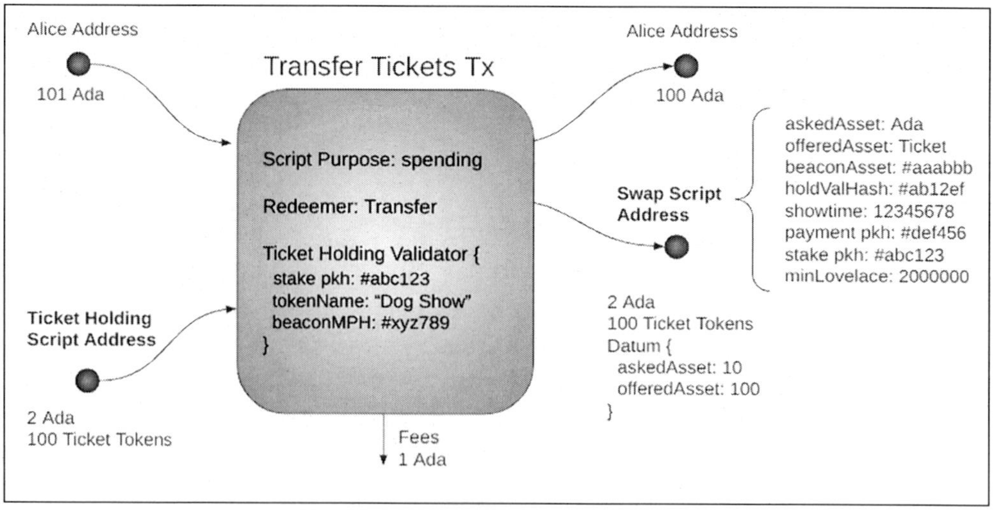

Figure 9.9: *Transfer Tickets Transaction*

As we recall from the previous section, the Beacon Token is used to easily find off-chain the swap script UTXOs. The Beacon Token minting policy outlined in *Figure 9.10* will be the same for all Beacons related to the marketplace owner, but each Beacon token name will be linked to a unique UTXO that is spent as part of the mint transaction. This is how we ensure the uniqueness of each Beacon Token. The stake **PKH** used to mint the event tickets must also sign the transaction when transferring ticket tokens to open a swap position.

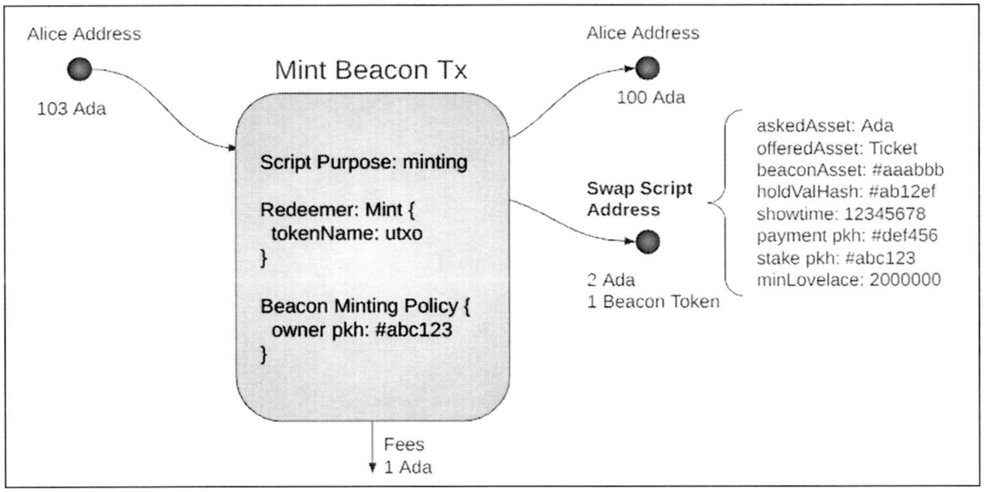

***Figure* 9.10:** *Mint Beacon Transaction*

Updating Swap

The user can update a swap position at any time if the following two conditions are true:

- The stake PKH of the wallet matches the stake **PKH** in the swap contract parameter.
- The Beacon Token specified as in the swap contract parameter is always returned to the script address.

If both conditions are true, then the smart contract will allow an update to the price, as shown in *Figure* 9.11. The types of assets being swapped, however, cannot be changed since this is hardcoded as a contract parameter.

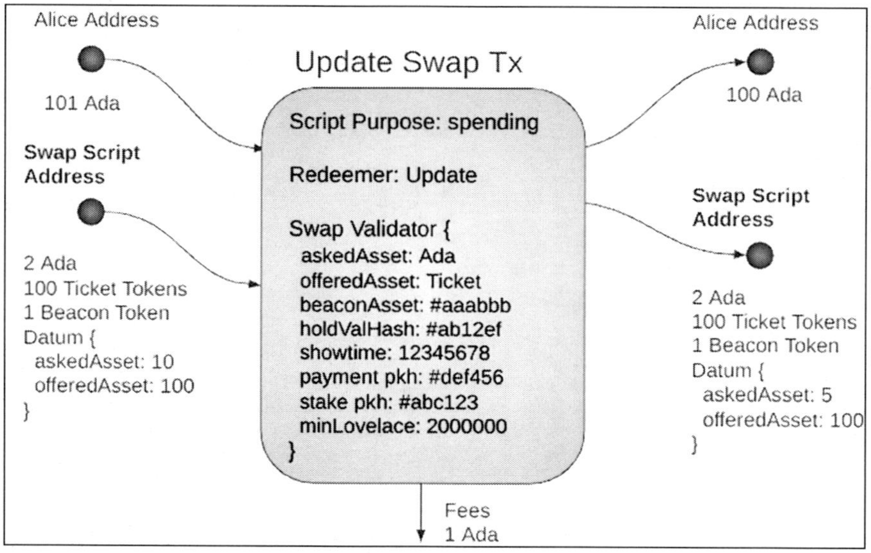

Figure 9.11: *Update Swap Transaction*

Executing Swap

Anyone can execute a swap provided that the price of **`askedAsset`** is met. The amount of **`offeredAsset`** (ticket tokens) available to purchase will be the amount of the ticket tokens locked in the swap UTXO, as shown in *Figure* 9.12. The swap validator will also ensure that the Beacon Token is always sent back to the validator script address, the seller receives the correct amount of **`askedAsset`** and the buyer receives the correct amount of **`offeredAsset`** (ticket tokens).

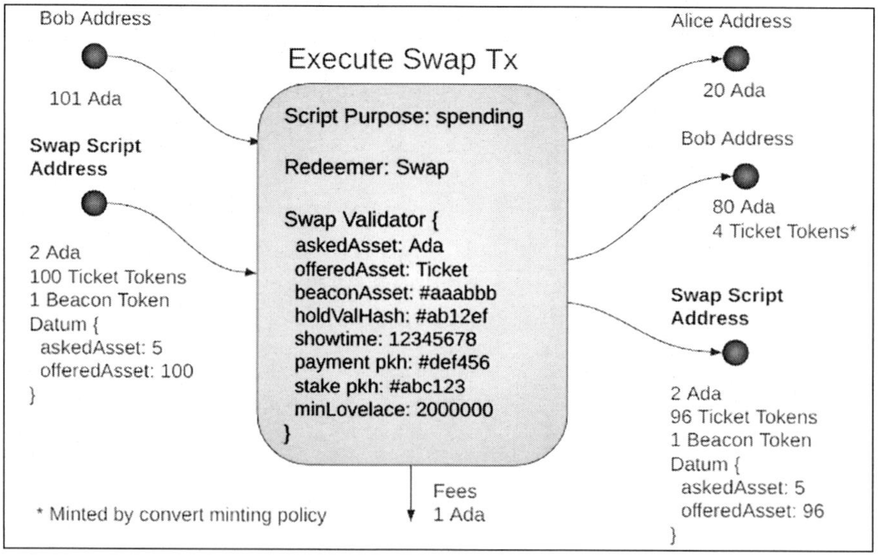

Figure 9.12: *Execute Swap Transaction*

During the swap Execute transaction, we must also convert the ticket token into a unique ticket token that can be marked *used* when entering the venue. We do this by both burning the original ticket token and minting a new one within the same transaction, as illustrated in *Figure* 9.13. The Reference Token Datum value is initially set to an empty string but will be populated with the payment PKH when the user prints their ticket.

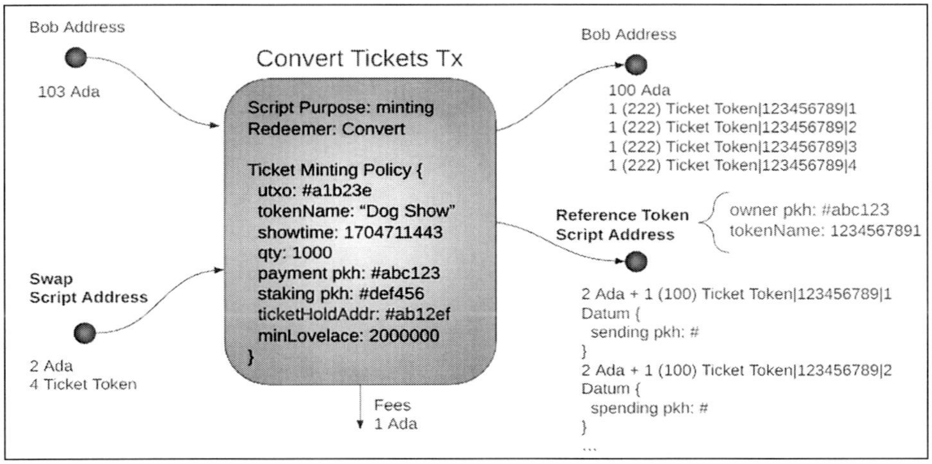

Figure 9.13: *Convert Ticket Transaction*

Closing Swap

A swap can be closed anytime by the seller, as shown in *Figure* 9.14.

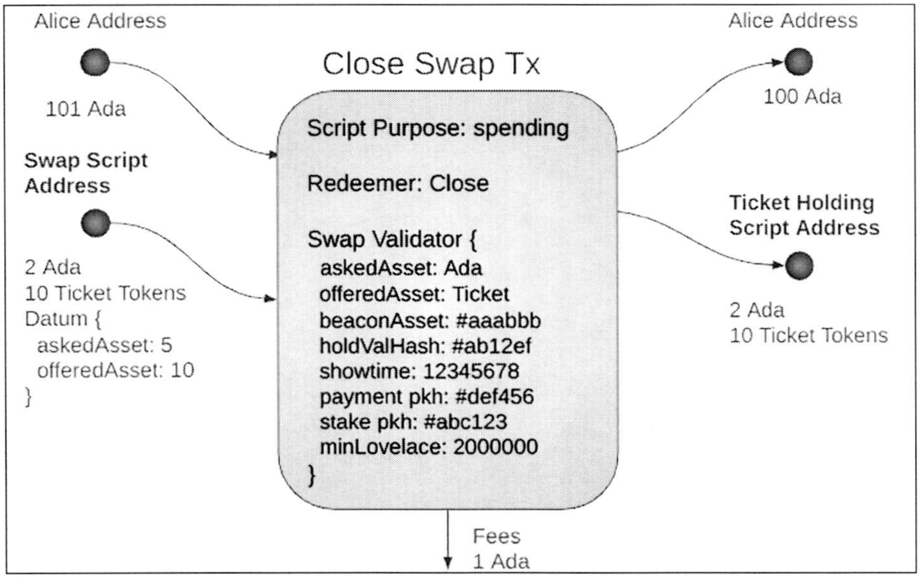

Figure 9.14: *Close Swap Transaction*

The ticket tokens must be returned to the token holding script address, defined as a swap script parameter. The Burn Beacon transaction detailed in *Figure* 9.15 must also be included in the Close Swap transaction.

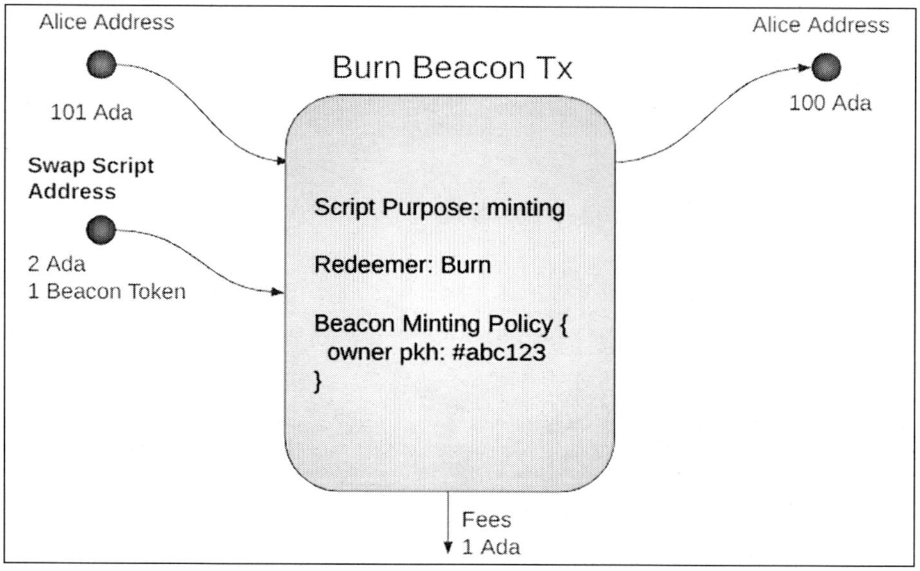

Figure 9.15: *Burn Beacon Token Transaction*

Print Ticket

To access an event, the user must prove that they, in fact, own the ticket token. This is done by using the Print Ticket transaction that will update the reference token datum with the spending PKH signed as part of the transaction, as shown in *Figure* 9.16. The application will create a QR code that can be shown later which includes a digital signature of the transaction.

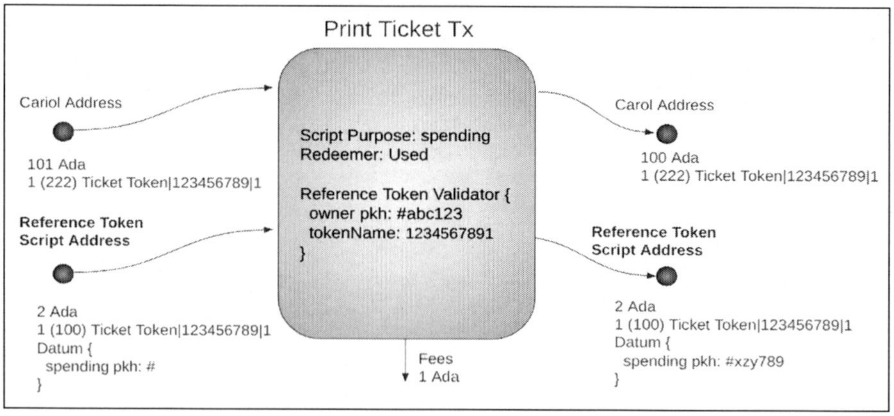

Figure 9.16: *Print Ticket*

Off-Chain Sequence Diagrams

The next section will review the high-level, happy path sequence diagrams that describe how different components within the application interact. Transactions are denoted by `[]`, and any values passed between components, if shown, are denoted by a `()`.

Minting Tickets

Minting event tickets using the application is shown in *Figure* 9.17. The first step is to get a list of UTXOs from the wallet and then build the Mint Ticket transaction. The user will sign the transaction with both their spending key to pay for the transaction costs and the staking key to prove they actually own the staking key. Once the transaction has been successfully submitted, the application database is updated to link the stake key with the new minting policy ID. An Event record is also created to show the new event to the user in the application.

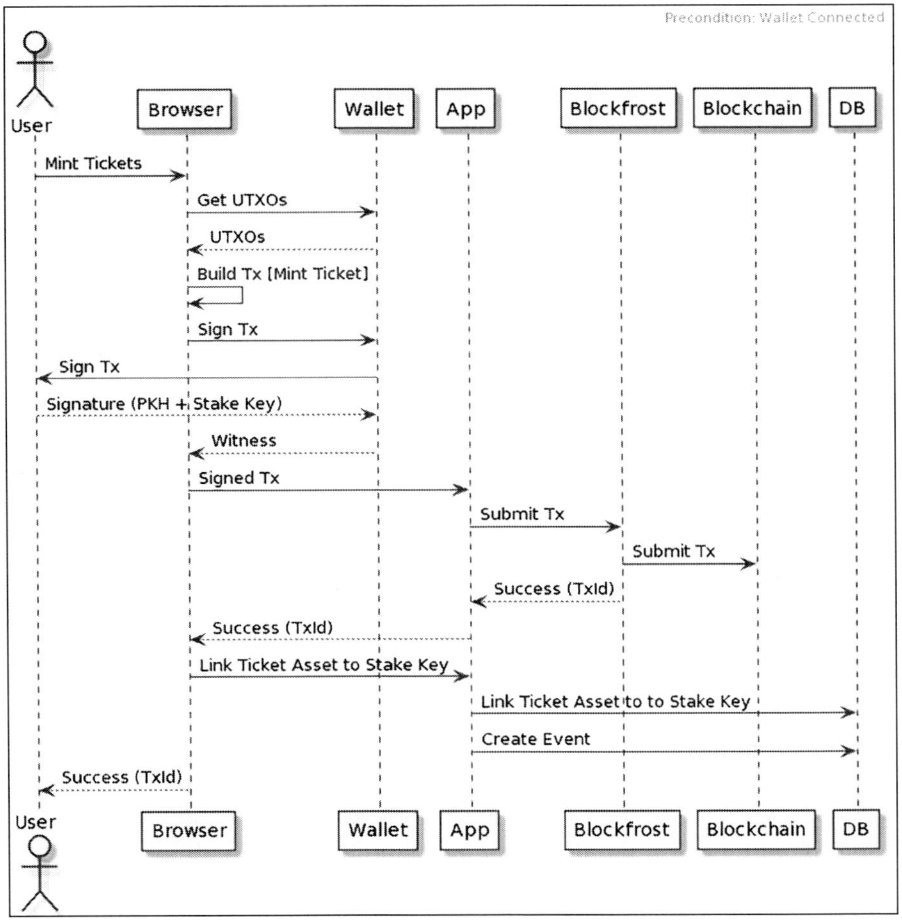

Figure 9.17: *Mint Tickets*

Connected Wallet

When a user connects with their wallet, they can see the list of events they have created, as shown in *Figure 9.18*. Additional security measures could be implemented such as requiring the user to sign with their stake key to see the list of events.

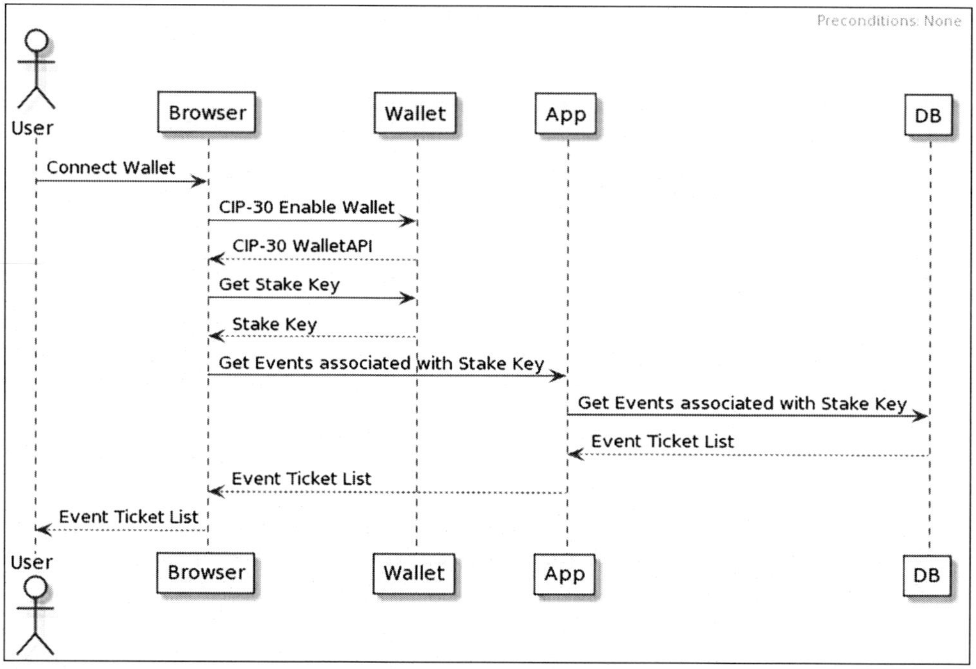

Figure 9.18: *Connect Wallet*

Opening Swap

After the tickets have been minted, the user can then decide to open a swap position and sell tickets, as shown in *Figure 9.19*. The first step is to determine what event Minting Policy Hashes (**MPHs**) belong to the user. Next, we rebuild the Ticket Holding validator to get the script address and UTXO. We then build the Transfer Ticket and Mint Beacon transaction using the wallet UTXOs, Ticket Holding UTXO, Ticket Holding, and Beacon Minting Policy scripts. The application must also sign the transaction with the owner **PKH** to be able to mint the beacon token. This is not required, but allows the application owner, if they need to, control who gets to sell tickets on the application. This could be used for a paywall, **KYC**, or fraud prevention.

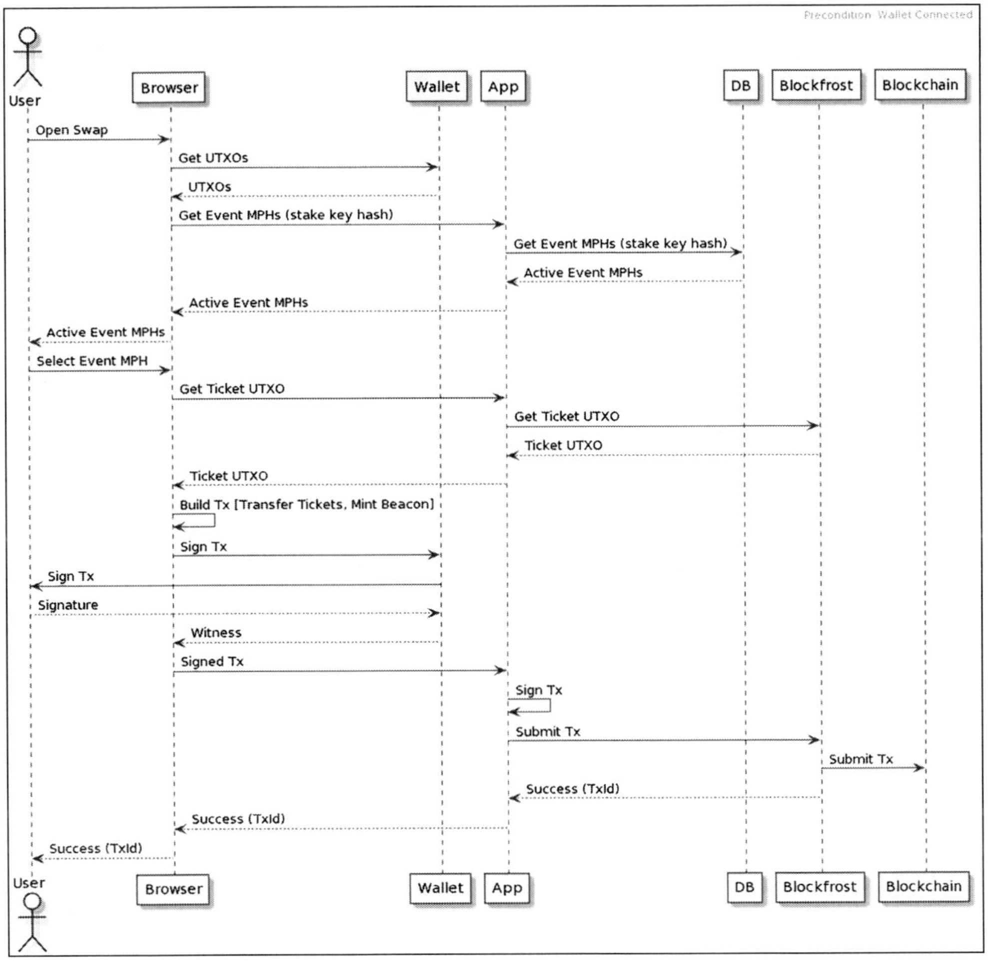

Figure 9.19: *Open Swap*

Viewing Swaps

All open swaps created by the application are available by querying the blockchain with the Beacon minting policy, as illustrated in *Figure* 9.20. The Beacon minting policy is derived from the application owner's public key hash, so anyone can query it and rebuild the minting policy script. Blockfrost will return all assets that belong to the beacon minting policy ID, which corresponds to all of the open swap positions. For our application, however, we have stored event and swap information in a database to reduce the latency and costs of each request. So, in our case, we will query the database directly to get the list of swaps, but remember that the blockchain is always the source of truth.

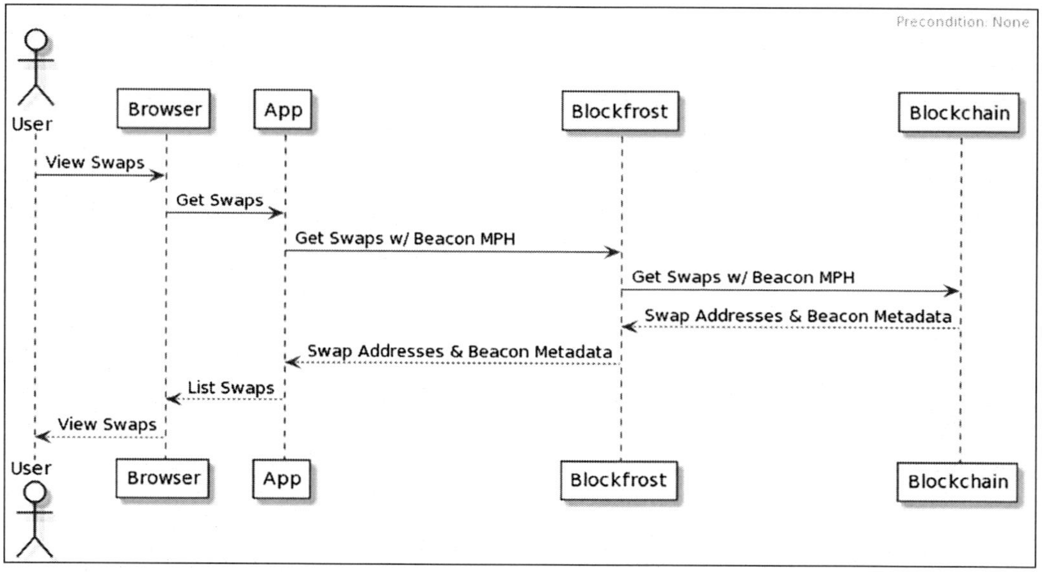

Figure 9.20: *View Swaps*

When using data replication in a local database, we need to make sure that we receive updates from the blockchain so we have current and accurate information, as shown in *Figure* 9.21.

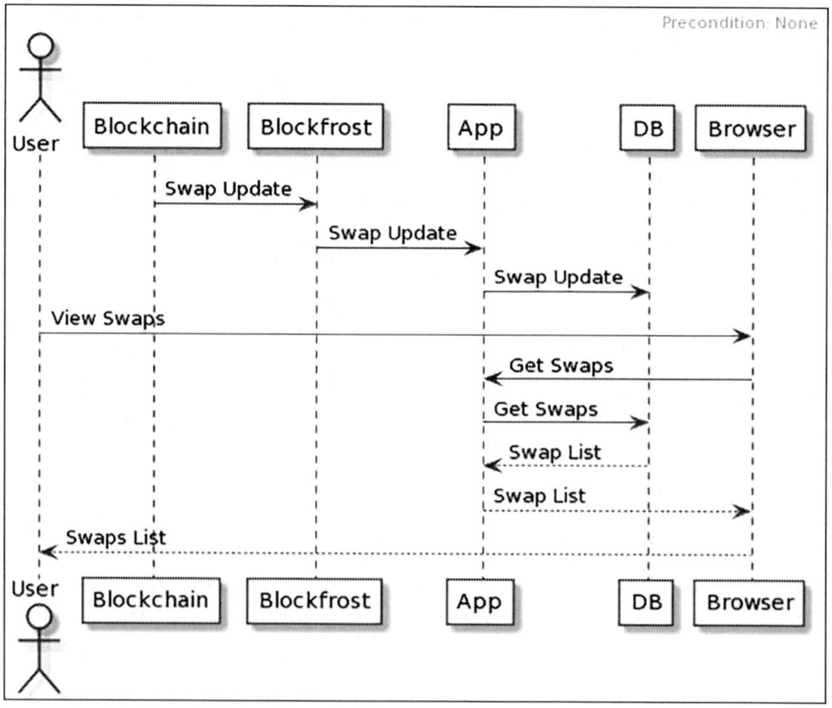

Figure 9.21: *Blockchain Swap Updates*

Updating Swap

The user can, at any time, update a swap position to change the price. They would select a swap from their own swaps, and update it with the new price (refer to *Figure 9.22*). The Beacon token for a swap is used to find the UTXO (and metadata) for a particular swap. Using the wallet UTXOs, swap UTXOS, swap metadata, and the swap script, the transaction can be built and submitted.

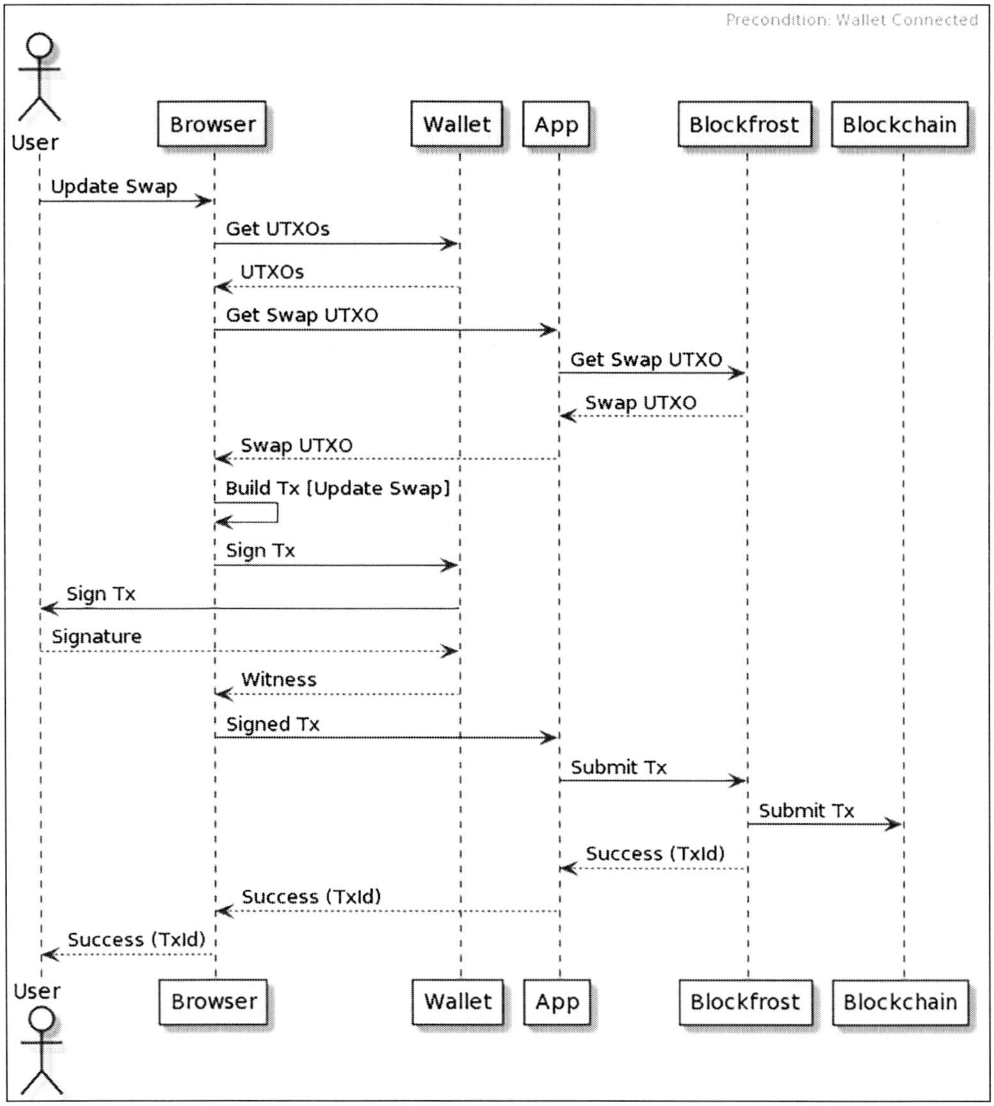

Figure 9.22: *Update Swap*

Executing Swap

A buyer can now go to the ticket application and view all available tickets for sale. If the price being paid is what is being asked for, and there is sufficient quantity for the order, then the swap will go through, as shown in *Figure* 9.23. Using the wallet UTXOs and the swap UTXO, the value paid for the ticket is sent directly to the seller's address and the buyer receives the ticket token(s). During the ticket conversion, a reference token is created for each unique ticket token minted. This reference token can only be updated by the application and contains a flag to indicate if a token has been used or not at an event.

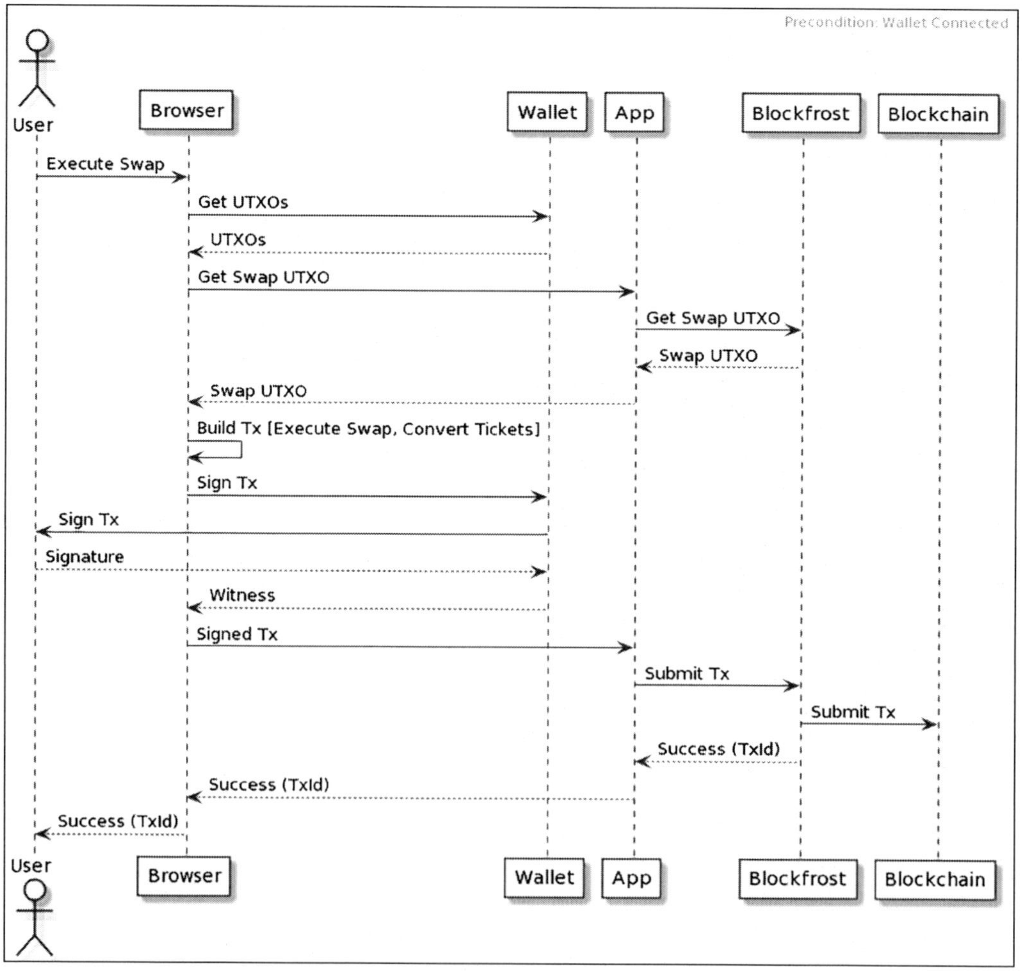

Figure 9.23: *Execute Swap*

Closing Swap

A seller will want to close a swap when either the amount of tickets in the swap is zero, or if they no longer want to make the tickets available for sale (refer to *Figure* 9.24). The Beacon asset is used to get the swap UTXO needed to build the swap transaction and send the ticket tokens (if any) back to the ticket holding address. The Beacon token is also burned as part of the close transaction, so the swap will no longer appear in the list of available swaps.

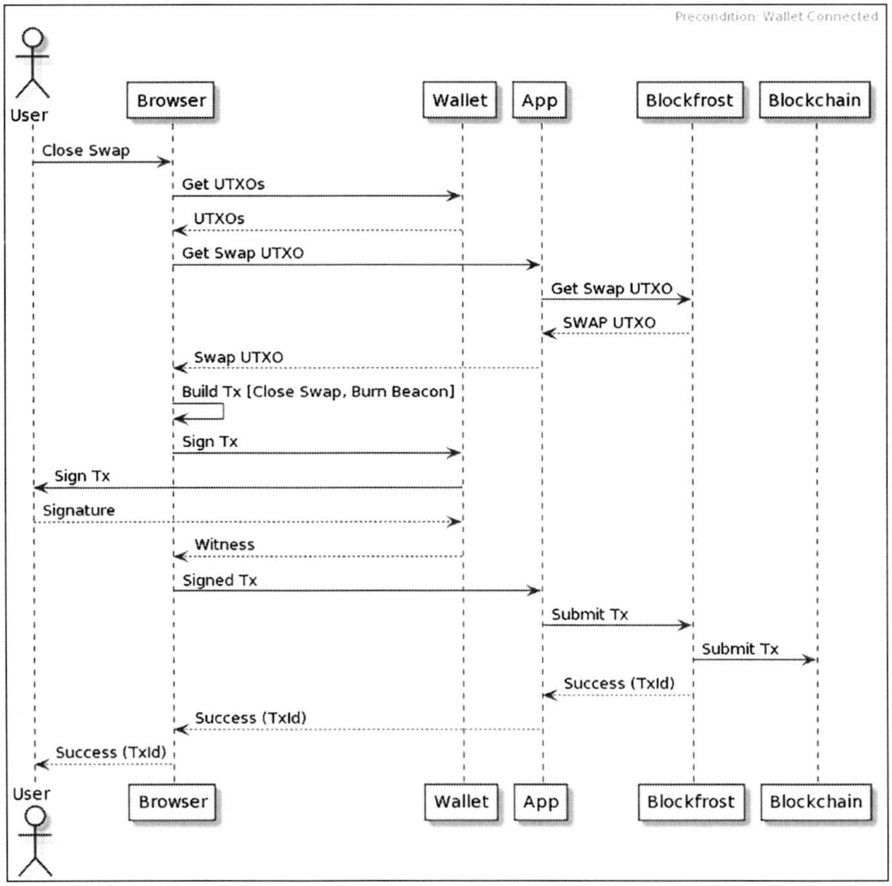

Figure 9.24: *Close Swap*

Print Ticket

The ticket application is also used to redeem event tickets to access an event. A user will show a QR code that verifies ownership and this can be done any time before (or at) the event. The QR code is a digital signature that is generated when they have signed a transaction with a wallet that has the ticket token. During the Print Ticket transaction, the reference token datum is updated with the wallet spending PKH. This is then used at the event to validate the spending PKH with the QR code shown. After verifying the QR code at the event, the ticket will be marked used in the application DB, as shown in *Figure 9.25*.

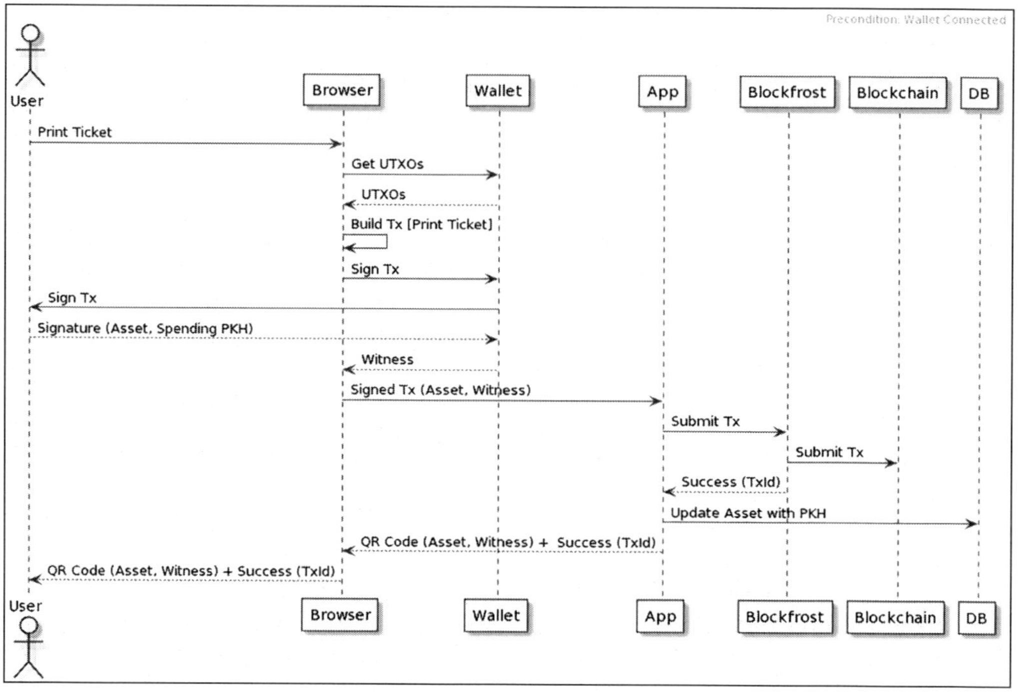

Figure 9.25: *Show Ticket*

Verifying Ticket

QR code generation can be done in advance. This avoids having the user bring their wallet to the event venue and submit blockchain transactions at the time of entry. Since the reference token datum may be updated with a payment **PKH** if printed, it is important that the ticket is verified before any secondary transfer. The application has an API that allows for querying the blockchain to confirm if a ticket has been shown or if it has been used to access an event, as shown in *Figure 9.26*.

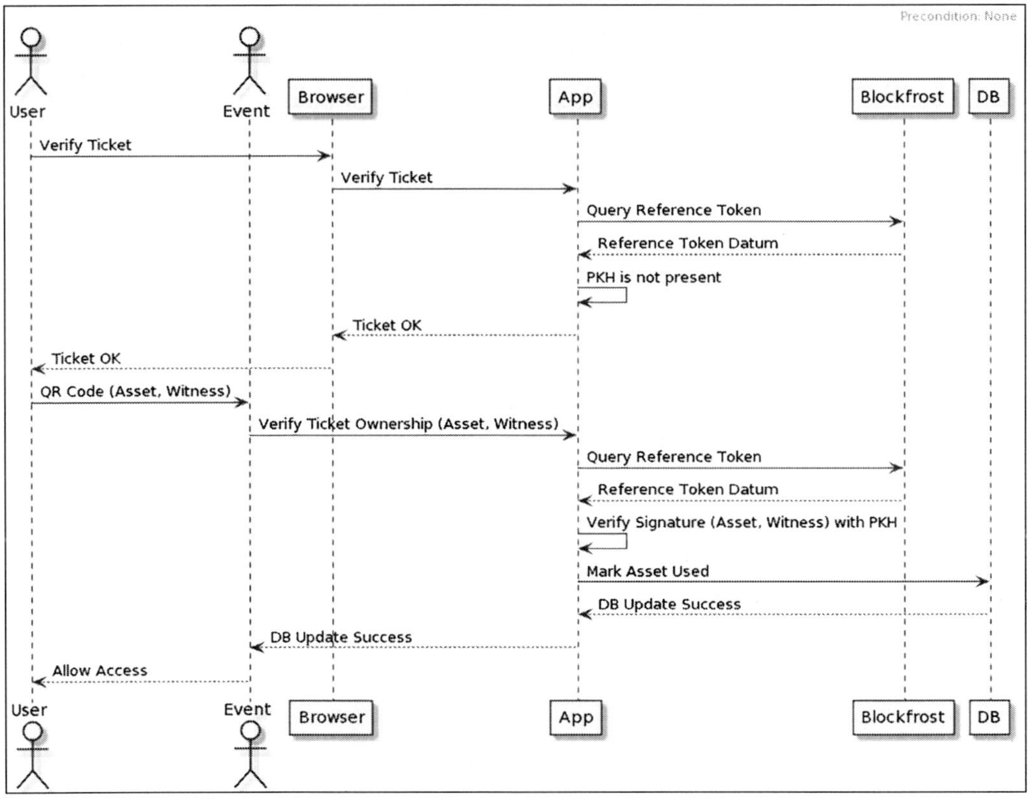

Figure 9.26: *Verify Ticket*

Conclusion

In this chapter, we understood the Thread Token, Beacon Token, and Order Book design patterns and how they leverage the benefits of EUTXO architecture. We looked at anti-patterns such as pools and batchers that typically lead to sub-optimal designs on UTXO blockchains such as Cardano. We explored several Cardano Improvement Proposals (CIPs) and how they relate to our application design. In particular, CIP-0068 was reviewed, as to how it provides a different way to store token metadata using datums. We then started to work on the design for the ticket application using the design patterns and standards reviewed in this chapter. Next, we created state transition diagrams with inputs and outputs for each use case. Then, we created sequence diagrams showing the interactions between system components. We are ready to implement the ticket application in the next chapter, *Chapter 10, Ticket Application Implementation.*

Points to Remember

- Account model design patterns are generally not well suited for an EUTXO architecture.
- The Thread Token design pattern uses a unique token to help isolate a specific UTXO locked at a script address.
- A Beacon Token design pattern uses a unique token to easily identify a particular UTXO off-chain.
- A Beacon Token can be used for both the Thread Token and Beacon Token design patterns.
- The Order Book design pattern is well suited for the EUTXO architecture because UTXOs are immutable, unique, and independent of each other.
- Identifying atomic swap pairs can be done using off-chain computation.
- A Swap is executed on-chain and does not involve any third party intermediary.
- Atomic swaps retain full self-custody and can be canceled at any time.
- An Order Book design pattern can be applied to many different use cases
- Liquidity Pools and Batches are examples of anti-patterns with sub-optimal performance and scalability
- The CIP-0068 Metadata standard uses Datums to store metadata for NFTs or FTs which can be updateable.
- The Mint Ticket transaction uses CIP-0025 transaction metadata to publish the minting script parameters.
- The Open Swap transaction needs to include both Transfer Ticket (**`ticket.hl`**) and Mint Beacon (**`beacon.hl`**) in the same transaction.
- The Execute Swap transaction needs to include both Execute Swap (**`swap.hl`**) and Convert Token (**`ticket.hl`**) in the same transaction.
- Convert Ticket uses CIP-0068 with a Datum value to save a payment PKH for event ticket verification.
- Update Swap and Close Swap can only be done by the wallet that created the swap and can be done at any time.
- When printing a ticket for an event, the user must sign a transaction with the wallet's public key to prove ownership of the ticket token.

Multiple Choice Questions

1. How can a Plutus script ensure a correct state transition?
    a. Use an on-chain oracle
    b. Use off-chain metadata
    c. Use a Thread Token
    d. Use a Reference Script
2. Why is EUTXO architecture well suited for Order Books?
    a. Uses an account model
    b. Uses local state
    c. Uses global state
    d. UTXO contention
3. What CIP allows a Smart Contract access to metadata?
    a. CIP-0068
    b. CIP-0031
    c. CIP-0025
    d. CIP-0033
4. How are Order Book swaps usually identified?
    a. Thread Token
    b. Metadata
    c. Beacon Token
    d. UTXO
5. Why must a user sign a transaction to verify ticket token ownership?
    a. Prove the ticket token is unique
    b. Show that the ticket has not already been used
    c. Prove that the ticket is located at the spending address of the wallet
    d. To prevent the ticket from being burned

Answers

1. c
2. b
3. a
4. c
5. c

Questions

1. What are some of the disadvantages of the Order Book design pattern?
2. When do you want to use Reference Scripts?
3. What was the motivation behind CIP-0068?
4. How do we avoid double spending when processing tickets at an event?
5. What will happen to the application if a blockchain rollback occurs?

Key Terms

- **Anti-Patterns:** Design patterns that should be avoided.
- **FT:** Fungible Token
- **KYC:** Know Your Customer
- **MPH:** Minting Policy Hash
- **NFT:** Non-Fungible Token
- **PKH:** Public Key Hash
- **P2P:** Peer-to-Peer communication
- **State Channel:** Segmenting a set of UTXOs to be processed off-chain chain that mirrors the same protocol as the base layer.
- **State Machine:** Describes system state transition lifecycles.
- **UTXO:** Unspent Transaction Outputs
- **UTXO Contention:** A concurrency issue with more than one transaction is trying to spend a UTXO input.
- **Zero Knowledge**: Uses cryptography to prove a claim without revealing the details of the claim.

CHAPTER 10
Ticket Application Implementation

Introduction

In this chapter, we will walk through the implementation of the ticket application, including blockchain integration. We will start with an overview of the system components and application stack, which include CharkraUI, Next.js, Redis DB, and Blockfrost. Next, we will look at the front-end and off-chain code that is used to build the transactions that we defined in *Chapter 9, Ticket Application Design*. Then, we will examine the corresponding Smart Contract on-chain code, business logic, and validation rules. We will look at the back-end components, such as the Redis DB schema set up to cache and query relevant blockchain data. We will also look at the application APIs and Blockfrost webhooks that are called when a blockchain event occurs. Finally, we will run through an end-to-end demo of the application.

Structure

In this chapter, we will discuss the following topics:

- Application Stack
- Application Resources
- Front-end Components
- Smart Contracts
- Back-end Components
- Application Demo
- Blockchain Benefits

Application Stack

In our ticketing application, we need the ability to search and filter on an arbitrary number of swaps that contain tickets for sale. This can be done efficiently if we store the swap details in an application database with indexes for quick access. The source of truth, however, will always be the blockchain, and the database is simply a cached copy of the blockchain data. By introducing data replication, we must ensure that the database is updated accordingly when a transaction is submitted to the blockchain. *Figure* 10.1 shows how swap searches are queried against the local application database, which is continually updated as new relevant blockchain data arrives via a Blockfrost webhook.

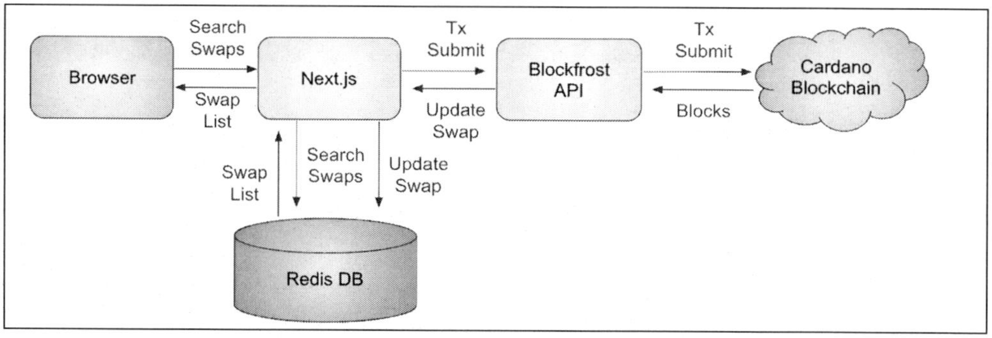

***Figure* 10.1:** *System Components*

Next.js will be used as the application server framework for building the html and JavaScript components. The application will also use a Redis DB with a **full stack JSON** and search modules for fast, in-memory database storage and retrieval. For improved error handling and troubleshooting, all transactions will be submitted using the Blockfrost API. This approach allows us to easily change the blockchain API service provider if required to do so. We will also use Blockfrost webhooks to monitor the blockchain for transaction confirmations that involve a swap created by the end user.

Application Resources

The application uses the Next.js directory structure, as shown in *Figure* 10.2.

```
└── ticket-app/
    ├── assets
    ├── common
    ├── components
    ├── config
    ├── init
    ├── lib
    ├── node_modules
    ├── pages/
    │   └── api
    ├── public/
    │   └── contracts
    └── schema
```

***Figure* 10.2:** *Next.js Directory Structure*

Common

The **`common`** folder contains client-side JavaScript code that may be used by one or more UI components. The following files are found in this directory:

- **`metadata.ts`**: used for creating transaction metadata
- **`network.ts`**: used for interacting with network APIs
- **`orders.ts`**: used for order calculations
- **`types.ts`**: defines custom data types
- **`utils.ts`**: includes utility functions

Components

All React **functional components** are located in this folder, which are used to build out the application web pages or popup windows.

Config

This folder defines the application settings, which include the list of supported wallets, network, theme settings, and compilation flags, if applicable.

Init

The **`init`** folder contains a command line script for generating the application owner's public and private keys. The owner public key is used when minting the beacon token so that we can identify all swaps created by this application instance.

Lib

The **`lib`** folder contains JavaScript libraries needed by the Redis connection library.

Node Modules

This folder stores all of the npm node modules and is created automatically when the **`npm install`** command is executed.

Pages

The **`pages`** folder contains all of the web pages and popup windows that are used in the application.

Pages / API

The **`api`** folder includes all of the application API interfaces called by client-side JavaScript and any webhooks called by Blockfrost. All client-side JavaScript network calls are made through these application APIs to avoid browser CORS errors and API key leakage.

Public

The public folder contains all static, publicly available resources such as icons and images.

Public/Contracts

The `contracts` folder contains all of the Smart Contract on-chain code. In particular, it contains all the business logic for the Smart Contracts that we need for this application:

- **`beacon.hl`**: Smart Contract for the beacon minting policy
- **`holding.hl`**: Smart Contract for the ticket holding validator
- **`swap.hl`**: Smart Contract for all swap operations (open, update, close, and execute)
- **`ticket.hl`**: Smart Contract for the ticket minting policy

Schema

The `schema` folder contains the database schemas used to define the data structures that will be stored in the Redis database. These include the following:

- **`beacon.ts`**: This schema is used to store and keep track of beacons created by the application so they can be retrieved easily.
- **`event.ts`**: The event schema is used to store event information locally that is linked to the stake key hash of the user.
- **`stake.ts`**: The stake schema maps all of the event assets created to a user's wallet stake key.
- **`swap.ts`**: The swap schema stores swap information so that the swap can be quickly retrieved, filtered, and shown to the user.

Front-end Application

The full source code is located on the GitHub repository, so this section will look at only code fragments to highlight the key aspects of the application. The application is a single-page application with React functional components, as shown in *Figure 10.3*. Chakra UI was chosen for its ease of use and out-of-the-box components and is used for all of the styles and front-end UI components. For more information on Chakra, please see their documentation.[1]

[1]https://chakra-ui.com/

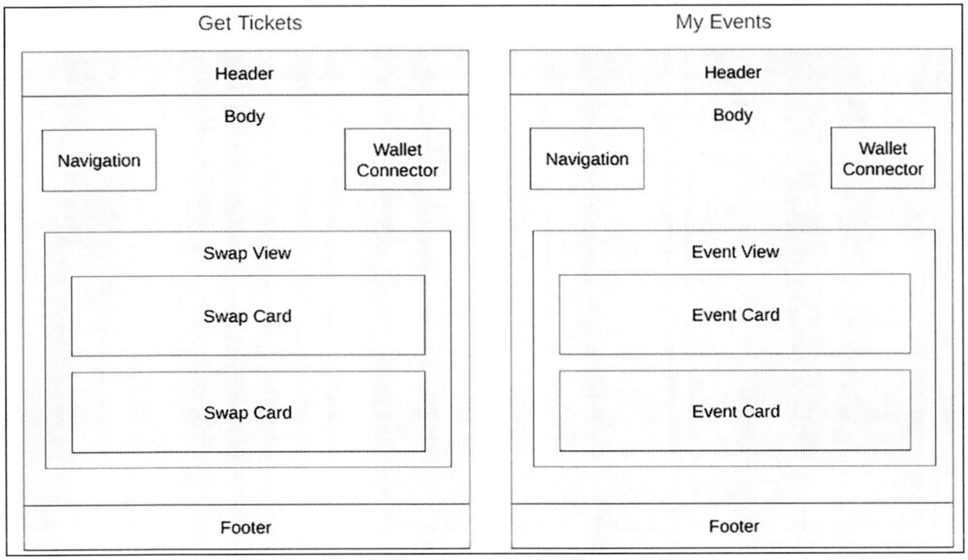

Figure 10.3*: React Functional Components*

The main entry point to the application is located in **`pages/index.tsx`** with a tab navigation containing the Get Tickets, My Events, and My Tickets views. The **`index.tsx`** page also contains the following global state variable information:

- **`walletAPI`**: The **`walletAPI`** JavaScript object for the browser extension wallet.
- **`walletInfo`** lists the wallet base address, stake address, lovelace balance, and event assets associated with this wallet.
- **`swapViewRefresh`** will trigger a **`useEffect`** to refresh the list of swaps to show to the user. This is called when a change is made to a swap such as opening, updating, or closing a swap.

Header and Footer

The Header and Footer components are included in the **`components/layout.tsx`** file and contain static information only.

Wallet Connector

The wallet connector is a key component and contains the logic to connect to the **`walletAPI`** object and saves the wallet information to a **`useState`** variable in **`pages/index.tsx`**. The **`walletAPI`** and **`walletInfo`** variables are made available to all other components by passing them as props to every child and sub-child component. We build upon the same code and logic for connecting to a user wallet as discussed in *Chapter 5, Transaction Builder*. To improve the user experience, a list of installed and supported browser wallets is presented to the user to select from, as shown in *Figure 10.4*.

```
async function getAvailableWallets (): Promise<WalletChoice[]> {
  const wallets: WalletChoice[] = [];
  walletSupported.forEach((wallet: WalletChoice) => {
    if (isValidName(wallet.name)) {
      if (window?.cardano && isValidAPI(wallet.api, window.cardano)) {
        wallets.push(wallet);
      }
    }
```

Figure 10.4: *Get Available Wallets*[2]

There also exists a Wallet Connect[3] component created by the Cardano Foundation. However, due to overlap and duplication with the off-chain transaction builder frameworks, we will not be using it.

Swap View

The swap view component obtains a list of swaps by calling **`getFilterSwaps()`** on line 43 in *Figure* 10.5. Filters will only be applied if they are set by the user using the **`Filter`** Button on the Get Tickets tab. SWR[4] is used to cache the list of Swaps unless the **`getFilterSwaps()`** returns a different result.

```
43  const { data } = useSWR(filter, getFilterSwaps, {
44    refreshInterval: 15000  // 15s refresh
45  });
46  const swapsPerPage = 2;
47  const startIndex = (page - 1) * swapsPerPage;
48  const endIndex = startIndex + swapsPerPage;
49  const displayedSwaps = data?.slice(startIndex, endIndex);
50  const { mutate } = useSWRConfig();
51  useEffect( () => {
52    const filterSwaps = async () => {
53        try {
54          await mutate(filter); // trigger cache refresh
55        } catch (err) {
56          console.log("No swaps found"); // No swaps found
57        }
58    }
59     filterSwaps();
60  }, [props.swapRefresh, filter]);
```

Figure 10.5: *Get FilterSwaps*[5]

[2] https://github.com/ava-orange-education/Mastering-Cardano-Smart-Contracts/blob/main/chapter_10/helios/ticket-app/pages/WalletPopup.tsx
[3] https://github.com/cardano-foundation/cardano-connect-with-wallet
[4] https://swr.vercel.app/
[5] https://github.com/ava-orange-education/Mastering-Cardano-Smart-Contracts/blob/main/chapter_10/helios/ticket-app/components/SwapView.tsx

The array of swaps returned populates each swap card and paginates the view if necessary. Filter parameters are defined as state variables in the **SwapView** component and applied to the database query. The list of filter parameters is shown in *Figure* 10.6.

```
const [filter, setFilter] = useState<Filter>({
    text: '',
    offeredAsset: '',
    offeredAssetQty: '',
    startDate: '',
    endDate: '',
    askedAsset:'',
    askedAssetQty:''
});
```

Figure 10.6: *Filter Parameters*[6]

The API call to **pages/api/getFilterSwaps.ts** first creates a record object of the key/value filter parameters, as shown in *Figure* 10.7.

```
if (req.method === 'POST') {
  try {
    let query = {};
    for (const key in req.body.filter) {
      if (Object.prototype.hasOwnProperty.call(req.body.filter, key)) {
          if (allowedFields.includes(key) && req.body.filter[key] !== '') {
              query = {
                ...query,
                [key]: req.body.filter[key]
              }
          }
      }
    }
    const swaps = await dynamicQuery(query);
    res.status(200).send(swaps);
```

Figure 10.7: *getFilterSwaps API*[7]

The record object is then passed to the **dynamicQuery()** function in *Figure* 10.8, which dynamically constructs the Redis database query and returns a filtered list of swaps.

[6]https://github.com/ava-orange-education/Mastering-Cardano-Smart-Contracts/blob/main/chapter_10/helios/ticket-app/components/SwapView.tsx
[7]https://github.com/ava-orange-education/Mastering-Cardano-Smart-Contracts/blob/main/chapter_10/helios/ticket-app/pages/api/getFilterSwaps.ts

```
async function dynamicQuery(criteria: Record<string, any>) {
  let query = swapRepository.search();
  for (const [key, value] of Object.entries(criteria)) {
    if (key === "offeredAsset" || key === "askedAsset") {
      query = query.where(key).equals(value);
    }
    if (key === "offeredAssetQty") {
      query = query.where(key).gte(value);
    }
    if (key === "askedAssetQty") {
      query = query.where(key).lte(value);
    }
    if (key === "startDate") {
      const time = (new Date(value)).getTime();
      query = query.where('deadline').gte(time);
    }
    if (key === "endDate") {
      const time = (new Date(value)).getTime();
      query = query.where('deadline').lte(time);
    }
    if (key === "text") {
      query = query.where('name').matches(value)
                   .or('location').matches(value)
                   .or('description').matches(value);
```

Figure 10.8: *Redis Database Dynamic Query*[8]

Swap Card

Each Swap Card is passed the **`swap`**, **`walletAPI`**, **`walletInfo,`** and **`setSwapViewRefresh`** as props, as shown in *Figure 10.9*. These variables and functions display the Swap Card and are also passed to the **`ExecuteSwap`**, **`UpdateSwap`**, or **`Close Swap`** popup windows to build and submit a transaction.

```
interface SwapViewProps {
  walletAPI: any,
  walletInfo: WalletInfo,
  swapRefresh: number,
  setSwapViewRefresh: (swapRefresh: number) => void;
}
```

Figure 10.9: *SwapCardProps Interface*[9]

To execute a swap, a user selects the "**`Buy`**" button that changes the **`buySwapOpen`** variable to true. When this occurs, the **`ExecuteSwapPopup`** page component is shown to the user (see *Figure 10.10*).

[8]https://github.com/ava-orange-education/Mastering-Cardano-Smart-Contracts/blob/main/chapter_10/helios/ticket-app/pages/api/getFilterSwaps.ts

[9]https://github.com/ava-orange-education/Mastering-Cardano-Smart-Contracts/blob/main/chapter_10/helios/ticket-app/components/SwapCard.tsx

```
                <ExecuteSwapPopup
                    isOpen={buySwapOpen}
                    onClose={setBuySwapOpen}
                    event={event}
                    swap={props.swap}
                    setSwapViewRefresh={props.setSwapViewRefresh}
                    buyQty={Number(buyQty)}
                    walletAPI={props.walletAPI}
                />
            </>
```

Figure 10.10: *Execute Swap Popup Component*[10]

Event View

The layout of the event page is similar to the swap view but requires the user to connect their wallet. Each event is linked to the wallet's stake key, so we must connect the wallet first before creating a new event or seeing events already created.

Event Card

The Event View contains Event Cards for each event linked to the connected wallet. The user can either sell tickets or archive the event. It also displays event statistics, such as the number of tickets allocated, released, and converted. All of this information is available on the blockchain, but we also update the database directly to provide faster, real-time updates within the application.

My Tickets

On the **`My Tickets`** screen, the user is able to see the tickets that they currently have in their browser wallet with relevant metadata information such as event image, name, location, and showtime. This is also where the user can print each ticket and view the verification QR code, as shown in *Figure 10.11*. The NFT event tickets are Cardano native tokens, so they can also be viewed directly within the wallet or transferred to any other wallet or dApp, just like Ada.

[10]https://github.com/ava-orange-education/Mastering-Cardano-Smart-Contracts/blob/main/chapter_10/helios/ticket-app/components/SwapCard.tsx

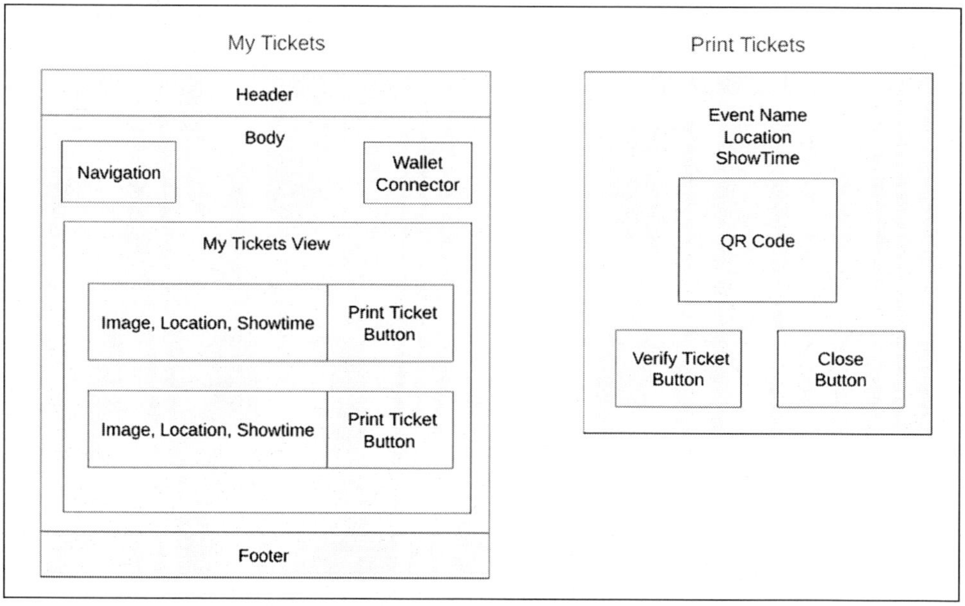

Figure 10.11: *My Tickets View*

Print Tickets

When the **`Print Ticket`** Button is selected, a **`Print Ticket`** popup window will appear and allow the user to generate the QR code. Once the transaction is signed and the reference ticket CIP-68 metadata is updated, the QR code will be displayed. The signing of the transaction proves that they control the private key corresponding to the public key that the ticket asset is locked at. When the QR code is presented to the venue, the unique ticket will be marked used in the application DB to prevent double-redeeming of the ticket.

The **`Verify`** Button in *Figure 10.11* can be used to simulate a ticket redemption and granting access to an event. The QR code can be generated and saved in advance, which avoids having the user bring their wallet to the event venue and submitting a blockchain transaction at the time of entry. If the event ticket token is subsequently transferred to another person, the reference token datum history should be checked to confirm that it has not already been printed (or redeemed). The QR code is a string that includes the ticket asset name (minting policy hash + token name), the transaction hash, and the **witness signature** for the transaction that was signed and submitted, as shown in *Figure 10.12*.

```
    toast({
      title: "Print Ticket Success",
      description: <Box fontSize='x-small'>TxId: {txHash}</Box>,
      duration: 10000,
      isClosable: true,
      position: 'bottom-right',
      status: 'success'
    })
    setIsLoading(false)

    const qrCode = props.ticket.asset + "|" + txHash + "|" + signatures[0].toCborHex()
    setQRCode(qrCode)
```

Figure 10.12: *QR Code Generation*[11]

Transaction Builder

The off-chain transaction builder code for swap operations such as open, update, execute, and close is done inside a popup window. When a popup window is enabled, a **`useEffect`** is triggered to call the appropriate function to build the off-chain transactions, as shown in *Figure* 10.13.

```
useEffect(() => {
  const executeSwapStart = async () => {
    await executeSwap();
  };
  if (props.isOpen) {
  executeSwapStart();
  }
}, [props.isOpen]);
```

Figure 10.13: *Execute Swap useEffect*[12]

The off-chain code follows a similar pattern to the off-chain builder code in previous chapters. For an Execute Swap transaction, we will apply the contract parameters to build the Plutus script. If the swap validation is successful, we use the ticket minting policy to convert each ticket. Following the CIP-68 Metadata NFT standard, both the NFT token and the reference token are minted. On lines 224–227 in *Figure* 10.14, both the NFT tokens and the reference tokens are added to arrays that contain the total number of tokens to mint.

[11]https://github.com/ava-orange-education/Mastering-Cardano-Smart-Contracts/blob/main/chapter_10/helios/ticket-app/pages/PrintTicketPopup.tsx
[12]https://github.com/ava-orange-education/Mastering-Cardano-Smart-Contracts/blob/main/chapter_10/helios/ticket-app/pages/ExecuteSwapPopup.tsx

```
// Build unique token name for each converted ticket
// and follow CIP-68 & CIP-67 label convention
const label222hex = "000de140";   // NFT Token Label
const label100hex = "000643b0";   // Reference Token Label
let ticketTokenNames: string[] = [];
let refTokenNames: string[] = [];
for(let i=0; i < props.buyQty; i++) {

  const nftTicketName = props.swap.name + "|" + orderId + "|" +  i.toString();
  const nftTicketNameLabel = label222hex + Buffer
                                    .from(nftTicketName)
                                    .toString('hex');
  const ticketToken = [hexToBytes(nftTicketNameLabel),
                       BigInt(1)] as [number[], bigint];

  const refTokenNameLabel = label100hex + Buffer
                                    .from(nftTicketName)
                                    .toString('hex');
  const refToken = [hexToBytes(refTokenNameLabel),
                    BigInt(1)] as [number[], bigint];
  ticketTokenNames.push(nftTicketNameLabel);
  ticketTokens.push(ticketToken);
  refTokenNames.push(refTokenNameLabel);
  refTokens.push(refToken);
```

Figure 10.14: *Convert Tickets*[13]

During the swap transaction, we update the datum and create the outputs that will satisfy the business logic in the swap validator. This will ensure that the asking price and the amount of offered assets are correct. The **`calcOrderDetails()`** function determines the values that must be sent to the buyer and seller and returned to the swap, as shown in *Figure* 10.15.

```
// Calc the values to be sent to the buyer, seller and swap
const orderDetails = await calcOrderDetails(swapUtxo,
                                            swapAskedAssetValue,
                                            props.swap);

// Construct the swap datum
const swapDatum = new (swapValidator.types.Datum)(
  orderDetails.askedAssetVal,     // askedAsset
  orderDetails.offeredAssetVal,    // offeredAsset
)
```

Figure 10.15: *Calc Order Details*[14]

In the ticket application, we also introduce the concept of time to ensure that a swap transaction is executed within a specific period of time. It is best practice to explicitly set the **time interval,** which must be set when checking for time constraints within a Plutus script. *Figure* 10.16 shows a typical off-chain validity interval.

[13]https://github.com/ava-orange-education/Mastering-Cardano-Smart-Contracts/blob/main/chapter_10/helios/ticket-app/pages/ExecuteSwapPopup.tsx
[14]https://github.com/ava-orange-education/Mastering-Cardano-Smart-Contracts/blob/main/chapter_10/helios/ticket-app/pages/ExecuteSwapPopup.tsx

```
    // Specify when this transaction is valid from. This is needed so
    // time is included in the transaction which will be use by the
    // scripts. Add two hours for time to live and offset the current time
    // by 5 mins.
    const currentTime = new Date().getTime();
    const earlierTime = new Date(currentTime - 5 * 60 * 1000);
    const laterTime = new Date(currentTime + 2 * 60 * 60 * 1000);

    tx.validFrom(earlierTime);
    tx.validTo(laterTime);
```

Figure 10.16: *Time Validity Interval*[15]

Once a validity interval has been set, a Plutus script can determine if a transaction occurs before, after, or during a specified time interval. In the next section, we will look at the on-chain code since we need to ensure the swap does not execute after a specific deadline (for example, showtime).

If the transaction is successfully built, signed, and submitted then we update the application database to increment the ticket converted amount and decrement the offered quantity in the swap. We will also include the transaction ID and set the confirmation flag to false on lines 481–482 in *Figure* 10.17. There will be a Blockfrost webhook to make a callback to the application after 3 block confirmations and to set the confirm flag to **`true`.** Finally, a call to **`handleClose()`** on line 493 is used to force a refresh of the swaps and events in the **`Swap View`** and **`Event View`**, respectively.

```
470       // Update event to DB
471       const eventUpdate = {
472         ...props.event,
473         released: props.event.released - props.buyQty,
474         converted: props.event.converted + props.buyQty
475       }
476       await updateEvent(eventUpdate);
477       // Update swap to DB
478       const swapUpdate = {
479           ...props.swap,
480           offeredAssetQty: props.swap.offeredAssetQty - props.buyQty,
481           txId: txHash.hex,
482           confirmed: false
483       }
484       await updateSwap(swapUpdate);
485       toast({
486         title: "Ticket Purchase Success",
487         description: <Box fontSize='x-small'>TxId: {txHash.hex}</Box>,
488         duration: 10000,
489         isClosable: true,
490         position: 'bottom-right',
491         status: 'success'
492       })
493       await handleClose()
```

Figure 10.17: *Swap and Event DB Updates*[16]

[15]https://github.com/ava-orange-education/Mastering-Cardano-Smart-Contracts/blob/main/chapter_10/helios/ticket-app/pages/ExecuteSwapPopup.tsx
[16]https://github.com/ava-orange-education/Mastering-Cardano-Smart-Contracts/blob/main/chapter_10/helios/ticket-app/pages/ExecuteSwapPopup.tsx

Smart Contracts

The ticket application on-chain code involves the following Plutus scripts:

- Beacon Minting Policy
- Ticket Minting Policy
- Holding Validator
- Swap Validator

Beacon Minting Policy

The beacon on-chain code is passed a transaction ID and index via the Redeemer to create a unique token name so we can easily locate all swaps. This is a different approach than what we saw in *Chapter 7, Minting*, where we used the transaction ID and index as contract parameters. The application owner's PKH is the only contract parameter in the beacon minting policy, as shown in *Figure* 10.18.

```
minting beacon
const version: String = "BTP v0.4"

enum Redeemer {
    Mint {
        txId: ByteArray
        txIdx: String
    }
    Burn
}

// Contract parameters
const OWNER_PKH: ByteArray = #

// Global variables
const ownerPKH: PubKeyHash = PubKeyHash::new(OWNER_PKH)
```

Figure 10.18: *Beacon Redeemer*[17]

In *Figure* 10.19, we determine the value of what was minted on line 22, and the value of the minting policy hash for the script itself on line 23. On line 28, we combine both the `TxId` and `TxIdx`, and then hash them using the **`blake2b`** hash algorithm. This follows what we do in the off-chain code so that the token names being minted are the same as the on-chain code. We also check that only 1 token was minted on line 36 and that no other tokens are minted as part of this minting policy.

[17]https://github.com/ava-orange-education/Mastering-Cardano-Smart-Contracts/blob/main/chapter_10/helios/ticket-app/public/contracts/beacon.hl

```
19 func main(redeemer: Redeemer, ctx: ScriptContext) -> Bool {
20     print(version.show());
21     tx: Tx = ctx.tx;
22     value_minted: Value = tx.minted;
23     mph: MintingPolicyHash = ctx.get_current_minting_policy_hash();
24     redeemer.switch {
25         red: Mint => {
26             txIdxBA: ByteArray = red.txIdx.serialize();
27             txIdxInt: Int = Int::parse(red.txIdx);
28             tn: ByteArray = (red.txId + txIdxBA.slice(1,txIdxBA.length)).blake2b();
29             txId: TxId = TxId::new(red.txId);
30             outputId: TxOutputId = TxOutputId::new(txId, txIdxInt);
31             assetclass: AssetClass = AssetClass::new(
32                     mph,
33                     tn
34                 );
35             // Check that the minted amount is equal to only 1 for this mint tx
36             (value_minted == Value::new(assetclass, 1)).trace("BTP1: ") &&
37             // Check that the transaction is signed by the owner
38             tx.is_signed_by(ownerPKH).trace("BTP2: ") &&
39             // Check that txId is part of the inputs
40             tx.inputs.any((input: TxInput) -> Bool {
41                         (input.output_id == outputId).trace("BTP3: ")
42                         }
43                 )
```

Figure 10.19: *Beacon Minting Policy*[18]

The Redeemer Mint code on lines 38–43 in *Figure* 10.19 confirms that the min transaction is signed by the application owner PKH and that the transaction ID and index correspond to a UTXO input. Requiring the owner's signature helps ensure that the PKH provided in the contract parameters is actually owned by the entity submitting the transaction. The Redeemer Burn allows the burning of any token that belongs to this minting policy, as shown in *Figure* 10.20.

```
        Burn => {
            // Allow the thread token to be burned
            tx.minted.get_policy(mph).all( (_, amount: Int) -> Bool {
                amount == -1
            }).trace("BTP4: ")
        }
```

Figure 10.20: *Beacon Burn*

Ticket Minting Policy

The Ticket Minting Policy has a Mint, Convert, and Burn Redeemer. The Convert Redeemer passes a number of tickets to convert, and a list of unique ticket tokens is minted, as shown in *Figure* 10.21. It should be noted that careful consideration is required when passing a list of an arbitrary length. The budget costs for executing this script will depend on how many tickets are included in the **`userTicketTokenName`** array. In our case, this is required because we are explicitly minting individual unique NFT tokens. Therefore, we need to know each ticket's name to be able to mint and validate them in the minting and validator script accordingly.

[18]https://github.com/ava-orange-education/Mastering-Cardano-Smart-Contracts/blob/main/chapter_10/helios/ticket-app/public/contracts/beacon.hl

```
minting ticket
const version: String = "TKP v0.4"

// The minting policy can either mint, convert or burn tickets
enum Redeemer {
    Mint
    Convert {
        qty: Int
        userTicketTokenNames: []ByteArray
        refTicketTokenNames: []ByteArray
    }
    Burn
}

// Contract parameters
const TX_ID: ByteArray = #
const TX_IDX: Int = 0
const TN: ByteArray = #
const SHOWTIME: Time = Time::new(0)
const QTY: Int = 1
const PAYMENT_PKH: PubKeyHash = PubKeyHash::new(#)
const STAKE_PKH: PubKeyHash = PubKeyHash::new(#)
const HOLD_VAL_HASH: ValidatorHash = ValidatorHash::new(#)
const MIN_LOVELACE: Int = 2_000_000
```

Figure 10.21: *Ticket Minting Policy*[19]

In *Figure* 10.22, on lines 27 and 28, a `TxOutputId` is created using the **`TX_ID`** and **`TX_IDX`** contract parameters. This will be used to ensure that the minting policy is unique for each event. The `totalAssetVal` function on line 31 is a recursive function that combines all of the NFT tokens and reference tokens into one Value.

```
26  // Global variables
27  const txId: TxId = TxId::new(TX_ID)
28  const outputId: TxOutputId = TxOutputId::new(txId, TX_IDX)
29  const minLovelaceVal: Value = Value::lovelace(MIN_LOVELACE)
30
31  func totalAssetVal( tokenNames: []ByteArray,
32                      refTokenNames: []ByteArray,
33                      mph: MintingPolicyHash,
34                      qty: Int) -> Value {
35
36      tokenAssetClass: AssetClass = AssetClass::new(
37          mph,
38          tokenNames.get(0)
39      );
40      refTokenAssetClass: AssetClass = AssetClass::new(
41          mph,
42          refTokenNames.get(0)
43      );
44      if (tokenNames.length == 1) {
45          Value::new(tokenAssetClass, 1) + Value::new(refTokenAssetClass, 1)
46      } else {
47          totalAssetVal(tokenNames.tail, refTokenNames.tail, mph, qty - 1)
48                  + (Value::new(tokenAssetClass, 1))
49                  + (Value::new(refTokenAssetClass, 1))
50      }
```

Figure 10.22: *Token List Value*[20]

[19]https://github.com/ava-orange-education/Mastering-Cardano-Smart-Contracts/blob/main/chapter_10/helios/ticket-app/public/contracts/ticket.hl
[20]https://github.com/ava-orange-education/Mastering-Cardano-Smart-Contracts/blob/main/chapter_10/helios/ticket-app/public/contracts/ticket.hl

The Mint Redeemer in *Figure* 10.23, lines 68 and 69, confirms that the **TX_ID** and **TX_IDX** contract parameters match a UTXO that is included as an input. On lines 73 and 75, the minting policy confirms that the transaction is signed by the event owner's stake key and the minted output is sent to the holding validator script. There is also an additional check on line 77 that will cause the transaction to fail if the mint occurs after the event showtime.

```
54 func main(redeemer: Redeemer, ctx: ScriptContext) -> Bool {
55     tx: Tx = ctx.tx;
56     mph: MintingPolicyHash = ctx.get_current_minting_policy_hash();
57     ticket_assetclass: AssetClass = AssetClass::new(
58         mph,
59         TN
60     );
61     value_minted: Value = tx.minted;
62     now: Time = tx.time_range.start;
63     redeemer.switch {
64         Mint => {
65             // Check that the contract parameter UTXO is included in the inputs
66             // and that the minted amount is equal to the quanty given
67             (value_minted == Value::new(ticket_assetclass, QTY)).trace("TKP1: ") &&
68             tx.inputs.any((input: TxInput) -> Bool {
69                                 (input.output_id == outputId).trace("TKP2: ")
70                                 }
71                     ) &&
72             // Check that the transaction is signed by stake key
73             tx.is_signed_by(STAKE_PKH).trace("TKP3: ") &&
74             // Check that the minted value is going to the holding validator
75             (tx.value_locked_by(HOLD_VAL_HASH) ==  value_minted + minLovelaceVal).trace
76             // Don't allow minting of ticket after showtime
77             (now < SHOWTIME).trace("TKP5: ")
78         },
```

Figure 10.23: *Ticket Mint Redeemer*[21]

The Convert Redeemer calls the **totalAssetVal** function on line 84 in *Figure* 10.24 and combines the NFT ticket tokens and reference tokens into one Value. By adding the minted NFT and reference tokens with the burned released tokens, we get the total amount minted and burned in this transaction. We also do a safety check to ensure that the quantity passed in the redeemer is always greater than 0 on line 91.

[21]https://github.com/ava-orange-education/Mastering-Cardano-Smart-Contracts/blob/main/chapter_10/helios/ticket-app/public/contracts/ticket.hl

```
        red: Convert => {
            // Construct the ticket token value to burn
            burnTokenValue: Value = Value::new(ticket_assetclass, (-1) * red.qty);
            mintTokenValue: Value = totalAssetVal(  red.userTicketTokenNames,
                                                    red.refTicketTokenNames,
                                                    mph,
                                                    red.qty);
            totalValue: Value = burnTokenValue + mintTokenValue;

            // Check that the amount of tokens to convert is greater than 0
            (red.qty > 0).trace("TKP6: ") &&
            // Check that the total value is what is actually minted/burned
            (value_minted == totalValue).trace("TKP7")

        },
        Burn => {
            // Allow any quantity of the minting policy to be burned in a transaction
            (value_minted.get_policy(mph).all( (_, amount: Int) -> Bool {
                amount < 0
            }).trace("TKP8: ")) &&
            // Burning only allowed by event owner
            tx.is_signed_by(STAKE_PKH).trace("TKP9: ")
        }
```

***Figure 10.24**: Ticket Convert Redeemer*[22]

The Burn Redeemer, in *Figure 10.24*, allows any amount of allocated, released, or converted tokens to be burned, but this transaction needs to be signed by the event owner's stake key.

Holding Validator

The **`Holding`** Validator script acts as a staging area for ticket tokens that have been minted but not yet released into swaps. They can only be spent by the event owner's stake key, which is hard-coded as a contract parameter, as shown in *Figure 10.25*. The implementation of the holding validator script was somewhat tricky because we wanted to ensure that there was no leakage of tokens when transferring back and forth to the swaps. The challenge is, that when the holding validator is created, the swap address is unknown. So, we run into the scenario with a **circular reference** where the holding script needs to know the swap address, the swap address needs to know the holding address and both should be contract parameters for each other.

To help mitigate this issue, we leverage the beacon token minting policy, which can be calculated in advance. As seen in *Figure 10.18*, the **`beaconMPH`** is set as a contract parameter on line 16. In *Figure 10.25*, we introduce a new helper function on line 19 called **`checkTokenOut`** that will return `true` if there are any tokens contained within a set of outputs, which will be used to check for token leakage.

[22]https://github.com/ava-orange-education/Mastering-Cardano-Smart-Contracts/blob/main/chapter_10/helios/ticket-app/public/contracts/ticket.hl

```
spending holding
const version: String = "HDV v0.3"

// The holding contract for ticket tokens
enum Redeemer {
    Transfer
    Return
    Burn
}
// Contract parameters
const STAKE_PKH: PubKeyHash = PubKeyHash::new(#)
const TN: ByteArray = #
const BEACON_MPH: ByteArray = #

// Global variables
const beaconMPH: MintingPolicyHash = MintingPolicyHash::new(BEACON_MPH)

// Check for any tokens in outputs
func checkTokensOut(outputs: []TxOutput) -> Bool {
    if(outputs.length == 0) {
        false
    } else if (outputs.get(0).value.get_assets().is_zero()) {
        checkTokensOut(outputs.tail)
    } else {
        true
```

Figure 10.25: *Holding Validator checkTokensOut*[23]

As seen in *Figure* 10.26, the **`Transfer`** Redeemer is used to transfer the ticket tokens from the holding script to a swap. The transaction must be signed by the event owners' stake key and must also contain a beacon token. As we recall, every swap must have a beacon token, which will help to ensure that these tickets go to a swap and nowhere else. Only outputs going to the swap and optional holding validator script for change should contain tokens. This rule is enforced on lines 43–49.

```
28  // Define the main validator function
29  func main(_, redeemer: Redeemer, ctx: ScriptContext) -> Bool {
30      print(version.show());
31      tx: Tx = ctx.tx;
32      vHash : ValidatorHash = ctx.get_current_validator_hash();
33      redeemer.switch {
34          Transfer => {
35              txOutputsContract : []TxOutput = tx.outputs_locked_by(vHash);
36              // Tx must be singed by the stake key
37              tx.is_signed_by(STAKE_PKH).trace("HDV1: ") &&
38              // Output to swap must have a beacon token
39              (tx.outputs.get(0).value.get_policy(beaconMPH)
40                          .all((_, amount: Int) -> Bool {
41                              amount == 1
42                          }).trace("HDV2: ")) &&
43              // If there is token change sent back to the holding script
44              (if (txOutputsContract.length == 1) {
45                  (!checkTokensOut((tx.outputs.tail).tail)).trace("HDV3: ")
46              // Otherwise, just check the remaining outputs for tokens
47              } else {
48                  (!checkTokensOut(tx.outputs.tail)).trace("HDV4: ")
49              })
50          },
```

Figure 10.26: *Holding Validator Transfer Redeemer*[24]

---

[23]https://github.com/ava-orange-education/Mastering-Cardano-Smart-Contracts/blob/main/chapter_10/helios/ticket-app/public/contracts/holding.hl
[24]https://github.com/ava-orange-education/Mastering-Cardano-Smart-Contracts/blob/main/chapter_10/helios/ticket-app/public/contracts/holding.hl

The **`Return`** Redeemer is similar to the **`Transfer`** redeemer and is used to validate that the ticket tokens from a closed swap are sent back directly to the holding script address. When a swap is closed, the beacon token is always burned, so we check for this condition in the transaction, as shown in *Figure* 10.27, on line 56. There is also only one output going to the holding script address, so we will make sure that this condition is true on line 62. We double-check that no other tokens are in any other outputs on line 64.

```
51          Return => {
52              txOutputsContract : []TxOutput = tx.outputs_locked_by(vHash);
53              // Tx must be singed by the stake key
54              tx.is_signed_by(STAKE_PKH).trace("HDV5: ") &&
55              // The transaction must be burning a beacon token
56              (tx.minted.value.get_policy(beaconMPH)
57                                  .all((_, amount: Int) -> Bool {
58                                      amount == (-1)
59                                  }).trace("HDV6: ")) &&
60              // Check that there is only one output that goes back to the
61              // holding script
62              (txOutputsContract.length == 1).trace("HDV7: ") &&
63              // Make sure that no other outputs contains tokens
64              (!checkTokensOut(tx.outputs.tail)).trace("HDV8: ")
65          },
66          Burn => {
67              // Tx must be singed by the stake key
68              tx.is_signed_by(STAKE_PKH).trace("HDV9: ") &&
69              // There must be only 1 change output and only contain Ada
70              (!checkTokensOut(tx.outputs)).trace("HDV10: ")
71          }
```

Figure 10.27: *Holding Validator Return Redeemer*[25]

The **`Burn`** Redeemer simply checks that the transaction is signed by the event owner's stake key and that no tokens exist in the outputs. When we archive an event, we burn all remaining allocated tokens.

Swap Validator

We define the datum of the **`swap`** validator to only contain two Values, the **`askedAssetVal`** and the **`offeredAssetVal`**, as shown in *Figure* 10.28. The **`askedAssetVal`** contains the asset class (in this case Ada) that we are asking for. The price for an offered asset is the amount set in **`askedAssetVal`**. So, **`askedAssetVal`** contains both the type of asset being asked for and the price for each offered asset. The swaps are designed so that an event owner (seller) can update the price of a swap at any time. If the user wants to change the asset they are selling or asking for, then they need to close the swap and create a new one.

[25]https://github.com/ava-orange-education/Mastering-Cardano-Smart-Contracts/blob/main/chapter_10/helios/ticket-app/public/contracts/holding.hl

The **offeredAssetVal** is used to indicate the asset that is for sale and the amount that is locked in the swap. The **offeredAssetVal** gets updated according to the amount of offered assets that leave the swap. *Figure* 10.28 shows the datum struct as well as the Redeemer for the swap script. The **Swap** Redeemer is passed a buyer public key hash as well as the quantity and token names that will be converted (minted) in this transaction on lines 11–14.

```
1   spending swap
2   const version: String = "SPV v0.3"
3
4   struct Datum {
5       askedAssetVal: Value
6       offeredAssetVal: Value
7   }
8
9   enum Redeemer {
10      Close
11      Swap {
12          buyerPkh: PubKeyHash
13          qty: Int
14          userTicketTokenNames: []ByteArray
15      }
16      Update
17  }
```

Figure 10.28: *Swap Validator Datum and Redeemer*[26]

Figure 10.29 shows the contract parameters and global variables used in the swap validator.

```
// Contract parameters
const ASKED_MPH: ByteArray = #
const ASKED_TN: ByteArray = #
const OFFERED_MPH: ByteArray = #
const OFFERED_TN: ByteArray = #
const BEACON_MPH: ByteArray = #
const BEACON_TN: ByteArray = #
const HOLD_VAL_HASH: ValidatorHash = ValidatorHash::new(#)
const SHOWTIME: Time = Time::new(0)
const PAYMENT_PKH: PubKeyHash = PubKeyHash::new(#)
const STAKE_PKH: PubKeyHash = PubKeyHash::new(#)
const MIN_LOVELACE: Int = 0

// Global variables
const beaconMPH: MintingPolicyHash = MintingPolicyHash::new(BEACON_MPH)
const beaconAssetClass: AssetClass = AssetClass::new(beaconMPH, BEACON_TN)
const minLovelaceVal: Value = Value::lovelace(MIN_LOVELACE)
```

Figure 10.29: *Swap Validator Contract Parameters*[27]

[26]https://github.com/ava-orange-education/Mastering-Cardano-Smart-Contracts/blob/main/chapter_10/helios/ticket-app/public/contracts/swap.hl
[27]https://github.com/ava-orange-education/Mastering-Cardano-Smart-Contracts/blob/main/chapter_10/helios/ticket-app/public/contracts/swap.hl

The **checkAdaVal** function, on line 38 in *Figure* 10.30, is used to add the minimum amount of Ada (lovelace) if a value contains a native token. For simplicity, we use a fixed minimum of 2,000,000 lovelace for all smart contract token interactions. As we recall, we can only send a native asset so long as there is a minimum amount of lovelace included. The exact amount of lovelace can be determined by calculating the bytes used in a particular UTXO. This amount can be larger or smaller depending on how many tokens are included in a UTXO. Therefore, we tightly control the outputs when sending native tokens to ensure that the correct minimum lovelace is always included.

We also create a function called **totalAssetVal** on line 46, in *Figure* 10.30, which is similar to the **totalAssetVal** in the ticket minting policy. For the **Swap** validator, however, we only need to include and validate the ticket tokens and not the reference tokens.

```
37  // If the value is not lovelace, then add minLovelace
38  func checkAdaVal(value: Value) -> Value {
39      if(value.get_lovelace() == 0) {
40          minLovelaceVal + value
41      } else {
42          value
43      }
44  }
45  // Calc the total value of the array of token names provided
46  func totalAssetVal( tokenNames: []ByteArray,
47                      mph: MintingPolicyHash,
48                      qty: Int) -> Value {
49
50      tokenAssetClass: AssetClass = AssetClass::new(
51          mph,
52          tokenNames.get(0)
53      );
54      if (tokenNames.length == 1) {
55          Value::new(tokenAssetClass, 1)
56      } else {
57          totalAssetVal(tokenNames.tail, mph, qty - 1)
58          + (Value::new(tokenAssetClass, 1))
59      }
60  }
```

Figure 10.30: *Swap Validator totalAssetVal*[28]

Inside the main swap validator function, we start off by obtaining the **ScriptContext** and the hash of the validator in *Figure* 10.31. Next, we create an `AssetClass` for both the asked assets and the offered assets, which will be used later in the program. On line 84, we get an array of all of the outputs locked at the swap address for this transaction. Fortunately, the order of the outputs is always set explicitly during the off-chain transaction construction. The same cannot be said about inputs that may be re-ordered canonically, so we try to avoid inspecting inputs as much as possible.

[28]https://github.com/ava-orange-education/Mastering-Cardano-Smart-Contracts/blob/main/chapter_10/helios/ticket-app/public/contracts/swap.hl

```
// Define the main validator
func main(datumIn: Datum, redeemer: Redeemer, ctx: ScriptContext) -> Bool {
    print(version.show());
    tx: Tx = ctx.tx;
    vHash : ValidatorHash = ctx.get_current_validator_hash();

    // Calculate the asked token
    askedMph: MintingPolicyHash = MintingPolicyHash::new(ASKED_MPH);
    askedAssetClass: AssetClass = AssetClass::new(
        askedMph,
        ASKED_TN
    );

    // Calculate the offered token
    offeredMph: MintingPolicyHash = MintingPolicyHash::new(OFFERED_MPH);
    offeredAssetClass: AssetClass = AssetClass::new(
        offeredMph,
        OFFERED_TN
    );

    // Get the outputs sent back to this script address
    txOutputsContract : []TxOutput = tx.outputs_locked_by(vHash);

```

Figure 10.31: *Swap Validator main function*[29]

The **Close** Redeemer in *Figure* 10.32 checks that the beacon token is burned, no outputs are sent back to the script address, and any offered assets are returned to the holding script address. It also confirms that only a transaction signed with the event owner's stake key can close a swap position.

```
    redeemer.switch {
        Close => {
            // Create beacon token value for burning
            beaconVal : Value = Value::new(beaconAssetClass, (-1));

            // Check that there is nothing sent back to swap adddress
            (txOutputsContract.length == 0).trace("SPV1.1: ") &&

            // Check that the transaction is siged by the stake key who created it
            tx.is_signed_by(STAKE_PKH).trace("SPV1.2: ") &&

            // Check that the beacon token is burned
            (tx.minted == beaconVal).trace("SPV1.3: ") &&

            // Check that the value of the swap is sent back to holding validator
            (tx.value_locked_by(HOLD_VAL_HASH))
            .contains(checkAdaVal(datumIn.offeredAssetVal))
            .trace("SPV1.4: ")
```

Figure 10.32: *Swap Validator Close Redeemer*[30]

The **Swap** Redeemer creates the beacon and ticket token values that will be part of the transaction outputs in *Figure* 10.33. Using the buyer's PKH and the event owner's PKH,

[29]https://github.com/ava-orange-education/Mastering-Cardano-Smart-Contracts/blob/main/chapter_10/helios/ticket-app/public/contracts/swap.hl
[30]https://github.com/ava-orange-education/Mastering-Cardano-Smart-Contracts/blob/main/chapter_10/helios/ticket-app/public/contracts/swap.hl

we obtain the outputs that are sent to the buyer and event owner (seller) addresses, respectively. On lines 121–127, we pull out the required values from the input and output datums, which will be used to validate the swap's spending conditions.

```
106   red: Swap => {
107       beaconVal : Value = Value::new(beaconAssetClass, (1));
108       mintTokenValue: Value = totalAssetVal(  red.userTicketTokenNames,
109                                               offeredMph,
110                                               red.qty);
111       txOutputsBuyer : []TxOutput = tx.outputs_sent_to(red.buyerPkh);
112       txOutputsSeller : []TxOutput = tx.outputs_sent_to(PAYMENT_PKH);
113
114       if (txOutputsContract.length == 1 &&
115           txOutputsBuyer.length >= 1 &&
116           txOutputsSeller.length >= 1) {
117
118           txOutputsContract.head.datum.switch {
119               datumOut: Inline => {
120
121                   datumOutData: Datum = Datum::from_data(datumOut.data);
122                   offeredAssetDiffVal: Value = datumIn.offeredAssetVal
123                                             - datumOutData.offeredAssetVal;
124                   offeredAssetDiffQty: Int = offeredAssetDiffVal.get(offeredAssetClass);
125                   swapVal: Value = checkAdaVal(datumOutData.offeredAssetVal) + beaconVal;
126                   buyerVal: Value = checkAdaVal(mintTokenValue);
127                   sellerVal: Value = checkAdaVal(datumIn.askedAssetVal * offeredAssetDiffQty);
128
```

Figure 10.33: *Swap Validator Swap Redeemer Datum Values*[31]

Now, we are ready to validate the core swap logic in *Figure* 10.34. On line 130, we first check that the asked asset does not change between the input and output datum. On lines 133–136, we check that the *asked asset* in the datum matches what was specified as the contract parameter. On line 140, we also check that the *offered asset* in the datum matches what was specified as a contract parameter as well. Lines 143–149 are the most critical business logic checks that ensure the correct values are sent to the swap, buyer, and seller, respectively. Finally, on line 152, we check that the amount of tokens to be converted matches what is recorded in the datums.

[31]https://github.com/ava-orange-education/Mastering-Cardano-Smart-Contracts/blob/main/chapter_10/helios/ticket-app/public/contracts/swap.hl

```
    // Check that the askedAsset datum value does not change
    (datumIn.askedAssetVal == datumOutData.askedAssetVal).trace("SPV2.1: ") &&

    // Check that the askedAsset in the datum is what is asked as part of this swap
    (if (datumIn.askedAssetVal.get_lovelace() > MIN_LOVELACE) {
       (ASKED_MPH.length == 0).trace("SPV2.3: ")
    } else {
        (datumIn.askedAssetVal.get(askedAssetClass) > 0).trace("SPV2.4: ")
    }) &&

    // Check that the offeredAsset in the datum is what is offered as part of this swap
    (datumIn.offeredAssetVal.get(offeredAssetClass) > 0).trace("SPV2.5: ") &&

    // Check that the remaining value sent back to swap is correct
    (tx.value_locked_by(vHash) == (swapVal)).trace("SPV2.6: ") &&

    // Check that buy receives the correct amount
    (buyerVal == txOutputsBuyer.head.value).trace("SPV2.7: ") &&

    // Check that the seller receives the correct amount
    (sellerVal == tx.value_sent_to(PAYMENT_PKH)).trace("SPV2.8: ") &&

    // Check that the qty minted matches the amount offered assets sold
    (offeredAssetDiffQty == red.qty).trace("SPV2.9: ")
```

Figure 10.34: *Swap Validator Swap Redeemer Logic*[32]

The **`Update`** Redeemer in *Figure* 10.35 verifies that the transaction is signed by the event owner's stake **`PKH`** on line 170. Any changes to the *asked assets* or *offered assets* will require a new swap and are checked on lines 176, 179, and 183. Similar to the Swap Redeemer, the Datum and output values are calculated on lines 165–168. Finally, the swap value is verified to return to the swap address on line 173.

```
160      Update => {
161          beaconVal : Value = Value::new(beaconAssetClass, (1));
162          if (txOutputsContract.length == 1) {
163              txOutputsContract.head.datum.switch {
164                  datumOut: Inline => {
165                      datumOutData: Datum = Datum::from_data(datumOut.data);
166                      offeredAssetValOut: Value = datumOutData.offeredAssetVal;
167                      askedAssetValOut: Value = datumOutData.askedAssetVal;
168                      swapVal: Value = checkAdaVal(offeredAssetValOut) + beaconVal;
169                      // Check that transaction was signed by the stake key
170                      tx.is_signed_by(STAKE_PKH).trace("SPV3.1: ") &&
171                      // Check that the offered asset type and quantity does not change
172                      // with a swap update, only the asking asset price
173                      (tx.value_locked_by(vHash) == (swapVal)).trace("SPV3.2: ") &&
174                      // Check that offered asset in datum does not change before
175                      // and after the update swap
176                      (datumIn.offeredAssetVal == datumOutData.offeredAssetVal) &&
177                      (if (askedAssetValOut.get_lovelace() > MIN_LOVELACE) {
178                          // Check that asked asset is in lovelace
179                          (ASKED_MPH.length == 0).trace("SPV3.3: ")
180                          }
181                      else {
182                          // Check that a non-Ada asked asset is greater than 0
183                          ((askedAssetValOut.get(askedAssetClass) > 0).trace("SPV3.4: "))
184                      })
```

Figure 10.35: *Swap Validator Swap Update Redeemer*[33]

[32]https://github.com/ava-orange-education/Mastering-Cardano-Smart-Contracts/blob/main/chapter_10/helios/ticket-app/public/contracts/swap.hl
[33]https://github.com/ava-orange-education/Mastering-Cardano-Smart-Contracts/blob/main/chapter_10/helios/ticket-app/public/contracts/swap.hl

Back-end Application

The following sections describe the back-end components that interact with the front-end code to provide blockchain data and state information.

Redis DB

Figure 10.36 shows the Redis DB schemas to support blockchain data replication and application state management. Access to the Redis DB is only done through API calls and is not directly accessed by the front-end code. Each schema has a corresponding class defined in **`common/types.ts`**. These classes help serialize and transmit the data structure from the front-end to the back-end API code.

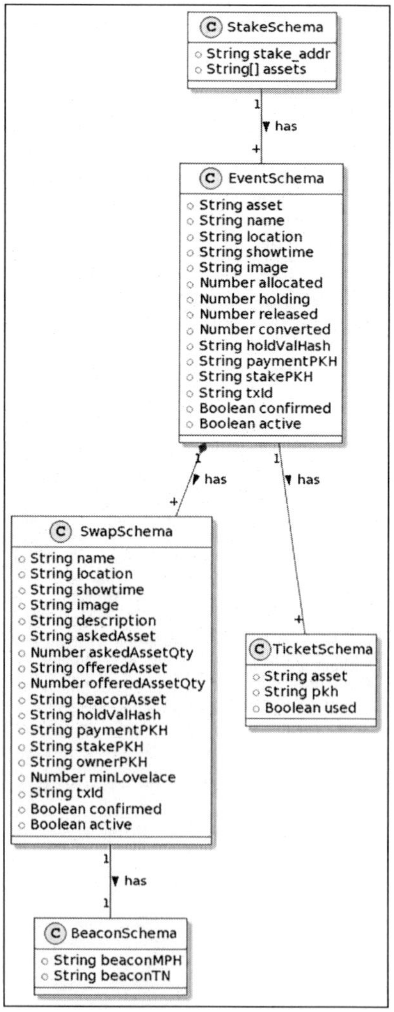

Figure 10.36: *Redis DB Schemas*

APIs

The following is a list of the APIs used to allow communication between the front-end and the back-end application components, such as the Redis DB and Blockfrost.

```
$ tree pages/api
```

```
pages/api
    ├── closeSwap.ts
    ├── getAssetUtxo.ts
    ├── getEvent.ts
    ├── getEvents.ts
    ├── getFilterSwaps.ts
    ├── getTicketMetadataCIP25.ts
    ├── getTicketMetadataCIP68.ts
    ├── getTicketPkh.ts
    ├── getWalletInfo.ts
    ├── printTicket.ts
    ├── setBeacon.ts
    ├── setEvent.ts
    ├── setStakeKey.ts
    ├── setSwap.ts
    ├── signSubmitTx.ts
    ├── submitTx.ts
    ├── updateEvent.ts
    ├── updateSwap.ts
    ├── updateTxStatus.ts
    └── verifyTicket.ts
```

All front-end API calls are made from the **`common/network.ts`** file, which uses axios[34] to make HTTP GET or POST requests. The Blockfrost webhook **`updateTxStatus.ts`** is called when there is a blockchain transaction matching the beacon minting policy. The webhook is configured to fire after three **blockchain confirmations**. When the Blockfrost webhook is called, it will update the event and swap that has the corresponding transaction ID and mark it confirmed.

Redis DB Setup

Before running the demo, a Redis DB instance with JSON stack must be created locally or using a cloud instance.

1. Go to https://redis.io/
2. Sign in or create an account.
3. Create a **`$0`** subscription.

[34]https://www.npmjs.com/package/axios

4. Create a new Redis Stack database (includes JSON stack).
5. Select the Databases navigation link on the left-hand side of the page.
6. Select **`Connect`** under the Endpoint column.
7. Then select **`Redis Client`** to obtain your credential information, as shown in *Figure 10.37*.

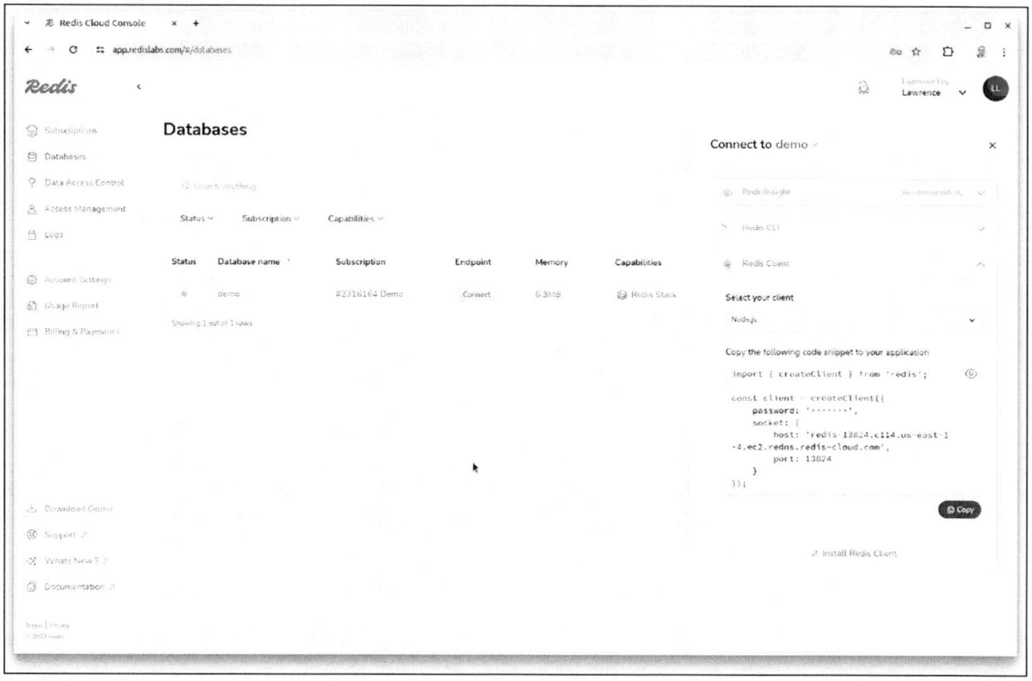

Figure 10.37: *Redis DB Setup*

Blockfrost Setup

1. Log into the Blockfrost dashboard and create a webhook.
2. Enter the URL of your application as the Endpoint URL:

   `https://your.host.domain.name/api/updateTxStatus`
3. Set the required number of blockchain confirmations.
4. Enter the Beacon Minting Policy ID as a trigger condition:

   `policy id = 421dacdd…e5ad68e76a6`
5. Create another webhook and use the same Endpoint URL, but use the event owner's stake key as the sender:

   `sender = stake_test1uqk6gt…6a5pj6p5qh6lc8v`

6. Copy the Auth Token and add it to the application environment variables:

   ```
   export WEBHOOK_AUTH_TOKEN=8e81d5...24e0f5
   ```

Application Owner Public/Private Key

You can use the **generatePrivateKey.mjs** utility in the init folder to create the application owner's public and private keys.

```
$ cd chapter_10/helios/ticket-app
$ nvm use 18.17.0
$ npm install
$ export ENTROPY="put your 24 word seed phrase here"
$ node ./init/generatePriveKey.mjs
$ export OWNER_PRIVATE_KEY=383be…b632341a4e
$ export NEXT_PUBLIC_OWNER_PKH=61942b…653a7d3cdb0
```

Demo

We will now run the application to demo the functionality of the ticket application on the Cardano preprod network. Please ensure the following bash environment variables are set with correct values before starting the application:

```
$ cat ~/.bashrc
export NEXT_PUBLIC_HOST=localhost
export NEXT_PUBLIC_PORT=:3000
export NEXT_PUBLIC_PROTOCOL=http
export NEXT_PUBLIC_ENV=dev
export NEXT_PUBLIC_NETWORK=preprod
export REDIS_PASSWORD=CnitD9...9UsOAQ
export REDIS_HOST=redis-13...labs.com
export REDIS_PORT=13633
export BLOCKFROST_API_KEY="prepro...hE1aMi"
export BLOCKFROST_API="https://cardano-preprod.blockfrost.io/api/v0"
export WEBHOOK_AUTH_TOKEN=8e81d5...24e0f5
export OWNER_PRIVATE_KEY=889c4a...7cf5d5
export NEXT_PUBLIC_OWNER_PKH=18b022...9e3aeb
```

Start the development server:

```
$ source ~/.bashrc
$ npm run dev
```

Use a browser and go to the external port to access the application.

Initial Startup

Figure 10.38 shows the initial view of the **Get Tickets** page when no swaps have been created. To first create an event, the user connects their wallet and selects the `My Events` tab.

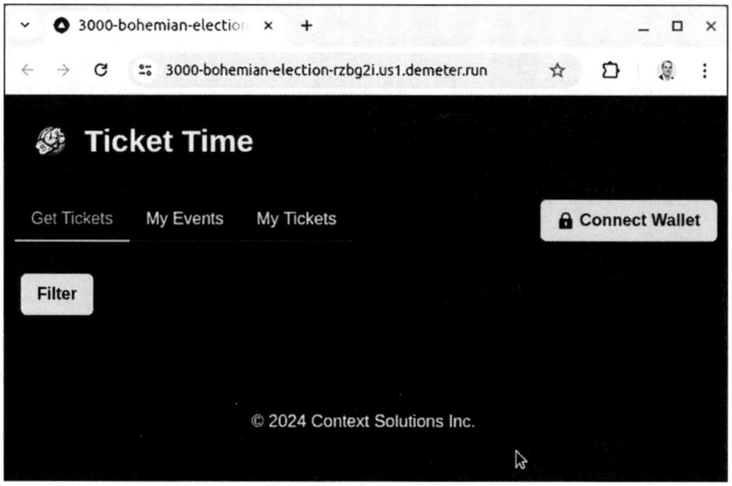

Figure 10.38: *Default Initial Ticket View*

Connect Wallet

When the user selects `Connect Wallet`, they are presented with a list of browser wallets that are supported and installed, as shown in *Figure* 10.39.

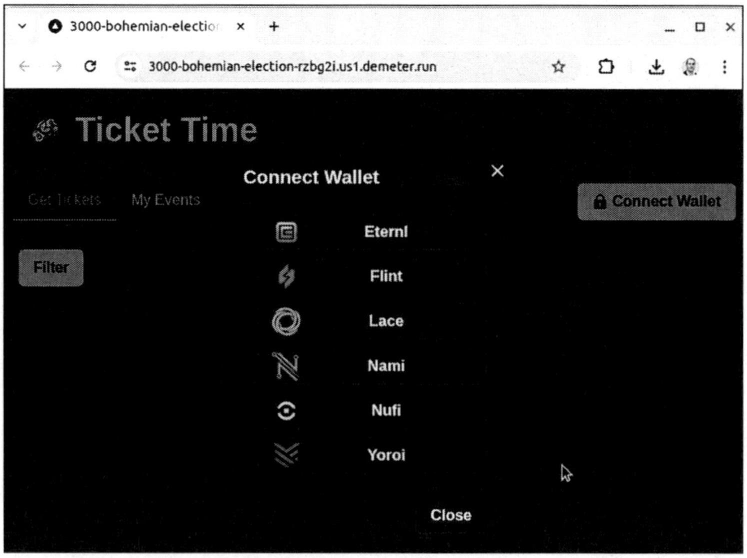

Figure 10.39: *Connect Wallet*

My Events

After the user has connected to their wallet, they can go to the `My Events` tab and will see the list of events they have created. Since we have not yet created any, we will see an empty list of events, as shown in *Figure 10.40*.

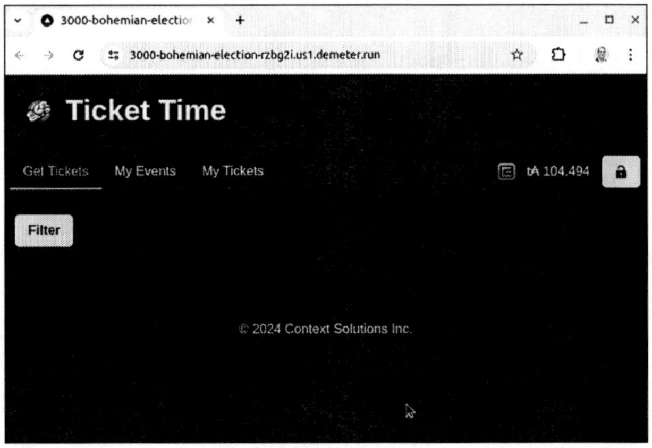

Figure 10.40: *My Events*

New Event

When a user selects the **`New Event`** button, they will see a popup window that allows them to enter the event details, as shown in *Figure 10.41*. When selecting the **`Mint Tickets`** button, the allocated tickets will be minted and sent to the ticket holding address. In addition, please note that there is a link to view the smart contract at the bottom of the popup window if a user wants to verify the smart contract independently.

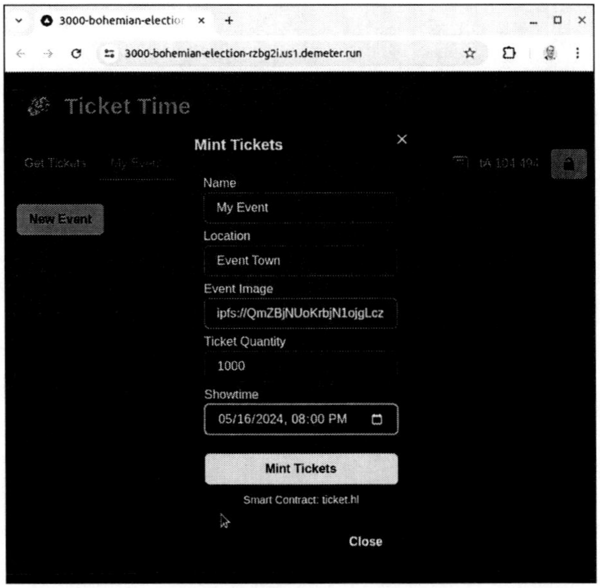

Figure 10.41: *New Event*

After the **`Mint Tickets`** button is pressed, the wallet prompts the user to sign a transaction to mint the event tickets. *Figure 10.42* shows the successful minting of a batch of 1000 tickets that are sent to the ticket holding script address.

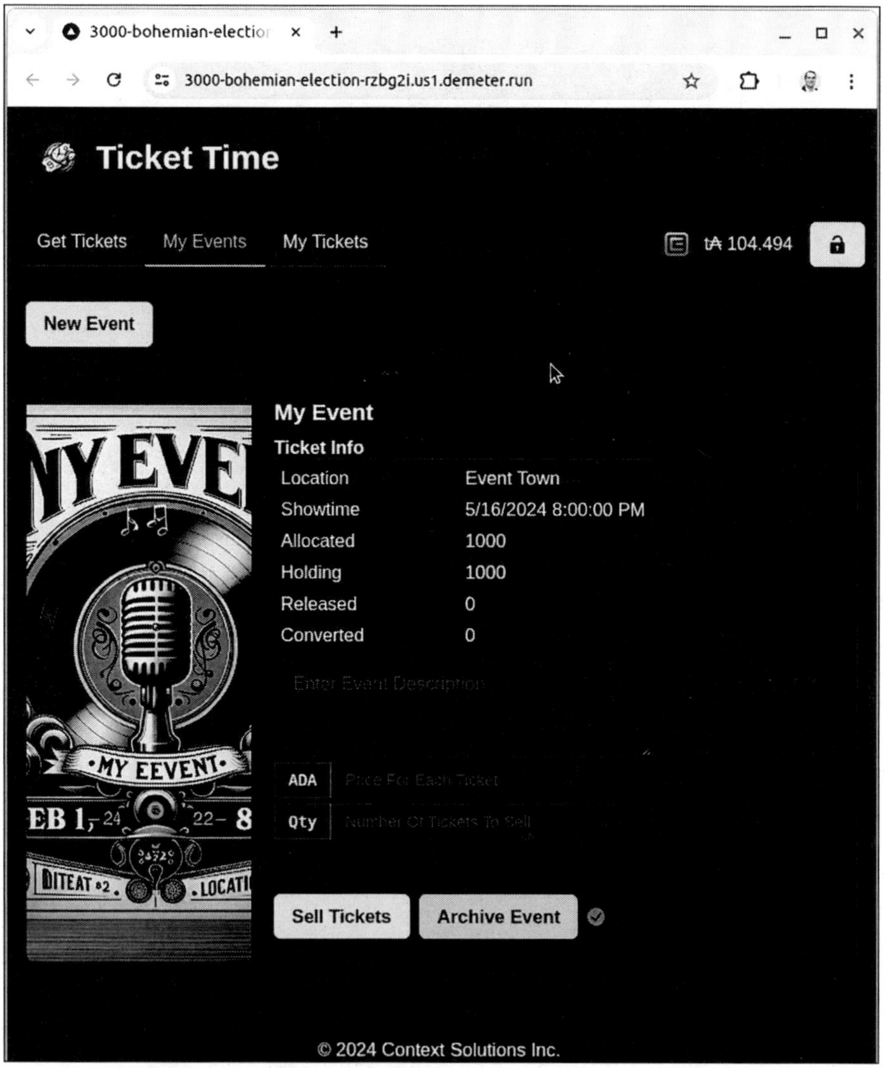

Figure 10.42: *Allocated Tickets*

Open Swap

Next, the tickets are made available for sale by opening a swap position, as shown in *Figure 10.43*. A description is also added and can be modified for each swap that is opened. The user may release some or all of the tickets from the ticket holding script and put them into the swap position. In this case, we will select 700 tickets to sell now.

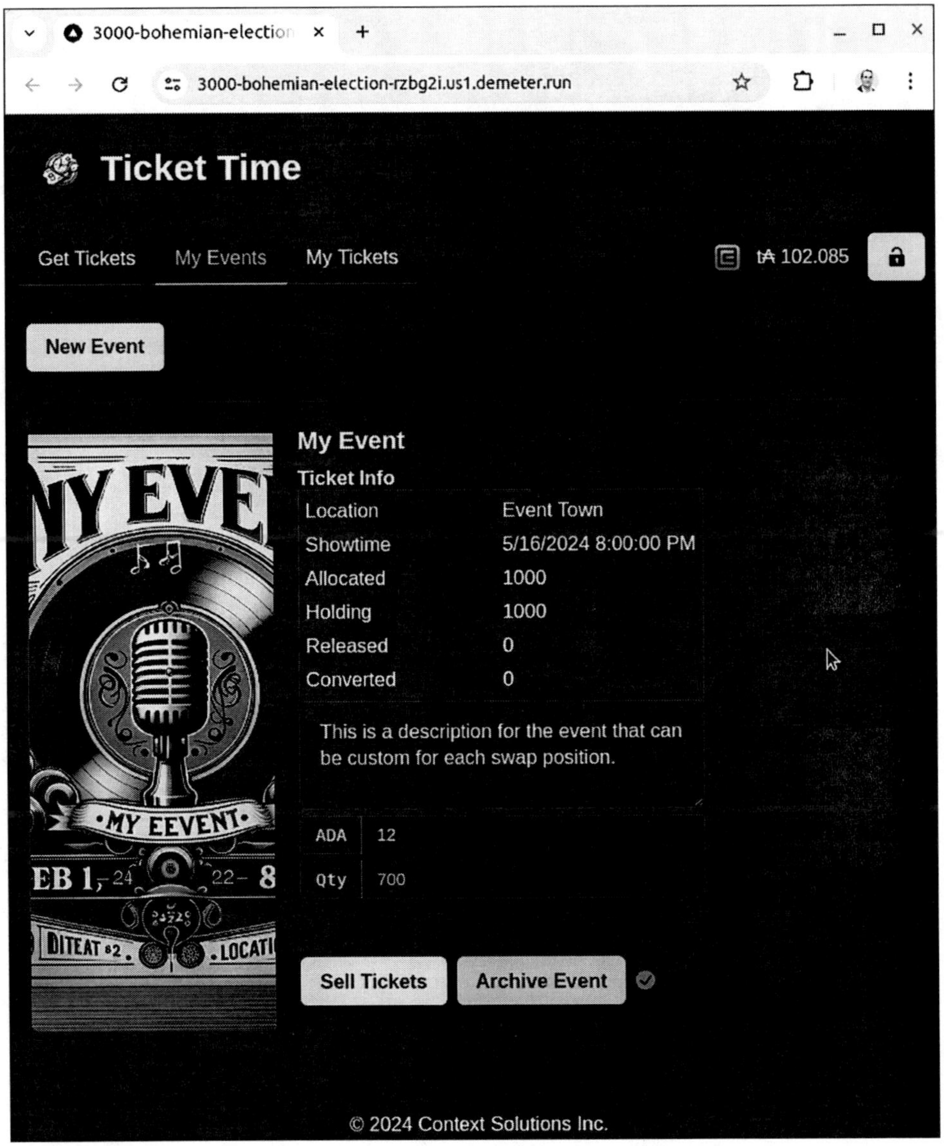

Figure 10.43: *Sell Tickets*

Get Tickets

After the user signs the open swap transaction, the tickets will appear in the **`Get Ticket`** screen, as shown in *Figure* 10.44. If the user is still connected to their wallet, the swap will show the ability to either update or close it. This is only available to the owner of the swap position with the correct staking key.

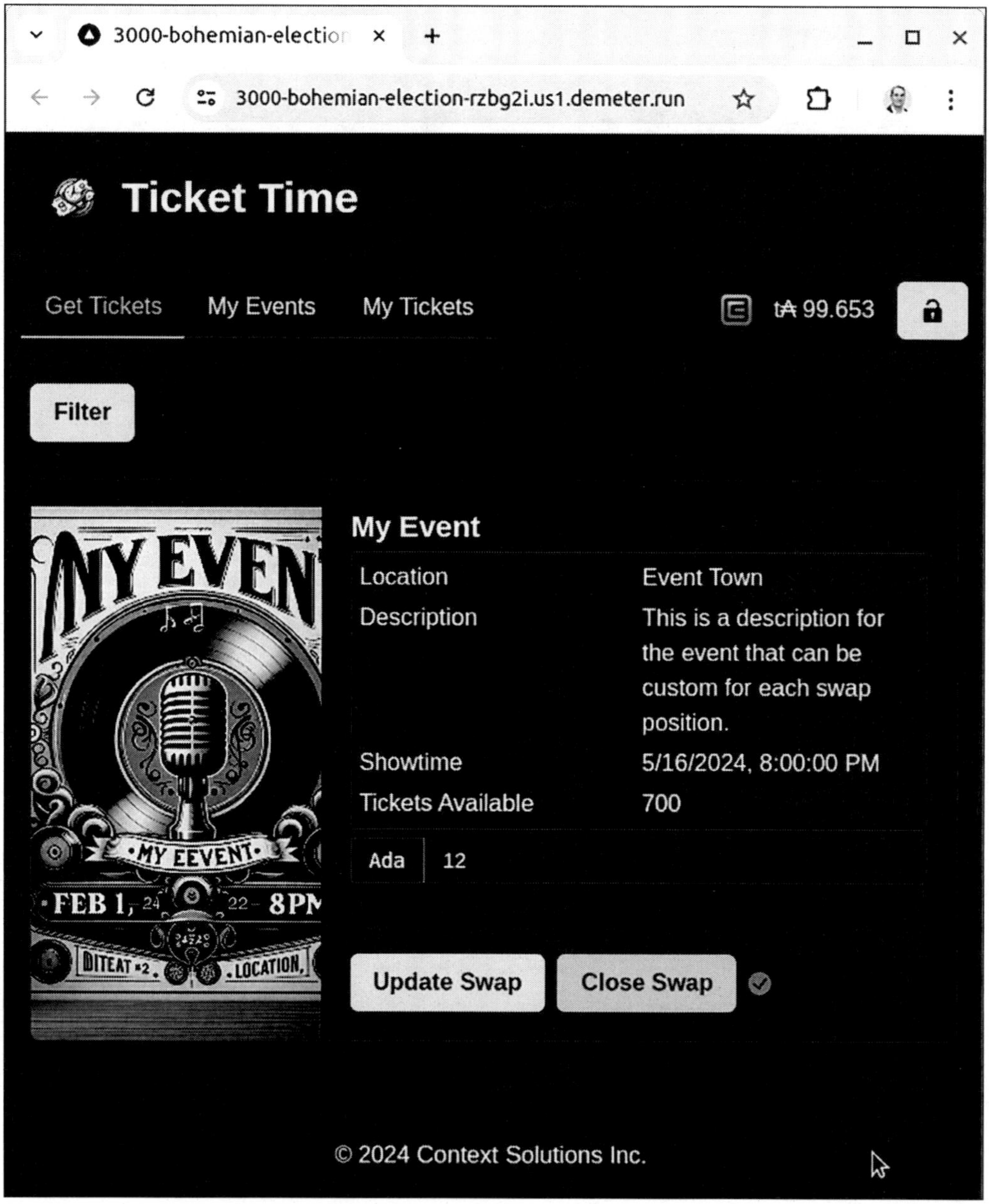

Figure 10.44: *Released Tickets*

Update Swap

Next, we will update the swap and change the price from 12 Ada to 15 Ada on the **`Get Tickets`** page. The update transaction is successful, as shown in *Figure* 10.45.

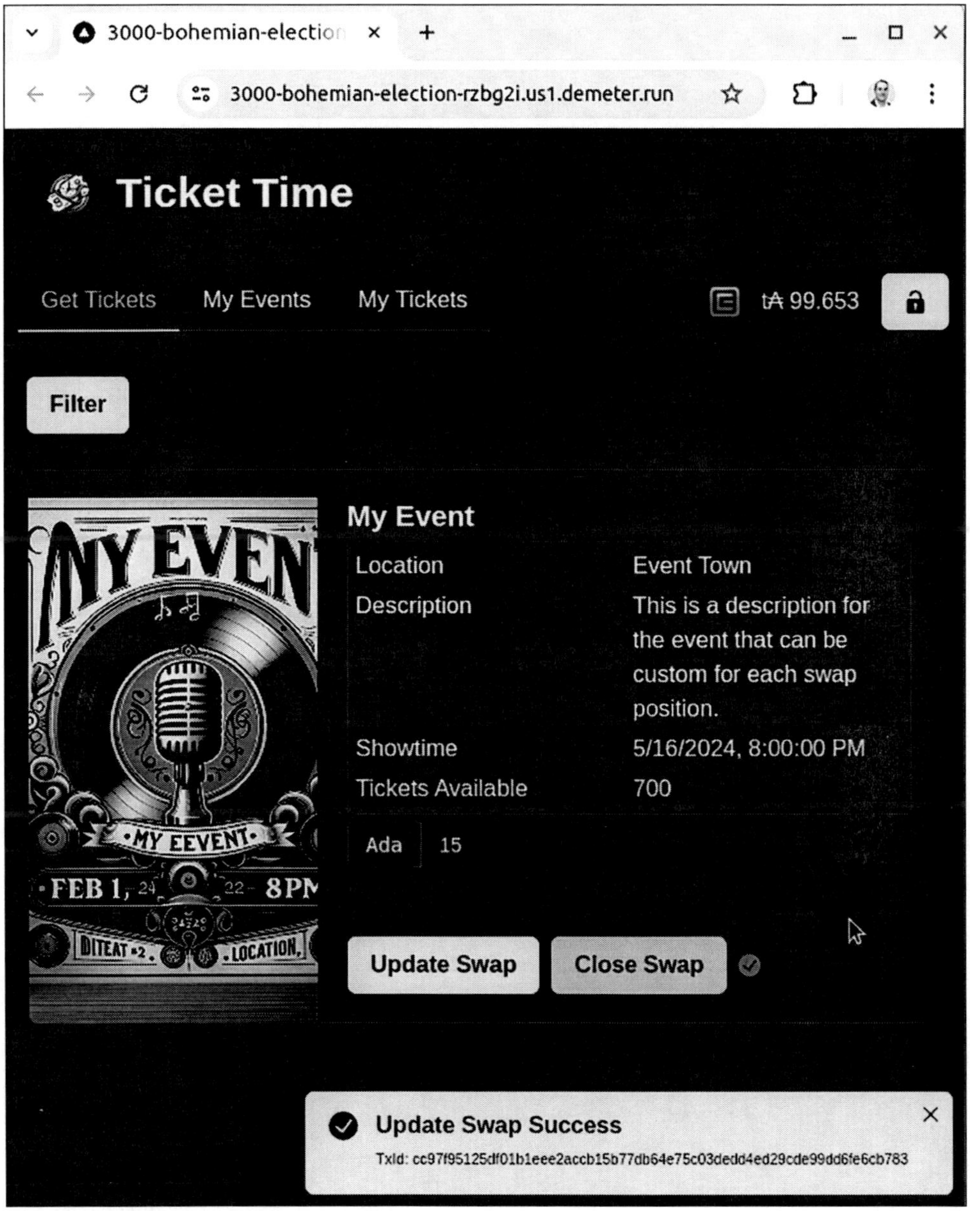

Figure 10.45: *Update Swap*

Buy Tickets

After connecting with the buyer's wallet, we select the **`Buy Tickets`** button, as shown in *Figure* 10.46. Remember to enable the buyer wallet account with dApp access if this is required in your wallet.

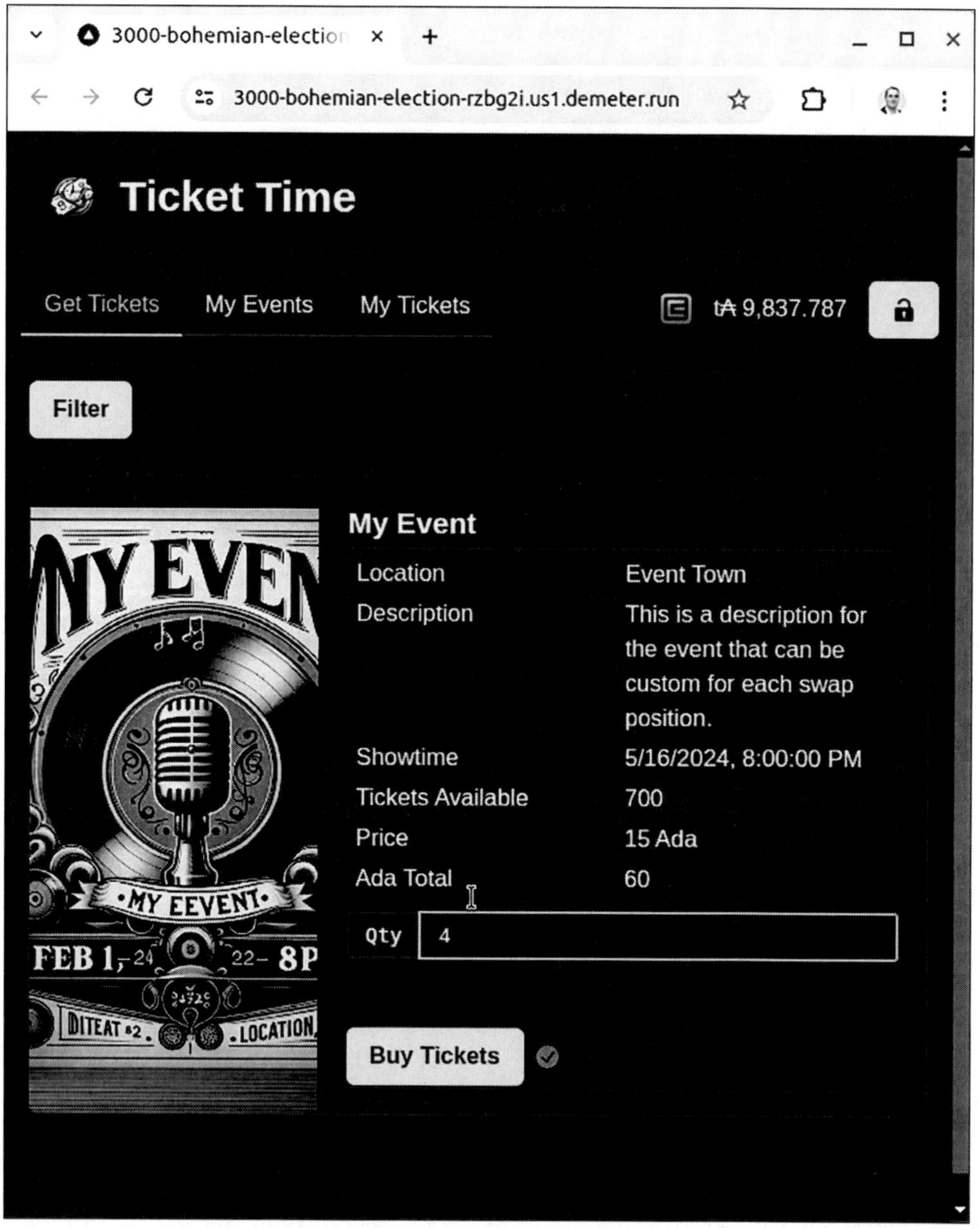

Figure 10.46: *Buy Tickets*

We will enter a quantity of four tickets and then select the **`Buy Tickets`** button. After signing the buy transaction, a purchase success message will appear. The current inventory available in the swap has changed to **`696`** since we purchased four tickets, as shown in *Figure* 10.47.

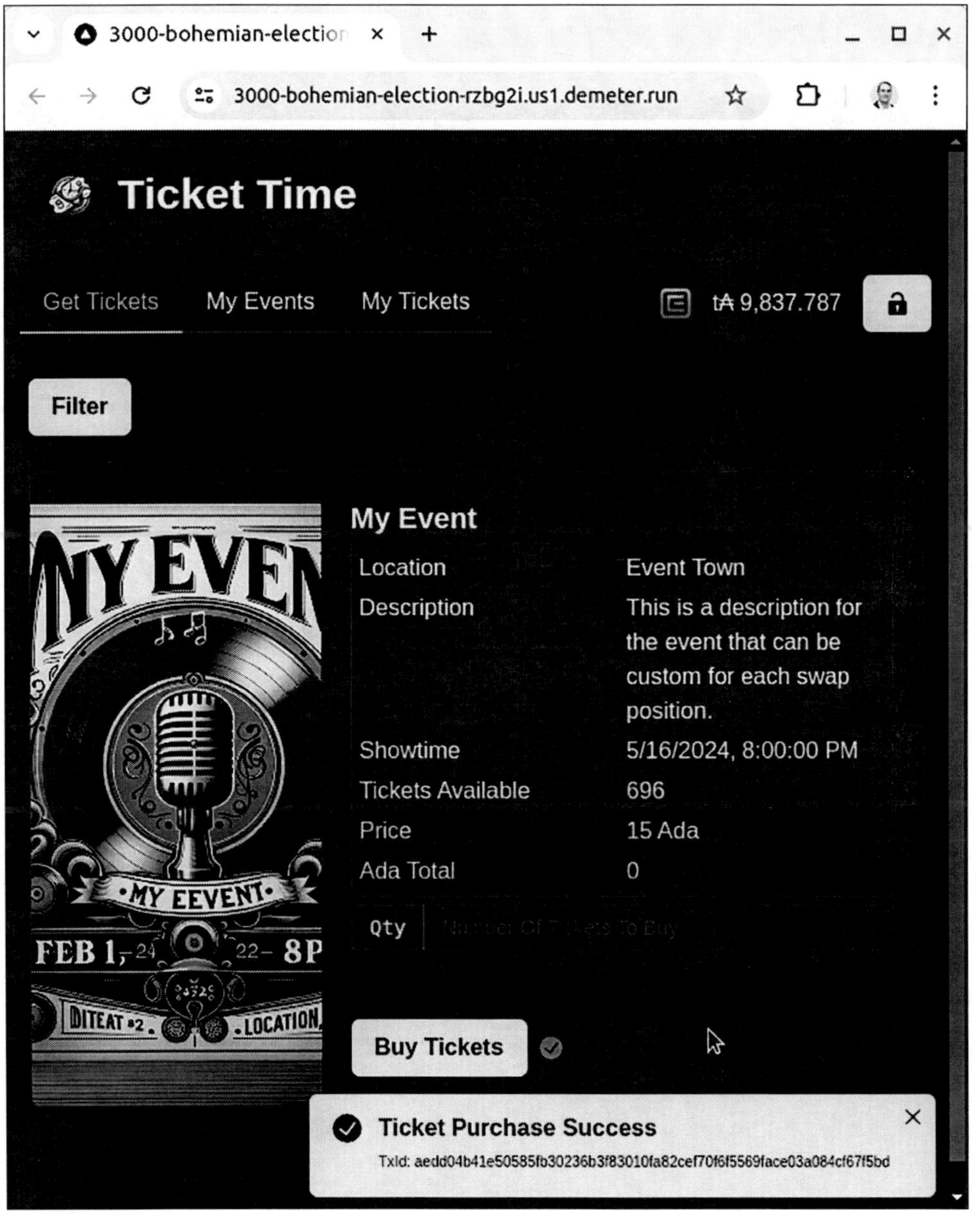

Figure 10.47: *Buy Tickets*

In the wallet transaction history shown in *Figure 10.48*, we can also see that 2 Plutus scripts were executed. This allowed us to burn 4 released tickets and mint 4 ticket tokens plus 4 reference tokens. This can also be viewed on a Cardano block explorer.[35]

---

[35]https://preprod.cexplorer.io/tx/aedd04b41e50585fb30236b3f83010fa82cef70f6f5569face03a084cf67f5bd

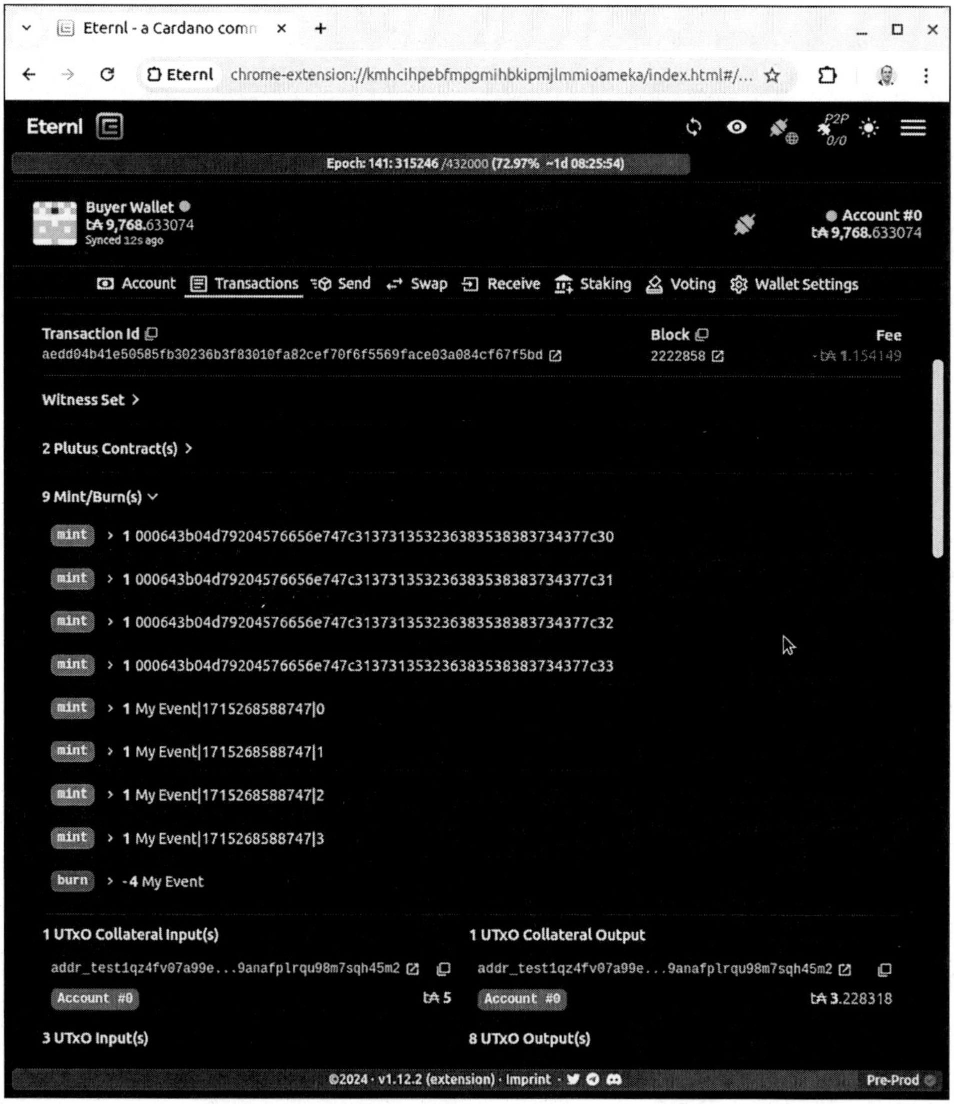

Figure 10.48: *Buy Tickets Wallet Transaction*

My Tickets

Once the transaction has been confirmed on the blockchain, the user can go to the `My Tickets` page to see the tickets in their wallet, as shown in *Figure* 10.49. Since the user owns the ticket tokens, they can also send them to another wallet or list them on a Cardano **DEX** for resale. Closer to the time of the event, the user will print their tickets to generate a unique QR code that they present at the event. The QR code is used to verify the ticket and will be marked as used when verified.

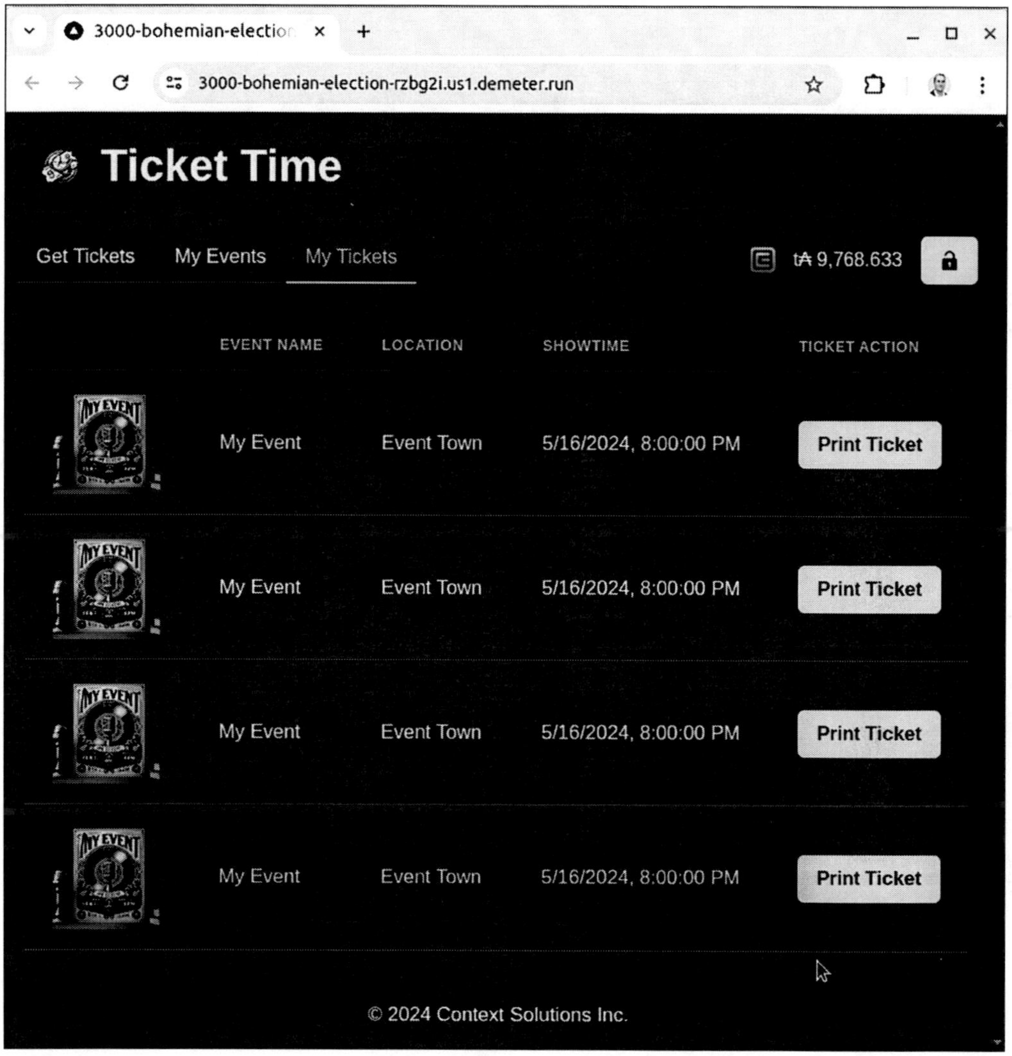

Figure 10.49: *My Tickets*

Print Ticket

When the user selects a `Print Ticket` button, they will need to sign a transaction that updates the reference token with the public key hash of the wallet. This way we know for sure that the user actually owns the ticket at the time of printing. If this transaction is successful, the user will be presented with a QR Code that they can save for later and present at the event, as shown in *Figure* 10.50.

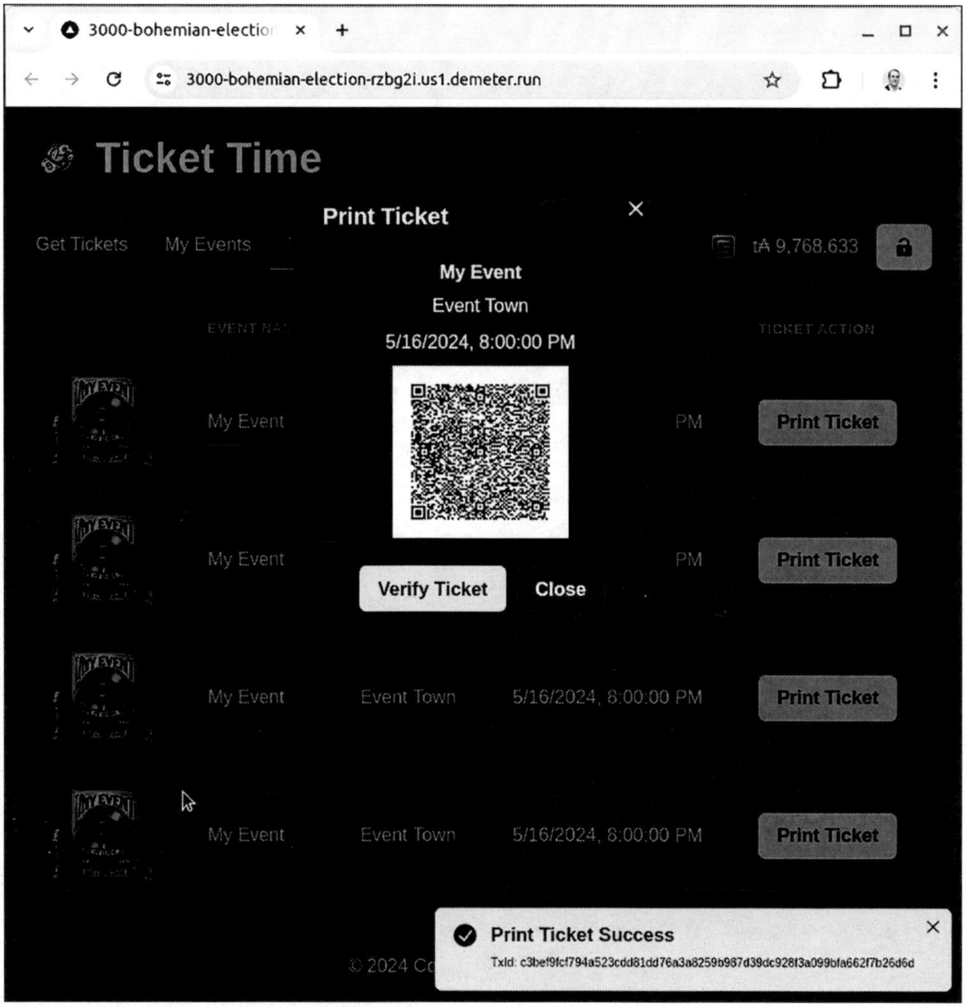

Figure 10.50: *Print Tickets*

Verify Ticket

To simulate verifying a ticket at an event, the `Print Ticket` popup window has a `Verify Ticket` button. When selected, it will check the QR Code signature and message to confirm that they match the public key hash in the database or reference token datum, as shown in *Figure 10.51*. Only a user with the corresponding private key could have generated this QR Code.

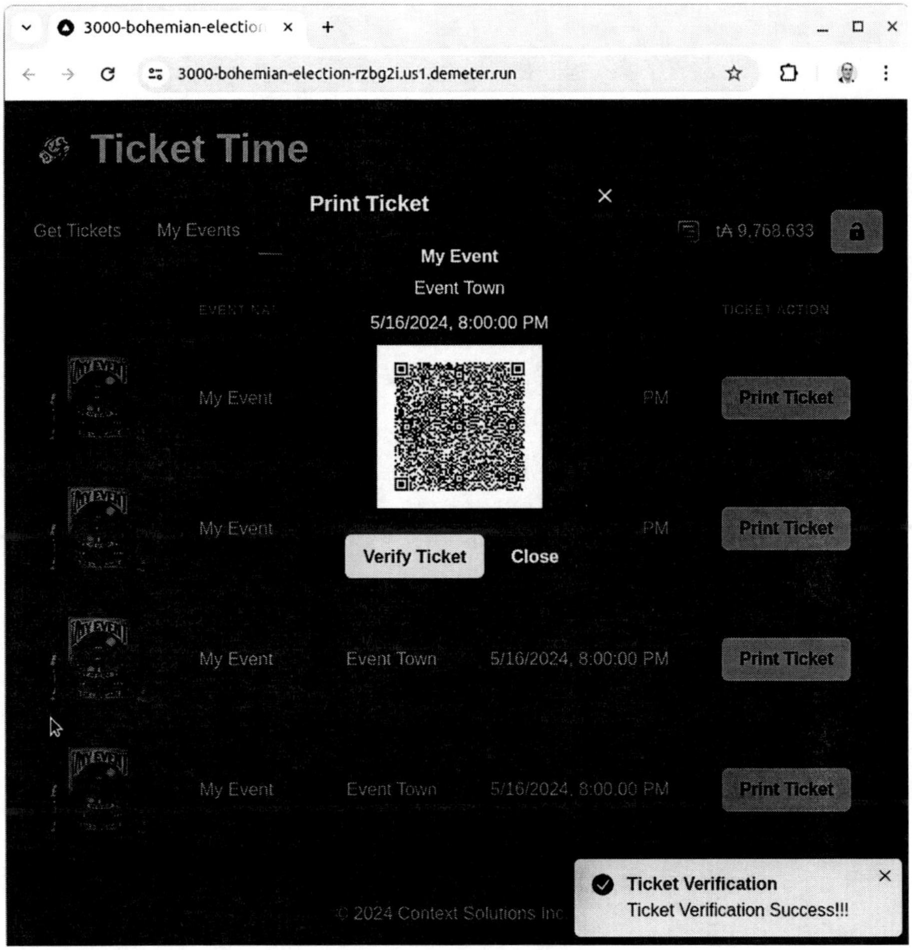

Figure 10.51: *Verify Ticket*

Close Swap

The last part of the demo is to close a swap position. Therefore, we will switch wallets back to the event owner wallet and go to the **`My Events`** page, as shown in *Figure* 10.52. We can now see that 4 tickets have been converted, 696 tickets are in released status, and 300 tickets are in the holding script.

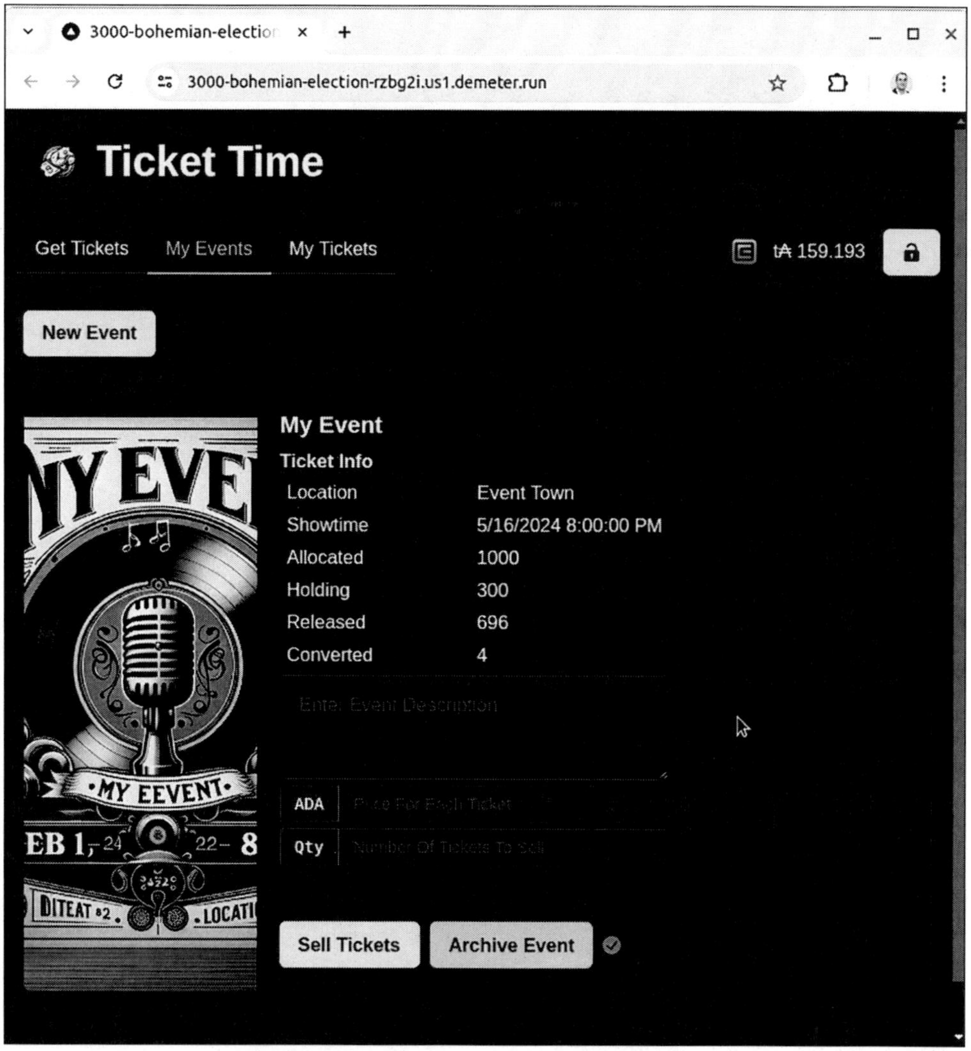

Figure 10.52: *Converted Tickets*

On the **`Get Tickets`** page, using the event owner's wallet, the swaps are displayed with a **`Close Swap`** button that returns the tickets back to the holding script, as shown in *Figure* 10.53.

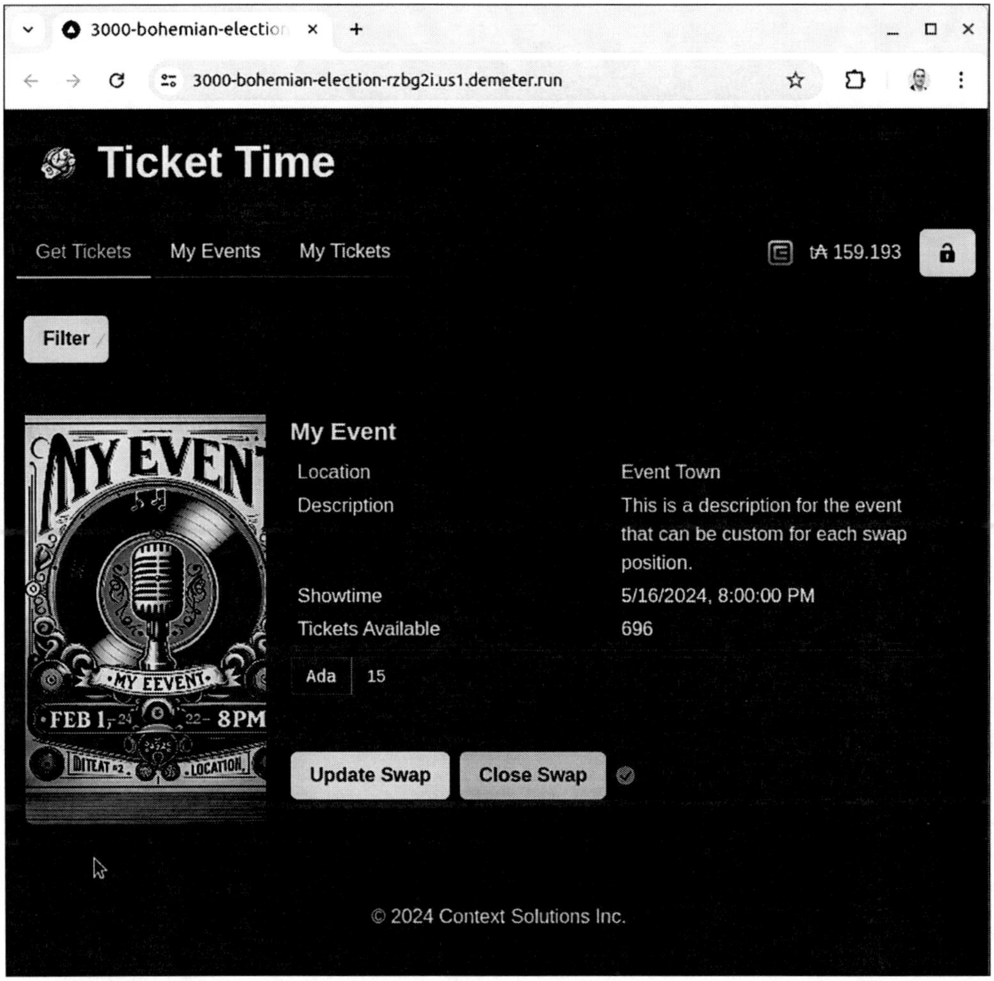

Figure 10.53: *Close Swap*

After the **`Close Swap`** transaction has been completed, the event owner will see that the number of tickets in the holding script is **`996`**, as shown in *Figure* 10.54.

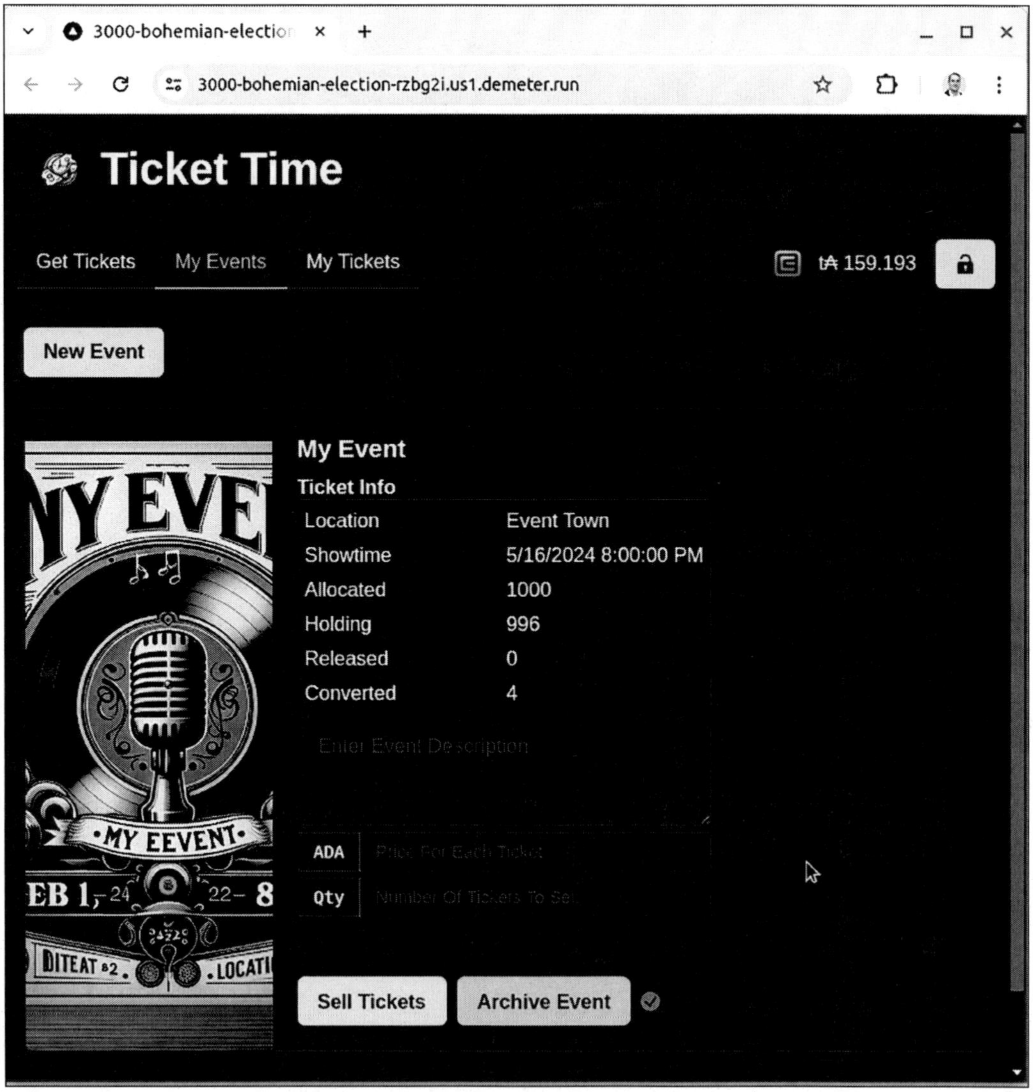

Figure 10.54: *Holding Tickets*

Search

The user is also able to search for open swaps using either a text-based search or filter on showtime or the number of tickets. In our demo, we now have two swaps open and will text search "`Jane Town`", which is only found in one of the swaps, as shown in *Figure 10.55*.

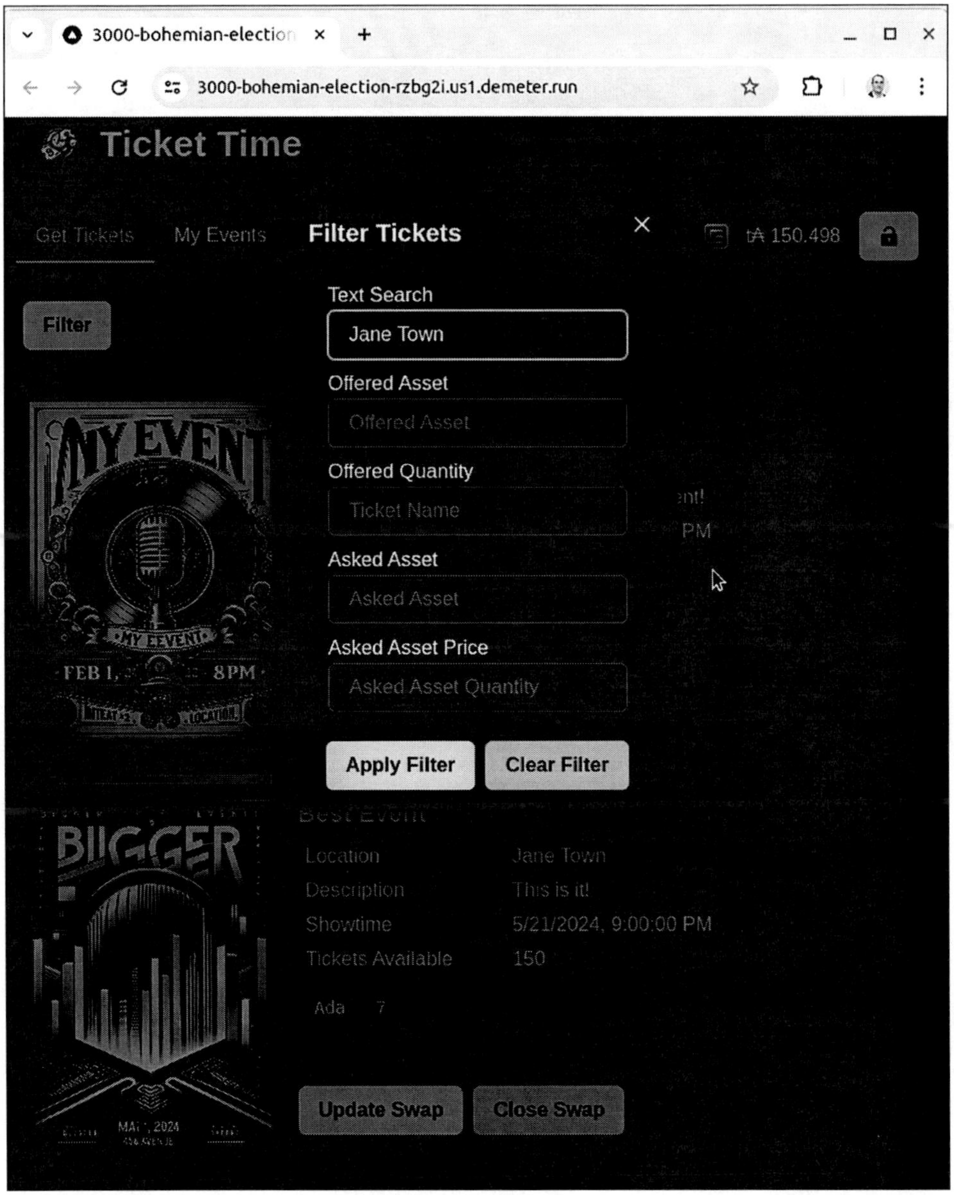

Figure 10.55: *Search Swaps*

Once the user has selected the **`Apply Filter`** button, only the ticket swaps that match the text are displayed, as shown in *Figure* 10.56. We are able to filter the swaps because we have replicated the blockchain swap data and metadata into our application database.

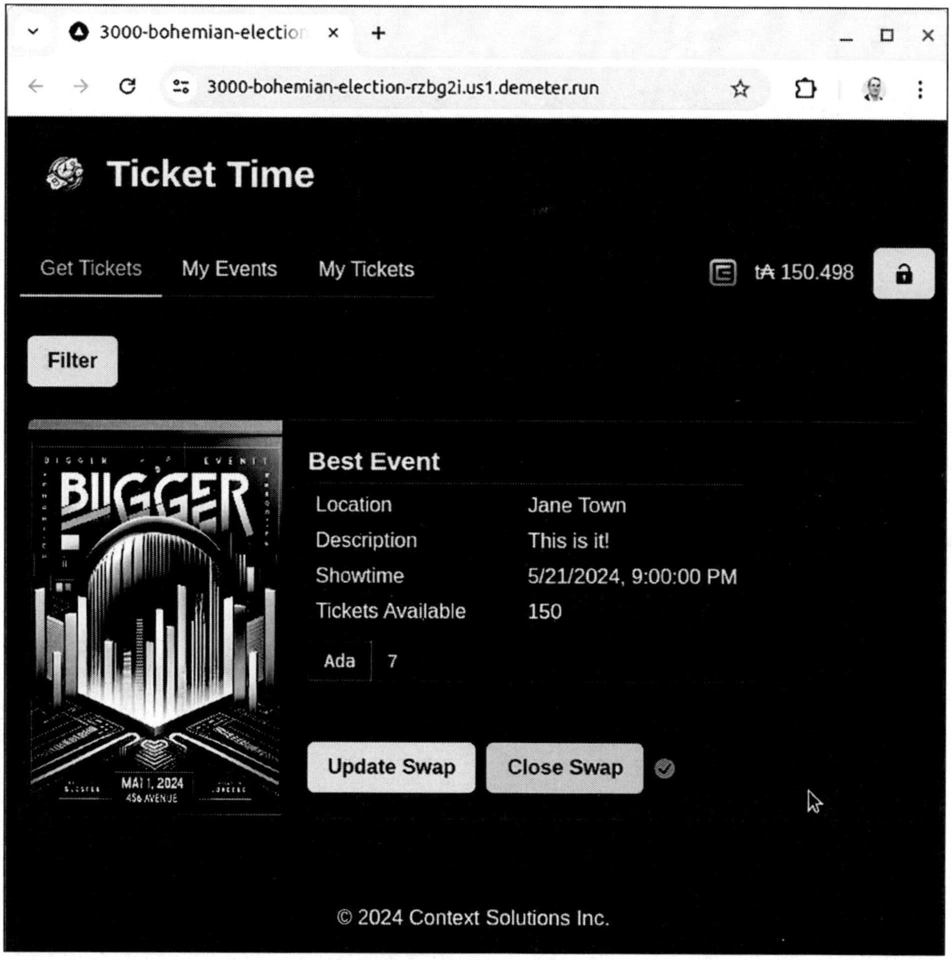

Figure 10.56: *Search Swaps*

Browser Wallet

The ticket tokens can also be viewed directly in the browser wallet, as shown in *Figure* 10.57. As previously mentioned, the ticket tokens are Cardano NFT native tokens and can be sent to another wallet or dApp directly without requiring a third party to facilitate the transaction.

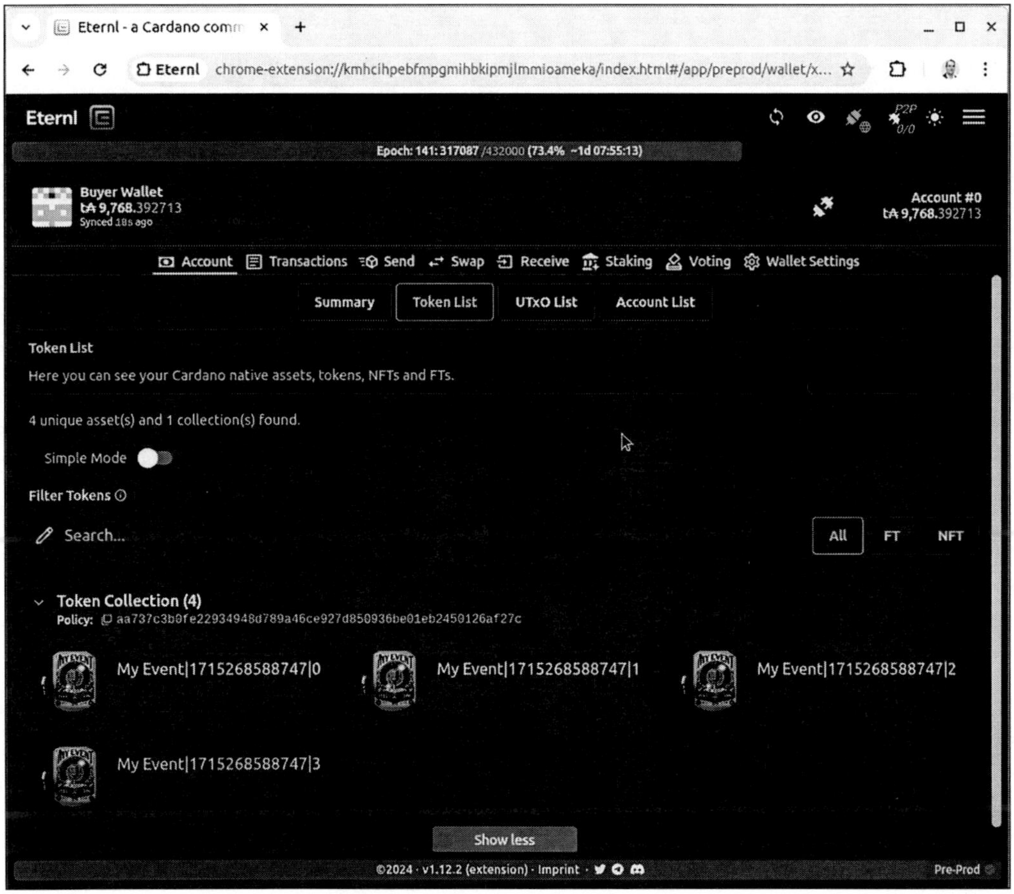

Figure 10.57: *Browser Wallet Tokens*

Blockchain Benefits

Currently, we have centralized, close-door event ticket providers with monopolistic control in the market that limits and stifles competition. Using blockchain, an event organizer can create their own ticket sales and redemption processes, leveraging the security and decentralization properties of blockchain. In particular, the advantages of a blockchain solution are as follows:

- Event data immutability
- Ticket asset uniqueness and authenticity
- Fair and transparent ticket allocation and distribution
- Genuine ticket resale verification
- Permissionless (or Permissioned) ticket token resellers
- Trustless auditing of ticket sales and attendance

- Ticket tokens can also be used for rewards and loyalty points
- Avoids third-party payment processors and settlement

Conclusion

In this chapter, we reviewed the implementation details of a more complex, multi-validator blockchain-based application. We explored the concepts of data replication to improve the user experience when dealing with blockchain data and events. We leveraged the technical stack of ChakraUI, Next.js, Redis DB, and Blockfrost to create a fully functional ticketing application. This included managing the complete ticketing lifecycle (mint, sell, buy, redeem). Using a QR code, we showed how the application is able to generate a digital signature to prove the ownership of a ticket for event redemptions. We also looked at some of the typical challenges with Smart Contract development such as circular references, inspecting inputs and outputs, and blockchain confirmations. We looked at how to implement a Redis DB schema to support the searching of blockchain swaps and creating APIs to support a dynamic blockchain-based React application. Finally, we finished with an end-to-end demo showcasing the features and benefits of a blockchain application. In the next chapter, we will look at testing techniques and how to write secure and scalable blockchain applications.

Points to Remember

- Pure client-side blockchain applications are more true to the principles of blockchain and provide the best transparency and auditability.
- The Redis DB contains the data models used by the application and is a copy of the relevant blockchain data.
- Redis DB is an in-memory database that allows for extremely fast read operations.
- Replicating blockchain data and metadata into an application database allows for an improved user experience and rich UI features such as multi-dimensional filters and searches.
- Global state information in Next.js is passed into child React components using props such as the walletAPI JavaScript object.
- UI changes can trigger real-time application and database changes while the application listens for blockchain block confirmations.
- The CIP-68 metadata standard prefixes a hex label to the token name to distinguish between a user token and a reference token.
- The swap datum contains an **`askedAssetValue`** and an **`offeredAssetValue`**.
- The **`askedAssetValue`** specifies the asset being asked for and the price for each of the offered assets.

- The `offeredAssetValue` specifies the asset being offered and the amount of the asset currently locked in the swap.
- Time validity intervals are needed when trying to evaluate deadline conditions within a Smart Contract.
- A thread token can be created using the transaction ID and index as contract parameters or as the token name.
- Circular references occur when a smart contract depends on knowing in advance the address of another smart contract and vice versa.
- A Blockfrost webhook calls the application when a blockchain event involving a beacon policy occurs.
- Ticket tokens once minted and converted are unique Cardano NFT native tokens.

Multiple Choice Questions

1. What are the advantages of a pure client-side blockchain application?
   a. Faster response times
   b. Easier to audit and trust
   c. Easier to build
   d. Does not require a browser
2. What are the advantages of replicating blockchain data in blockchain applications?
   a. Simplified architecture
   b. Improve decentralization
   c. Better user experience
   d. Better vendor support
3. What is the difference between CIP-25 and CIP-68?
   a. They are the same and both record transaction metadata
   b. CIP-25 uses a datum to record transaction metadata
   c. CIP-68 uses transaction metadata to record NFT metadata
   d. CIP-68 uses a reference token with a datum to record NFT metadata

4. Why are time validity intervals needed?
    a. The Cardano blockchain can only confirm if a range of time is valid for a particular transaction
    b. The Cardano blockchain uses Oracles for time
    c. The Cardano blockchain is non-deterministic
    d. A Cardano Block is created approximately every 20 seconds
5. When can a circular reference occur?
    a. A Plutus Script uses a reference script
    b. Cardano is deterministic, so this is not a valid scenario
    c. A Plutus script references another Plutus script and vice versa
    d. Using a pointer address

Answers

1. b
2. c
3. d
4. a
5. c

Questions

1. What are some of the approaches to improve the user experience while maintaining audibility and transparency?
2. How do CIP-0067 and CIP-0068 relate to each other?
3. How do you calculate the correct minimum lovelace for a particular UTXO?
4. How are inputs sorted, and why is it difficult to know in advance?
5. Are there other approaches to resolving the circular reference problem?

Key Terms

- **Blake2B:** Produces cryptographic hashes optimized for 64-bit architectures.
- **Blockchain Confirmation:** The acceptance of a block to the Cardano blockchain network.
- **DEX:** Decentralized Exchange.
- **Functional Components:** A React UI component.
- **Redis JSON full stack:** Optional components to the Redis DB to store JSON objects.
- **Time Interval:** The start and end time in milliseconds.
- **Trustless Model:** Ability to self-audit and does not require trusting an application.
- **`useEffect`:** Triggers and actions based on a page mount or variable change.
- **Witness Signature:** Contains both the message and the signature and proves the message was signed by the given public key.

CHAPTER 11
Testing, Security, and Scaling

Introduction

This chapter will show how to test Smart Contracts and include them in a popular testing framework such as Vitest. We will look at both the traditional testing and property-based testing approaches. Next, we will focus on security and review vulnerabilities that have been identified in real-world audits of Cardano applications. We will look in detail with code examples of how to make your Smart Contract code more robust and more resilient to such attacks. Finally, we will close the chapter with a discussion around scaling and some tools and techniques to improve dApp performance.

Structure

In this chapter, we will discuss the following topics:

- Testing Frameworks
    - Test Strategy
    - Test Cases
    - Property-Based Testing
- Secure Smart Contracts
    - Double Satisfaction
    - Invalid Datums
    - Token Leakage
    - Audits
- Scaling
    - Avoiding UTXO Contention
    - Reference Scripts

- Advanced Smart Contract Designs
- Hydra
- Mithril
- Input Endorsers

Testing Frameworks

Testing Smart Contracts is always tricky because code is executed on distributed nodes across the Cardano network. Fortunately, most Smart Contract developer tooling includes a local emulator that allows us to catch many errors that would otherwise occur on the node. Typically this involves generating traces when the code is executed. Traces are, however, disabled by default and removed for production builds to optimize performance. That said, there may be situations where an error only occurs in production and in those cases, you may need to turn on traces to obtain additional debugging information. Traces are enabled for Helios when the **`optimization`** flag is set to **`false`**, and for Aiken by executing **`aiken build`** with the flags **`--trace-level`** or **`--filter-traces.`**

In this section, we will look at how to use Vitest,[1] a popular testing framework, to test both the on-chain and off-chain code. Vitest is fast and has an interactive web page for inspecting passed and failed test cases. It is suitable for watching any changes in off-chain code and re-running the tests automatically. Vitest can also be part of an overall application testing framework that can test the entire application and not just the Smart Contracts. A disadvantage of Vitest is that it does not work well with Webpack because Vitest uses Vite, which does not use Webpack. There are other testing frameworks such as Jest[2] that do support Webpack, but Jest has its own challenges with setup and configuration.

We will use the vesting example in *Chapter 6, Validators*, to demonstrate how to use Vitest and test Smart Contracts. Before we can start, we first need to refactor the code to pull out the off-chain code from the front-end user interface (**UI**) code. This has two benefits:

- Clean separation of the **UI** from off-chain transaction building.
- Creates functions that can be used by the front-end and testing framework without any modifications.

The new folder structure to support this separation of **UI** and off-chain code is shown in *Figure 11.1*.

[1]https://vitest.dev/
[2]https://jestjs.io/

```
vesting/
├── components
│   ├── Cancel.tsx
│   ├── LoadingSpinner.tsx
│   ├── Lock.tsx
│   ├── Unlock.tsx
│   ├── WalletConnector.tsx
│   └── WalletInfo.tsx
├── contracts
│   ├── config
│   │   ├── protocolParams.ts
│   │   └── settings.ts
│   ├── off-chain
│   │   ├── cancel.ts
│   │   ├── lock.ts
│   │   ├── network.ts
│   │   ├── types.ts
│   │   ├── unlock.ts
│   │   └── utils.ts
│   ├── tests
│   └── validators
│       └── vesting.hl
├── pages
│   ├── _app.tsx
│   └── index.tsx
│
```

Figure 11.1: *Refactored Vesting Project*

All **UI** code is located in the **`pages/index.tsx`** and components directory. The **UI** code will contain all **UI** elements and application state information, such as what wallet is connected, wallet balance, and more. All off-chain code is located in **`contracts/off-chain`**, and the on-chain code is located in **`contracts/validators`** directories. The **`contracts/config`** folder defines the network we connect to (for example, Mainnet, Preprod, and so on) and the protocol parameters.

Testing Strategy

The testing strategy uses both traditional testing and property-based testing.[3] Traditional testing involves creating specific test cases to confirm that the Smart Contract correctly implements the requirements. This can include both positive and negative test cases. Property-based testing will attempt to exploit inputs into the Smart Contract and test conditions that are not expected.[4] We will use fast-check[5] for typescript that integrates well with Vitest. One consideration in doing this type of testing is that the off-chain transaction builder framework performs validity checks before **UPLC** evaluation. So, some of your failed tests will be the error handling of the off-chain transaction builder and not the Smart Contract. A potential solution is to have off-chain tooling to avoid any checks while still building and submitting a

[3]Gabriel Lebec, "The Magic of Generative Testing: Fast-Check in JavaScript"
[4]John Hughes, "Testing smart contracts with QuickCheck by John Hughes"
[5]https://fast-check.dev/

transaction. Making this type of change is outside of the scope of this book, but it may be considered as a future feature request to enable this option. With Aiken, you can modify the script context for traditional and property-based testing. However, the downside to this approach is that it does not integrate well into a testing framework such as Vitest and is time-consuming to set up.

The test cases for the vesting application are shown in *Figure* 11.2.

```
├── tests
    ├── cancel.test.ts
    ├── lock.property.test.ts
    ├── lock.test.ts
    ├── unlock.property.test.ts
    ├── unlock.test.ts
    ├── utils.ts
    ├── vitest.config.all.ts
    ├── vitest.config.property.ts
    └── vitest.config.test.ts
```

Figure 11.2: *Vesting Test Cases*

The test cases that confirm the business logic and negative test cases are located in **`cancel.test.ts,`** **`lock.test.ts`**, and **`unlock.test.ts`**. The property-based tests are located in **`lock.property.test.ts`** and **`unlock.property.test.ts`**. The **`vitest.config.*`** files specify what tests are included in each test run. To execute a test run locally, issue the following commands:

```
$ cd chapter_11/helios/vesting
$ npm install
$ npm run test:ui
```

This will start up Vitest in watcher mode and display the test execution results, as shown in *Figure* 11.3.

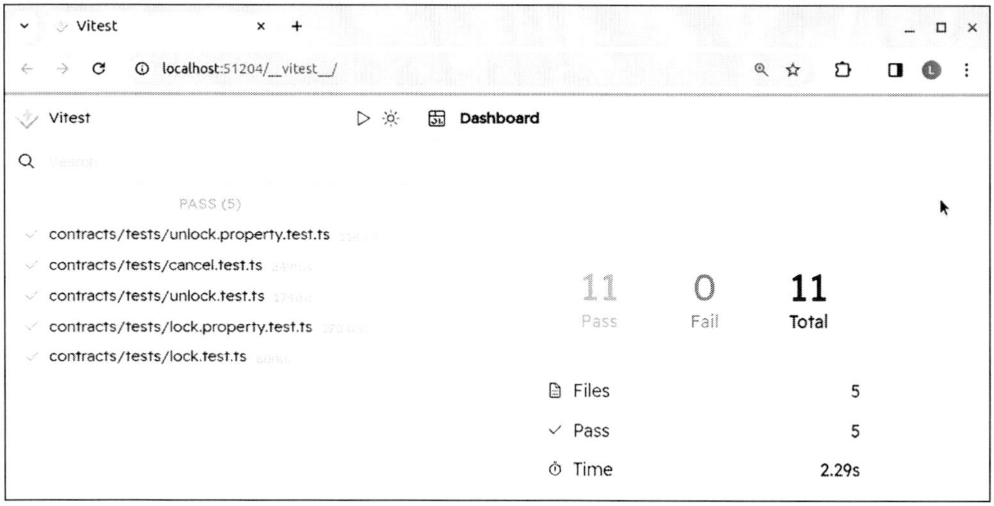

Figure 11.3: *Vitest Watcher*

We can then drill down into any passed or failed scenarios to see each individual test execution, as shown in *Figure 11.4*.

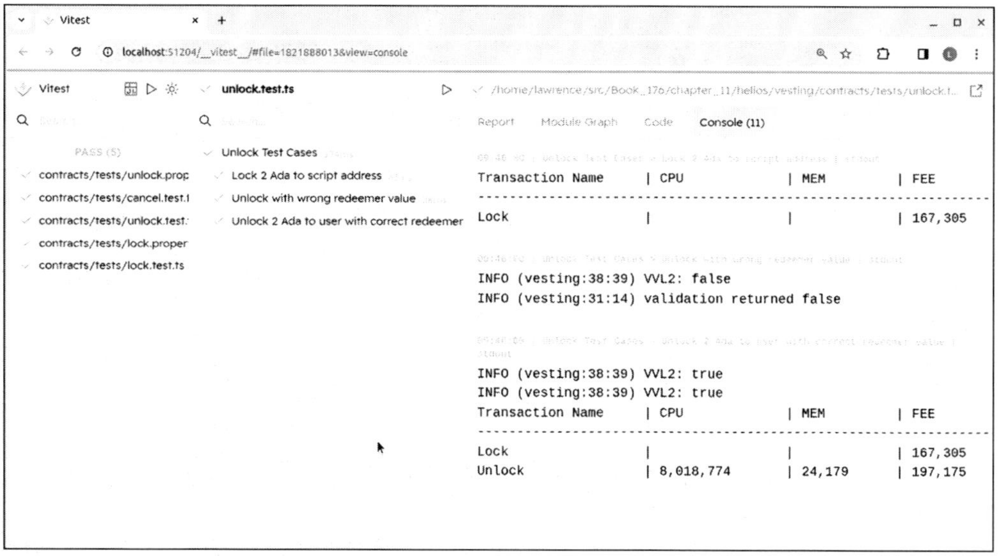

Figure 11.4: *Vitest Test Details*

In Figure 11.4, we selected the unlock test scenario, which executed three test cases:

- Lock 2 Ada test case
- Unlock 2 Ada with an incorrect redeemer
- Unlock 2 Ada with a correct redeemer

The console view on the right shows the executed transactions and the fee, CPU, and memory costs. Locking 2 Ada to a vesting script address does not invoke the Smart Contract, so no script execution units are used. Only the unlock (or cancel) transactions invoke the Smart Contract and will show `cpu` and `mem` values. We have also included trace information inside the Smart Contract, which is shown on the console view in *Figure* 11.4. This allows us to easily find what in the validator script is failing.

Test Cases

The Helios and Lucid + Aiken test case source code and setup are almost identical. The Lucid provider, however, is slightly easier to switch between a real network and an emulator network. Therefore, we will show the Lucid + Aiken code in this section. In *Figure* 11.5, the first step is to create an emulator with two test accounts, as shown on lines 41 and 42.

```
41  const ACCOUNT_0 = await generateAccount({ lovelace: 30000000000n });
42  const ACCOUNT_1 = await generateAccount({ lovelace: 60000000000n });
43
44  let exCosts = [] as ReturnType[]
45
46  /**
47  * Unlock Test Cases
48  */
49  describe('Unlock Test Cases', async () => {
50
51    const emulator = new Emulator([ACCOUNT_0, ACCOUNT_1 ], protocolParams);
52
53    // Create an instance of NetworkEmulator
54    const lucid = await Lucid.new(emulator, 'Custom');
55
56    // Read in the validator script and determine the script address
57    const validator = await readValidator();
58    const contractAddress = lucid.utils.validatorToAddress(validator);
```

Figure 11.5: *unlock.test.ts*[6]

On line 49, we specify the test scenario, which includes one or more test cases. The lucid provider created on line 54 will use the emulator instance we created on line 51. The first test case is to lock Ada on line 63 in *Figure* 11.6. We test for pre-conditions to ensure that the amount locked at the Smart Contract and wallet balance beforehand is correct.

```
63    test('Lock 2 Ada to script address', async () => {
64
65      // Pre-condition
66      let lockedAssetStart = { lovelace: 0n } as Assets;
67      const contractUtxosStart = await lucid.utxosAt(contractAddress);
68      const contractAssetsStart = contractUtxosStart.reduce((acc, utxo) =>
69        addAssets(acc, utxo.assets), { lovelace: 0n } as Assets
70      );
71
72      assert.deepEqual(contractAssetsStart, lockedAssetStart);
73
74      // Connect to wallet 0
75      lucid.selectWalletFromSeed(ACCOUNT_0.seedPhrase);
76      const walletUtxoStart = await lucid.wallet.getUtxos();
77      const walletAssetsStart = walletUtxoStart.reduce((acc, utxo) =>
78        addAssets(acc, utxo.assets), { lovelace: 0n } as Assets
79      );
```

Figure 11.6: *Lock 2 Ada Test Case Part 1*[7]

The next step is to call the **`lock`** off-chain function on line 81 in Figure 11.7. This is the same function that is called from the front-end **UI**, except that the lucid provider is connected to an emulator network. Once the **`lock`** function has been executed, we check if the return status is true on line 86 and then update the execution cost

[6]https://github.com/ava-orange-education/Mastering-Cardano-Smart-Contracts/blob/main/chapter_11/aiken/vesting/contracts/tests/unlock.test.ts

[7]https://github.com/ava-orange-education/Mastering-Cardano-Smart-Contracts/blob/main/chapter_11/aiken/vesting/contracts/tests/unlock.test.ts

counters, which will be used in the test case reports. We must also manually create an emulator block on line 89. Finally, we check that the 2 Ada has been successfully locked at the Smart Contract address on line 99.

```
81    const result = await lock({
82      lovelace: lockAmount,
83      lucid: lucid,
84      validator: validator
85    });
86    expect(result.status == 200).toBeTruthy();
87
88    exCosts.push(result);
89    emulator.awaitBlock(10);
90
91    // Post conditions
92    let lockedAssetEnd = { lovelace: lockAmount } as Assets;
93    const contractUtxosEnd = await lucid.utxosAt(contractAddress);
94    const contractAssetsEnd = contractUtxosEnd.reduce((acc, utxo) =>
95      addAssets(acc, utxo.assets), { lovelace: 0n } as Assets
96    );
97
98    // 2 Ada is locked at script address
99    assert.deepEqual(contractAssetsEnd, lockedAssetEnd);
```

Figure 11.7: *Lock 2 Ada Test Case Part 2*[8]

The unlock (or cancel) test case is very similar to the lock test case, except that we need to pass a message to the redeemer on line 168 in *Figure* 11.8. We also include pre- and post-conditions for the user's wallet to confirm that the user (or owner for cancel) received the locked 2 Ada, minus the transaction fees.

```
158    // Correct message
159    const message = "Hello World!"
160
161    // Connect to wallet 1
162    lucid.selectWalletFromSeed(ACCOUNT_1.seedPhrase);
163    const walletUtxoStart = await lucid.wallet.getUtxos();
164    const walletAssetsStart = walletUtxoStart.reduce((acc, utxo) =>
165      addAssets(acc, utxo.assets), { lovelace: 0n } as Assets
166    );
167
168    const result = await unlock({
169      message: message,
170      lucid: lucid,
171      validator: validator
172    })
173    expect(result.status == 200).toBeTruthy();
174
175    exCosts.push(result);
176    emulator.awaitBlock(10);
```

Figure 11.8: *Unlock 2 Ada Test Case*[9]

[8]https://github.com/ava-orange-education/Mastering-Cardano-Smart-Contracts/blob/main/chapter_11/aiken/vesting/contracts/tests/unlock.test.ts

[9]https://github.com/ava-orange-education/Mastering-Cardano-Smart-Contracts/blob/main/chapter_11/aiken/vesting/contracts/tests/unlock.test.ts

Property-Based Testing

To perform property testing, we typically need to build the transaction using off-chain code to directly feed inputs into the Smart Contract redeemer, datum, or contract parameters. The unlock test case, as shown in *Figure* 11.9, involves sending invalid redeemer messages to the off-chain unlock function. To use the fast-check library, we must call **`fc.assert`** on line 163, which will wrap the **`fc.asyncProperty.`** It is inside the **`asyncProperty`** that fast-check will generate pseudo-random strings that we can pass into the unlock function as the message. We expect this to fail every time, so the property test passes when every execution attempt fails.

```
160    // Connect to wallet 1
161    lucid.selectWalletFromSeed(ACCOUNT_1.seedPhrase);
162
163    fc.assert(
164      fc.asyncProperty(fc.string(), async (message) => {
165        try {
166          // Arrange
167          // Act
168          let status = await unlock(message);
169          // Assert
170          expect(status).toBeFalsy();
171        } catch (err) {
172          expect(true).toBeTruthy();
173        }
174      }),
175      { verbose: 2 }
176    )
```

Figure 11.9: *Unlock Property Test Case*[10]

Both Helios and Aiken also have native property-based testing frameworks. Helios has a helper class called FuzzyTest[11] that allows you to create randomized data, which can be fed into your Plutus script. Aiken has excellent support for unit- and property-based testing, including a report coverage report. The following is an example of an Aiken unit test and a fuzzy test:[12]

```
use aiken/fuzz

fn answer_of_life(n: Int) -> Bool {
  n == 42
}

test question_of_life() {
   answer_of_life(42) == True
}
```

[10]https://github.com/ava-orange-education/Mastering-Cardano-Smart-Contracts/blob/main/chapter_11/aiken/vesting/contracts/tests/unlock.property.test.ts
[11]https://www.hyperion-bt.org/helios-book/api/reference/classes/FuzzyTest.html
[12]https://aiken-lang.org/language-tour/tests

```
test prop_bool_distribution(predicate via fuzz.bool()) {
  fuzz.label(
    if predicate {
      @"True"
    } else {
      @"False"
    },
  )
  True
}
```

When the **`aiken check`** command is run, the following report will be generated:

```
┍━ aiken_test ━━━━━━━━━━━━━━━━━━━━━━━━━━━━━━━━━━━━━
│ PASS [mem: 1802, cpu: 680589] question_of_life
│ PASS [after 100 tests] prop_bool_distribution
│ · with coverage
│ │ False  53.0%
│ │ True   47.0%
┕ with --seed=4272986809 → 2 tests | 2 passed | 0 failed

  Summary 101 checks, 0 errors, 0 warnings
```

Aiken property tests allow you to specify a predicate to evaluate, which is included in the report. In this example, we can verify that **`True`** and **`False`** values are generated and have a good distribution.

Secure Smart Contracts

The most important aspect of Smart Contract development is security. Smart contracts can be responsible for the value transfer of millions of dollars or for validating the results of an election. Therefore, special consideration is required in designing and writing Smart Contracts in the most secure way possible. This can only be done if you are aware of what *not to do* and examples and best practices on what *to do*. This section will review some of the common pitfalls that have been identified through audits on Cardano.

Double Satisfaction

One of the most frequent vulnerabilities in Cardano Smart Contracts is the double satisfaction vulnerability, as shown in *Figure 11.10*. In this simple NFT swap implementation, the validator script looks at the datum values in each swap to validate the business logic. The assumption is that only one NFT swap is executed at one time. However, there is nothing preventing a transaction from having two swaps included in the same transaction. When this occurs, the swap validator validates each UTXO separately and both hold true so the amount of Ada that goes to Alice is double counted. She should receive 250 Ada for both NFTs but only receives 150 Ada. This is because the higher amount of 150 Ada satisfies both the NFT swap conditions, hence the double satisfaction vulnerability.

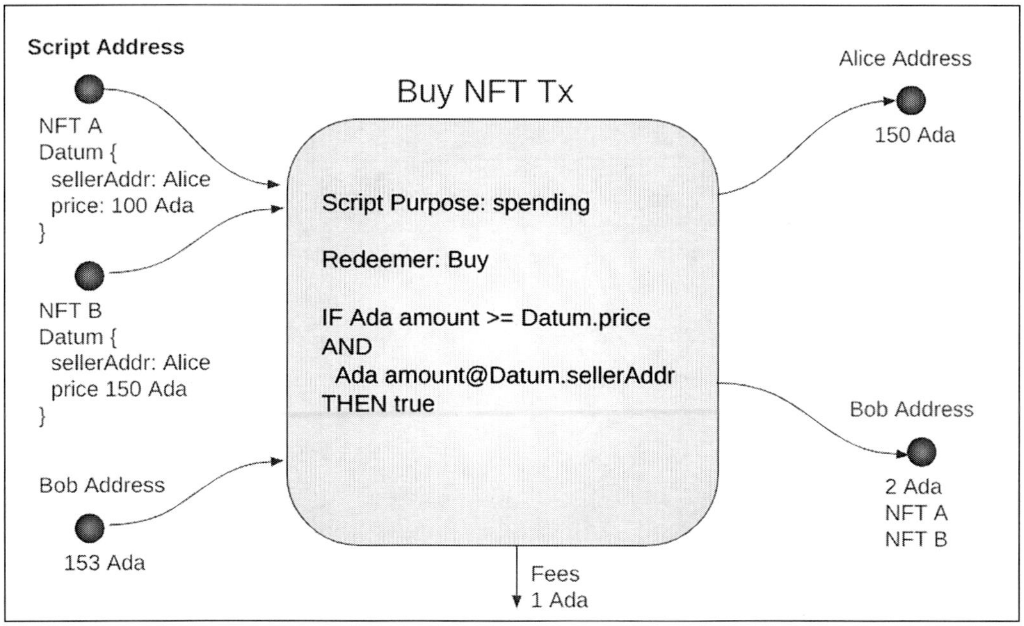

Figure 11.10: *Double Satisfaction Validator*

There are several approaches we can take to address this exploit:

1. Create a unique address for each swap script corresponding to the NFT being sold.
2. Match inputs to outputs so there is a one-to-one correspondence between them.
3. Verify and restrict the outputs that if Alice gets 150 Ada, Bob only gets one NFT B.
4. Use a validity token such that if it is present, the transaction can proceed because validation has occurred elsewhere.
5. We should also restrict other transaction types such as Minting and Withdraws unless there is specific business logic.

Figure 11.11 shows a code example written in Helios for this vulnerability. On line 15, the check to see if the amount sent to the seller is at or above the price is performed.

```
spending buy

struct Datum {
    sellerPKH: PubKeyHash
    price: Value
}
enum Redeemer {
    Buy
}
func main(datum: Datum, redeemer: Redeemer, ctx: ScriptContext) -> Bool {
    tx: Tx = ctx.tx;
    redeemer.switch {
        Buy => {
            // Amount sent to seller must be great or equal to price
            (tx.value_sent_to(datum.sellerPKH) >= datum.price).trace("BVL1: ")
        }
    }
}
```

Figure 11.11: *Double Satisfaction Code Exploit*[13]

To fix this code and avoid the double satisfaction vulnerability, we add a few additional checks, as shown in *Figure* 11.12. First, we require the **PKH** of the buyer in the redeemer on line 8. Second, we define contract parameters to hard code the **NFT** minting policy hash and token name for the validator script on lines 10 and 11. We also create a utility function on line 15 to recursively go through the given outputs and return the total value. Inside the main function, we check that the **NFT** value is sent to the buyer's address using the **PKH** provided by the redeemer. Then, we calculate the total value of all of the outputs, subtract the **NFT** going to the buyer, and verify the remaining value. If the remaining value contains no other tokens, we know that the transaction only had one **NFT** in the outputs and that it went to the buyer.

```
7   enum Redeemer {
8       Buy { buyerPKH: PubKeyHash }
9   }
10  const NFT_TN: ByteArray = #
11  const NFT_MPH: MintingPolicyHash = MintingPolicyHash::new(#)
12  const nftAssetClass: AssetClass = AssetClass::new(NFT_MPH, NFT_TN)
13  const nftValue: Value = Value::new(nftAssetClass, 1)
14
15  func totalValue(outputs: []TxOutput) -> Value {
16      if (outputs.length == 0) {
17          Value::ZERO
18      } else {
19          outputs.get(0).value + totalValue(outputs.tail)
20      }
21  }
22  func main(datum: Datum, redeemer: Redeemer, ctx: ScriptContext) -> Bool {
23      tx: Tx = ctx.tx;
24      redeemer.switch {
25          red: Buy => {
26              // Amount sent to seller must be great or equal to price
27              (tx.value_sent_to(datum.sellerPKH) >= datum.price).trace("BVL1: ") &&
28              (tx.value_sent_to(red.buyerPKH).get_assets() == nftValue).trace("BVL2: ") &&
29              (totalValue(tx.outputs) - nftValue).get_assets().is_zero().trace("BVL3: ")
30          }
```

Figure 11.12: *Double Satisfaction Fix*[14]

[13]https://github.com/ava-orange-education/Mastering-Cardano-Smart-Contracts/blob/main/chapter_11/helios/double-satisfaction-exploit/buy.hl

[14]https://github.com/ava-orange-education/Mastering-Cardano-Smart-Contracts/blob/main/chapter_11/helios/double-satisfaction-fix/buy.hl

Invalid Datums

We saw in the design patterns in *Chapter 9*, *Ticket Application Design*, that a state machine is frequently used in UTXO architecture. It involves maintaining the state in a datum and ensuring the correct datum state is updated as part of a transaction. It is always important to remember that anyone can create a UTXO and lock it at a script address with a malicious datum. Therefore, it is extremely important that a Plutus script always checks whether the inbound and outbound datums are valid. The example we will look at is a multi-sig contract for controlling when the funds can be spent by a beneficiary. It is a two-step process to exploit the vulnerability. The first step is for each required signature to sign a transaction and update the datum with their **PKH**, as shown in *Figure 11.13*.

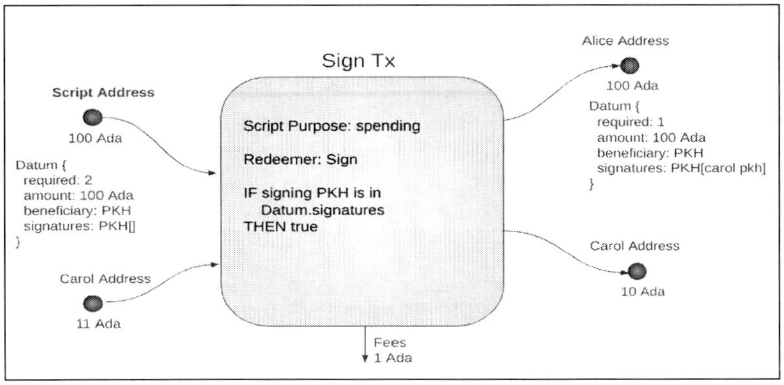

Figure 11.13: *Invalid Datum Sign Tx*

Although there is a check that the **PKH** of the signer is included in the outbound Datun, there is no check that the other Datum fields are not modified. This leads to the exploit where Carol changes the required number of signers from 2 to 1. Now, Bob the beneficiary can release the funds and not have to wait for the second signature, as shown in *Figure 11.14*.

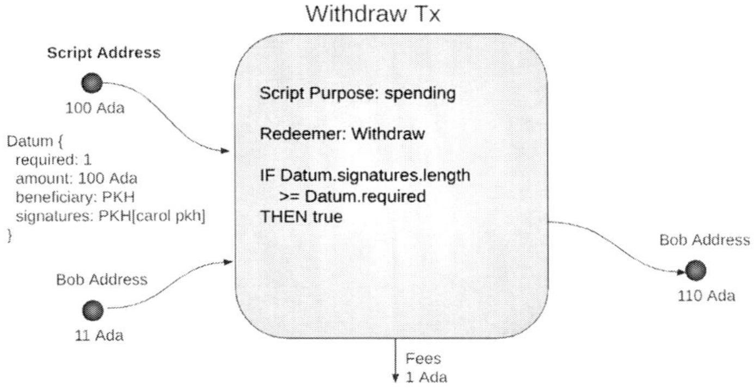

Figure 11.14: *Invalid Datum Withdraw Tx*

Let's examine the code that contains the vulnerability, as shown in *Figure* 11.15. We define the **Datum** on line 3 and the **Redeemer** on line 9 accordingly. The two signatures allowed to sign and update the datum are hard coded as contract parameters.

```
1    spending multisig
2
3    struct Datum {
4        required: Int
5        amount: Value
6        beneficiary: PubKeyHash
7        signatures: []PubKeyHash
8    }
9    enum Redeemer {
10       Sign {
11           pkh: PubKeyHash
12       }
13       Withdraw
14   }
15   const ALICE_PKH: PubKeyHash = PubKeyHash::new(#)
16   const CAROL_PKH: PubKeyHash = PubKeyHash::new(#)
```

Figure 11.15: *Invalid Datum Exploit Datum*[15]

The business logic is contained in the main function in *Figure* 11.16. In particular, line 31 checks that the datum created for the output contains the signers **PKH** in the signatures array.

```
18   func main(datum: Datum, redeemer: Redeemer, ctx: ScriptContext) -> Bool {
19       tx: Tx = ctx.tx;
20       vHash: ValidatorHash = ctx.get_current_validator_hash();
21
22       redeemer.switch {
23           red: Sign => {
24               txOutputContract : []TxOutput = tx.outputs_locked_by(vHash);
25               datumData: Data = txOutputContract.head.datum.get_inline_data();
26               datumOut: Datum = Datum::from_data(datumData);
27               // Each signaure must be signed and then added to the datum
28               (tx.is_signed_by(red.pkh)).trace("MSV1: ") &&
29               (red.pkh == ALICE_PKH || red.pkh == CAROL_PKH).trace("MSV2: ") &&
30               (txOutputContract.head.value == datum.amount).trace("MSV3: ") &&
31               (datumOut.signatures.any((pkh: PubKeyHash)
32                                   -> Bool {pkh == red.pkh})).trace("MSV4: ")
33           },
34           Withdraw => {
35               // Confirm required signatures and only allow beneficiary to spend
36               (datum.signatures.length == datum.required).trace("MSV5: ") &&
37               (tx.is_signed_by(datum.beneficiary)).trace("MSV6: ")
38           }
39       }
```

Figure 11.16: *Invalid Datum Exploit*[16]

[15]https://github.com/ava-orange-education/Mastering-Cardano-Smart-Contracts/blob/main/chapter_11/helios/invalid-datum-exploit/multisig.hl
[16]https://github.com/ava-orange-education/Mastering-Cardano-Smart-Contracts/blob/main/chapter_11/helios/invalid-datum-exploit/multisig.hl

As we can see, the exploit allows the signer (Carol in this case) to change the required number of signatures so that Alice's signature is no longer required. Fixing this vulnerability requires checking *all* datum values and not just the one that is getting updated. In *Figure* 11.17, we create what the output Datum is supposed to look like on line 24. We only look for an output UTXO that matches the new datum on line 30. We perform the same check that the signing **PKH** is included in the updated signatures array on line 32 but tighten the restriction to make sure there are no duplicate signatures on line 38. Finally, we ensure that the signatures list has increased by 1 on line 39.

```
18  func main(datum: Datum, redeemer: Redeemer, ctx: ScriptContext) -> Bool {
19      tx: Tx = ctx.tx;
20      vHash: ValidatorHash = ctx.get_current_validator_hash();
21
22      redeemer.switch {
23          red: Sign => {
24              newDatum: Datum = Datum {
25                  required: datum.required,
26                  amount: datum.amount,
27                  beneficiary: datum.beneficiary,
28                  signatures: datum.signatures.prepend(red.pkh)
29              };
30              txOutput: []TxOutput = tx.outputs_locked_by_datum(vHash, newDatum, true);
31              datumOut: Datum = Datum::from_data(txOutput.head.datum.get_inline_data());
32              filterSigs: []PubKeyHash = datumOut.signatures.filter((pkh: PubKeyHash)
33                                                          -> Bool {pkh == red.pkh});
34              // Each signaure must be signed and then added to the datum
35              (tx.is_signed_by(red.pkh)).trace("MSV1: ") &&
36              (red.pkh == ALICE_PKH || red.pkh == CAROL_PKH).trace("MSV2: ") &&
37              (txOutput.head.value == datum.amount).trace("MSV3: ") &&
38              (filterSigs.length == 1).trace("MSV4: ") &&
39              (datum.signatures.length == datumOut.signatures.length - 1).trace("MSV5: ")
40          },
```

***Figure* 11.17**: *Invalid Datum Fix*[17]

Token Leakage

Another common vulnerability we will delve into is token leakage. This can seriously impact state machines or liquidity pools that rely on a unique token being minted. Smart Contracts may incorrectly validate a transaction if more than one unique token is minted. A high-profile Cardano example was with MinSwap,[18] where this type of vulnerability was identified. Fortunately, no funds were lost, thanks to WingRiders[19] and their quick action. An excellent write-up was provided by Tweag, who performed an audit on the code.[20]

There are variations of this type of vulnerability, and we will look at one particular type in Figure 11.18. It can be difficult to spot these types of vulnerabilities in multi-contract, complex applications.

[17]https://github.com/ava-orange-education/Mastering-Cardano-Smart-Contracts/blob/main/chapter_11/helios/invalid-datum-fix/multisig.hl
[18]https://minswap.org/
[19]https://www.wingriders.com/
[20]https://www.tweag.io/blog/2022-03-25-minswap-lp-vulnerability/

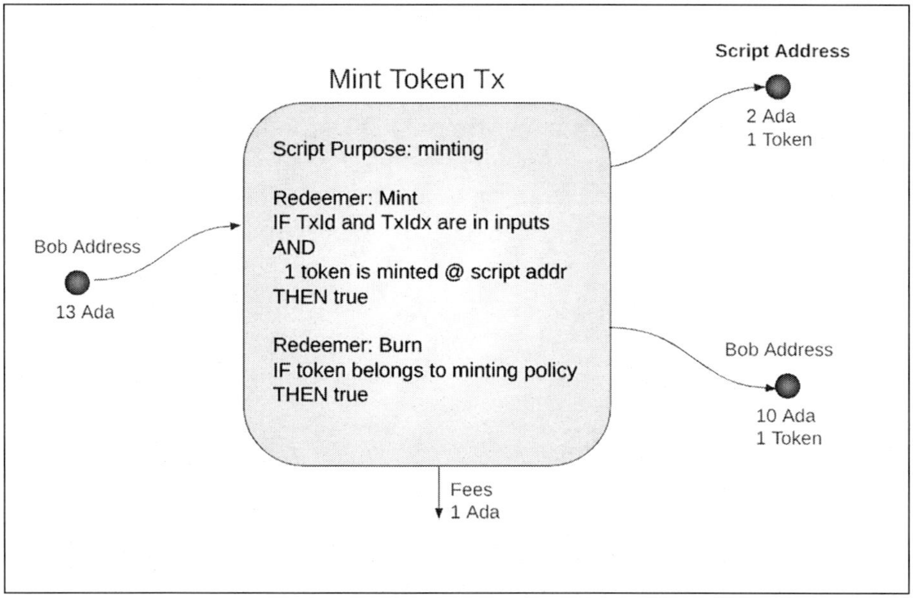

***Figure 11.18:** Token Leakage*

The code in *Figure 11.19* contains an exploit allowing an attacker to mint their thread token. The **`Mint Redeemer`** correctly tests that the Value of what is being minted is the thread token and is a quantity of one. So, the vulnerability actually lies in the Burn redeemer used for burning a thread token. The Burn allows any token to be burned as long as it has the minting policy on line 29.

```
11  func main(redeemer: Redeemer, ctx: ScriptContext) -> Bool {
12      tx: Tx = ctx.tx;
13      mph: MintingPolicyHash = ctx.get_current_minting_policy_hash();
14      tt_assetclass: AssetClass = AssetClass::new(
15          mph, "Thread Token".encode_utf8()
16      );
17      value_minted: Value = tx.minted;
18      redeemer.switch {
19          Mint => {
20              // Only mint 1 asset and confirm TxId and TxIdx are in the inputs
21              (value_minted == Value::new(tt_assetclass, 1)).trace("TTP1: ") &&
22              tx.inputs.any((input: TxInput) -> Bool {
23                          (input.output_id == outputId).trace("TTP2: ")
24                          }
25                      )
26          },
27          Burn => {
28              // Allow the thread token to be burned
29              value_minted.contains_policy(mph).trace("TTP3: ")
30          }
```

***Figure 11.19:** Thread Token Exploit*[21]

[21]https://github.com/ava-orange-education/Mastering-Cardano-Smart-Contracts/blob/main/chapter_11/helios/token-leakage-exploit/threadToken.hl

The issue is that we are not checking the token quantity that is actually being burned; only the minted value contains a particular minting policy. To fix this issue, explicitly check the quantity that is being minted and confirm that it is negative. The code for the fix is shown in *Figure 11.20*, lines 29–31. It looks at the value that is being minted and then iterates through a **map** to check that every entry has a value of negative one.

```
11  func main(redeemer: Redeemer, ctx: ScriptContext) -> Bool {
12      tx: Tx = ctx.tx;
13      mph: MintingPolicyHash = ctx.get_current_minting_policy_hash();
14      tt_assetclass: AssetClass = AssetClass::new(
15          mph, "Thread Token".encode_utf8()
16      );
17      value_minted: Value = tx.minted;
18      redeemer.switch {
19          Mint => {
20              // Only mint 1 asset and confirm TxId and TxIdx are in inputs
21              (value_minted == Value::new(tt_assetclass, 1)).trace("TTP1: ") &&
22              tx.inputs.any((input: TxInput) -> Bool {
23                                  (input.output_id == outputId).trace("TTP2: ")
24                                  }
25                          )
26          },
27          Burn => {
28              // Allow the thread token to be burned
29              tx.minted.get_policy(mph).all( (_, amount: Int) -> Bool {
30                  amount == -1
31              }).trace("TTP3: ")
```

Figure 11.20: *Thread Token Fix*[22]

Audits

It is very important to have an extra pair of eyes to review your code to help spot and identify potential vulnerabilities. This is typically the role of an auditor, and there are several auditing companies that can help with Cardano Smart Contracts.[23] It is also highly recommend to explore the excellent repository by Vacuum Labs, which provides more examples of vulnerabilities from real-world audits using Aiken.[24] Finally, you should also review completed audits to understand the types of common vulnerabilities known to exist fully. Although the Smart Contract code language may be different, such as Haskell or Plutarch, the concepts are the same. The following is a list of published audits for further reading:

- Vacuum Labs[25]
- Tweag[26]
- Mlabs[27]

[22]https://github.com/ava-orange-education/Mastering-Cardano-Smart-Contracts/blob/main/chapter_11/helios/token-leakage-fix/threadToken.hl
[23]https://github.com/cardano-foundation/CIPs/tree/master/CIP-0052
[24]https://github.com/vacuumlabs/cardano-ctf/tree/main
[25]https://github.com/vacuumlabs/audits
[26]https://github.com/tweag/tweag-audit-reports
[27]https://library.mlabs.city/common-plutus-security-vulnerabilities

Scaling

There are several ways to scale smart contracts on the Cardano Blockchain, which we will review in this section. When improving scalability, one must typically consider the trade-offs between decentralization and security. An application is always constrained by the underlying blockchain architecture and that is why choosing what blockchain to use is critical. As we know, Cardano uses the UTXO architecture, which in turn uses local state and not global state. We will leverage this property to increase the scalability of our application.

Avoiding UTXO Contention

For the ticket application in *Chapter 10, Ticket Application Implementation*, we can easily handle many events running simultaneously without any UTXO contention or bottlenecks. However, if there was an extremely popular event, there could be UTXO contention if all of the event tickets were located in one swap UTXO. The way to mitigate this is by creating multiple swaps with batches of tickets that can be accessed in parallel. Much like having multiple ticket windows at a stadium, the off-chain code would need to be modified to route or surface swaps not currently waiting for block confirmations. By distributing event tickets across multiple swaps without any changes to the Smart Contracts, the application scaling limits would directly depend on the underlying blockchain block size and frequency.

Reference Scripts

All of the examples we have looked at so far require spending the UTXO inputs as part of a transaction. With the Vasil hard fork in September 2022, Reference Inputs[28] were introduced, allowing read-only UTXOs to be included in a transaction and not have to be spent. This is particularly useful if you only need to read a datum value and not update it. It dramatically improves concurrency because multiple scripts can simultaneously include and use a reference input. The final benefit paved the way for Reference Scripts,[29] which allows a Plutus script to be included in a UTXO on-chain. By using reference scripts, a transaction does not need to include the Plutus CBOR payload, which will reduce the overall transaction size. As long as the Plutus script is included as a UTXO Reference Input, the transaction will be able to evaluate and execute the Plutus script that is stored on-chain.

Using the vesting example, we will show how to submit a reference script with Helios in *Figure 11.21*. The reference script is put on-chain as a one-time activity inside the `lock` function. On line 89, we first check to see if there already exists a reference script, and if not, then build the output that contains the compiled Plutus script

[28]https://github.com/cardano-foundation/CIPs/tree/master/CIP-0031
[29]https://github.com/cardano-foundation/CIPs/tree/master/CIP-0033

(**`compiledProgram`**) on line 91. We must also evaluate the cost of storing the Plutus script on-chain on line 99. The fee is included in the overall transaction costs and is calculated using the **`coinsPerUTxOWord`** from the network parameters.

```
88      // Only add reference utxo if it does not already exist
89      if (!vestingRefUtxo) {
90          // Construct the output for the reference script
91          const scriptOutput = new TxOutput(
92            Address.fromHashes(compiledProgram.validatorHash),
93            new Value(BigInt(5_000_000)),      // dummy vaule
94            undefined,                         // no datum required
95            compiledProgram
96          );
97
98          // Calculate the Min Lovelace for the output
99          scriptOutput.correctLovelace(params);
100
101         // Now add the reference outputs
102         tx.addOutput(scriptOutput);
103     }
104   }
```

Figure 11.21: *Lock With Reference Script*[30]

Once the reference script has been submitted on-chain, we create a reference input in *Figure* 11.22. On line 83, inside the UnLock function, we query the blockchain for the reference script UTXO. Then, on line 88, we add it to the transaction using **`addRefInput`**, which includes the reference script UTXO and a copy of the original **UPLC** script (**`uplcProgram)`**. The included script will not be submitted to the network and is only used for local evaluation to ensure the transaction is valid before submitting it to the network.

```
79    // Get the UTXO(s) locked at the vesting contract (if any)
80    const vestingUtxo = await getVestingUtxo(
81        Address.fromHashes(uplcProgram.validatorHash)
82    );
83    const vestingRefUtxo = await getVestingRefUtxo(
84        Address.fromHashes(uplcProgram.validatorHash)
85    );
86    // Check that UTXO inputs exists
87    if (vestingUtxo && vestingRefUtxo) {
88        tx.addRefInput(vestingRefUtxo, uplcProgram);
89        tx.addInput(vestingUtxo, vestingRedeemer);
90    } else {
91        throw console.error("No UTXOs found at vesting contract address: ",
92            Address.fromHashes(uplcProgram.validatorHash).toBech32);
93    }
```

Figure 11.22: *UnLock With Reference Script*[31]

[30]https://github.com/ava-orange-education/Mastering-Cardano-Smart-Contracts/blob/main/chapter_11/helios/vesting-reference-script/contracts/off-chain/lock.ts
[31]https://github.com/ava-orange-education/Mastering-Cardano-Smart-Contracts/blob/main/chapter_11/helios/vesting-reference-script/contracts/off-chain/unlock.ts

Advanced Smart Contract Designs

When Smart Contracts were first launched on Cardano, the inefficient Plutus scripts made creating and deploying real-world decentralized applications very difficult. As a result, there were a number of clever ways to reduce the Plutus script size and computation overhead. Some of these advanced techniques are still applicable today, but they come at a cost of added complexity and reduced readability. In situations that require additional performance gains beyond applying the best practices in this chapter, please look at the excellent examples provided by Anastasia Labs[32] for further study.

Hydra

There are two general approaches to scaling a layer 1 blockchain: rollups and layer 2 side chains. Rollups involve processing transactions off-chain, which can be done faster and more efficiently and then applied as one transaction at a later point in time. Layer 2 side chains involve creating a blockchain network similar to layer 1, with faster block creation and settlement times but less decentralization and security. Hydra is a layer 2 scaling solution that creates isomorphic state channels.[33] This means that it has similar ledger rules and a Plutus evaluator that can run most Smart Contracts without any modifications. Hydra is a suite of protocols with the Hydra Head protocol involving the creation (and destruction) of a layer 2 network and the transferring of value back and forth to layer 1.[34]

Hydra's design traces back to the original concepts of the settlement layer and the computation layer for Cardano. There will be situations that require a dedicated layer for computation at the expense of decentralization and security. For example, a Hydra Head could be created for the ticket application discussed in *Chapters* 9 and 10 when there is a planned high-demand ticket sale, as shown in *Figure* 11.23. The Hydra head would be managed by the application with a potential use case as follows:

1. Users who want to participate in a high-profile ticket sale would lock Ada into a Hydra Smart Contract and obtain vouchers (tokens inside the Hydra Head) representing the amount of Ada they have locked.
2. The ticket tokens would be minted in advance on the Cardano layer 1 network and locked into a Hydra Head Smart Contract, so that they are available for sale inside the Hydra Head.
3. Users would interact with the ticket swaps running in the Hydra Head using a custodial wallet managed by the Ticket Application.

---

[32]https://github.com/Anastasia-Labs/design-patterns
[33]https://iohk.io/en/blog/posts/2022/08/05/layer-1-layer-2-all-you-need-to-know/
[34]https://iohk.io/en/blog/posts/2021/09/17/hydra-cardano-s-solution-for-ultimate-scalability/

4. Once the ticket sale is over, the tickets purchased in the Hydra Head are transferred back to the Cardano layer 1 blockchain to the new owners.
5. Any unspent vouchers are converted to Ada on layer 1 and returned to the original owner.

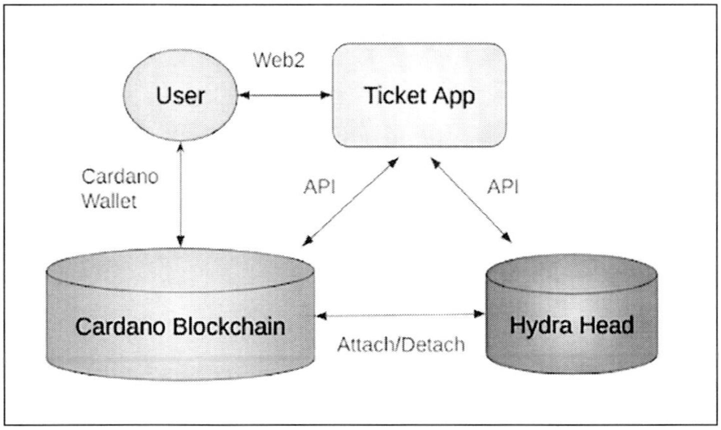

Figure 11.23: *Hydra Head*

The disadvantage of this type of architecture is that the user needs to trust the application owner while the Hydra head is being used. Hydra is currently available for Mainnet but is still early in adoption and maturity. For more information on Hydra, please check out their documentation and discord channel.[35]

Mithril

Mithril is an important development for blockchain scalability, wallets, and Stake Pool Operators (SPOs). It is a solution that allows a client to obtain the current state of the blockchain without having to download and replay all of the transactions from the Genesis block.[36] The core innovation behind Mithril is using stake-based threshold multisignatures[37] (**STM**) to create a certificate by an honest majority of stakeholders that a Cardano snapshot is valid. Using this certificate, a light client or SPO can verify a snapshot with security properties that are similar to a fully synchronized node.[38]

Input Endorsers

Input Endorsers, as documented in Ouroboros Leios, are an ambitious and profound design extension of the Cardano Ouroboros protocol.[39] In particular, it focuses on

[35]https://hydra.family/head-protocol/
[36]Jean-Philippe Raynaud, "Light, fast, efficient, and secure - Mithril"
[37]Pyrros Chaidos et al., "Mithril: Stake-based Threshold Multisignatures", 1
[38]Olga Hryniuk, "How Mithril facilitates strong security settings"
[39]Duncan Coutts, et al., "Ouroboros Leios: design goals and concepts", 1

maximizing the utilization of the network by parallelizing block production and transaction selection.[40] This would significantly increase block production throughput while minimizing additional resource demands on the network. *Figure 11.24* illustrates the current underutilization of the Cardano network and areas for optimization.

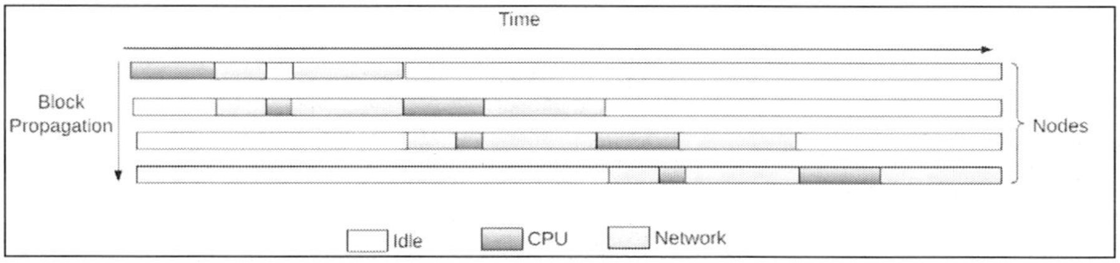

Figure 11.24: *Network Utilization*[41]

Ouroboros Leios introduces three new block types:

- Input Blocks
- Endorsement Blocks
- Ranking Blocks

At a high level, Input Blocks contain the list of transactions taken from the mempool of a block-producing node. This can be done asynchronously during the idle periods, as shown in *Figure 11.24*. Endorsement Blocks then generate certificates of valid Input Blocks. Ranking Blocks then use Endorsement certificates and form a chain of Endorsement Blocks. The ledger state is then based on the order of the Ranking Blocks. It should be noted that Input Endorsers do not change the consensus mechanism of determining the longest chain.[42] For a more detailed and thorough description of Input Endorsers, please refer to the Ouroboros Leios research paper.[43]

Conclusion

We should now have a good understanding of how to test Smart Contracts and include them as part of an overall testing framework. Traditional and property-based testing were examined using tools like Vitest and fast-check. Next, we reviewed code examples from real-world audits and how to avoid common Smart Contract vulnerabilities. Finally, we discussed scaling and some tools and techniques such as avoiding UTXO contention, Reference Scripts, Hydra, and Mithril. We also reviewed layer 1 scalability improvements using Input Endorsers that will significantly increase block production while maintaining security and minimizing additional network resource demands. In the next chapter, we will review troubleshooting tools and techniques that can be used when writing Cardano Smart Contracts.

---

[40]Duncan Coutts, et al., "Ouroboros Leios: design goals and concepts", 7
[41]Duncan Coutts, et al., "Ouroboros Leios: design goals and concepts", 4
[42]Cardaniansio, "Understanding Input Endorsers"
[43]Duncan Coutts, et al., "Ouroboros Leios: design goals and concepts",

Points to Remember

- Testing Smart Contracts is difficult because code is executed on distributed nodes across the network.
- Application design best practices separate UI code from off-chain and back-end code.
- A test strategy can include both traditional testing and property-based testing.
- Security is the most important aspect of Smart Contract development.
- A Double Satisfaction vulnerability involves spending two or more inputs while only validating (satisfying) one input condition.
- An Invalid Datum vulnerability occurs when not all datum fields are checked and verified.
- Token Leakage involves minting more than one unique Thread or Validity token.
- Audits are a key part of production readiness and should be used to review Smart Contract source code.
- Application scaling techniques include avoiding UTXO contention and making use of Reference Scripts.
- Hydra is a layer 2 scaling solution but impacts security and decentralization properties.
- Input Endorsers is a Cardano layer 1 scaling solution to significantly increase block production throughput.

Multiple Choice Questions

1. What techniques would you use to debug a Smart Contract in production?
   a. Use VS Code debugger
   b. Open a support ticket
   c. Enable tracing in production
   d. Restart the Cardano node
2. Property testing test is used for?
   a. Testing unexpected inputs
   b. Testing expected inputs
   c. Regression testing
   d. Non-functional testing

3. Where can Token leakage occur?
    a. Minting script only
    b. Validator or Minting scripts
    c. Validator scripts only
    d. None of the above
4. Reference Scripts are only possible because of _______.
    a. Native Assets
    b. Determinism
    c. Shelly Hard Fork
    d. Reference Inputs
5. What statement about Hydra is correct?
    a. Only a limited number of Hydra heads can be opened
    b. An unlimited number of Hydra heads can be opened
    c. Joining a Hydra head is permissionless
    d. Minted tokens on a Hydra network will be created in the base layer

Answers

1. c
2. a
3. b
4. d
5. a

Questions

1. What are other approaches to testing Smart Contracts?
2. Can you list three other documented vulnerabilities and describe what was involved in the exploit?
3. What are some other use cases for Hydra?
4. What else can Mithril be used for?
5. What are some of the potential risks of Input Endorsers?

Key Terms

- **UPLC:** Untype Plutus Core, the compiled language generated from Helios or Aiken.
- **Map:** A dictionary data type that contains a list of key and value pairs.
- **PKH:** Public Key Hash
- **NFT:** Non-Fungible Token
- **SPO:** Stake Pool Operator
- **STM:** Stake-based Threshold Multi-signatures
- **UI:** User Interface
- **UTXO:** Unspent Transaction Output

CHAPTER 12
Troubleshooting

Introduction

This chapter aims to walk through debugging tools and techniques for Helios and Lucid + Aiken. We will look at generating CBOR for a transaction and comparing data types against formal specifications. We will address reducing the computational overhead of a Plutus script that exceeds the execution budget. We will also examine compiler errors and how transaction builders provide robust error-handling support. Furthermore, Cardano Node errors will be discussed, along with the best strategies for understanding them if they occur. Finally, the chapter will conclude with a brief review of browser-based wallet errors.

Structure

In this chapter, we will discuss the following topics:

- Trace and Print
  - Helios
  - Aiken
- CBOR Analysis
  - Helios
  - Lucid + Aiken
- Execution Budget Errors
- Compiler Errors
- Transaction Builder Errors
- Cardano Node Errors
- Wallet Errors

Trace and Print

When your smart contract is not working correctly, the best way (at the time of writing) to troubleshoot is to use print and traces inside your smart contract. This allows you to write the console log and see what is getting executed in your Smart Contract. We will focus on the Helios and Lucid + Aiken Smart Contract development toolkits used in this book.

Helios

For Helios, as an example, you can print out the value being minted with a particular transaction using the **`print`** and **`show`** functions. The Helios **`optimize`** flag must be set to false to enable tracing.

```
func main(redeemer: Redeemer, ctx: ScriptContext) -> Bool {
   tx: Tx = ctx.tx;
   print("tx.minted: " + tx.minted.show());
```

This will generate the following output when running the Plutus script.

```
INFO (ticket:13:10) tx.minted: lovelace: 0
INFO (ticket:13:10) 0af9021a0…d93cba53ecf15.546872656164205 46f6b656e: 2
```

The line number of the Helios script is also shown in the **`INFO`** brackets. The **`trace()`** function can also be used to emit an output to test a boolean condition.

```
value_minted.contains_policy(mph).trace("TTP3: ")
```

This will generate an output of the evaluation when the Plutus script is executed.

```
INFO (ticket:33:52) TTP3: true
```

If the Smart Contract fails and returns a false boolean value, a stack trace is generated in *Figure 12.1*, which allows you to see where and why it failed.

```
INFO (ticket:32:21) TTP3: false
ERROR (ticket:19:14) validation returned false
    at evalCek (file:///home/lawrence/src/Book_176/chapter_1
helios/helios.js:14935:10)
    at async UplcProgram.runInternal (file:///home/lawrence/
e_modules/@hyperionbt/helios/helios.js:15159:10)
    at async UplcProgram.run (file:///home/lawrence/src/Book
s/@hyperionbt/helios/helios.js:15187:11)
    at async UplcProgram.profile (file:///home/lawrence/src/
dules/@hyperionbt/helios/helios.js:15284:16)
    at async TxWitnesses.executeRedeemer (file:///home/lawre
/node_modules/@hyperionbt/helios/helios.js:49744:20)
    at async TxWitnesses.executeRedeemers (file:///home/lawr
x/node_modules/@hyperionbt/helios/helios.js:49846:17)
    at async TxWitnesses.executeScripts (file:///home/lawren
node_modules/@hyperionbt/helios/helios.js:49772:3)
    at async Tx.executeRedeemers (file:///home/lawrence/src/
dules/@hyperionbt/helios/helios.js:47812:3)
    at async Tx.finalize (file:///home/lawrence/src/Book_176
yperionbt/helios/helios.js:48258:3)
    at async mint (file:///home/lawrence/src/Book_176/chapte
```

Figure 12.1: *Helios Trace()*

Aiken

When you build an Aiken script you can specify what type of tracing you want to include, as illustrated in *Figure* 12.2.

```
-f, --filter-traces <FILTER_TRACES>
        Filter traces to be included in the generated program(s).
          - user-defined: only consider traces that you've explicitly
          defined (either through the
          'trace' keyword of via the trace-if-false ('?') operator.
          - compiler-generated: only included internal traces generated by
          the Aiken compiler, for
          example in usage of 'expect'.
          - all: include both user-defined and compiler-generated traces.
        [optional] [default: all] [possible values: user-defined,
        compiler-generated, all]
-t, --trace-level <TRACE_LEVEL>
        Choose the verbosity level of traces:
          - silent: disable traces altogether
          - compact: only culprit line numbers are shown on failures
          - verbose: enable full verbose traces as provided by the user or
          the compiler
        [optional] [default: silent] [possible values: silent, compact,
        verbose]
```

Figure 12.2: *Aiken Build Trace Options*

To emit **`print`** statements, use the **`trace`** function.

```
trace "redeemer message: "

trace string.from_bytearray(msg)
```

To emit a trace when a condition is evaluated to be false, you use the **`?`** operator.

```
some_expression_a? && some_expression_b?
```

In this example, it can help isolate what expression is failing because if either condition evaluates to false, the entire script will fail.

An example of emitting **`trace`** information is shown in *Figure* 12.3.

```
validator {
  fn vesting(datum: Datum, redeemer: Redeemer, context: ScriptContext) -> Bool {
    when redeemer is {
      Cancel ->
        // Tx must be singed by pkh in datum
        list.has(context.transaction.extra_signatories, datum.owner)?
      Claim { msg } ->
        trace "redeemer message: "
        trace string.from_bytearray(msg)
        // Redeemer must match the message to spend this UTXO
        (msg == message)?
    }
```

Figure 12.3: *Aiken Traces*

The validator script is compiled using the **-t** flag.

```
$ aiken build -t verbose
```

The following output is generated when the script is executed when the validator fails, as shown in *Figure 12.4*.

```
err: Redeemer (Spend, 1): The provided Plutus code called 'error'.

ExBudget {
    mem: 21079,
    cpu: 9252632,
}

redeemer message:
You Rock!
msg == message ? False
Validator returned false
```

Figure 12.4: *Aiken Traces*

CBOR Analysis

As we learned in previous chapters, a Plutus script is compiled into **UPLC** and converted into the **CBOR** format. We typically inspect **CBOR** using the hexadecimal representation of the underlying bytes. This binary format is stored and executed on-chain, so looking at this when troubleshooting is helpful.

Helios

Helios has excellent support for **CBOR** serialization and deserialization and you can easily view any part of the transaction in **CBOR** format.

```
await tx.finalize(networkParams, alice.address, utxos);
console.log("tx final: ", tx.toCborHex());
```

You can also easily deserialize a transaction or any transaction component back into a Helios object using `fromCbor()`.

```
const txCbor = tx.toCborHex();
const newTx = Tx.fromCbor(txCbor);
console.log("tx from cbor: ", newTx.dump());
```

Lucid + Aiken

Aiken provides the **`cbor.diagnostic()`** function to help generate **CBOR** that can be used for troubleshooting. To print out the **CBOR** representation of the **`msg`** in *Figure 12.3*, we can use:

```
trace cbor.diagnostic(msg)
```

This will generate the **CBOR** representation of a bytearray:

```
h'596F7520526F636B21'
```

We can also print out the **CBOR** representation of the entire transaction easily using Lucid.

```
const signedTx = await tx.sign().complete();
console.log("signedTx: ", signedTx.toString());
```

The **CBOR** output in hexadecimal can then be used in https://cbor.nemo157.com/ to inspect and analyze the **CBOR** elements. Once you have the **CBOR** elements, you can compare them against the formal **CDDL** specifications[1] to see if there are any discrepancies. As we can recall from *Chapter* 5, *Transactions*, the **CDDL** is the Concise Data Definition Language used to describe the structure of a transaction.

Execution Budget Errors

If you have not encountered execution budget errors, you will eventually.

```
CekError An error has occurred:  User error:\\\\nThe machine terminated
part way through evaluation due to overspending the budget.\\\\nThe budget
when the machine terminated was:\\\\n({ cpu: -447572\\\\n| mem: 5302\\\\n}
```

Execution budget errors are typically detected during transaction construction, so the off-chain transaction builder framework generates a more user-friendly error. The preceding error *can also* occur when the off-chain framework has not supplied the correct budget values in the redeemer for each Plutus script being executed. This will result in an execution budget mismatch, which the Cardano node rejects.

There is another scenario where the order of the inputs is different between what is executed locally and what is executed on the Node. The order of the inputs will be re-ordered to follow the canonical **CBOR** order format.[2] However, the ordering of the *outputs* will remain the same as when they were created during off-chain transaction construction. This is why it is preferred to inspect outputs rather than inputs. For more information on this subject, please refer to CIP-0021[3] , which documents the canonical ordering and how it relates to hardware wallets and tokens.

---

[1]https://github.com/IntersectMBO/cardano-ledger/blob/master/eras/babbage/impl/cddl-files/babbage.cddl
[2]https://datatracker.ietf.org/doc/html/rfc7049#section-3.9
[3]https://github.com/cardano-foundation/CIPs/tree/master/CIP-0021

In the previous chapter, we showed how to include CPU and memory units in your testing so you can keep track of a transaction's execution budget. Remember that a Plutus script is resource-constrained to minimize the hardware requirements for the node operators. This, in turn, promotes decentralization since anyone can run a node without requiring specialized hardware or infrastructure.

When you trigger a CPU or memory execution limit error using Helios, the error message will be displayed, as shown in *Figure* 12.5. It indicates what was exceeded and the current values of the protocol parameters during the evaluation. This is helpful so you can isolate exactly what contributes to the **cpu** and **mem** units and tune accordingly.

```
Error: execution budget exceeded for cpu (11957505917 > 10000000000)
  MintingRedeemer 0: mem=946122, cpu=11957505917
    builtins
      mkNilData: mem=32, cpu=22558
      mkNilPairData: mem=32, cpu=16563
      unBData: mem=64, cpu=62440
      bData: mem=128, cpu=4000
      ...
      fstPair: mem=96, cpu=241308
      equalsData: mem=2, cpu=2284352
      chooseUnit: mem=920, cpu=10675910
    terms
      startup: mem=100, cpu=100
      call: mem=180600, cpu=41538000
      lambda: mem=12000, cpu=2760000
      variable: mem=103300, cpu=23759000
      builtin: mem=51400, cpu=11822000
      const: mem=47700, cpu=10971000
      force: mem=51100, cpu=11753000
      delay: mem=1600, cpu=368000
```

***Figure* 12.5**: *Helios Execution Units Error*

Protocol parameters can be changed by network updates, so it is best to query the network to get the current value. This can be done using a tool like https://cexplorer.io/params or **cardano-cli**, as shown in *Figure* 12.6.

```
cardano-cli query protocol-parameters --testnet-magic 1

...
"maxTxExecutionUnits": {
    "memory": 14000000,
    "steps": 10000000000
},
"maxTxSize": 16384,
...
```

***Figure* 12.6**: *Network Protocol Parameters*

In general, the following guidelines will help you optimize your Plutus script:

- Compile Helios scripts with **optimize=true** and **aiken build** without any traces or logging levels.
- Avoid unnecessary data conversions and work directly with the serialized data structures.

- Avoid iterating through the list of UTXO inputs if possible and focus on specific UTXO outputs.
- If you encounter script size or CPU and memory execution limit errors, split out validator logic across multiple scripts using separate transactions.
- Use reference scripts to reduce the transaction size.

Compiler Errors

Both Helios and Aiken handle errors well during script compilation. A typical error generated using Helios creates a stack trace that shows you exactly what and where the error occurred.

Here is an example of invalid syntax for assigning a variable using Helios.

```
tx = ctx.tx;
```

Figure 12.7 shows the error message, which states the type of error, the script name, and the line number.

```
UserError: (ticket:12:8) TypeError: unable to infer type of assignment rhs
    at UserError.new (file:///home/lawrence/src/Book_176/chapter_11/helios/
yperionbt/helios/helios.js:1592:10)
    at UserError.typeError (file:///home/lawrence/src/Book_176/chapter_11/h
les/@hyperionbt/helios/helios.js:1638:30)
    at Site.typeError (file:///home/lawrence/src/Book_176/chapter_11/helios
hyperionbt/helios/helios.js:1513:20)
    at AssignExpr.typeError (file:///home/lawrence/src/Book_176/chapter_11/
ules/@hyperionbt/helios/helios.js:1855:21)
    at AssignExpr.evalInternal (file:///home/lawrence/src/Book_176/chapter_
modules/@hyperionbt/helios/helios.js:30905:10)
    at AssignExpr.eval (file:///home/lawrence/src/Book_176/chapter_11/helic
@hyperionbt/helios/helios.js:30105:23)
    at FuncLiteralExpr.evalInternal (file:///home/lawrence/src/Book_176/cha
node_modules/@hyperionbt/helios/helios.js:32048:32)
    at file:///home/lawrence/src/Book_176/chapter_11/helios/token-leakage-e
s/helios.js:36276:24
    at TypeParameters.evalParametricFuncType (file:///home/lawrence/src/Boc
-exploit/node_modules/@hyperionbt/helios/helios.js:34994:16)
    at TypeParameters.evalParametricFunc (file:///home/lawrence/src/Book_17
loit/node_modules/@hyperionbt/helios/helios.js:35011:21)
```

Figure 12.7: *Helios Builder Error*

Here is an example of an invalid variable assignment for Aiken.

```
let { transaction, purpose } = context
```

This will generate an error and indicate the line number and reason for the error (refer to *Figure* 12.8).

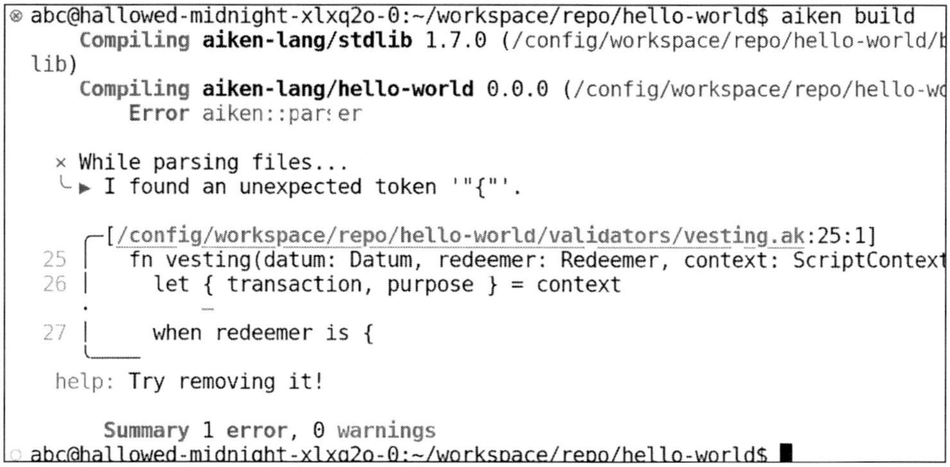

Figure 12.8: *Aiken Builder Error*

Transaction Builder Errors

Both Helios and Lucid have good transaction-building error messages, and there are a lot of error conditions and different reasons why an error may occur. The most common error is insufficient funds because a transaction is not balanced. This can occur because there is insufficient Ada to cover transaction fees or if there are not enough tokens being minted to match the outputs. Luckily these errors can be debugged using a local debugger and you should be able to identify the problem. If you still have issues, search and ask questions on the Cardano stack exchange[4] or the Helios[5] and Lucid/Translucent[6] discord channels accordingly.

Cardano Node Errors

Unfortunately, Cardano Node (Ledger) errors are the most challenging to diagnose. This is because you will see unfamiliar error messages that are poorly formatted, making them difficult to read[7] and understand. *Figure* 12.9 provides an example of a Cardano Node error you may see when a transaction fails.

[4]https://cardano.stackexchange.com/
[5]https://discord.gg/uARRRGXNRr
[6]https://discord.gg/A4cpwNXzEC
[7]https://github.com/IntersectMBO/cardano-node/issues/3126

```
{code: 2, info: 'Wallet could not send the tx.', message: '"transaction submit error
ShelleyTxValidationError…evLASPi7yrah51Ichh5ZP03///+CCAA=\\" :| []))))))])"'}
        code: 2
        info: "Wallet could not send the tx."
        message: "\"transaction submit error ShelleyTxValidationError
        ShelleyBasedEraBabbage (ApplyTxError [UtxowFailure (UtxoFailure
        (FromAlonzoUtxoFail (UtxosFailure (ValidationTagMismatch (IsValid True)
        (FailedUnexpectedly (PlutusFailure \\\"\\\\nThe 2 arg plutus script
        (PlutusScript PlutusV2 ScriptHash
        \\\\\\\"639f8f9051a92e9f39f9157af2c048f8bbcab6a1e7521c861e593f4d\\\\\\\")
        fails.\\\\nCekError An error has occurred:  User error:\\\\nThe machine
        terminated part way through evaluation due to overspending the
        budget.\\\\nThe budget when the machine terminated was:\\\\n({ cpu:
        -447572\\\\n| mem: 5302\\\\n})\\\\nNegative numbers indicate the overspent
        budget; note that this only indicatessthe budget that was needed for the next
        step, not to run the program to completion.\\\\nThe protocol version is:
        ProtVer {pvMajor = 8, pvMinor = 0}\\\\nThe redeemer is: Constr 0 []\\\\nThe
        second data argument, does not decode to a context\\\\nConstr 0 [Constr 0
        [List [Constr 0 [Constr 0 [Constr 0 [B
        \\\\\\\"\\\\\\\\138|bb9\\\\\\\\183\\\\\\\\202\\\\\\\\203Tj\\\\\\\\168~\\\\\\\
        \133\\\\\\\\GS\\\\\\\\220\\\\\\\\134P\\\\\\\\156\\\\\\\\SO4\\\\\\\\196J\\\\\\
        \\EOT\\\\\\\\247\\\\\\\\254xUQ\\\\\\\\r}\\\\\\\\158\\\\\\\\128\\\\\\\"],I
```

***Figure 12.9**: Cardano Node Error*

To better understand what the error messages mean, you may need to refer to the Cardano Ledger[8] source code written in Haskell. You will see the code and comments that can explain why an error occurs. The example in *Figure* 12.9 is fairly straightforward and is an execution budget error. There are other errors not as obvious and may require looking at the code to understand what the error means. Fortunately, most of these errors are now caught by the off-chain transaction builder, so encountering Cardano Node errors is not as common as it used to be.

Wallet Errors

The last type of error we will review is wallet error. These occur when using a browser extension wallet and are listed in *Table* 12.1.

Error Types	Error Name	Description	Value
API Error	`InvalidRequest`	Inputs are not valid and do not conform to the CIP-0030 specification	-1
	`InternalError`	An internal error occurred during this request	-2
	`Refused`	The dApp was not approved to access the browser wallet	-3
	`AccountChange`	The wallet account has been changed	-4

[8]https://github.com/IntersectMBO/cardano-ledger/tree/master/eras/babbage/impl/src/Cardano/Ledger/Babbage/Rules

Data Sign Error	`ProofGeneration`	The data could not be signed by the wallet	1
	`AddressNotPK`	The address was invalid and not a public key hash address	2
	`UserDeclined`	The user declined to sign the data	3
PaginateError	`maxSize`	The maximum size supported for pagination. Will return the amount supported if the amount requested has exceeded the limit	maxSize
Tx Send Error	`Refused`	The wallet refuses to send the tx (for example, it could be rate limiting)	1
	Failure	The Wallet could not send the tx	2
Tx Sign Error	`ProofGeneration`	The Wallet was not able to sign the transaction	1
	`UserDeclined`	The user declined to sign the transaction	2

Table 12.1: *Browser Extension Wallet Errors*[9]

Conclusion

This chapter provided an overview of debugging tools and techniques for Helios and Lucid + Aiken. We explored how to generate **CBOR** for a transaction and data types to compare it against formal specifications. We also looked at what to do if the Plutus script exceeds the CPU and memory execution limits and suggestions to improve script performance. We then explored how Helios and Lucid + Aiken frameworks provide error messages when we build and submit a transaction. Cardano Node errors were also examined and why we may need to look at the Cardano Ledger source code to troubleshoot if they occur. Finally, we closed the chapter by reviewing browser-based wallet errors that follow the CIP-0030 specification. In the next chapter, we will explore and review the Cardano ecosystem and the resources available to help you build an application on the Cardano blockchain.

Points to Remember

- Debugging Smart Contracts involves emitting traces that can print variables and state information.
- Both Helios and Aiken support traces and have the capability to trace boolean expressions.

[9]https://github.com/cardano-foundation/CIPs/tree/master/CIP-0030#error-types

- **`Trace`** and **`print`** statements in Helios are removed if the **`optimize`** flag is set to `true`.
- Traces in Aiken are removed by default and only present if enabled during the `aiken build`.
- Converting a transaction to **CBOR** is helpful because you can then compare the transaction structure to the **CDDL** specifications for correctness.
- CPU and memory execution budget errors are usually detected by the off-chain transaction builder framework.
- By querying the chain using cardano-cli or blockchain explorers, you can find the current protocol parameters.
- Unbalanced transactions are the most common error when using off-chain transaction builders.
- Errors occurring only on the Cardano Node and not caught by the off-chain transaction builder are rare but can happen.
- Wallet errors are well-documented and return a status code that will map back to a well-defined error message and description.

Multiple Choice Questions

1. When can you use a local IDE debugger to help troubleshoot a Smart Contract?
   a. An error that only occurs on the Cardano Node
   b. Off-chain transaction builder error
   c. Plutus smart contact error
   d. All of the above
2. When would you want to turn on traces in production?
   a. To help troubleshoot a production issue
   b. To improve performance
   c. To capture user analytics
   d. None of the above
3. Where can you find the latest protocol parameters?
   a. The `shelley-genesis.json` file
   b. The `alonzo-genesis.json` file

   c. The node `config.json` file

   d. An active Cardano network

4. Execution budget errors can occur because?

   a. A difference between what was calculated locally and the Cardano node

   b. Cardano is non-deterministic

   c. It depends on what Cardano node is executing the script

   d. Different Cardano node versions

5. CBOR uses what type of ordering?

   a. FIFO

   b. Lexical

   c. LIFO

   d. Canonical

Answers

1. b
2. a
3. d
4. a
5. d

Questions

1. What are other common sources of errors when writing Cardano Smart Contracts?
2. What additional optimization techniques exist to improve Plutus script performance?
3. Why was the Cardano Node written in Haskell?
4. Why are outputs and inputs sorted differently?
5. What are some new ways to help debug Plutus scripts?

Key Terms

- **UPLC:** Untype Plutus Core, the compiled language generated from Helios or Aiken
- **CBOR:** Concise Binary Object Representation
- **CDDL**: Concise Data Definition Library
- **UTXO**: Unspent Transaction Output

CHAPTER 13
Cardano Ecosystem

Introduction

This chapter will first review the state of Cardano with the most recently published report by Messari[1]. Next, we will look at the Cardano GitHub repositories containing all the source code and specifications for the Cardano blockchain. We will examine the Cardano Improvement Process (**CIP**) and how the Cardano blockchain changes and improvements are made. Then, we will look at the newly created Intersect and the creation of a Members-Based Organization (**MBO**) for Cardano. Next, we will explore the era of Voltaire and CIP-1694 regarding Cardano governance. We will then discuss on-chain governance actions such as protocol parameter changes, hard forks, and treasury withdrawals. We will also review the Stake Pool Operator's (SPO) role and where to find additional information on them. Furthermore, we will also examine Project Catalyst, one of the largest decentralized innovation platforms that provides grant funding to Cardano projects. Next, we will review Atala Prism, which enables decentralized identity and provides Self Sovereign Identity (**SSI**) solutions. We will also look at Midnight, a data-protection sidechain being built using the Cardano partner chain framework. Finally, we will discuss additional Cardano Smart Contract development languages and learning resources.

Structure

In this chapter, we will discuss the following topics:

- State of Cardano
- Cardano GitHub Repositories
- Cardano Improvement Process (**CIP**)
- Member Based Organization (Intersect)
- CIP-1694
- Stake Pool Operators
- Project Catalyst

---

[1]https://messari.io/

- Atala Prism (HyperLedger Identus)
- Midnight
- Additional Smart Contract Languages
- Learning Resources

State of Cardano

Messari released its latest Q4, 2023 report on Cardano, and it is worth reviewing some of the key insights of that report.[2]

- The Cardano Total Value Locked (TVL) of Ada in DeFi protocols increased 223.6% year over year. When converted to USD, this ranked Cardano TVL 11th compared to all other blockchains. It is important to mention that staking is not included in Cardano TVL, whereas it is on other blockchains.
- Circulating market capitalization is at 21.1B USD, a 145.3% YoY increase
- The Treasury balance is 1.43B Ada (or 861.4M USD)
- The Nakamoto coefficient was at 31 which is higher (better) than other **PoS** blockchains. It is important to be aware that it is not always possible to determine if multiple pools are in fact operated by the same entity.[3] This was one of the reasons why the Edinburgh Decentralization Index (**EDI**) was created.[4]

One of the best ways to explore the Cardano ecosystem is to use a website like Cardano Cube.[5] The website breaks down the ecosystem into the following categories and has project logos and links in each category, including:

- AI
- Community and DAO
- DeFi
- Developer Tools
- Dex - Liquidity
- Education
- Gaming
- Identity and Data
- Infrastructure
- Launchpad

[2]Red Sheehan, "State of Cardano Q4 2023"
[3]https://nakaflow.io/
[4]https://www.ed.ac.uk/informatics/blockchain/edi
[5]https://www.cardanocube.com/cardano-ecosystem-interactive-map

- Lending and Borrowing
- Marketplaces
- Meme Coins
- Metaverse
- Payment and Stablecoins
- Social
- Tools and Explorers
- Wallets

Year after year, the Cardano ecosystem continues to expand, grow, and mature.

Cardano GitHub Repositories

The Cardano blockchain was built by **IOG** (formerly IOHK), and they controlled and maintained the Cardano GitHub repositories. In Q4 of 2023, these repositories were handed over to Intersect, which oversees the Cardano Membership Based Organization (**MBO**). The Cardano blockchain source code is fully open-source and built with Haskell. Haskell is a very powerful functional programming language and an excellent choice for building high-assurance, complex software that can be linked back to a formal verification or specification.[6] The following is a list of the core Cardano blockchain GitHub repositories[7]:

- Cardano API[8]
- Cardano Base[9]
- Cardano Ledger[10]
- Cardano Node[11]
- Formal Ledger Specifications[12]
- Ouroboros Consensus[13]
- Ouroboros Network[14]
- Plutus Core[15]

---

[6]https://why.cardano.org/en/science-and-engineering/formal-specification-and-verification/
[7]https://github.com/orgs/IntersectMBO/repositories
[8]https://github.com/IntersectMBO/cardano-api.git
[9]https://github.com/IntersectMBO/cardano-base.git
[10]https://github.com/IntersectMBO/cardano-ledger.git
[11]https://github.com/IntersectMBO/cardano-node.git
[12]https://github.com/IntersectMBO/formal-ledger-specifications.git
[13]https://github.com/IntersectMBO/ouroboros-consensus.git
[14]https://github.com/IntersectMBO/ouroboros-network.git
[15]https://github.com/IntersectMBO/plutus

Cardano Improvement Process (CIP)

The Cardano Improvement Process is the mechanism to request and implement changes on the Cardano blockchain. It is important to mention that the **CIP** process focuses on how to get changes done on the Cardano blockchain and not the governance or prioritization of what changes should be done and when. The **CIPs** are located on GitHub[16] and have the following states:

- **Proposed:** Meets all of the **CIP** criteria but not yet active
- **Active:** Is ready for, or in production
- **Inactive**: No longer relevant or has been withdrawn
- **Draft**: Is no longer used, but some older **CIP**s may still be in this state. It is similar to a Proposed **CIP** pull request that has not been merged due to missing or incomplete information.

The onus to obtain feedback and alignment from impacted teams is on the **CIP** author. Cardano is a large, complex system so it may not always be clear who the impacted teams are and they may change over time. That said, the steps to get a **CIP** from concept to implementation are as follows:

1. The **CIP** author opens a pull request with the required CIP information and format.
2. The **CIP** author seeks feedback and input from impacted teams.
3. **CIP** editors review incoming **CIP**s and respond with feedback.
5. **CIP** editors may invite authors and other relevant teams/individuals for reviews to facilitate discussions, feedback, and alignment.
6. Once the **CIP** pull request contains all required information, including sufficient detail, feedback, impact analysis, and a path to active, it will be merged with the main CIP branch.
7. When the **CIP** status changes to Active, it will be implemented following the **CIP**'s documented implementation plan.

CIP Editors are responsible for safeguarding the **CIP** process and will form groups to help enforce the standards outlined in CIP-0001.[17] **CIP** Reviewers may be subject matter experts who are engaged to provide feedback and review a particular **CIP**. **CIP** Editors are not expected to be experts in all areas of Cardano, and it is the responsibility of the **CIP** author to ensure the satisfactory involvement of the required reviewer(s) of a **CIP**. **CIP** Editors can be nominated by existing **CIP** editors or community members if they have shown active contributions to the **CIP** process regularly.[18]

[16]https://github.com/cardano-foundation/CIPs
[17]https://github.com/cardano-foundation/CIPs/tree/master/CIP-0001#editors
[18]https://github.com/cardano-foundation/CIPs/tree/master/CIP-0001#nomination

There is a lot more detailed information on **CIP**s and the **CIP** process that the reader must review[19] thoroughly before proceeding with a **CIP** pull request. A Cardano Problem Statement (**CPS**)[20] has also been introduced to help capture and document a particular problem, which can be used to help create a **CIP**. A **CPS** is not required but is advisable when requesting a change via the **CIP** process.

Member-Based Organization (Intersect)

Intersect was launched in July 2023 and is the Member-Based Organization (**MBO**) of Cardano. Using community governance, Intersect will prioritize and allocate Cardano treasury funding for future maintenance and development of the Cardano Blockchain. To achieve this goal, Intersect focuses on five key areas[21]:

- Support the community and growth of the Cardano ecosystem.
- Administer and advocate on-chain governance as documented by CIP-1694.[22]
- Oversee the delivery of the Cardano Technical Roadmap.
- Facilitate the continuity of Cardano system stability.
- Coordinate open-source development of Cardano core technologies.

Intersect is a non-profit corporation based in Wyoming, United States. Wyoming has favorable legislation[23] regarding the legal structure of a decentralized autonomous organization (**DAO**), and that is why Intersect was incorporated in that state.[24] There is a board of directors for Intersect, and they meet monthly with meeting notes published on the Intersect website.[25] Any Ada holder can join Intersect[26] with community announcements, committee working groups, and meeting information shared on Discord once you become a member.

CIP-1694

Cardano is now in the Voltaire era of the Cardano roadmap which will use on-chain governance to allow the Cardano network to become a self-sustaining system.[27] CIP-1694 documents how an on-chain governance system should work and what would be required for an initial bootstrapping phase known as Minimal Viable Governance

[19]https://github.com/cardano-foundation/CIPs/tree/master/CIP-0001
[20]https://github.com/cardano-foundation/CIPs/tree/master/CIP-9999
[21]https://docs.intersectmbo.org/intersect-overview/what-is-intersect
[22]https://github.com/cardano-foundation/CIPs/tree/master/CIP-1694
[23]Taras Zharun, "Wyoming LLC as a DAO Legal Wrapper: What You Need to Know
[24]https://docs.intersectmbo.org/intersect-overview/intersects-structure
[25]https://docs.intersectmbo.org/intersect-overview/intersects-structure/intersect-governance/governing-board-meetings
[26]https://www.intersectmbo.org/join
[27]https://roadmap.cardano.org/en/voltaire/

(**MVG**). The most important aspect of CIP-1694 is the confirmation that one Ada equals one vote when on-chain voting occurs.

There are three governing bodies documented in CIP-1694 and each play a key role in the governance process.[28]

- Delegated Representative (**DRep**)
- Stake Pool Operator (**SPO**)
- Constitutional Committee (**CC**)

These governing bodies will vote to approve or reject an on-chain proposal depending on the type of proposal being voted on. On-chain governance tooling is currently (as of writing) being tested on the Sanchonet Testnet.[29] Tooling is needed to allow **DReps** and **SPOs** to participate in on-chain governance easily and conveniently.

Delegated Representatives (DReps)

For an Ada holder to vote on an on-chain proposal, they would delegate their voting power like a user delegates their staked Ada to a Stake Pool Operator. Any Ada holder can submit an on-chain proposal, but typically **DReps** with their delegated Ada voting power will cast votes. **DReps** will then vote on proposals and the outcome will indicate whether the vote has been approved or not by the **DRep** governing body.

Stake Pool Operators (SPOs)

SPOs play a critical role in maintaining the network's security by operating the nodes that process and distribute blocks in the Cardano blockchain. As a result, they will have a vote when there are on-chain proposals that involve a hard fork which in turn requires upgrading a network node.[30] They also participate in votes regarding changes to the constitutional committee. Similar to DReps, the collective **SPO** voting power is used to determine if a vote has been approved or not by the **SPO** governing body.

Constitutional Committee (CC)

The **CC** is a group of members elected to the committee for a fixed period. The role of the **CC** is to vote only on the constitutionality of a particular proposal.[31] For example, if the constitution states that a treasury must always exist with 0.125% of all Ada in circulation, then the CC would be opposed to a vote withdrawing Ada from the treasury that violates this threshold. The **CC** can be dissolved at any time with a vote of

[28]https://github.com/cardano-foundation/CIPs/tree/master/CIP-1694
[29]https://sancho.network/
[30]https://www.essentialcardano.io/infographic/cip-1694-in-a-nutshell
[31]https://github.com/cardano-foundation/CIPs/tree/master/CIP-1694#the-constitutional-committee

no confidence, on which only **DReps** and **SPOs** can vote. The **CC** quorum parameters will be used to determine if a vote has been approved or not by the **CC** governing body.

There are seven governance actions documented in CIP-1694 and shown in *Table 13.1*:

Governance Action	Purpose	Who Can Vote
Motion of no-confidence	Used to dissolve the CC	DRep, SPO
New CC or CC threshold changes	Elect members to the CC or change the CC quorum requirements or term limits	DRep, SPO
Update to the Constitution	Make changes to the constitution	DRep, CC
Hard-fork initiation	Approval for a hard fork	DRep, SPO, CC
Protocol parameter changes	Approval for protocol parameter changes	DRep, CC
Treasury withdrawal	Approval to make a withdrawal from the treasury	DRep, CC
Info	Creates on-chain info only record	DRep, CC

Table 13.1: *Governance Actions*[32]

Stake Pool Operators

A key aspect of the success of Cardano's Proof-Of-Stake protocol is the role of the staking and the Stake Pool Operator (**SPO**). A lot of analysis and design went into the mechanics of how an Ada holder can easily and securely delegate their Ada to a stake pool operator while still retaining self-custody. As a result, there is now a large community of Stake Pool Operators that you can stake your Ada with. Most Cardano wallets will provide you with a list of Stakepool operators ranked by Return Of Stake (**ROS**) that you can choose. The following is a list of online tools that allow searching and filtering of Cardano **SPOs**:

- PoolTool[33]
- ADASTAT[34]
- CExplorer[35]
- AdaPool[36]

[32]https://github.com/cardano-foundation/CIPs/tree/master/CIP-1694#governance-actions
[33]https://pooltool.io/
[34]https://adastat.net/pools
[35]https://cexplorer.io/pool
[36]https://adapools.org/pool

- CardanoScan[37]
- Pool.pm[38]

Setting up a Stake Pool is outside of the scope of this book, but there are a lot of great resources online and communities that can help you get started:

- Operate A Stake Pool[39]
- Guild Operators[40]
- CoinCashew[41]
- IOG Academy[42]

Project Catalyst

One of the most interesting aspects of the Cardano ecosystem is Project Catalyst. Project Catalyst started as an experiment to give grants to projects based on voting by Ada holders. There have been 11 Funding rounds, with Fund 1 announced in September 2020[43]. The amount of funding has increased between Fund 1 and Fund 9 and is now currently set at 50 Million Ada per funding round. Using the IdeaScale platform[44] Project Catalyst claims to be one of the largest decentralized innovation funds in the world.[45]

A funding round typically lasts approximately 4 months, allowing the community to participate in various ways and receive compensation in Ada. The community can participate as reviewers, project submitters, voters, or milestone verifiers. The format has changed over time and will continue to evolve based on community feedback and input. Anyone can submit a proposal and form a team; this is one of the main drivers of attracting and retaining talent in the ecosystem. Please refer the following for more information on project catalyst:

- Cardano IdeaScale[46]
- Project Catalyst Website[47]

---

[37]https://cardanoscan.io/pools
[38]https://pool.pm/
[39]https://developers.cardano.org/docs/operate-a-stake-pool/
[40]https://cardano-community.github.io/guild-operators/
[41]https://www.coincashew.com/coins/overview-ada/guide-how-to-build-a-haskell-stakepool-node
[42]Crypto Carlos, "Node course | Creating a stake pool, the setup"
[43]https://iohk.io/en/blog/posts/2020/09/16/project-catalyst-introducing-our-first-public-fund-for-cardano-community-innovation/
[44]https://cardano.ideascale.com/c/landing
[45]Tim Richmond, "Project Catalyst - A virtuous cycle of Cardano ecosystem development"
[46]https://cardano.ideascale.com/c/landing
[47]https://projectcatalyst.io/

- **IOG (IOHK)** YouTube Channel[48]
- Project Catalyst Announcements Telegram Channel[49]

A typical Project Catalyst timeline is shown in *Figure* 13.1:

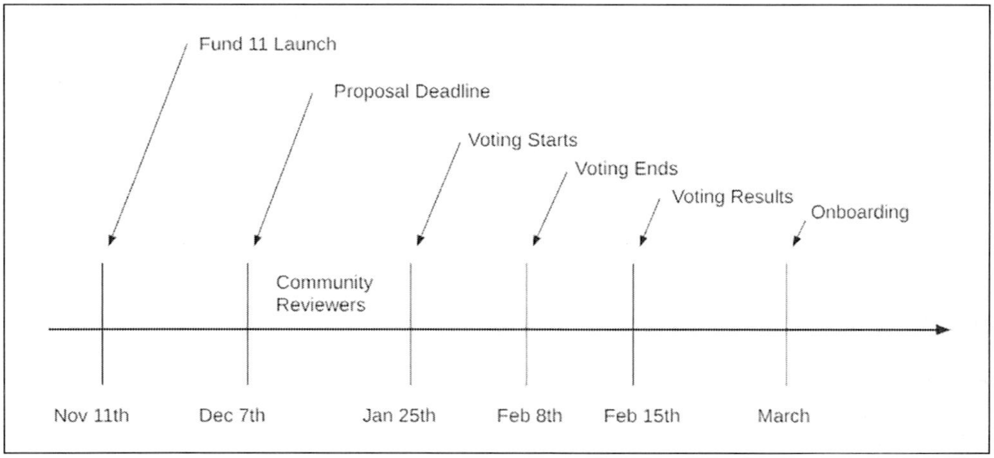

***Figure* 13.1**: *Fund 11 Timeline*

Atala Prism (HyperLedger Identus)

Digital Identity and Self-Sovereign Identity (**SSI**) have the potential to become the next killer app in the blockchain space. Using a secure and decentralized blockchain, an identity solution can allow users to control and own their identity. This is a significant shift from today where a handful of tech companies own your digital identity and where you have no control over how it is used. Furthermore, social media platforms are littered with bots, scammers, and impersonators because **SSI** systems are not used. Social media companies are not financially incentivized to fix this issue because their revenue is based on users on the platform, whether real people or not.

The challenge and the opportunity is that people will start demanding assurances that the person or entity they are interacting with is genuine and accurate. Second, users will want to control who has access to their identity. The Atala Prism **SSI** framework which follows the **W3C-DID** standard[50], allows you to build secure, private, and verifiable interactions.[51] Using **SSI**, you can solve both problems, verify who you are dealing with, and control who has access to your identity. Atala Prism has recently been open-sourced and renamed to HyperLedger Identus.[52]

[48]https://www.youtube.com/@IohkIo
[49]https://t.me/cardanocatalyst
[50]https://www.w3.org/TR/did-core/
[51]https://atalaprism.io/#why
[52]https://github.com/hyperledger/identus

Midnight

Midnight is a data-protection blockchain using zero-knowledge proofs to transact with a public permissionless blockchain while keeping sensitive data private.[53] This has several advantages and can be used in use cases such as identity verification, tokenized asset privacy, AI modules, credit scoring, and voting.[54] Midnight is being built using Parity Technologies' Substrate stack which lays the foundation for additional partner chains in the future.[55] The concept of partner chains will help realize the goal of separation of the Cardano Settlement Layer (**CSL**) and the Cardano Computation Layer (**CCL**).[56] Cardano also has other side chains[57] such as Milkomeda C1[58], Wanchain[59], and World Mobile[60].

Additional Cardano Smart Contract Languages

Although this book has focused on Helios and Lucid + Aiken for Cardano Smart Contract development, other options are available to developers, including:

- **PlutusTx** is a Haskell Module and was the first way to write Cardano Smart Contracts. Several resources, including the Plutus Developer Portal[61] and the Plutus Pioneer Program[62], are available for writing smart contracts using PlutusTx in Haskell.
- **PyCardano + OpShin**[63] allows you to write Cardano Smart Contracts using Python for both the off-chain and on-chain code respectively.
- **Plu-ts**[64] also allows you to write both the on-chain and off-chain code for Cardano Smart Contracts but in typescript.

Learning Resources

There are many excellent resources available to help you learn about Cardano.

---

[53]https://midnight.network/
[54]Neil Burgess, "Calling trailblazers to Midnight"
[55]Mike Ward, "Partner chains are coming to Cardano"
[56]Mike Ward, "Partner chains are coming to Cardano"
[57]Red Sheehan, "State of Cardano Q4 2023"
[58]https://milkomeda.com/
[59]https://www.wanchain.org/
[60]https://worldmobile.io/en
[61]https://developers.cardano.org/docs/smart-contracts/plutus
[62]https://www.youtube.com/playlist?list=PLnPTB0CuBOBypVDf1oGcsvnJGJg8h-LII
[63]https://developers.cardano.org/docs/smart-contracts/opshin
[64]https://developers.cardano.org/docs/smart-contracts/plu-ts

- **Cardano Academy**[65]**,** created by the Cardano Foundation is an excellent all-around resource on blockchain and Cardano.
- **IOG Academy**[66], created by IOG (IOHK), contains a collection of videos on Cardano, Haskell, and the Plutus Pioneers Program.
- **Emurgo Academy**[67], created by Emurgo is a paid program with some of the best developer resources in the ecosystem.
- **Gimbalabs**[68], a pioneer in the open education space in Cardano, focuses on project-based learning and online coding sessions for learning and collaboration.
- **Learn Cardano**[69] always has great topics and speakers on its show, making it a go-to resource for keeping up to date on the Cardano ecosystem.
- **Cardano With Paul**[70] has been creating great Cardano content for years. It continues to showcase exciting new projects and keeps up-to-date with the latest developments in Cardano.
- And many more...

Conclusion

We started the chapter by reviewing the state of Cardano and looking at the published Messari Q4, 2023 report. Next, we reviewed the public GitHub repositories transferred to Intersect, which contained the Cardano blockchain source code. The **CIP** process and how changes are made to the Cardano blockchain using a CIP pull request, with the required information, were examined in the correct format. Intersect, the Cardano Members Based Organization (**MBO**), and the five areas it focuses on were also discussed. Next, we discussed the Voltaire era and how CIP-1694 captures the mechanics of on-chain voting for Cardano governance. We reviewed the list of governance actions such as protocol parameter changes, hard forks, and treasury withdrawals. We also looked at **SPO** return on stake (ROS) rankings and the role of Project Catalyst in the Cardano ecosystem. We also introduced Atala Prism, a Self-Sovereign Identity (**SSI**) solution built on Cardano, and the benefits and opportunities it can provide. Finally, we discussed Midnight, the first type of partner chain on Cardano, as well as additional Smart Contract languages and learning resources. The next and final chapter will discuss the ethos and social impact of Cardano and how blockchain is following the five stages of technology adoption.

---

[65]https://academy.cardanofoundation.org/
[66]https://www.youtube.com/channel/UCX9j__vYOJu0OiqBrCzecVw
[67]https://education.emurgo.io/
[68]https://gimbalabs.com/gimbalgrid
[69]https://www.youtube.com/@LearnCardano
[70]https://www.youtube.com/@CardanoWithPaul

Points to Remember

- Cardano Total Value Locked (**TVL**) does not include the 22.68B Ada staked in the Cardano network.
- Nakamoto coefficients can be misleading because the entities controlling a stake pool are not always known.
- The public Cardano GitHub repositories are now managed by Intersect.
- The **CIP** process is about making changes on the Cardano network, not governing or prioritizing such requests.
- The **CIP** author is responsible for securing feedback and alignment on a proposed **CIP**.
- Intersect, a non-profit **DAO** is the Cardano Members Based Organization.
- CIP-1694 documents how Cardano on-chain voting should work and the initial bootstrapping phase known as Minimal Viable Governance (**MVG**).
- **DRep**, **SPO**, and **CC** are the three governing bodies of on-chain voting.
- Different governing bodies will be required to vote depending on the governance action.
- **DRep**s use delegated voting power from Ada holders to cast a vote, which is aggregated into a yes or no DRep vote for a governance action.
- The **CC** can be dissolved when a governance action of no confidence is passed.
- The **CC** members, quorum requirements, and term limits are voted on by DReps and **SPO**s.
- Project Catalyst, one of the largest decentralized innovation funds in the world, allows Ada holders to vote on projects that will receive grant funding from the treasury.
- There have been 11 Project Catalyst funds, with the last two funds having 50M in Ada available for grants.
- Atala Prism is a Self-Sovereign Identity (**SSI**) solution built on the Cardano blockchain.
- **SSI** allows users to control their identity and who has access to it.
- Midnight is a data protection side chain built using zero-knowledge-proof technology.
- Midnight is an example of a Cardano partner chain that separates the Cardano Settlement Layer from the Cardano Computation Layer.

Multiple Choice Questions

1. Who manages the Cardano open-source code repositories?
    a. Intersect
    b. IOHK
    c. Cardano Foundation
    d. All of the above
2. What example would not be well suited for a CIP?
    a. Suggest a change to the ledger to accommodate a feature request
    b. Suggest a change to the protocol parameters to improve performance
    c. Request a treasury funding withdrawal
    d. Document on-chain governance processes
3. What is the goal of CIP-1694?
    a. Create the Cardano constitution
    b. Finalize Cardano governance and end the Voltaire era
    c. Elect members to the constitutional committee
    d. Document the on-chain governance processes and establish MVG
4. What is false about DReps?
    a. Ada holders will be able to delegate their Ada voting power to a DRep
    b. Ada holders will not be able to change their Ada delegation to a DRep
    c. Ada holders can change or withdraw their Ada delegation by submitting a transaction
    d. Ada holders will be able to see what governance actions their DRep has voted on
5. What statement is true about Project Catalyst?
    a. Project catalyst controls the funds in the Cardano Treasury
    b. Most of the Cardano treasury is spent by Project Catalyst
    c. 20% of transaction fees go to Project Catalyst
    d. The Project Catalyst operations team is funded by Project Catalyst

Answers

1. a
2. c
3. d
4. b
5. d

Questions

1. Why did IOG (formerly IOHK) decide to transfer ownership of the Cardano open-source repositories to Intersect?
2. What improvements or suggestions do you have for the CIP process?
3. What other jurisdictions would have been suitable to incorporate Intersect in?
4. Why is CIP-1694 only focused on Minimal Viable Governance?
5. Can a user be a DRep, Stake Pool Operator, and CC member simultaneously? If so, why is this (or not) an issue?
6. What are some of the difficulties and challenges of running Project Catalyst?
7. What are the barriers to widespread adoption of SSI?
8. What are the risks of using data-protection blockchains?

Key Terms

- **CC:** Constitutionals Committee
- **CCL:** Cardano Computation Layer
- **CIP:** Cardano Improvement Process
- **CPS**: Cardano Problem Statement
- **CSL:** Cardano Settlement Layer
- **DAO:** Decentralized Autonomous Organization
- **DID:** Decentralized Identifier
- **DReps:** Delegated Representatives
- **IOG:** Input Output Global
- **IOHK:** Input Output Hong Kong

- **MBO:** Members Based Organization
- **MVG:** Minimal Viable Governance
- **ROS:** Return On Stake
- **SPO:** Stake Pool Operator
- **SSI:** Self Sovereign Identity
- **TVL:** Total Value Locked
- **W3C:** World Wide Web Consortium

CHAPTER 14
Closing Remarks

Introduction

This chapter will review the ethos of Cardano and how it relates to the peer review process and formal methods. We will examine the software industry standards and how these standards fall short for high-assurance software. We will see how semi-formal methods were used to build Cardano and how cryptographic associations like **IACR** facilitate the peer review process. Next, we will look at the potential for social good using Cardano with real-world examples. We will also discuss regulatory and compliance risks and what to be aware of. Then, we will review the five stages of technology adoption and how they apply to blockchain. Finally, we will discuss the Cardano journey and the road to get here.

Structure

In this chapter, we will discuss the following topics:

- Cardano Ethos
- Software Industry Standards
  - Blockchain Risks
  - Semi-Formal Methods
  - IACR
- Potential For Social Good
- Regulatory and Compliance Risks
- Technology Adoption
- The Cardano Journey

Cardano Ethos

Openness and transparency are the ethos of Cardano[1] and are one of the reasons why there is such an emphasis on peer review and formal methods. The peer review

[1]https://roadmap.cardano.org/en/

process for organizations such as The International Association for Cryptographic Research (**IACR**)[2] uses a double-blind process that makes both the author and the reviewer anonymous to each other.[3] This helps eliminate biases and promotes fairness and transparency during the review process. In addition to the peer review process, **IOG (IOHK)** applies formal methods that rigorously use mathematical techniques to ensure that software works as intended.[4] For example, the Cardano ledger code, written in Haskell, can be linked back to the formal specification which has been peer-reviewed. This level of traceability and transparency is unparalleled in the blockchain industry and is typically only used in high-assurance software found in the space, airline, and financial industries.[5]

Fundamentally, blockchain technology is about giving agency and self-control to the edges. The benefits of empowering the edges (people or employees) lead to higher productivity, better engagement, and social outcomes.[6] Since the underlying cryptocurrency token is free to trade, this will, however, result in speculation. This speculation is frequently abused where blockchains (and projects) masquerade as permissionless and decentralized with the primary purpose of extracting value. This has been an issue since the earliest days of Bitcoin with ICOs.[7] Therefore, it is advisable to align with blockchains and projects that focus on the service of others, eventually leading to correct price discovery, value, and market fit.

Software Industry Standards

Quality, resilience, and bug-free are not typically associated with most software, particularly that has been recently released. This "*Industry Standard*" is a low bar and is usually addressed by regular software updates to improve the quality of the software over time. This approach does not work well for blockchains! Blockchains, by their nature, are immutable, and once deployed, a *true* decentralized and permissionless blockchain cannot be stopped, reset, or patched by a central authority. Furthermore, blockchains can involve millions of dollars of value that can be stolen by exploiting a bug found in the software.

Blockchain Risks

Let us first look at what can go wrong when designing and deploying a blockchain. The following is a list of issues that could occur:[8]

[2]https://iacr.org/
[3]Aggelos Kiayias, "Why Peer Review?"
[4]https://roadmap.cardano.org/en/
[5]https://en.wikipedia.org/wiki/Formal_methods
[6]David Marquet, "How Great Leaders Serve Others: David Marquet at TEDxScottAFB"
[7]Joi Ito, "Highlight: Joi Ito on ICOs at Scaling Bitcoin"
[8]Duncan Coutts, "IOHK PlutusFest 2018 | Duncan Coutts Presentation & Rebecca Valentine Closing Remarks"

- Flawed protocol design
- Incorrect implementation of the design
- Typical software mistakes
- Amateur cryptography implementations
- Missing performance deadlines
- Collapse under load
- Failure to scale
- DoS failures
- Vulnerability to economic attacks
- Social or voting collapse
- Macroeconomic collapse
- and more...

Semi-Formal Methods

As we can see, there are many pitfalls when designing and building a permissionless and decentralized blockchain. **IOG (IOHK)** mitigated these issues by linking together a semi-formal specification, a Haskell specification, and the Haskell implementation code, as illustrated in *Figure* 14.1.

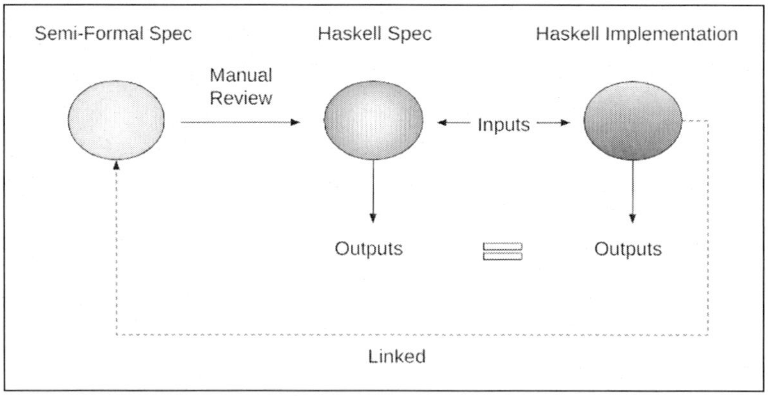

Figure 14.1: *Chain Of Evidence*[9]

A semi-formal specification for the ledger defines transition types and transition rules which make it formal, but not machine-checked.[10] By creating a Haskell specification, test cases can be run that compare the outputs of the specification executable to those created by the implementation executable. If the two outputs match, we can

[9]Duncan Coutts, "IOHK PlutusFest 2018 | Duncan Coutts Presentation & Rebecca Valentine Closing Remarks"

[10]Philipp Kant et al., "Flexible Formality Practical Experience with Agile Formal Methods" ,104

have reasonably high assurances that the implementation code implements the semi-formal specification. **IOG** continues to improve the formal verification process and has recently released a paper titled, *"Formal specification of the Cardano blockchain ledger, mechanized in Agda."*[11] The goal is to use Agda to create formal specifications going forward, with a work-in-progress version located on GitHub.[12]

IACR

The International Association for Cryptographic Research **(IACR)** is a non-profit scientific organization that advances cryptology and related fields.[13] It organizes three leading conferences that are used by academics in the field to present and review scientific papers:

- Crypto
- Eurocrypt
- Asiacrypt

IACR also runs four additional specialized conferences, one symposium, and a series of cryptography training schools.[14] The Journal of Cryptography is the flagship journal of the **IACR** and provides a forum for the publication of original work in modern information security.[15]

Potential for Social Good

Cardano's mission to bank the unbanked goes back to Charles Hoskinson's TED talk in 2014 before Cardano even existed.[16] Cardano began with a vision of a world without intermediaries, where individuals have control over their own data and how they can transact.[17] This has resonated with many in the Cardano community and is why there are great synergies with companies like World Mobile, which are connecting the unconnected.[18] Aspiring to be the financial operating system of the world,[19] Cardano has significant potential for social good.

[11]Andre Knispel, et. all., "Formal specification of the Cardano blockchain ledger, mechanized in Agda"
[12]https://github.com/IntersectMBO/formal-ledger-specifications
[13]https://iacr.org/
[14]https://iacr.org/meetings/
[15]https://iacr.org/jofc/
[16]Charles Hoskinson, "The future will be decentralized | Charles Hoskinson | TEDxBermuda"
[17]https://cardano.org/discover-cardano#purpose
[18]Alex Hamilton, "Connecting the unconnected, banking the unbanked"
[19]Input Output, "How Do You Explain The Mission Of Cardano?"

World Mobile

There are almost 3 billion people unconnected in the world, with 40% in developing countries not having access to a mobile network.[20] World Mobile is creating a sharing economy for telecommunications which is only possible because of blockchain.[21] World Mobile nodes can be purchased and receive World Mobile Tokens (WMT) from network transaction fees and token staking that incentivizes the network buildout. The mobile network is a Cardano sidechain that uses Decentralized Identifiers (**DIDs**) for provisioning and billing.[22] World Mobile has deployed networks in countries such as Tanzania and Zanzibar.[23]

Empowa

Homeownership in Africa is out of reach for most people because of the high cost of borrowing (45%), which in turn leads to a housing supply shortage.[24] Empowa is a decentralized property development and collectibles platform that provides microfinancing to underserved communities in Africa.[25] Empowa has used the Cardano blockchain to finance affordable homes in Mozambique.[26]

Crypto Green Research

Cardano ranks as one of the highest-scoring blockchains from an **ESG** perspective. [27]It has very low energy consumption and electronic waste. It is best in class in transparent governance, with a good distribution of token assets and a low barrier to entry.[28] As a result, Cardano scores on the following blockchain metrics.

- **Environment:** A-
- **Social:** A-
- **Governance:** A+

Social Good Projects

Following is a list of additional examples of using Cardano for social good:

[20]https://worldmobile.io/en
[21]https://worldmobiletoken.com/WhitePaper.pdf, p2
[22]https://worldmobiletoken.com/WhitePaper.pdf, p3
[23]https://worldmobile.io/en
[24]https://empowa.io/our-mission/
[25]mpowa Whitepaper, "Empowering African Communities"
[26]https://empowa.io/
[27]https://www.greencryptoresearch.com/blockchains
[28]https://www.greencryptoresearch.com/blockchains/cardano-(ada)

- **IOG (IOHK)** issues digital identities to Ethiopian students as a pilot program with the Education Ministry in Ethiopia[29].
- Community groups such as **WADA** focus on blockchain education hubs in Ghana, and Cameroon and future plans for other countries in West and Central Africa.[30]
- A community of stake pool operators called Climate Neutral Cardano is committed to using 100% renewable energy.[31]
- UNHCR awarded the Cardano Foundation and Switzerland recognition for allowing 80% of staking rewards to go toward refugees in pressing need.[32]
- Sustainable Ada maintains a repository of social impact Cardano projects.[33]
- AdaFilms has a collection of short documentaries on real, impactful use cases using the Cardano blockchain.[34]

Regulatory and Compliance Risks

The regulatory climate in the US has been particularly difficult and challenging for all blockchain companies located there. This is why most blockchain companies or foundations have headquarters outside the US in crypto-favorable jurisdictions such as Switzerland. Regulatory clarity has improved over the last few years and will continue to do so as legitimate use cases are realized and the benefits of blockchain are advocated.

Compliance risks, particularly KYC and AML regulations, are not always compatible with a pseudonymous, decentralized, permissionless blockchain. The Cardano blockchain is a toolbox with many tools that can address various functional and non-functional requirements, including KYC and AML if required. So, always be aware of your users' regulatory environment and tailor your solution accordingly. Also, be aware that there may be reporting requirements or outright bans on holding cryptocurrency assets in certain jurisdictions.

Technology Adoption

Blockchain appears to be following a similar trajectory to other disruptive innovations such as cell phones, the Internet, and social media, as illustrated in *Figure* 14.2. The innovators are first in this space, pioneering and championing the first iterations of

[29]Olga Hryniuk, "Atala PRISM: pioneering digital identity with decentralized solutions"
[30]https://www.wada.org/
[31]https://climateneutralcardano.org/
[32]Alex Maaza, "Cardano Foundation and Switzerland for UNHCR Recognized for Philanthropy Innovation"
[33]https://sustainableada.com/
[34]https://www.adafilms.art/

the technology. Then comes the early adopters who see the potential and evangelize the benefits. Next, the expectation is that the early majority will arrive and that this will usher in a new era with mass adoption.

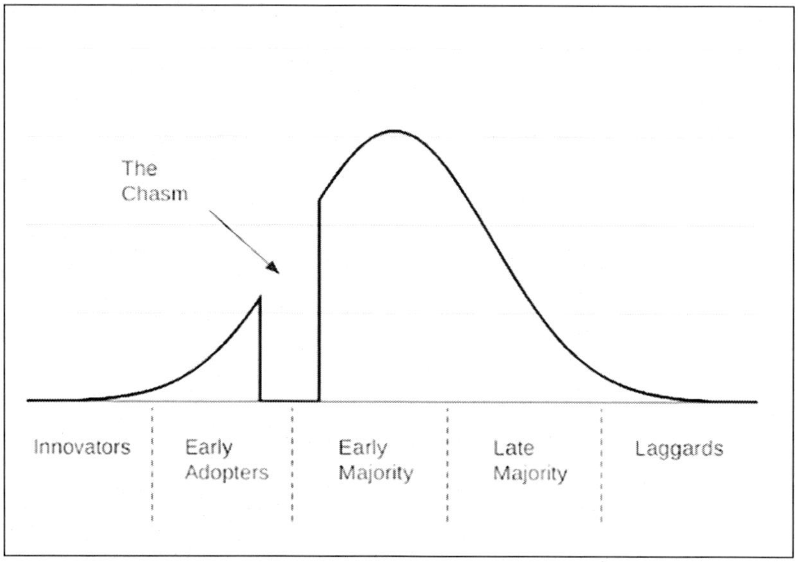

***Figure 14.2**: Technology Adoption Curve*

Unfortunately, this does not happen and instead, the chasm occurs. The early interest and excitement fade and the technology is discarded by many as a passing fad. But the builders keep building during this phase, strong with conviction that this new technology has significant potential. At some point in the future, "*killer*" applications are created that realize the unique value proposition of this new technology. It fundamentally changes how society views solutions to previously unsolvable problems. At this point, the early majority arrives and mass adoption occurs at scale. By the late majority phase, the technology is no longer novel and is accepted as the new normal. Finally, there will be the laggards who will remain skeptical of the technology but will have no choice but to use it to stay connected with the rest of the world.

The Cardano Journey

The road to get here was not easy for the teams involved in building and deploying the Cardano blockchain. Delays, setbacks, resets, and pivots caused a lot of friction and frustration. This is not uncommon for new, complex, highly integrated systems. What made this and other cryptocurrency projects more challenging than most, is that it is built in public with many people having a direct financial stake in the outcome. Throughout it all, however, **IOG (IOHK)**[35] and Charles Hoskinson[36] provided regular

[35]https://www.youtube.com/c/iohkio
[36]https://www.youtube.com/user/charleshoskinson

updates on YouTube and blog posts. Constantly having to dispel the naysayers, respond to the critics, and reassure the community that progress was being made. It was truly amazing to be part of this journey, watching and participating in it in real-time, and looking forward to what comes next.

Conclusion

In this chapter, we reviewed the ethos of Cardano and why there is such an emphasis on the peer review process and formal methods. We looked closely at software industry standards and how the current quality mitigation approaches are unsuitable for blockchains. We looked at how semi-formal methods are used to link high-assurance software back to the formal specification. We also examined how cryptographic associations like **IACR** promote and advance cryptographic research through conferences and publications. Next, we looked at how Cardano has significant potential for social good with real-world examples. We discussed the regulatory and compliance risks when creating a blockchain-based application. We also reviewed the five stages of technology adoption and how it applies to blockchain. Finally, we discussed the road to get here as part of the Cardano journey.

Points to Remember

- The Cardano ethos is openness and transparency.
- The peer review process is important to Cardano because it aligns with the Cardano ethos and best practices for high-assurance software.
- Haskell was chosen as the language to write the Cardano blockchain because of its similarity to the mathematical proofs of correctness.
- Blockchain empowers and gives agency to the edges of the network.
- Blockchains (and projects) focusing on the service others will typically succeed in the long run and the market will determine price, value, and product fit.
- The current software industry standards for quality are unsuitable for high-assurance software.
- A true decentralized and permissionless blockchain has no central authority to shut down, restart, or patch a network.
- A blockchain software bug can result in millions of dollars lost or stolen.
- A semi-formal method is an approach used by **IOG** (**IOHK**), in which a specification executable generates outputs that can be compared to implementation executable outputs.
- The International Association of Cryptographic Research (**IACR**) is a non-profit organization that advances cryptography.

- Cardano's mission to bank the unbanked goes back to the earliest days of Cardano.
- The potential for social good using Cardano is significant, and many real-world examples exist.
- Regulatory risks need to be monitored and assessed for each jurisdiction that is applicable to an application.
- Understanding **KYC** and **AML** regulations for a system or application's users is important for a project's success.
- The five stages of technology adoption include the innovators, early adopters, early majority, late majority, and the laggards.
- The chasm typically occurs between the early adopters and the early majority, a period when expected growth and user adoption do not occur at the expected pace.
- The Cardano journey has been long and has faced many challenges, which are not uncommon when creating a new, complex, and highly integrated platform.

Multiple Choice Questions

1. What is the ethos of Cardano?
   a. Creating value
   b. Banking the unbanked
   c. Openness and transparency
   d. All of the above
2. What are the benefits of the peer review process?
   a. Facilitates the sharing and collaboration of ideas
   b. Provides unbiased feedback and review of published papers
   c. Advances the field through scientific study and research
   d. All of the above
3. What statement is false?
   a. Software industry standards are suitable for high-assurance software
   b. Blockchain gives agency to the edges of the network
   c. IACR is a non-profit organization
   d. Cryptocurrency speculation first started with ICOs

4. What are the five stages of technology adoption?
    a. Innovators, Early Adopters, Early Majority, Late Majority, Laggards
    b. Innovators, Early Majority, Later Majority, Late Adopters, Laggards
    c. Early Adopters, Early Innovators, Early Majority, Late Majority, Laggards
    d. Innovators, Early Adopters, Early Majority, Middle Majority, Laggards
5. Why is it difficult to build a blockchain?
    a. A cryptocurrency token will include speculation and financial stakeholders
    b. Building is done in public where anyone can see the last open-source code
    c. It is a highly complex, secure, and integrated system
    d. All of the above

Answers

1. c
2. d
3. a
4. a
5. d

Questions

1. Why is the peer review process not typically done in other blockchains?
2. What other languages could have Cardano been written in and what are the pros and cons of each?
3. Why are 3 billion people in the world unbanked?
4. What are the difficulties of using formal methods in software development?
5. Can agile software development methodologies and formal methods coexist?
6. Why does the chasm appear in the five stages of technology adoption?

Key Terms

- **AML:** Anti-Money Laundering
- **DID:** Decentralized Identifier
- **ESG:** Environmental, Social and Governance
- **IACR:** International Association of Cryptographic Research
- **ICO:** Initial Coin Offering
- **IOG:** Input Output Global
- **IOHK:** Input Output Hong Kong
- **KYC:** Know Your Customer
- **UNHCR:** United National High Commissioner for Refugees
- **WADA:** Africa, Diaspora and Beyond

Bibliography

Alden, L., "Broken Money."

Timestamp Press, 2023

Badertscher, C., Gazi1 C.,Kiayias A.,Russell A. and Zikas V., "Ouroboros Chronos: Permissionless Clock Synchronization via Proof-of-Stake"

IACR, May 15, 2019
Available online via: https://eprint.iacr.org/2018/1132.pdf

Badertscher, C.,Gazi, P., Kiayias, A., Russell, A. and Zikas V, "Ouroboros Genesis: Composable Proof-of-Stake Blockchains with Dynamic Availability"

IACR, February 22, 2019
Available online via: https://eprint.iacr.org/2018/378.pdf

Bailly, A., "Time handling on Cardano, part 1. About Ouroboros and the importance of determinism"

IOHK, December 6, 2022
Available online via: https://iohk.io/en/blog/posts/2022/12/07/time-handling-on-cardano-part-1-about-ouroboros-and-the-importance-of-determinism/

Bano S., Sonnino A., Al-Bassam M.,Azouvi S.,McCorry P.,Meiklejohn S. and Danezis1 D. "SoK: Consensus in the Age of Blockchains"

November 14, 2017
Available online via: https://arxiv.org/pdf/1711.03936.pdf

Britannica, Encyclopaedia of, "cipher"

Encyclopaedia of Britannica, Jan 03, 2008
Available online via: https://www.britannica.com/topic/cipher

Bernstein, D.J., Duif, N., Lange, T. et al. "High-speed high-security signatures."

J Cryptogr Eng 2, 77–89 (2012).
Available online via: https://doi.org/10.1007/s13389-012-0027-1

Brunjes, L. and Betrin, M. "Building UTxO optimized Dapps"

Genius Yield, December 8, 2022
Available online via: https://www.youtube.com/watch?v=MYMha1C0o1g

Burgess, N., "Calling trailblazers to Midnight"

IOHK, October 4, 2023
Available online via: https://iohk.io/en/blog/posts/2023/10/05/calling-trailblazers-to-midnight/

Buterin, V., "Ethereum: A Next-Generation Smart Contract and Decentralized Application Platform"

Ethereum.org, 2014
Available online via: https://ethereum.org/content/whitepaper/whitepaper-pdf/Ethereum_Whitepaper_-_Buterin_2014.pdf

Cardanians.io, "Understanding Input Endorsers"

CExplorer.io, June 10, 2023
Available online via: https://cexplorer.io/article/understanding-input-endorsers

Cardanians.io, "There is 1.23B ADA in Cardano's treasury"

CExporer.io, November, 11, 2023
Available online via: https://cexplorer.io/article/there-is-1-23b-ada-in-cardano-s-treasury

CertiK, "The Blockchain Trilemma: Decentralized, Scalable, and Secure?"

Medium, October 4, 2019
Available online via: https://medium.com/certik/the-blockchain-trilemma-decentralized-scalable-and-secure-e9d8c41a87b3

Chaidos, P. and Kiaias, A., "Mithril: Stake-based Threshold Multisignatures"

IACR, May, 2021
Available online via: https://eprint.iacr.org/2021/916.pdf

Chainalysis, "2022 Biggest Year Ever For Crypto Hacking with $3.8 Billion Stolen, Primarily from DeFi Protocols and by North Korea-linked Attackers"

Chainalysis.com, February 1, 2023
Available online via: https://www.chainalysis.com/blog/2022-biggest-year-ever-for-crypto-hacking/

Chapman, J.,Kireev R.,Nester C.,Wadler, P., "System F in Agda, for fun and profit"

Mathematics of Program Construction: 13th International Conference, MPC 2019, Porto, Portugal, October 7–9, 2019, Proceedings

10.1007/978-3-030-33636-3_10

Available online via: https://iohk.io/en/research/library/papers/system-f-in-agda-for-fun-and-profit/

Coutts, D., "IOHK PlutusFest 2018 | Duncan Coutts Presentation & Rebecca Valentine Closing Remarks"

Input Output, January 30, 2019
Available online via: https://www.youtube.com/watch?v=wW1CI9zt1tg

Coutts, D., Panagiotakos, G. and Fitzi, M. , "Ouroboros Leios: design goals and concepts"

IOHK, October, 2022
Available online via: https://iohk.io/en/research/library/papers/ouroboros-leios-design-goals-and-concepts/

Crypto Carlos, "Node course | Creating a stake pool, the setup"

IOG Academy, March 21, 2023
Available online via: https://www.youtube.com/watch?v=6AQaPdmxnfo

Crypto Carlos., "Ourobors protocol. The heart of Cardano"

Crypto Carlos, May 21, 2019
Available online via: https://www.youtube.com/watch?v=U92Ks8rucDQ

Cryptopedia, "The Blockchain Trilemma: Fast, Secure, and Scalable Networks"

Gemini.com, June 28, 2022,
Available online via: https://www.gemini.com/cryptopedia/blockchain-trilemma-decentralization-scalability-definition

Dai, W., "b-money"

Weidia.com, February 19, 1999
Available online via: http://www.weidai.com/bmoney.txt

David B., Gazi P., Kiayias A. and Russell A., "Ouroboros Praos: An adaptively-secure, semi-synchronous proof-of-stake blockchain"

IACR, April 27, 2023
Available online via: https://eprint.iacr.org/2017/573.pdf

Empowa Whitepaper, "Empowering African Communities"

Empowa.io, 2021,
Available online via: https://drive.google.com/filed/1ei_0eQFCK5wKGMQgVcyNlTQYUQ4ky-xT/edit

Finney, H. "RPOW - Reusable Proofs of Work"

Satoshi Nakamoto Institute, August 15, 2004
Available online via: https://nakamotoinstitute.org/rpow/

Kiayias, A., "Why Peer Review?"

Input Output, June 22, 2018
Available online via: https://www.youtube.com/watch?v=MV8ANlktGoI

Knispel, A., Melkonian, O., Chapman, J., Hill, A., Jääger, J., DeMeo, W., Norell, U., "Formal specification of the Cardano blockchain ledger, mechanized in Agda"

Input Output, March 2024
Available online via: https://iohk.io/en/research/library/papers/formal-specification-of-the-cardano-blockchain-ledger-mechanized-in-agda/

Gauba A., Finality in Blockchain Consensus

Medium, Aug 30, 2018
Available online: https://medium.com/mechanism-labs/finality-in-blockchain-consensus-d1f83c120a9a

Gaži, P., "Presenting Ouroboros at MIT"

Input Output, March 13, 2018
Available online via: https://www.youtube.com/watch?v=PoNaw-Mtxgo

Goldwasser, S. and Mihir, B., "Lecture Notes on Cryptography"

MIT, July 2008
Available online via: https://cseweb.ucsd.edu/~mihir/papers/gb.pdf

Haber, S. and Stornetta, W. S., "How To Time-Stamp a Digital Document."

Journal of Cryptology, 1991
Available online via: https://link.springer.com/article/10.1007/BF00196791

Hamilton, A., "Connecting the unconnected, banking the unbanked"

IOHK, August 10, 2021
Available online via: https://iohk.io/en/blog/posts/2021/08/11/connecting-the-unconnected-banking-the-unbanked/

Hirniak, J., "Axo Protocol Whitepaper: The New era of trading"

axo.trade, October 21, 2021
Available online via: https://www.axo.trade/whitepaper.pdf

Hoskinson, C. "Cardano whiteboard; overview with Charles Hoskinson"

Input Output, October 26, 2017
Available online via: https://www.youtube.com/watch?v=Ja9D0kpksxw

Hoskinson, C., "The future will be decentralized | Charles Hoskinson | TEDxBermuda"

TEDx Talks, December 4, 2014
Available online via: https://www.youtube.com/watch?v=97ufCT6lQcY

Hryniuk, O., "Atala PRISM: pioneering digital identity with decentralized solutions"

IOHK, May 10, 2023
Available online via: https://iohk.io/en/blog/posts/2023/05/11/atala-prism-pioneering-digital-identity-with-decentralized-solutions/

Hryniuk, O., "How Mithril facilitates strong security settings"

IOHK, August 22, 2023
Available online via: https://iohk.io/en/blog/posts/2023/08/23/how-mithril-facilitates-strong-security-settings/

Hryniuk O., "From Classic to Chronos: the implementations of Ouroboros explained"

IOHK, June 2, 2022
Available online vai: https://iohk.io/en/blog/posts/2022/06/03/from-classic-to-chronos-the-implementations-of-ouroboros-explained/

Hughes, J., "Testing smart contracts with QuickCheck by John Hughes"

Func Prog Sweden, May 27, 2021
Available online via: https://www.youtube.com/watch?v=V9_14jjJiuQ

Input Output, "How Do You Explain The Mission Of Cardano?"

Input Output, January 29, 2021
Available online via: https://www.youtube.com/watch?v=l_Nv0-PVrnM

Ito, J., "Highlight: Joi Ito on ICOs at Scaling Bitcoin"

Seoul Bitcoin, June 15, 2018
Available online via: https://www.youtube.com/watch?v=-whIh7n4Yqc

Kant, P. et al., "Flexible Formality Practical Experience with Agile Formal Methods."

In: Byrski, A., Hughes, J. (eds) Trends in Functional Programming. TFP 2020. Lecture Notes in Computer Science(), vol 12222. Springer, Cham.
Available online via: https://doi.org/10.1007/978-3-030-57761-2_5

Kerber, T., Kohlweiss†, M., Kiayias, A. and Zikas V. "Ouroboros Crypsinous: Privacy-Preserving Proof-of-Stake"

IACR, May 15, 2019
Available online via: https://eprint.iacr.org/2018/1132.pdf

Khovratovich, D. and Law, J., "BIP32-Ed25519: Hierarchical Deterministic Keys over a Non-linear Keyspace,"

2017 IEEE European Symposium on Security and Privacy Workshops (EuroS&PW), Paris, France, 2017, pp. 27-31, doi: 10.1109/EuroSPW.2017.47. keywords: {Public key;Bitcoin;Proposals;Privacy;Standards;Encoding},
Available online via: https://input-output-hk.github.io/adrestia/static/Ed25519_BIP.pdf

Kiayias, A. and Russell A., "Ouroboros-BFT:A Simple Byzantine Fault Tolerant Consensus Protocol"

IACR, November 26, 2018
Available online via: https://eprint.iacr.org/2018/1049.pdf

Kiayias, A., Russell A., David B. and Oliynyko R., "Ouroboros: A Provably Secure Proof-of-Stake Blockchain Protocol"

IACR, July 20, 2019
Available online via: https://eprint.iacr.org/2016/889.pdf

Knispel, A., Vinogradova, P., "Formal Specification of the Cardano Ledger with Plutus Integration",

IOHK, February 28th, 2021
Available online via: https://github.com/input-output-hk/cardano-ledger/releases/latest/download/alonzo-ledger.pdf

Lamport, L.; Shostak, R.; Pease, M., "The Byzantine Generals Problem."

ACM Transactions on Programming Languages and Systems. 4 (3): 382–401. July 1982.
Available online via: https://lamport.azurewebsites.net/pubs/byz.pdf

Lebec, G., "Lambda Calculus - Fundamentals of Lambda Calculus & Functional Programming in JavaScript"

Fullstack Academy, August 25, 2017
Available online via: https://www.youtube.com/watch?v=3VQ382QG-y4

Lebec, G., "The Magic of Generative Testing: Fast-Check in JavaScript"

Fullstack Academy, July 2, 2019
Available online via: https://www.youtube.com/watch?v=a2J_FSkxWKo

LLFOURN, "Introduction To Ouroboros"

Medium, Feb 17, 2018
Available online via: https://medium.com/unraveling-the-ouroboros/introduction-to-ouroboros-1c2324912193

Maaza, A., "Cardano Foundation and Switzerland for UNHCR Recognized for Philanthropy Innovation"

Cardano Foundation, February 6, 2024
Available online via: https://cardanofoundation.org/blog/cardano-foundation-and-switzerland-for-unhcr-recognized-for-philanthropy-innovation/

Marquet, D., "How Great Leaders Serve Others: David Marquet at TEDxScottAFB"

TEDx Talks, June 21, 2012
Available online via: https://www.youtube.com/watch?v=DLRH5J_93LQ

Mazieres, D. and Shasha, D., "Building secure file systems out of Byzantine storage."

NYU Department of Computer Science, 2006
Available online via: https://cs.nyu.edu/~shasha/papers/mazpodc.pdf

Menezes, A., Oorschot, P. van and Vanstone, S. "Handbook of Applied Cryptography"

CRC Press, 1996
Available online via: https://cacr.uwaterloo.ca/hac/about/chap8.pdf

Nakamoto, S., "Bitcoin: A Peer-to-Peer Electronic Cash System"

Bitcoin.org, October 31st, 2008
Available online via: https://bitcoin.org/bitcoin.pdf

Pittalia, P. P., "A comparative study of hash algorithms in cryptography"

Int. J. Comput. Sci. Mobile Comput., vol. 8, no. 6, pp. 147-152, 2019
Available online via: https://ijcsmc.com/docs/papers/June2019/V8I6201928.pdf

Plutus Core Team, DRAFT "Formal Specification of the Plutus Core Language"

IOHK, September 1st, 2023
Available online: https://ci.iog.io/build/1230997/download/1/plutus-core-specification.pdf

Raynaud, J., "Light, fast, efficient, and secure - Mithril"

Input Output, December 7, 2022
Available online via: https://www.youtube.com/watch?v=VyxsqwNWZt4

Richmond, T., "Project Catalyst - A virtuous cycle of Cardano ecosystem development"

IOHK, May 9, 2022
Available online via: https://iohk.io/en/blog/posts/2022/05/10/project-catalyst-a-virtuous-cycle-of-cardano-ecosystem-development-investing-in-great-ideas-to-make-positive-real-world-changes/

Sheehan, R., "State of Cardano Q4 2023"

Messari.io, Feb 14, 2024
Available online via: https://messari.io/report/state-of-cardano-q4-2023

Simmons, G. J., "History of cryptography"

Encyclopedia Britannica, Apr 15, 2004
Available online via: https://www.britannica.com/topic/cryptology/The-Data-Encryption-Standard-and-the-Advanced-Encryption-Standard

Upadhyay, D., Gaikwad, N., Zaman, M. and Sampalli, S., "Investigating the Avalanche Effect of Various Cryptographically Secure Hash Functions and Hash-Based Applications,"

IEEE Access, vol. 10, pp. 112472-112486, 2022, doi: 10.1109/ACCESS.2022.3215778.
Available online via: https://ieeexplore.ieee.org/document/9923931

Wadler, P., "Functional smart contracts on Cardano"

Input Output, July 21, 2020
Available online via: https://www.youtube.com/watch?v=MpWeg6Fg0t8

Ward, M., "Partner chains are coming to Cardano"

IOHK, November 2, 2023
Available online via: https://iohk.io/en/blog/posts/2023/11/03/partner-chains-are-coming-to-cardano/

Zharun, T., "Wyoming LLC as a DAO Legal Wrapper: What You Need to Know"

Legal Nodes, January 26, 2024
Available online via: https://legalnodes.com/article/wyoming-dao-llc

Index

A

Absolute Finality (PBFT) 23
address 32
address, types
  base address 32, 33
  enterprise address 33
  reward address 33, 34
Aiken 92, 93
Aiken, libraries
  lucid cancel, function 95
  lucid off-chain,
    unlocking 94, 95
  on-chain,
    validating 93, 94
anti-pattern, approaches
  batchers, utilizing 155
  liquidity, pools 154
AssetClass 107

B

back-end, components
  Blockfrost setup 204
  public key,
    optimizing 205
  Redis DB 202
Beacon Token 152
Bitcoin Whitepaper 3, 4
Blockchain, Benefits 223, 224
Blockchain Trilemma
  about 7
  approaches 8
  decentralizing 8
  scalability 8
  security 8
Blockchain, use cases
  DAO 13
  DEX 13
  financial, products 13
  insurance 13
  market, capital 13
  marketplaces 13
  media, entertaining 13
  reward 13
  storage,
    decentralizing 13
  system, identity 13
  tokenization 13
Blockfrost
  reference link 125
builtin 49
Byzantine Generals Problem
    (BGP) 2

C

Cancel.tsx 95
Cardano
  GitHub repositories,
    preventing 267
  history 286
  resources,
    learning 274, 275
  state, utilizing 266, 267
Cardano Blockchain
  about 127
  challenge 128
  Kupo 136-138
  node, component 128-130
  Ogmios 133-135
  setup 138

Cardano Blockchain, aspects
endorsers,
containing 247, 248
Hydra, analyzing 246, 247
Mithril 247
scripts, referencing 244
smart contract,
preventing 246
UTXO Contention,
avoiding 244, 245
cardano-cli 130
Cardano Improvement Process
(CIP)
about 268
concepts 268, 269
states 268
Cardano, industries
Crypto research,
optimizing 284
Empowa 284
social project,
utilizing 284, 285
World Mobile Tokens
(WMT) 284
Cardano Node 259, 260
Cardano, risks 285
Cardano Roadmap 11
Cardano Testnet
reference link 63
chain sequence diagram,
concepts
application, executing 170
Becon, viewing 167, 168
swap, closing 171
swap, opening 166
swap, updating 169
ticket, printing 171
tickets, minting 165
transaction, verifying 172
wallet, connecting 166
Charles Hoskinson
concepts 6
interoperability 6, 7
scalability 6
sustainability 7
CIP-1694 269
CIP-1694, key role
Constitutional Committee
(CC) 270
Delegated Representatives
(DReps) 270
Stake Pool Operators
(SPOs) 270
CIPs, best practices
CIP-0003 Key,
generating 155
CIP-0030 Web,
bridging 156
CIP-0032 Inline,
datums 156
CIP-0040 Collateral,
expliciting 156
CIP-0068 Metadata 156, 157
Coin Selection
about 105
process, utilizing 106
Collateral 56
Concise Binary Representation
(CBOR)
about 50
Datum, configuring 54
Plutus, scripting 53
Redeemer, utilizing 53
transaction,
analyzing 51, 52
Cryptography
about 18
Hashes 19
Public Key Encryption 18

D

Dandelion 127
Datums 40
Demeter.run 60, 67
Design Patterns
about 151
Beacon Token 152
order book 152, 153
thread token 151
Digital Signatures 19, 20

Distributed Ledger Technology
about 2
Byzantine Generals Problem (BGP) 2, 3
concept 3
dynamicQuery() 183

E

Ethereum Whitepaper 4, 5
EUTXO Design Patterns
architecture, utilizing 158
chain sequence diagram 165
state machine diagram 158
Execution budget
errors 256-258

F

Front-end UI, components
event, viewing 185
header/footer 181
swap card, containing 184
swap, viewing 182, 183
tickets, printing 185, 186
transaction, building 187-189
wallet, connecting 181, 182

H

Hashes 19
Helios
about 70
GitHub, initializing 71
UTXO, locking 72

J

JavaScript Application
common folder, analyzing 179
components 179
init folder, optimizing 179
lib, containing 179
models, preventing 179
Pages/API, utilizing 179
public/contracts 180
schema, analyzing 180
wallet, configuring 179

K

Koios 127
Kupo 136-138

L

lam function 49
Local Devnet
about 138, 139
docker, installing 139-143
environment, utilizing 139
resources, utilizing 146
Lucid + Aiken
advantage 77
Blockfrost API, utilizing 77
code, initializing 77, 78
off-chain, coding 79, 80

M

Maestro 125
Maestro, features
Blockchain, indexing 125
transaction, managing 125
turbo, transaction 125
Member-Based Organization (MBO) 269
Metadata 38, 39
Midnight 274
Minting Policy, use case
Aiken On-Chain 111, 112
Lucid Off-Chain 112-114
Off-Chain, burning 110, 111
Off-chain, minting 108-110
On-chain Helios 107, 108
Mithril 247

N

Next.js
reference link 70
Non-Fungible Token (NFT)
about 103
approaches 103
metadata, utilizing 103
validator, setup 115-119

O

off-chain, coding 70
offeredAssetVal 197
Ogmios 133, 134
order book, principles 153
order book, process 152
Ouroboros PoS, protocol
  Byzantine Fault Tolerance (BFT) 24
  chronos 26
  classic 24
  crypsinous 25
  genesis, addressing 25
  Verifiable Random Function (VRF) 25
Ouroboros Protocol, lifecycle
  register 26
  staking 26, 27
  time 26

P

Plutus Budget, executing 55, 56
Plutus Script, concepts
  Beacon Policy, minting 190, 191
  ticket policy, minting 191-194
  validator, holding 194-196
  validator, swapping 196-201
Plutus Scripts 40
Preprod Testnet
  reference link 63
Probabilistic Finality (Chain-based) 23
Proof-of-Stake (PoS) 22, 23
Proof-of-Stake, protocols
  Absolute Finality (PBFT) 23
  Probabilistic Finality (Chain-based) 23
Proof-of-Work (PoW) 21, 22
PubKeyHash 85
Public Key Encryption 18

R

Redeemers 40, 41
Redis DB
  about 202
  API, utilizing 203
  setup 203, 204

S

ScriptContext 84, 86
ScriptHash 32
smart contract, aspect
  Aiken 254, 255
  Helios 253
Smart Contract development 236
Smart Contract development, concept
  audits, optimizing 243
  datum, analyzing 239-241
  token, leakage 241-243
  vulnerabilities, satisfying 236-238
Software Industry, trends
  Blockchain, risks 281
  IACR 283
  semi-formal method, specifying 282, 283
Stake Pool Operator (SPO)
  about 271
  project, varifying 272
  tools 271
stake_reference 34
state machine diagram, concepts
  asset, executing 162, 163
  burning 159
  print, transaction 164
  swap, closing 163, 164
  swap, opening 160, 161
  swap, updating 161
  ticket, minting 159

swap, setup
  even, organizing 206
  script, modifying 208
  ticket, converting 217-219
  ticket, getting 209
  tickets, buying 211-213
  ticket, verifying 216
  transaction, updating 210
  wallet, connecting 206

T

testing framework
  about 229
  benefits 229
  directory, utilizing 230
  property, testing 235, 236
  strategies 230-232
  test, cases 232-234
Testnet, types
  preprod 62
  preview 62
thread token 151
Token
  about 101
  CIP-25 104
  CIP-68 105
  minting, policy 102
  Native Assets 101
  Non-Fungible Token (NFT) 103
Token Bundles 101, 102
Token, components
  naming 101
  policy, identifying 101
  quantity, utilizing 101
Tokenomics
  about 8
  rate, inflation 11
  Token, allocating 8
  Token, comparing 10
  Token, distributing 9
Token Registry 103
Transaction Builder Errors 259

U

Unlock.tsx 87
Untyped Plutus Lambda Core (UPLC)
  about 47
  example, simplifying 50
  grammar, utilizing 49
  types 48
UTXO
  about 35
  input, transaction 36
  output, transaction 36-38
UTXO, lifecycle 60, 61
UTXO, script purposes
  certifying 86
  minting 86
  rewarding 86
  spending 86

V

Validators 84
Validators, components
  function, analyzing 90, 91
  off-chain, code 87-89
  on-chain, code 85-87
  URL, scripting 91

W

wallet
  about 61, 62
  CIP-30 67
  path, derivating 64, 65
  seed, phrasing 62
  staking 65, 66
  Testnets 62-64
walletAPI 72
WalletConnect.tsx 79
WalletInfo 114
witnesses, types 41, 42

Made in United States
North Haven, CT
05 November 2026

21778840R10180